From Bacteria to Plants: Teacher's Edition

Contents in Brief

W9-AUI-732

Teacher's Edition

See Program Component List on page ii

Student Edition

Prentice Hall Science Explorer

Series Tables of Contents

Life Science

The Nature of Science and Technology

1. What Is Science?
2. The Work of Scientists
3. Technology and Engineering

From Bacteria to Plants

1. Living Things
2. Viruses and Bacteria
3. Protists and Fungi
4. Introduction to Plants
5. Seed Plants

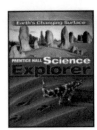

Animals

1. Sponges, Cnidarians, and Worms
2. Mollusks, Arthropods, and Echinoderms
3. Fishes, Amphibians, and Reptiles
4. Birds and Mammals
5. Animal Behavior

Cells and Heredity

1. Cell Structure and Function
2. Cell Processes and Energy
3. Genetics: The Science of Heredity
4. Modern Genetics
5. Changes Over Time

Human Biology and Health

1. Bones, Muscles, and Skin
2. Food and Digestion
3. Circulation
4. Respiration and Excretion
5. Fighting Disease
6. The Nervous System
7. The Endocrine System and Reproduction

Environmental Science

1. Populations and Communities
2. Ecosystems and Biomes
3. Living Resources
4. Land, Water, and Air Resources
5. Energy Resources

Earth Science

Inside Earth

1. Plate Tectonics
2. Earthquakes
3. Volcanoes
4. Minerals
5. Rocks

Earth's Changing Surface

1. Mapping Earth's Surface
2. Weathering and Soil Formation
3. Erosion and Deposition
4. A Trip Through Geologic Time

Earth's Waters

1. Earth: The Water Planet
2. Freshwater Resources
3. Ocean Motions
4. Ocean Zones

Weather and Climate

1. The Atmosphere
2. Weather Factors
3. Weather Patterns
4. Climate and Climate Change

Astronomy

1. Earth, Moon, and Sun
2. Exploring Space
3. The Solar System
4. Stars, Galaxies, and the Universe

Physical Science

Chemical Building Blocks

1. Introduction to Matter
2. Solids, Liquids, and Gases
3. Elements and the Periodic Table
4. Exploring Materials

Chemical Interactions

1. Atoms and Bonding
2. Chemical Reactions
3. Acids, Bases, and Solutions
4. Carbon Chemistry

Motion, Forces, and Energy

1. Motion
2. Forces
3. Forces in Fluids
4. Work and Machines
5. Energy
6. Thermal Energy and Heat

Electricity and Magnetism

1. Magnetism
2. Electricity
3. Using Electricity and Magnetism
4. Electronics

Sound and Light

1. Characteristics of Waves
2. Sound
3. The Electromagnetic Spectrum
4. Light

Teacher's Edition

From Bacteria to Plants

PRENTICE HALL Science Explorer

PEARSON
Prentice Hall

Needham, Massachusetts
Upper Saddle River, New Jersey

Copyright © 2005 by Pearson Education, Inc., publishing as Pearson Prentice Hall, Upper Saddle River, New Jersey 07458.
All rights reserved. Printed in the United States of America. This publication is protected by copyright, and permission should be obtained
from the publisher prior to any prohibited reproduction, storage in a retrieval system, or transmission in any form or by any means, electronic,
mechanical, photocopying, recording, or likewise. For information regarding permission(s), write to: Rights and Permissions Department.

Pearson Prentice Hall™ is a trademark of Pearson Education, Inc.
Pearson® is a registered trademark of Pearson plc.
Prentice Hall® is a registered trademark of Pearson Education, Inc.
Lab zone™ is a trademark of Pearson Education, Inc.

Planet Diary® is a registered trademark of Addison Wesley Longman, Inc.

Discovery Channel School® is a registered trademark of Discovery Communications, Inc., used under license.
The Discovery Channel logo is a trademark of Discovery Communications, Inc.

SciLinks® is a trademark of the National Science Teachers Association. The SciLinks® service includes copyrighted
materials and is owned and provided by the National Science Teachers Association. All rights reserved.

Science News® is a registered trademark of Science Services, Inc.

ISBN 0-13-181119-3   1 2 3 4 5 6 7 8 9 10   08 07 06 05 04

Pacing Options

SCIENCE EXPLORER offers many aids to help you plan your instruction time, whether regular class periods or block scheduling. Section-by-section lesson plans for each chapter include suggested times for Student Edition activities. TeacherExpress™ and the Lab zone™ Easy Planner CD-ROM will help you manage your time electronically.

PRENTICE HALL
TeacherEXPRESS™
Plan • Teach • Assess

Lab zone™

Pacing Chart

	PERIODS	BLOCKS		PERIODS	BLOCKS
Careers in Science: Disease Detective Solves Mystery	1	$^1/_2$	**Chapter 4 Introduction to Plants**		
Chapter 1 Living Things			Chapter 4 Project *Design and Build an Interactive Exhibit*	Ongoing	Ongoing
Chapter 1 Project *Mystery Object*	Ongoing	Ongoing	1 The Plant Kingdom	3–4	$1^1/_2$–2
1 What Is Life?	2–3	1–$1^1/_2$	2 Integrating Physics: Photosynthesis and Light	2–3	1–$1^1/_2$
2 Classifying Organisms	1–2	$^1/_2$–1	3 Mosses, Liverworts, and Hornworts	2–3	1–$1^1/_2$
3 Domains and Kingdoms	3–4	$1^1/_2$–2	4 Ferns, Club Mosses, and Horsetails	2–3	1–$1^1/_2$
4 Integrating Earth Science: The Origin of Life	1–2	$^1/_2$–1	Chapter 4 Review and Assessment	1	$^1/_2$
Chapter 1 Review and Assessment	1	$^1/_2$	**Chapter 5 Seed Plants**		
Chapter 2 Viruses and Bacteria			Chapter 5 Project *Cycle of a Lifetime*	Ongoing	Ongoing
Chapter 2 Project *Be a Disease Detective*	Ongoing	Ongoing	1 The Characteristics of Seed Plants	3–4	$1^1/_2$–2
1 Viruses	2–3	1–$1^1/_2$	2 Gymnosperms	2–3	1–$1^1/_2$
2 Bacteria	3–4	$1^1/_2$–2	3 Angiosperms	1–2	$^1/_2$–1
3 Integrating Health: Viruses, Bacteria, and Your Health	2–3	1–$1^1/_2$	4 Plant Responses and Growth	1–2	$^1/_2$–1
Chapter 2 Review and Assessment	1	$^1/_2$	5 Integrating Technology: Feeding the World	1–2	$^1/_2$–1
Chapter 3 Protists and Fungi			Chapter 5 Review and Assessment	1	$^1/_2$
Chapter 3 Project *A Mushroom Farm*	Ongoing	Ongoing	Interdisciplinary Exploration: Corn—The Amazing Grain	2–3	1–$1^1/_2$
1 Protists	3–4	$1^1/_2$–2			
2 Integrating Environmental Science: Algal Blooms	2–3	1–$1^1/_2$			
3 Fungi	1–2	$^1/_2$–1			
Chapter 3 Review and Assessment	1	$^1/_2$			

Research-Based and Proven to Work

As the originator of the small book concept in middle school science, and as the nation's number one science publisher, Prentice Hall takes pride in the fact that we've always listened closely to teachers. In doing so, we've developed programs that effectively meet the needs of your classroom.

As we continue to listen, we realize that raising the achievement level of all students is the number one challenge facing teachers today. To assist you in meeting this latest challenge, Prentice Hall has combined the very best author team with solid research to create a program that meets your high standards and will ensure that no child is left behind.

With Prentice Hall, you can be confident that your students will not only be motivated, inspired, and excited to learn science, but that they will also achieve the success needed in today's environment of the No Child Left Behind (NCLB) legislation and testing reform.

On the following pages, you will read about the key elements found throughout *Science Explorer* that truly set this program apart and ensure success for you and your students.

> As we continue to listen, we realize that raising the achievement level of all students is the number one challenge facing teachers today.

A Science Program Backed by Research

In developing Prentice Hall *Science Explorer*, we used research studies as a central, guiding element. Research on *Science Explorer* indicated key elements of a textbook program that ensure students' success: support for reading and mathematics in science, consistent opportunities for inquiry, and an ongoing assessment strand. This research was conducted in phases and continues today.

1. Exploratory: Needs Assessment

Along with periodic surveys concerning state and national standards as well as curriculum issues and challenges, we conducted specific product development research, which included discussions with teachers and advisory panels, focus groups, and quantitative surveys. We explored the specific needs of teachers, students, and other educators regarding each book we developed in Prentice Hall *Science Explorer*.

2. Formative: Prototype Development and Field-Testing

During this phase of research, we worked to develop prototype materials. Then we tested the materials by field-testing with students and teachers and by performing qualitative and quantitative surveys. In our early prototype testing, we received feedback about our lesson structure. Results were channeled back into the program development for improvement.

3. Summative: Validation Research

Finally, we conducted and continue to conduct long-term research based on scientific, experimental designs under actual classroom conditions. This research identifies what works and what can be improved in the next revision of Prentice Hall *Science Explorer*. We also continue to monitor the program in the market. We talk to our users about what works, and then we begin the cycle over again. The next section contains highlights of this research.

A Science Program With Proven Results

In a year-long study in 2000–2001, students in six states using Prentice Hall *Science Explorer* outscored students using other science programs on a nationally normed standardized test.

The study investigated the effects of science textbook programs at the eighth-grade level. Twelve eighth-grade science classes with a total of 223 students participated in the study. The selected classes were of similar student ability levels.

Each class was tested at the beginning of the school year using the TerraNova CTBS Basic Battery Plus, and then retested at the end of the school year. The final results, shown in the graph, show a significant improvement in test scores from the pre-test to the post-test evaluation.

• All tests were scored by CTB/McGraw-Hill, the publisher of the TerraNova exam. Statistical analyses and conclusions were performed by an independent firm, Pulse Analytics, Inc.

In Japan, Lesson Study Research has been employed for a number of years as a tool for teachers to improve their curriculum. In April 2003, Prentice Hall adapted this methodology to focus on a lesson from this edition. Our goal was to test the effectiveness of lesson pedagogy and improve it while in the program development stage. In all three classrooms tested, student learning increased an average of 10 points from the pre- to the post-assessment.

• Detailed results of these studies can be obtained at **www.PHSchool.com/research.**

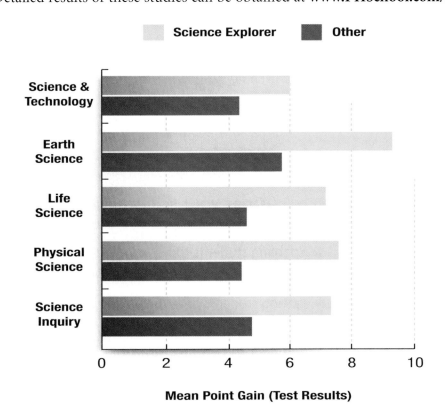

Mean Point Gain (Test Results)

Foundational Research: Inquiry in the Science Classroom

"How do I know if my students are inquiring?" "If students are busy doing lots of hands-on activities, are they using inquiry?" "What is inquiry, anyway?" If you're confused, you are not alone. Inquiry is the heart and soul of science education, with most of us in continuous pursuit of achieving it with our students!

Defining Science Inquiry

What is it? Simply put, inquiry is the intellectual side of science. It is thinking like a scientist—being inquisitive, asking why, and searching for answers. The National Science Education Content Standards define inquiry as the process in which students begin with a question, design an investigation, gather evidence, formulate an answer to the original question, and communicate the investigative process and results. Since it is often difficult to accomplish all this in one class period, the standards also acknowledge that at times students need to practice only one or two inquiry components.

Understanding Inquiry

The National Research Council in Inquiry and the National Science Education Standards (2000) identified several "essential features" of classroom inquiry. We have modified these essential features into questions to guide you in your quest for enhanced and more thoughtful student inquiry.

1. *Who asks the question?* In most curricula, these focusing questions are an element given in the materials. As a teacher you can look for labs that, at least on a periodic basis, allow students to pursue their own questions.

2. *Who designs the procedures?* To gain experience with the logic underlying experimentation, students need continuous practice with designing procedures. Some labs in which the primary target is content acquisition designate procedures. But others should ask students to do so.

3. *Who decides what data to collect?* Students need practice in determining the data to collect.

4. *Who formulates explanations based upon the data?* Students should be challenged to think—to analyze and draw conclusions based on their data, not just copy answers from the text materials.

5. *Who communicates and justifies the results?* Activities should push students not only to communicate but also to justify their answers. Activities also should be thoughtfully designed and interesting so that students want to share their results and argue about conclusions.

Making Time for Inquiry

One last question—Must each and every activity have students do all of this? The answer is an obvious and emphatic "No." You will find a great variety of activities in *Science Explorer*. Some activities focus on content acquisition, and thus they specify the question and most of the procedures. But many others stress in-depth inquiry from start to finish. Because inquiry is an intellectual pursuit, it cannot merely be characterized by keeping students busy and active. Too many students have a knack for being physically but not intellectually engaged in science. It is our job to help them engage intellectually.

Michael J. Padilla, Ph.D.
Program Author of *Science Explorer*
Professor of Science Education
University of Georgia
Athens, Georgia

"Because inquiry is an intellectual pursuit, it cannot merely be characterized by keeping students busy and active."

Evaluator's Checklist

Does your science program promote inquiry by—

✔ Enabling students to pursue their own questions

✔ Allowing students to design their own procedures

✔ Letting students determine what data are best to collect

✔ Challenging students to think critically

✔ Pushing students to justify their answers

Inquiry in *Science Explorer*

Science Explorer offers the most opportunities to get students to think like a scientist. By providing inquiry opportunities throughout the program, *Science Explorer* enables students to enhance their understanding by participating in the discovery.

Student Edition Inquiry

Six lab and activity options are included in every chapter, structured from directed to open-ended—providing you the flexibility to address all types of learners and accommodate your class time and equipment requirements. As Michael Padilla notes, some activities focus on content acquisition, and thus the question and most of the procedures are specified. But many others stress in-depth inquiry from start to finish. The graph below shows how, in general, inquiry levels are addressed in the Student Edition.

Science Explorer encourages students to develop inquiry skills across the spectrum from teacher-guided to open-ended. Even more opportunities for real-life applications of inquiry are included in Science & Society, Science & Technology, Careers in Science, and Interdisciplinary Exploration features.

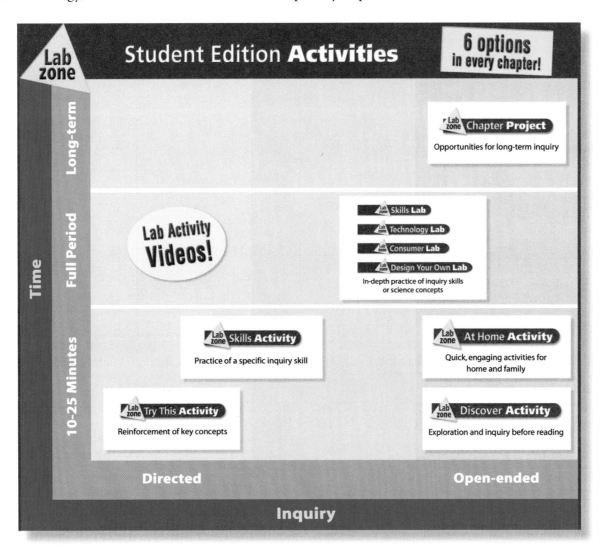

Inquiry Skills Chart

SCIENCE EXPLORER provides comprehensive teaching, practice, and assessment of science skills, with an emphasis on the process skills necessary for inquiry. This chart lists the skills covered in the program and cites the page numbers where each skill is covered.

	Student Text: Projects and Labs	Student Text: Activities	Student Text: Caption and Review Questions	Teacher's Edition: Extensions
Basic Process SKILLS				
Observing	4–5, 15, 25, 58–59, 87, 102–103, 120–121, 125, 134–135, 158–159	14, 20, 29, 40, 50, 57, 74, 83, 88, 114, 119, 124, 138, 164	17, 52	9, 28, 43, 76, 77, 79, 81, 82, 91, 94, 107, 109, 110, 115, 129, 138, 140, 143, 151
Inferring	4–5, 25, 58–59, 96–97, 125, 158–159	19, 30, 40, 48, 79, 104, 126, 128, 146, 148, 160	12, 14, 24, 29, 30, 33, 36, 45, 46, 57, 78, 89, 95, 100, 111, 115, 129, 132, 138, 153, 172	63, 143, 147, 152, 155, 156, 162, 166
Predicting	47, 87	19, 40, 46, 53, 60, 80, 84, 106, 122, 163, 165	24, 36, 56, 65, 70, 86, 95, 100, 111, 119, 132, 150, 172	43, 64, 160
Classifying	4–5, 25, 158–159	8, 16, 24, 136	27, 29, 36, 46, 70, 83, 94, 111, 118, 157	17, 20, 21, 23, 50, 91, 108, 109
Making Models	47, 102–103, 158–159	92		32, 41, 42, 78, 80, 139, 143, 153, 161
Communicating	38–39, 47, 59, 72–73, 87, 97, 102–103, 121, 125, 134–135, 159, 169	57, 83, 119, 124, 150, 164		43, 45, 61, 77, 139
Measuring	96–97, 125, 134–135, 158–159, 168–169	42, 46		
Calculating	47, 125	19, 48, 94, 142, 156	42, 157, 172	118
Creating Data Tables	15, 58–59, 87, 96–97, 134–135, 168–169	14		
Graphing		53, 94, 106, 163	132	
Advanced Process SKILLS				
Posing Questions	38–39, 121, 134–135			107
Developing Hypotheses	72–73, 97	164	36, 65, 70, 164	
Designing Experiments	15, 59, 72–73, 97, 120–121, 168–169	13, 164	36, 70	53, 93, 107, 115

	Student Text: Projects and Labs	Student Text: Activities	Student Text: Caption and Review Questions	Teacher's Edition: Extensions
Controlling Variables	15, 58–59, 87, 120–121		10, 36	11
Forming Operational Definitions		6, 26, 151		
Interpreting Data	15, 38–39, 97	19, 53, 94, 106, 163	37, 70, 100, 132, 172	148
Drawing Conclusions	15, 25, 38–39, 47, 58–59, 72–73, 96–97, 120–121, 159, 169	53, 106, 163, 164	22, 100, 132, 172	28, 52, 54, 56, 93, 154

Critical Thinking SKILLS

	Student Text: Projects and Labs	Student Text: Activities	Student Text: Caption and Review Questions	Teacher's Edition: Extensions
Comparing and Contrasting	59	26, 84	9, 29, 46, 69, 70, 75, 83, 86, 91, 95, 100, 111, 124, 129, 131, 132, 145, 150, 157, 164, 172	10, 23, 27, 28, 42, 50, 51, 75, 77, 89, 104, 110, 115, 127, 137, 140, 154, 165
Applying Concepts	134–135	150	14, 24, 33, 36, 57, 65, 119, 132, 145, 162, 164, 172	9, 56, 93
Interpreting Diagrams, Graphs, Photographs, and Maps		19, 53, 94, 106, 163	21, 36, 49, 70, 80, 81, 100, 101, 105, 111, 123, 128, 133, 143, 148, 154, 156, 172, 173	7, 21, 22, 44, 45, 53, 56, 61, 62, 76, 77, 81, 86, 90, 91, 110, 115, 118, 123, 124, 127, 128, 138, 141, 142, 143, 144, 148, 149, 155, 161, 163
Relating Cause and Effect		84, 160	36, 46, 65, 85, 93, 100, 107, 119, 124, 132, 141, 145, 164, 166, 172	117
Making Generalizations			7, 19, 28, 83	
Making Judgments	121, 168–169		83, 100, 150, 157, 167	
Problem Solving	168–169		70, 100	

Informational Organizational SKILLS

	Student Text: Projects and Labs	Student Text: Activities	Student Text: Caption and Review Questions	Teacher's Edition: Extensions
Concept Maps			35, 171	7, 34, 68, 98, 130, 153, 170
Compare/Contrast Tables		26, 84	86, 131	28
Venn Diagrams			69, 98	32, 82
Flowcharts				11, 85, 148
Cycle Diagrams			111, 133, 148, 154	

The *Science Explorer* program provides additional teaching, reinforcement, and assessment of skills in the *Inquiry Skills Activities Book* and the *Integrated Science Laboratory Manual*.

A National Look at Science Education

Project 2061 was established by the American Association for the Advancement of Science (AAAS) as a long-term project to improve science education nationwide. A primary goal of Project 2061 is to define a "common core of learning"—the knowledge and skills we want all students to achieve. Project 2061 published *Science for All Americans* in 1989 and followed this with *Benchmarks for Science Literacy* in 1993. *Benchmarks* recommends what students should know and be able to do by the end of grades 2, 5, 8, and 12. Project 2061 clearly states that *Benchmarks* is not a curriculum but a tool for designing successful curricula.

The National Research Council (NRC) used *Science for All Americans* and *Benchmarks* to develop the National Science Education Standards (NSES), which were published in 1996. The NSES are organized into six categories (Content, Teaching, Assessment, Professional Development, Program, and System) to help schools establish the conditions necessary to achieve scientific literacy for all students.

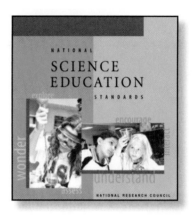

Michael Padilla, the program author of *Science Explorer,* guided one of six teams of teachers whose work led to the publication of *Benchmarks.* He also was a contributing writer of the National Science Education Standards. Under his guidance, *Science Explorer* has implemented these standards through its inquiry approach, a focus on student learning of important concepts and skills, and teacher support aligned with the NSES teaching standards.

Neither *Benchmarks* nor the NSES requires a single, uniform national curriculum, and in fact there is a great diversity nationwide in science curricula. The correlations that follow are designed to help you use the *Science Explorer* program to meet your particular curriculum needs.

Meeting the National Science Education Standards

LIVING THINGS

Science as Inquiry (Content Standard A)

● **Identify questions that can be answered through scientific investigations** Students develop a list of characteristics shared by living things. *(Chapter Project—Mystery Object)*

● **Design and conduct a scientific investigation** Students devise a system for determining if an object is alive. *(Chapter Project—Mystery Object)*

● **Communicate scientific procedures and explanations** Students report on the results of the investigation of the mystery object. *(Chapter Project—Mystery Object)*

Life Science (Content Standard C)

● **Reproduction and heredity** Reproduction is a fundamental characteristic of living things. *(What Is Life?)*

History and Nature of Science (Content Standard G)

● **History of science** Redi and Pasteur established that life comes from life. The observations of Darwin established that living things evolve. Miller and Urey demonstrated that conditions in Earth's early atmosphere could have produced complex organic molecules. *(What Is Life?; Classifying Organisms; Integrating Earth Science: The Origin of Life)*

VIRUSES AND BACTERIA

Science as Inquiry (Content Standard A)

● **Use mathematics in all aspects of scientific inquiry** How many viruses fit on a pin? *(Skills Lab—How Many Viruses Fit on a Pin?)*

● **Use appropriate tools and techniques to gather, analyze, and interpret data** Students investigate how well disinfectants control the growth of bacteria. *(Real-World Lab—Do Disinfectants Work?)*

Life Science (Content Standard C)

● **Diversity and adaptations of organisms** Students learn the main characteristics of viruses and how they reproduce. *(Viruses)* Students learn the main characteristics of bacteria and how they reproduce. *(Bacteria)*

● **Populations and ecosystems** Students learn that bacteria function as decomposers of dead organic matter. *(Bacteria)*

● **Structure and function in living systems** Students learn that the cells of bacteria are different from those of other organisms. *(Bacteria)* Students learn that disease is often the result of infection by bacteria and viruses. *(Integrating Health: Viruses, Bacteria, and Your Health)*

A National Look at Science Education *(continued)*

PROTISTS AND FUNGI

Science as Inquiry (Content Standard A)

● **Ask questions that can be answered by scientific investigations** How does the amount of fertilizer affect algae growth? *(Skills Lab—An Explosion of Life)* How does the presence of sugar or salt affect the activity of yeast? *(Skills Lab—What's for Lunch?)*

● **Design and conduct a scientific investigation** Students design and conduct an investigation about how light and moisture affect the growth of mushrooms. *(Chapter Project—A Mushroom Farm)*

Life Science (Content Standard C)

● **Structure and function of living systems** Students learn the main characteristics of protists and the differences among the protist groups. *(Protists)* Students learn the characteristics of fungi, how they obtain food, and their role in the living world. *(Fungi; Chapter Project—A Mushroom Farm)*

● **Populations and ecosystems** Students learn about the effects of the rapid growth of algae in the ocean and on a pond or a lake. *(Integrating Environmental Science: Algal Blooms)*

● **Diversity and adaptations of organisms** Students learn about the diversity among protists and fungi. *(Protists; Fungi)*

INTRODUCTION TO PLANTS

Science as Inquiry (Content Standard A)

● **Design and conduct a scientific investigation** Students design experiments to identify the raw materials and conditions that are involved in photosynthesis. *(Design Your Own Lab—Eye on Photosynthesis)*

● **Communicate scientific procedures and explanations** Students create an interactive exhibit that teaches young children how a plant becomes a useful product. *(Chapter Project—Design and Build an Interactive Exhibit)*

Physical Science (Content Standard B)

● **Transfer of energy** Light can pass through objects, be absorbed by objects, or be reflected by objects. The energy from the sun is stored in plants during photosynthesis. *(Photosynthesis and Light; Design Your Own Lab—Eye on Photosynthesis)*

Life Science (Content Standard C)

● **Structure and function in living systems** Plants are multicellular and have a variety of structures that carry out life functions. *(The Plant Kingdom; Integrating Physics: Photosynthesis and Light; Mosses, Liverworts, and Hornworts; Ferns, Club Mosses, and Horsetails; Chapter Project—Design and Build an Interactive Exhibit; Design Your Own Lab—Eye on Photosynthesis; Skills Lab—Masses of Mosses)*

● **Reproduction and heredity** Mosses and ferns have life cycles that include gametophyte and sporophyte stages. *(Mosses, Liverworts, and Hornworts; Ferns, Club Mosses, and Housetails)*

● **Diversity and adaptations of organisms** There are many kinds of plant species. Mosses and ferns evolved adaptations that allowed them to survive on land. *(The Plant Kingdom; Mosses, Liverworts, and Hornworts; Ferns, Club Mosses, and Horsetails; Skills lab—Masses of Mosses)*

SEED PLANTS

Science and Technology (Content Standard E)

● **Design a solution or product** Students design a system for growing plants without soil. *(Technology Lab—Design and Build a Hydroponic Garden)*

Life Science (Content Standard C)

● **Structure and function in living systems** Seed plants have specialized tissues, such as xylem and phloem, that carry out specific functions. *(The Characteristics of Seed Plants)* Gymnosperms and angiosperms have different structures involved in reproduction. *(Gymnosperms; Angiosperms; Skills Lab—A Close Look at Flowers)* Hormones are chemicals that govern growth and development *(Plant Responses and Growth)*

● **Reproduction and heredity** Seeds are specialized structures for reproduction. *(The Characteristics of Seed Plants)* Most gymnosperms sexually reproduce using cones. *(Gymnosperms)* Angiosperms sexually reproduce using flowers and fruit. *(Angiosperms; Chapter Project—Cycle of a Lifetime; Skills Lab—A Close Look at Flowers)*

Science in Personal and Social Perspectives (Content Standard F)

● **Populations, resources, and environments** Overpopulation may lead to a food shortage. *(Integrating Technology: Feeding the World)*

Note: To see how the benchmarks are supported by *SCIENCE EXPLORER,* go to **PHSchool.com.**

Reading Comprehension in the Science Classroom

Q&A

Q: Why are science texts often difficult for students to read and comprehend?

A: In general, science texts make complex literacy and knowledge demands on learners. They have a more technical vocabulary and a more demanding syntax, and place a greater emphasis on inferential reasoning.

Q: What does research say about facilitating comprehension?

A: Studies comparing novices and experts show that the conceptual organization of experts' knowledge is very different from that of novices. For example, experts emphasize core concepts when organizing knowledge, while novices focus on superficial details. To facilitate comprehension, effective teaching strategies should support and scaffold students as they build an understanding of the key concepts and concept relationships within a text unit.

Q: What strategies can teachers use to facilitate comprehension?

A: Three complementary strategies are very important in facilitating student comprehension of science texts. First, guide student interaction with the text using the built-in strategies. Second, organize the curriculum in terms of core concepts (e.g., the **Key Concepts** in each section). Third, develop visual representations of the relationships among the key concepts and vocabulary that can be referred to during instruction.

Nancy Romance, Ph.D.
Professor of Science Education
Florida Atlantic University
Fort Lauderdale, Florida

"Effective teaching strategies should support and scaffold students as they build an understanding of the key concepts and concept relationships within a text unit."

Reading Support in *Science Explorer*

The latest research emphasizes the importance of activating learners' prior knowledge and teaching them to distinguish core concepts from less important information. These skills are now more important than ever, because success in science requires students to read, understand, and connect complex terms and concepts.

Before students read—
Reading Preview introduces students to the key concepts and key terms they'll find in each section. The **Target Reading Skill** is identified and applied with a graphic organizer.

During the section—
Boldface Sentences identify each key concept and encourage students to focus on the big ideas of science.

Reading Checkpoints reinforce students' understanding by slowing them down to review after every concept is discussed.

Caption Questions draw students into the art and photos, helping them connect the content to the images.

After students read—
Section Assessment revisits the **Target Reading Skill** and encourages students to use the graphic organizer.

Each review question is scaffolded and models the way students think, by first easing them into a review and then challenging them with increasingly more difficult questions.

Evaluator's Checklist

Does your science program promote reading comprehension with—

✔ Text structured in an outline format and key concepts highlighted in boldface type

✔ Real-world applications to activate prior knowledge

✔ Key concepts, critical vocabulary, and a reading skill for every section

✔ Sample graphic organizers for each section

✔ Relevant photos and carefully constructed graphics with questions

✔ Reading checkpoints that appear in each section

✔ Scaffolded questions in section assessments

Math in the Science Classroom

Why should students concern themselves with mathematics in your science class?

Good science requires good data from which to draw conclusions. Technology enhances the ability to measure in a variety of ways. Often the scientist must measure large amounts of data, and thus an aim of analysis is to reduce the data to a summary that makes sense and is consistent with established norms of communication—i.e., mathematics.

Calculating measures of central tendency (e.g., mean, median, or mode), variability (e.g., range), and shape (graphic representations) can effectively reduce 500 data points to 3 without losing the essential characteristics of the data. Scientists understand that a trade-off exists between precision and richness as data are folded into categories, and so margins of error can be quantified in mathematical terms and factored into all scientific findings.

Mathematics is the language used by scientists to model change in the world. Understanding change is a vital part of the inquiry process. Mathematics serves as a common language to communicate across the sciences. Fields of scientific research that originated as separate disciplines are now integrated, such as happened with bioengineering. What do the sciences have in common? Each uses the language of mathematics to communicate about data and the process of data analysis. Recognizing this need, *Science Explorer* integrates mathematics practice throughout the program and gives students ample opportunity to hone their math skills.

Clearly, mathematics plays an important role in your science classroom!

William Tate, Ph.D.
Professor of Education and Applied Statistics and Computation
Washington University
St. Louis, Missouri

> "Mathematics is the language used by scientists to model change in the world."

Integrated Math Support

In the Student Edition

The math instruction is based on principles derived from Prentice Hall's research-based mathematics program.

Sample Problems, Math Practice, Analyzing Data, and a Math Skills Handbook all help to provide practice at point of use, encouraging students to Read and Understand, Plan and Solve, and then Look Back and Check.

Color-coded variables aid student navigation and help reinforce their comprehension.

In the Teacher's Edition

Math teaching notes enable the science teacher to support math instruction and math objectives on high-stakes tests.

In the Guided Reading and Study Workbook

These unique worksheets help students master reading and enhance their study and math skills. Students can create a record of their work for study and review.

Evaluator's Checklist

Does your science program promote math skills by—

✔ Giving students opportunities to collect data

✔ Providing students opportunities to analyze data

✔ Enabling students to practice math skills

✔ Helping students solve equations by using color-coded variables

✔ Using sample problems to apply science concepts

Technology and Design

Technology and Design in the Science Classroom

Much of the world we live in is designed and made by humans. The buildings in which we live, the cars we drive, the medicines we take, and often the food we eat are products of technology. The knowledge and skills needed to understand the processes used to create these products should be a component of every student's basic literacy.

Some schools offer hands-on instruction on how technology development works through industrial arts curricula. Even then, there is a disconnect among science (understanding how nature works), mathematics (understanding data-driven models), and technology (understanding the human-made world). The link among these fields of study is the engineering design process—that process by which one identifies a human need and uses science knowledge and human ingenuity to create a technology to satisfy the need. Engineering gives students the problem-solving and design skills they will need to succeed in our sophisticated, three-dimensional, technological world.

As a complement to "science as inquiry," the National Science Education Standards (NRC, 1996) call for students at all age levels to develop the abilities related to "technology as design," including the ability to identify and frame a problem and then to design, implement, and evaluate a solution. At the 5–8 grade level, the standards call for students to be engaged in complex problem-solving and to learn more about how science and technology complement each other. It's also important for students to understand that there are often constraints involved in design as well as trade-offs and unintended consequences of technological solutions to problems.

As the *Standards for Technological Literacy* (ITEA, 2000) state, "Science and technology are like conjoined twins. While they have separate identities they must remain inextricably connected." Both sets of standards emphasize how progress in science leads to new developments in technology, while technological innovation in turn drives advances in science.

Ioannis Miaoulis, Ph.D.
President
Museum of Science
Boston, Massachusetts

"Engineering gives students the problem-solving and design skills they will need to succeed in our sophisticated, three-dimensional, technological world."

Evaluator's Checklist

Does your science program promote technology and design by—

✔ Incorporating technology and design concepts and skills into the science curriculum

✔ Giving students opportunities to identify and solve technological design problems

✔ Providing students opportunities to analyze the impact of technology on society

✔ Enabling students to practice technology and design skills

Technology and Design

Technology and Design in *Science Explorer*

How often do you hear your students ask: "Why do I need to learn this?" Connecting them to the world of technology and design in their everyday life is one way to help answer this question. It is also why so many state science curricula are now emphasizing technology and design concepts and skills.

Science Explorer makes a special effort to include a technology and design strand that encourages students to not only identify a need but to take what they learned in science and apply it to design a possible solution, build a prototype, test and evaluate the design, and/or troubleshoot the design. This strand also provides definitions of technology and engineering and discusses the similarities and differences between these endeavors and science. Students will learn to analyze the risks and benefits of a new technology and to consider the tradeoffs, such as safety, costs, efficiency, and appearance.

In the Student Edition

Integrated Technology & Design Sections

Sections throughout *Science Explorer* specifically integrate technology and design with the content of the text. For example, students not only learn how seismographs work but also learn what role seismographs play in society and how people use the data that are gathered.

Technology Labs

These labs help students gain experience in designing and building a device or product that meets a particular need or solves a problem. Students follow a design process of Research and Investigate, Design and Build, and Evaluate and Redesign.

Chapter Projects

Chapter Projects work hand-in-hand with the chapter content. Students design, build, and test based on real-world situations. They have the opportunity to apply the knowledge and skills learned to building a product.

Special Features

This technology and design strand is also reflected in Technology & Society and Science & Society features as well as Technology & History timelines. These highly visual features introduce a technology and its impact on society. For example, students learn how a hybrid car differs from a traditional car.

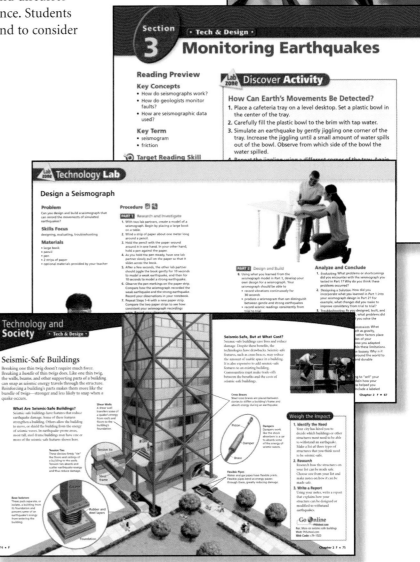

Assessment in the Science Curriculum

No Child Left Behind clearly challenges school districts across the nation to raise expectations for all students with testing of student achievement in science beginning in 2007–2008.

A primary goal of NCLB is to provide classroom teachers with better data from scientifically valid assessments in order to inform instructional planning and to identify students who are at risk and require intervention. It has been a common practice to teach a science lesson, administer a test, grade it, and move on. This practice is a thing of the past. With the spotlight now on improving student performance, it is essential to use assessment results as a way to identify student strengths and challenges. Providing student feedback and obtaining student input is a valuable, essential part of the assessment process.

Assessment is a never-ending cycle, as is shown in the following diagram. Although you may begin at any point in the assessment cycle, the basic process is the same.

An important assessment strategy is to ensure that students have ample opportunities to check their understanding of skills and concepts before moving on to the next topic. Checking for understanding also includes asking appropriate, probing questions with each example presented. This enables students and teachers to know whether the skills or concepts being introduced are actually understood.

Eileen Depka
Supervisor of Standards and Assessment
Waukesha, Wisconsin

"Meeting the NCLB challenge will necessitate an integrated approach to assessment with a variety of assessment tools."

Use a variety of assessment tools to gain information and strengthen student understanding.

Implement the plan with a focus on gathering and using assessment information throughout.

Analyze assessment results to create a picture of student strengths and challenges.

Identify strategies to achieve the target, create a plan for implementation, and choose assessments tools.

Choose a target to create a focused path on which to proceed.

IMPLEMENT · ASSESS · ANALYZE · TARGET · STRATEGIZE

Evaluator's Checklist

Does your science program include assessments that—

✔ Are embedded before, during, and after lesson instruction

✔ Align to standards and to the instructional program

✔ Assess both skill acquisition and understanding

✔ Include meaningful rubrics to guide students

✔ Mirror the various formats of standardized tests

Assessment in *Science Explorer*

Science Explorer's remarkable range of strategies for checking progress will help teachers find the right opportunity for reaching all their students.

The assessment strategies in *Science Explorer* will help both students and teachers alike ensure student success in content mastery as well as high-stakes test performance. A wealth of opportunities built into the Student Edition help students monitor their own progress. Teachers are supported with ongoing assessment opportunities in the Teacher's Edition and an easy-to-use, editable test generator linked to content objectives. These integrated, ongoing assessment tools assure success.

Especially to support state and national testing objectives, Prentice Hall has developed test preparation materials that model the NCLB approach.

- **Diagnostic Assessment** tools provide in-depth analysis of strengths and weaknesses, areas of difficulty, and probable underlying causes that can help teachers make instructional decisions and plan intervention strategies.

- **Progress Monitoring** tools aligned with content objectives and state tests provide ongoing, longitudinal records of student achievement detailing individual student progress toward meeting end-of-year and end-of-schooling grade level, district, or state standards.

- **Outcomes** tools that mimic state and national tests show whether individual students have met the expected standards and can help a school system judge whether it has made adequate progress in improving its performance year by year.

Caption Questions enhance critical thinking skills

Reading Checkpoints reinforce students' understanding

Scaffolded Section Assessment Questions model the way students think

Comprehensive Chapter Reviews and Assessment provide opportunities for students to check their own understanding and practice valuable high-stakes test-taking skills

Exam*View*®, Computer Test Bank CD-ROM provides teachers access to thousands of modifiable test questions in English and Spanish

Test Preparation Blackline Masters and Student Workbook include diagnostic and prescription tools, progress-monitoring aids, and practice tests that help teachers focus on improving test scores.

Section 3 Assessment

Target Reading Skill Sequencing Refer to your flowchart about seismographs as you answer Question 1.

Reviewing Key Concepts

1. a. **Defining** What is a seismogram?
   b. **Explaining** How can geologists tell apart the different types of seismic waves on a seismogram?
   c. **Comparing and Contrasting** Two identical seismographs are located 1,000 km and 1,200 km from an earthquake's epicenter. How would the two seismograms for the earthquake compare?

2. a. **Reviewing** What changes are measured by the instruments used to monitor faults?
   b. **Describing** How are satellites used to measure movements along a fault?
   c. **Inferring** A satellite that monitors a fault detects an increasing tilt in the land surface along the fault. What could this change in the land surface indicate?

3. a. **Listing** What are three ways in which geologists use seismographic data?
   b. **Explaining** How do geologists use seismographic data to make maps of faults?
   c. **Making Generalizations** Why is it difficult to predict earthquakes?

Writing in Science

Dialogue Geologists in Alaska have just detected an earthquake and located the earthquake's epicenter. Write a dialogue in which the geologists notify a disaster response team that will help people in the earthquake area.

Chapter 2 F ◆ 65

Standardized Test Prep

Test-Taking Tip

When answering questions about diagrams, read all parts of the diagram carefully, including title, captions, and labels. Make sure that you understand the meaning of arrows and other symbols. Determine exactly what the question asks. Then eliminate those answer choices that are not supported by the diagram.

Practice answering this question.
The diagram shows how stress affects a mass of rock in a process called
   A compression.
   B tension.
   C squeezing.
   D shearing.
The correct answer is **D** because the arrows show rock being pulled in opposite directions.

Choose the letter that best answers the question or completes the statement.

1. In a strike-slip fault, rock masses along the fault move
   A in the same direction.
   B down only.
   C together.
   D sideways past each other.

2. Stress will build until an earthquake occurs if friction along a fault is
   F decreasing.   G high.
   H low.   J changed to heat.

Use the information below and your knowledge of science to answer Questions 3 and 4.

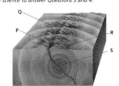

Seismic waves

3. When an earthquake occurs, seismic waves travel
   A from P in all directions.
   B from R to S.
   C from S in all directions.
   D from Q to P.

4. At point R, seismic waves from an earthquake would be
   F weaker than at P.
   G likely to cause little damage.
   H weaker than at Q.
   J likely to cause the most damage.

5. To estimate the total energy released by an earthquake, a geologist should use the
   A Mercalli scale.   B Richter scale.
   C epicenter scale.   D moment magnitude scale.

Constructed Response

6. A geologist discovers a large fault beneath a major city. Why would this information be helpful in determining earthquake risk in the area? What three safety steps should the geologist recommend?

Chapter 2 F ◆ 79

Master Materials List

SCIENCE EXPLORER offers an abundance of activity options in the Student Edition so you can pick and choose those that suit your needs. Prentice Hall has worked with Neo/SCI Corporation to develop Consumable Kits and Nonconsumable Kits that precisely match the needs of the *SCIENCE EXPLORER* labs. Use this Master Materials List or the Materials Ordering CD-ROM to help order your supplies. For more information on materials kits for this program, contact your local Prentice Hall sales representative or Neo/SCI Corporation at 1-800-526-6689 or **www.neosci.com**.

Consumable Materials

Description	Textbook Section(s)	Quantity per Class	Description	Textbook Section(s)	Quantity per Class
Agar, nutrient, sterile, 225 mL	2-2 (Lab)	1	*Gloves, plastic, box	2-3 (DIS)	1
Bag, plastic, clear, sealable	1-1 (CP), 1-1 (Lab), 3-3 (DIS), 5-5 (DIS)	20	Goldfish	1-1 (CP)	5
			Glue	4-2 (DIS)	5
Balloon, round, large	3-3 (TT), 3-3 (Lab)	30	Larvae, insect	1-1 (CP)	5
Beans, dried (kidney, lima, or navy)	2-2 (DIS), 5-1 (TT)	5	*Leaves, variety	1-2 (Lab), 4-1 (DIS), 5-2 (DIS)	40
*Bottle, plastic soda, 2 L	5-5 (Lab)	5			
Bottles, plastic, narrow-necked, small	3-3 (Lab)	25	*Lemon, slice	1-1 (TT)	5
*Box, shoe	4-2 (DIS)	5	Lens paper 4x6"	5-3 (Lab)	5
*Bread, without preservatives, bag	1-1 (Lab)	1	Marker, permanent	3-2 (Lab), 3-3 (Lab)	5
*Bread, moldy	3-3 (DIS)	5	Methylene blue, 30 mL	2-2 (TT)	1
Celery	5-1 (SA)	5	Modeling clay, white, 1 lb	3-3 (TT)	1
Chlorella, coupon for	3-1 (TT)	1	Mold, bread	1-1 (CP)	5
Cone, pine, female	5-2 (TT)	5	Mold, slime	1-1 (CP)	5
Container, wide-mouthed	4-2 (Lab), 5-1 (SA)	10	Moss Clump, coupon for	4-3 (Lab)	10
Cotton Balls, bag	3-1 (TT), 3-3 (TT)	1	Mushroom, growing kit	3-1 (CP)	5
Cotton swabs, pkg	5-1 (CP)	1	*Mushroom, spores, package	3-1 (CP)	1
Coverslip, 1 oz	1-1 (CP), 2-2 (TT), 3-1 (DIS), 3-1 (TT), 5-1 (SA), 5-3 (Lab)	1	Nutrient solution	5-5 (Lab)	5
			Paper, construction, green, sheet	3-2 (DIS)	25
Cup, paper, 7 oz	2-2 (DIS)	40	*Paper, white, ream	2-1 (Lab), 4-2 (DIS), 5-2 (TT)	1
Cup, plastic, 10 oz	2-3 (DIS)	5			
*Disinfectants, household	2-2 (Lab)	2	Paramecium, coupon for	3-1 (TT)	1
Dropper, plastic, pkg/10	1-1 (CP), 1-1 (Lab), 2-2 (TT), 2-2 (Lab), 2-3 (DIS), 3-1 (DIS), 3-1 (TT), 4-3 (DIS), 4-3 (Lab), 4-4 (DIS), 4-4 (TT), 5-1 (SA), 5-3 (Lab)	13	Peanuts, shelled	5-1 (TT)	1
			Peas, dried	5-1 (TT)	1
			Peat moss, bag	4-3 (DIS)	1
			*Pencil	2-1 (Lab), 5-4 (DIS)	10
			Pencil, wax	2-2 (Lab), 4-2 (Lab)	5
Elodea plants, coupon for	4-2 (Lab)	1	Petri dish, plastic, pkg/20	1-1 (CP), 2-2 (Lab), 3-1 (SA), 3-2 (Lab), 4-4 (DIS)	1
Euglena, coupon for	3-1 (SA)	1			
*Fern	4-4 (TT)	5	Phenol Red Sodium Salt, 30 mL	2-3 (DIS)	1
Fertilizer, liquid, 8 oz	3-1 (CP), 3-2 (Lab)	1	Pin, straight	2-1 (Lab), 3-3 (TT)	5
*Flower, large	5-3 (Lab)	5	Plant, green, potted	1-1 (CP), 1-3 (DIS)	5
Foil, aluminum, roll	3-1 (SA)	1	*Plant, variety, potted	5-4 (DIS), 5-5 (Lab)	20
Food coloring, red, 30 mL	4-4 (DIS), 5-1 (SA)	1	Plant, touch-sensitive	5-4 (DIS)	1
*Food items	5-1 (DIS)	15	Plate, paper	1-1 (Lab)	10
*Fruit	5-3 (DIS)	15	Pond Culture, coupon for	3-1 (DIS)	1
*Fruit, moldy	3-3 (DIS)	5	Potato, slice	1-1 (SA)	5

KEY: * = School Supplied

Quantities based on five groups of six students per class.

Master Materials List

Consumable Materials (continued)

Description	Textbook Section(s)	Quantity per Class	Description	Textbook Section(s)	Quantity per Class
Potting soil, large bag	5-1 (CP)	1	Straw, plastic	3-3 (Lab)	25
Potting tray	5-1 (CP)	5	String, ball	3-3 (Lab)	1
Raisins, box	5-5 (DIS)	1	Substrate, lacking nutrients	3-1 (CP)	1
Ruler, 15 cm	5-3 (Lab)	5	Sugar, 454 g	1-1 (CP), 3-3 (Lab)	1
Salt, 737 g	3-3 (Lab)	1	Tags, one per student	5-5 (DIS)	1
Salts, soluble, "crystal garden" kit	1-1 (CP)	5	Tape, masking, roll	2-1 (Lab), 3-3 (DIS), 3-3 (TT), 5-3 (Lab)	1
Sand, white, fine, 3 lb. bag	4-3 (DIS)	1	Tape, packing, roll	1-1 (Lab)	1
Scalpel	5-3 (Lab)	5	*Tape, transparent, roll	2-2 (Lab)	1
Sea animal (i.e., tropical fish, starfish, anemone)	1-3 (DIS)	5	Toothpicks, pkg/250	4-3 (Lab)	1
Seeds, tomato or pea, pkt	5-1 (CP)	5	*Towel, paper, roll	1-1 (CP), 1-1 (SA), 5-3 (Lab), 5-5 (Lab)	1
Shrimp, brine	1-1 (CP)	1	Water, aquarium	3-2 (SA)	
Slide, microscope, glass, pkg/72	1-1 (CP), 2-2 (TT), 3-1 (DIS), 3-1 (TT), 5-3 (Lab)	1	Water, distilled, bottle	2-3 (DIS)	1
			Worm, live	1-3 (DIS)	5
Sodium bicarbonate solution, 15 mL	4-2 (Lab)	1	Yeast, dry active, powdered, 7 g	1-1 (CP), 3-3 (Lab)	1
Sodium hydroxide solution, 0.01 mL	2-3 (DIS)	1	*Yogurt, plain, unpasteurized (container, small)	2-2 (TT)	5
Spoons, plastic, pkg	5-1 (SA)	1			
Stick, craft, 30 cm	3-3 (TT)	5			

Nonconsumable Materials

Description	Textbook Section(s)	Quantity per Class	Description	Textbook Section(s)	Quantity per Class
*Apron, safety	2-2 (TT), 2-3 (DIS), 5-1 (SA), 5-3 (DIS)	30	*Lamp	1-1 (CP), 4-2 (Lab)	5
			Meter stick, 1/2	2-1 (Lab)	5
*Balance	1-1 (SA)	5	*Microscope	1-1 (CP), 2-2 (TT), 3-1 (DIS), 3-1 (TT), 3-1 (SA), 5-3 (Lab)	5
Beaker, 400 mL	3-3 (Lab)	5			
Bottle, spray	3-1 (CP)	1			
*Calculator	2-1 (Lab), 5-1 (SA)	5	Mirror, 7.5 x 12.5 cm	1-1 (TT), 1-1 (SA), 4-2 (DIS)	5
*Goggles, safety	2-3 (DIS), 4-4 (DIS)	30			
Graduated cylinder, polypropylene, 50	3-2 (Lab), 3-3 (Lab), 4-3 (DIS)	15	Prism, 25mm x 50 mm	4-2 (DIS)	5
			Ruler, 15 cm	1-1 (CP), 1-2 (Lab), 3-3 (Lab), 4-3 (Lab), 5-2 (DIS), 5-3 (DIS), 5-3 (SA)	5
*Hair dryer	1-1 (SA)	5			
Hand lens	1-1 (CP), 1-2 (Lab), 3-3 (DIS), 4-1 (DIS), 4-3 (Lab), 4-4 (TT), 5-1 (TT), 5-2 (DIS), 5-2 (TT), 5-3 (DIS), 5-3 (Lab)	5	Scissors	1-1 (CP), 2-1 (Lab)	5
			Stopwatch	4-3 (DIS)	1
			Test tube, 18x150 mm	4-2 (Lab)	15
			Thermometer	3-1 (CP)	1
*Hole punch	3-2 (DIS)	5	Timer	5-1 (SA)	1
*Jar, glass with lid	3-2 (Lab)	20	Toy, wind-up	1-1 (DIS)	5
*Key, with matching lock	2-1 (DIS)	5	Tube, glass, 75 mm, pkg/100	4-4 (DIS)	1

KEY: * = School Supplied

Quantities based on five groups of six students per class.

From Bacteria to Plants

Book-Specific Resources

Student Edition
Interactive Textbook
Teacher's Edition
All-in-One Teaching Resources
Color Transparencies
Guided Reading and Study Workbook
Student Edition on Audio CD
Discovery Channel Video
Lab Activity Video
Consumable and Nonconsumable Materials Kits

Program Print Resources

Integrated Science Laboratory Manual
Computer Microscope Lab Manual
Inquiry Skills Activity Books
Progress Monitoring Assessments
Test Preparation Workbook
Test-Taking Tips With Transparencies
Teacher's ELL Handbook
Reading in the Content Area

Program Technology Resources

TeacherExpress™ CD-ROM
Interactive Textbook
Presentation Pro CD-ROM
ExamView®, Computer Test Bank CD-ROM
Lab zone™ Easy Planner CD-ROM
Probeware Lab Manual With CD-ROM
Computer Microscope and Lab Manual
Materials Ordering CD-ROM
Discovery Channel DVD Library
Lab Activity DVD Library
Web Site at PHSchool.com

Spanish Print Resources

Spanish Student Edition
Spanish Guided Reading and Study Workbook
Spanish Teaching Guide With Tests

Acknowledgments appear on page 214, which constitutes an extension of this copyright page.

Cover
Ferns grow among giant redwood trees in Redwood National Park in California (top). Although these colorful fly agaric mushrooms might look harmless, they are extremely poisonous (bottom).

ISBN 0-13-115086-3

2 3 4 5 6 7 8 9 10   08 07 06 05 04

Program Authors

Michael J. Padilla, Ph.D.
Professor of Science Education
University of Georgia
Athens, Georgia

Michael Padilla is a leader in middle school science education. He has served as an author and elected officer for the National Science Teachers Association and as a writer of the National Science Education Standards. As lead author of Science Explorer, Mike has inspired the team in developing a program that meets the needs of middle grades students, promotes science inquiry, and is aligned with the National Science Education Standards.

Ioannis Miaoulis, Ph.D.
President
Museum of Science
Boston, Massachusetts

Originally trained as a mechanical engineer, Ioannis Miaoulis is in the forefront of the national movement to increase technological literacy. As dean of the Tufts University School of Engineering, Dr. Miaoulis spearheaded the introduction of engineering into the Massachusetts curriculum. Currently he is working with school systems across the country to engage students in engineering activities and to foster discussions on the impact of science and technology on society.

Martha Cyr, Ph.D.
Director of K–12 Outreach
Worcester Polytechnic Institute
Worcester, Massachusetts

Martha Cyr is a noted expert in engineering outreach. She has over nine years of experience with programs and activities that emphasize the use of engineering principles, through hands-on projects, to excite and motivate students and teachers of mathematics and science in grades K–12. Her goal is to stimulate a continued interest in science and mathematics through engineering.

Book Author

Jan Jenner, Ph.D.
Science Writer
Talladega, Alabama

Contributing Writers

James Robert Kaczynski, Jr.
Science Instructor
Jamestown School
Jamestown, Rhode Island

Evan P. Silberstein
Science Instructor
The Frisch School
Paramus, New Jersey

Joseph Stukey, Ph.D.
Department of Biology
Hope College
Holland, Michigan

Consultants

Reading Consultant

Nancy Romance, Ph.D.
Professor of Science
Education
Florida Atlantic University
Fort Lauderdale, Florida

Mathematics Consultant

William Tate, Ph.D.
Professor of Education and
Applied Statistics and
Computation
Washington University
St. Louis, Missouri

Reviewers

Teacher Reviewers

David R. Blakely
Arlington High School
Arlington, Massachusetts

Jane E. Callery
Two Rivers Magnet Middle
    School
East Hartford, Connecticut

Melissa Lynn Cook
Oakland Mills High School
Columbia, Maryland

James Fattic
Southside Middle School
Anderson, Indiana

Dan Gabel
Hoover Middle School
Rockville, Maryland

Wayne Goates
Eisenhower Middle School
Goddard, Kansas

Katherine Bobay Graser
Mint Hill Middle School
Charlotte, North Carolina

Darcy Hampton
Deal Junior High School
Washington, D.C.

Karen Kelly
Pierce Middle School
Waterford, Michigan

David Kelso
Manchester High School Central
Manchester, New Hampshire

Benigno Lopez, Jr.
Sleepy Hill Middle School
Lakeland, Florida

Angie L. Matamoros, Ph.D.
ALM Consulting, INC.
Weston, Florida

Tim McCollum
Charleston Middle School
Charleston, Illinois

Bruce A. Mellin
Brooks School
North Andover, Massachusetts

Ella Jay Parfitt
Southeast Middle School
Baltimore, Maryland

Evelyn A. Pizzarello
Louis M. Klein Middle School
Harrison, New York

Kathleen M. Poe
Fletcher Middle School
Jacksonville, Florida

Shirley Rose
Lewis and Clark Middle School
Tulsa, Oklahoma

Linda Sandersen
Greenfield Middle School
Greenfield, Wisconsin

Mary E. Solan
Southwest Middle School
Charlotte, North Carolina

Mary Stewart
University of Tulsa
Tulsa, Oklahoma

Paul Swenson
Billings West High School
Billings, Montana

Thomas Vaughn
Arlington High School
Arlington, Massachusetts

Susan C. Zibell
Central Elementary
Simsbury, Connecticut

Safety Reviewers

W. H. Breazeale, Ph.D.
Department of Chemistry
College of Charleston
Charleston, South Carolina

Ruth Hathaway, Ph.D.
Hathaway Consulting
Cape Girardeau, Missouri

Douglas Mandt, M.S.
Science Education Consultant
Edgewood, Washington

Activity Field Testers

Nicki Bibbo
Witchcraft Heights School
Salem, Massachusetts

Rose-Marie Botting
Broward County Schools
Fort Lauderdale, Florida

Colleen Campos
Laredo Middle School
Aurora, Colorado

Elizabeth Chait
W. L. Chenery Middle School
Belmont, Massachusetts

Holly Estes
Hale Middle School
Stow, Massachusetts

Laura Hapgood
Plymouth Community
    Intermediate School
Plymouth, Massachusetts

Mary F. Lavin
Plymouth Community
    Intermediate School
Plymouth, Massachusetts

James MacNeil, Ph.D.
Cambridge, Massachusetts

Lauren Magruder
St. Michael's Country
    Day School
Newport, Rhode Island

Jeanne Maurand
Austin Preparatory School
Reading, Massachusetts

Joanne Jackson-Pelletier
Winman Junior High School
Warwick, Rhode Island

Warren Phillips
Plymouth Public Schools
Plymouth, Massachusetts

Carol Pirtle
Hale Middle School
Stow, Massachusetts

Kathleen M. Poe
Fletcher Middle School
Jacksonville, Florida

Cynthia B. Pope
Norfolk Public Schools
Norfolk, Virginia

Anne Scammell
Geneva Middle School
Geneva, New York

Karen Riley Sievers
Callanan Middle School
Des Moines, Iowa

David M. Smith
Eyer Middle School
Allentown, Pennsylvania

Gene Vitale
Parkland School
McHenry, Illinois

Contents

From Bacteria to Plants

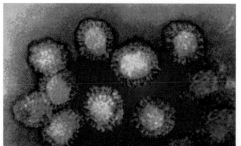
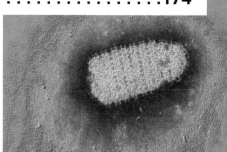

Reference Section

Enhance understanding through dynamic video.

Preview Get motivated with this introduction to the chapter content.

Field Trip Explore a real-world story related to the chapter content.

Assessment Review content and take an assessment.

Get connected to exciting Web resources in every lesson.

SCᴵLINKS｡ Find Web links on topics relating to every section.

Active Art Interact with selected visuals from every chapter online.

Planet Diary® Explore news and natural phenomena through weekly reports.

Science News® Keep up to date with the latest science discoveries.

Experience the complete textbook online and on CD-ROM.

Activities Practice skills and learn content.

Videos Explore content and learn important lab skills.

Audio Support Hear key terms spoken and defined.

Self-Assessment Use instant feedback to help you track your progress.

Activities

Disease Detective Solves Mystery

Inquiry and Vocabulary

Dr. Cindy Friedman works at the Centers for Disease Control and Prevention. She is a physician and investigator who studies the transmission of infectious diseases throughout the world. By reading about her work on a particular case, students will gain insights about how Dr. Friedman investigates disease outbreaks. They will read about how Dr. Friedman plans and conducts her investigations. They will also learn about fieldwork involved in her investigations, including interviewing, sampling, and collecting data. The skills that Dr. Friedman uses every day are the same inquiry skills that students need to become successful young scientists.

Build Background Knowledge

Knowledge about Salmonella

Have students write *What I Know about Salmonella* on the top of a sheet of paper. Give them five minutes to record whatever facts and information they know or think they know about salmonella. At the end of the five minutes, have students share the items on their lists, making a cumulative list on the board.

Introduce the Career

Before students read the feature, tell students that salmonella is one of the most common intestinal infections in the United States. However, only a small percentage of salmonella cases are officially reported every year. Ask: **Why do you suppose such a small number of salmonella cases are reported each year?** (*Student responses will vary but may include ideas such as it is difficult to diagnose or people do not realize they are infected.*) **In what ways might a scientist research how a group of people have been infected by salmonella?** (*Student responses will vary but may include ideas such as talking to those that have been infected, collecting samples, and testing samples for the bacteria.*)

Disease Detective Solves Mystery

The Colorado Health Department had a problem. Seven children had become sick with diarrhea, stomach cramps, fever, and vomiting. Within days, another 43 people had the same symptoms.

Tests indicated that they all had become infected with salmonella. Salmonella are bacteria that are usually transmitted through foods such as contaminated meat or eggs.

How did these children become infected with salmonella? To find the answer, Colorado health officials called in Dr. Cindy Friedman. Dr. Friedman works at the Centers for Disease Control and Prevention (CDC), a United States government agency that tracks down and studies the transmission of diseases throughout the world.

Cindy Friedman studies outbreaks of diseases in groups of people rather than in individuals. Her specialty is infectious diseases, illnesses that spread from person to person. She has investigated outbreaks of disease in such places as rural Bolivia in South America, Cape Verde Islands off the coast of Africa, and a Vermont farm.

Career Path

Cindy Friedman grew up in Brooklyn, New York. After receiving a B.S. in biology at Purdue University, she earned an M.D. at Ross University on the Caribbean island of Dominica. She is a physician and investigator in the Foodborne and Diarrheal Diseases Branch of the Centers for Disease Control and Prevention (CDC).

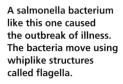

A salmonella bacterium like this one caused the outbreak of illness. The bacteria move using whiplike structures called flagella.

x ◆ A

Background

Facts and Figures Salmonella is a type of bacteria that is usually transmitted through contaminated foods such as poultry and eggs. It can also be transmitted through animals such as reptiles, cats, dogs, birds, and other animals. The type of salmonella illness most common today is called salmonellosis. This illness acts like the flu. People infected with the salmonella bacteria often have diarrhea, stomach cramps, fever, and vomiting. Once infected, the symptoms usually appear within 6 hours to 48 hours, but they can appear as late as 10 days after infection. Infection from salmonella can be prevented by preparing food correctly and by washing hands, kitchen counters, and utensils with soap and water.

Talking With
Dr. Cindy Friedman

? How did you get started in science?

When I was young, we always had pets around the house and a lot of books about medicine and science. I wanted to be a veterinarian. In college I decided that I loved animals but didn't want to practice medicine on them. I'd rather keep them as a hobby and devote my career to human medicine.

? Why did you specialize in infectious diseases?

Out of all the subjects I studied in medical school, I liked microbiology the best—learning about different viruses and bacteria. Then, when I did my medical training in New Jersey, we had a lot of patients from Latin America. So I saw quite a few tropical and exotic diseases, which further heightened my interest.

? What do you enjoy about your job?

I really like being able to help more than one patient at a time. We do this by figuring out the risk factors for a disease and how to prevent people from getting it. Sometimes the answer is complicated, like adding chlorine to the water. Sometimes it's simple measures, like washing your hands or cooking your food thoroughly.

? What clues did you have in the Colorado case?

At first, state investigators thought the bacteria came from some contaminated food. But when they questioned the children, they couldn't identify one place where the children had all eaten.

? What experience did the children share?

The investigators did a second set of interviews and learned that the children had all visited the zoo the week before they got sick. They didn't eat the same food at the zoo. But they all went to a special exhibit at the reptile house.

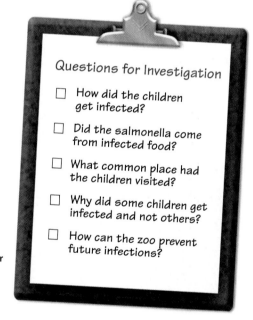

Questions for Investigation

☐ How did the children get infected?

☐ Did the salmonella come from infected food?

☐ What common place had the children visited?

☐ Why did some children get infected and not others?

☐ How can the zoo prevent future infections?

Cindy needed to answer questions like these to figure out what caused the illness.

Explore the Career

Choose from among the teaching strategies on these pages as you help your students explore the practical application of inquiry skills.

Use Maps Use a map to show where Dr. Friedman has investigated outbreaks of disease: Bolivia, South America; Cape Verde Islands off the coast of Africa; Vermont; Colorado. Ask: **Are there any similarities between these areas that would lead one to believe there is a pattern to disease outbreak?** *(No, each of these areas probably has its own special circumstances for disease outbreak.)*

Connect Culture The Centers for Disease Control and Prevention report that foodborne illnesses, such as salmonella, are serious health problems across the world. Because of changes in human food preferences, changes in food production and distribution, and increases in trade and travel opportunities across the world, there is now a greater risk of contracting and spreading foodborne illnesses. Physicians now play an even greater role in helping to prevent and control the outbreak of these illnesses.

Build Inquiry Skills Dr. Friedman studies outbreaks of diseases in groups of people rather than individuals. Ask: **Why is it important for physicians like Dr. Friedman to study diseases in groups of people rather than individuals?** *(By studying groups of people, physicians can look for patterns in disease outbreaks and begin to figure out risk factors and ways to prevent others from being infected.)*

Research Interested students may want to investigate other cases where salmonella has affected a group of people and how scientists came to understand the cause of each salmonella outbreak.

A ◆ 1

Discuss Ask: **Why do you think it is important to determine the cause of infection when a group of people become ill?** *(In order to stop additional outbreaks from occurring, it is necessary for scientists to try and determine the cause of infections. Determining the cause of infection can keep future outbreaks from occurring at the site of the original outbreak. It can also provide people with additional information in other areas around the world to prevent outbreaks from occurring elsewhere.)*

Use Visuals Show students spot maps, line listings, or histograms that are used by disease detectives to piece together clues to an outbreak. Samples of these charts can be found at www.cdc.gov/global/field2.htm. Ask: **How might these charts help disease detectives to understand the cause of the infectious outbreak?** *(These charts allow scientists to piece together information about the sick. They can begin to see patterns when they study these charts.)*

Discuss Some people may think that being a scientist like Dr. Friedman is not very exciting because it involves dealing with sick people. Have students recall what they read in the feature. Ask: **What is it about Dr. Friedman's job that sounds interesting and exciting?** *(Dr. Friedman gets to travel all over the world to solve mysteries. Her work is like detective work, trying to figure out which clues are important to understanding the outbreak and how those clues can lead to a prevention for further outbreaks.)*

? Did you think the exhibit might be a new clue?

Yes. It was a clue because reptiles frequently carry the salmonella bacteria without becoming ill. In the special exhibit, there were four baby Komodo dragons, meat-eating lizards from the island of Komodo in Indonesia. They were displayed in a pen filled with mulch, surrounded by a wooden barrier about two feet high. We tested the Komodo dragons and found that one of them had salmonella bacteria. But it wasn't a petting exhibit, so I couldn't understand how the children got infected.

? How did you gather new data?

I questioned the children who became ill and compared their answers with those of children who didn't become ill. I asked about their behavior at the exhibit—where they stood, what they touched, and whether they had anything to eat or drink there. I also asked all the children if they washed their hands after visiting the exhibit. Those who did destroyed the bacteria. It was only the children who didn't wash their hands who became ill.

These images suggest ways to fight harmful bacteria that cause diseases.

Wash your hands often.

Avoid using your fingers and double dipping.

? What was the source of the contamination?

I found that anyone who touched the wooden barrier was much more likely to have gotten sick. Children would go up to the barrier and put their hands on it. Then some of them would put their hands in their mouth or would eat without washing their hands first. Those were the children who became infected with salmonella.

The Komodo dragon is the largest lizard species in existence. Found on Komodo Island in Indonesia, it is nearly extinct.

2 ◆ A

Background

Integrating Science Salmonella bacteria can be found wherever animals live. The bacteria can live in hot and cold weather, rainy areas, and dry areas. It can be passed from animal to person or person to person. Some animals that are infected with salmonella bacteria do not show signs of infection. However, the bacteria can be passed on to a person, causing that person to become ill. Scientists are now finding that antibiotics used to treat serious cases of salmonella infection may not be as effective as they once were. Bacteria are becoming resistant to antibiotics, which concerns the American Medical Association.

Keep picnic food cold.

Refrigerate food promptly.

Cook meat thoroughly.

? What's it like being a disease detective?

It's more the old-fashioned idea of medicine. What I do is examine the patients and listen to the stories they tell—where they've traveled, what they ate, and what they were exposed to. Then I try to figure out what caused their illness.

After Cindy swabbed the barrier at the zoo, she then tested the sample at the CDC labs.

? How did you test your hypothesis?

We took cultures—swabs from the top of the barrier where the children put their hands. When we tested those cultures in the lab, we found salmonella bacteria.

? What did you conclude about the bacteria?

The infected Komodo dragon left its droppings in the mulch and the animals walked in it. Then they would stand on their hind legs, bracing themselves by putting their front paws on top of the barrier.

? What recommendations did you make?

We didn't want to tell zoos not to have reptile exhibits, because they're a good thing. And children should be able to get close to the animals. But at this particular exhibit, the outbreak could have been prevented with a double barrier system, so that the reptiles and the children couldn't touch the same barrier. And hand-washing is really important. Zoos should have signs instructing people to wash their hands after going to that kind of exhibit. In homes and schools with pet reptiles, hand-washing is important, too.

Writing in Science

Career Link Review the scientific process that Cindy used to solve the case of salmonella infections. What makes her a disease detective? Write a paragraph describing the steps Cindy follows and the skills she uses in her career as an investigator of infectious diseases.

Go Online
PHSchool.com
For: More on this career
Visit: PHSchool.com
Web Code: ceb-1000

A ◆ 3

Discuss Ask: **Why is it important for disease detectives to continue their work in the field?** (*As our world changes we need to continue to look at infectious outbreaks and determine the causes of them. The information we gain from studying these outbreaks will allow us to educate the world against future outbreaks of similar infections.*)

Research Have students work in small groups or pairs to research additional information about disease detectives. Disease detectives study not only foodborne illnesses, but also illnesses caused by other things such as insects.

Writing in Science

Writing Mode Description
Scoring Rubric
4 Includes detailed, complete, and accurate information
3 Includes complete and accurate information with several details
2 Includes complete and accurate information but no details
1 Includes inaccurate or incomplete information

Go Online
PHSchool.com
For: More on this career
Visit: PHSchool.com
Web Code: ceb-1000

Students can research this career and others that are related to the study of infectious diseases.

Chapter at a Glance

PRENTICE HALL
TeacherEXPRESS™
Plan • Teach • Assess

 **Chapter Project** *Mystery Object*

Technology

Local Standards

Teaching Resources
- Chapter Project Teacher Notes, pp. 38–39
- Chapter Project Student Overview, pp. 40–41
- Chapter Project Student Worksheets, pp. 42–43
- Chapter Project Scoring Rubric, p. 44

 DISCOVERY CHANNEL SCHOOL

 Section 1

What Is Life?

2–3 periods
1/2 block

A.1.1.1 List the characteristics all living things share
A.1.1.2 Explain where living things come from
A.1.1.3 Identify what all living things need to survive

 Go Online
active art

Section 2

Classifying Organisms

1–2 periods
1/2–1 block

A.1.2.1 Tell why biologists classify organisms
A.1.2.2 Relate the levels of organisms to the relationships between organisms
A.1.2.3 Explain how taxonomic keys are useful
A.1.2.4 Explain the relationship between evolution and classification

 DISCOVERY CHANNEL SCHOOL
Video Field Trip

Go Online
PHSchool.com

Section 3

Domains and Kingdoms

3–4 periods
1 1/2–2 blocks

A.1.3.1 List characteristics used to classify organisms
A.1.3.2 Contrast bacteria and archaea
A.1.3.3 Name the kingdoms within Eukarya

 Go Online
SC*LINKS* NSTA

 Section 4

The Origin of Life

1–2 periods
1/2–1 block

A.1.4.1 Contrast the atmosphere of early Earth with today's atmosphere
A.1.4.2 Describe how scientists hypothesize that life arose on Earth

Go Online
SC*LINKS* NSTA

 Review and Assessment

Teaching Resources
- Key Terms Review, p. 79
- Transparency A9
- Performance Assessment Teacher Notes, p. 85
- Performance Assessment Scoring Rubric p. 86
- Performance Assessment Student Worksheet, p. 87
- Chapter Test, pp. 88–91

 DISCOVERY CHANNEL SCHOOL
Video Assessment

Go Online
PHSchool.com

Test Preparation

Test Preparation Blackline Masters

Lab zone Chapter Activities Planner

For more activities

LAB ZONE Easy Planner CD-ROM

Student Edition	Inquiry	Time	Materials	Skills	Resources
Chapter Project p. 5	Open-Ended	1 to 2 weeks	**All in One Teaching Resources** See p. 38	Observing, inferring, classifying	**Lab zone Easy Planner** **All in One Teaching Resources** Support pp. 38–44
Section 1					
Discover Activity, p. 6	Guided	10 minutes	Wind-up toys	Forming operational definitions	**Lab zone Easy Planner**
Try This, p. 8	Guided	10 minutes	Lemon slices, small mirrors	Classifying	**Lab zone Easy Planner**
Skills Activity, p. 13	Open-Ended	30 minutes	Balance, hair dryer, paper towels, thin potato slices, small mirrors	Designing an experiment	**Lab zone Easy Planner**
Skills Lab, p. 15	Directed	Prep: 20 minutes Class: 20 minutes the first day, then 5 minutes for each of the next 5 days	Paper plates, plastic dropper, bread without preservatives, sealable plastic bags, tap water, packing tape	Observing, controlling variables	**Lab zone Easy Planner Lab Activity Video** Skills Lab: *Please Pass the Bread,* pp. 53–54
Section 2					
Discover Activity, p. 16	Guided	15 minutes	Items such as envelopes, erasers, paper, paper clips, pencils, rubber bands, stamps, tape	Classifying	**Lab zone Easy Planner**
Skills Activity, p. 20	Guided	10 minutes	None	Observing	**Lab zone Easy Planner**
Skills Lab, p. 25	Guided	Prep: 30 minutes Class: 30 minutes	A variety of leaves, hand lens, metric ruler	Observing, classifying, inferring	**Lab zone Easy Planner Lab Activity Video** **All in One Teaching Resources** Skills Lab: *Living Mysteries,* pp. 63–65
Section 3					
Discover Activity, p. 26	Guided	15 minutes	Green plant, insect or worm, mushroom, sea animal (urchin, cultivated coral, anemone)	Classifying	**Lab zone Easy Planner**
Section 4					
Discover Activity, p. 30	Guided	10 minutes	Two covered plastic jars; one containing a plant, the other, an animal	Inferring	**Lab zone Easy Planner**

Section 1 What Is Life?

 2–3 periods, 1/2 blocks

ABILITY LEVELS
L1 Basic to Average
L2 For All Students
L3 Average to Advanced

Objectives

A.1.1.1 List the characteristics all living things share.
A.1.1.2 Explain where living things come from.
A.1.1.3 Identify what all living things need to survive.

Local Standards

Key Terms

• organism • cell • unicellular • multicellular • stimulus • response
• development • spontaneous generation • controlled experiment
• autotroph • heterotroph • homeostasis

Preteach

Build Background Knowledge

Invite students to describe the most unusual thing they have seen and describe it as a plant, animal, or other life form.

 Discover Activity *Is It Living or Nonliving?*

Targeted Print and Technology Resources

All in One Teaching Resources

L2 Reading Strategy Transparency A1: Using Prior Knowledge

O **Presentation-Pro CD-ROM**

Instruct

The Characteristics of Living Things Use questions to link the lesson subheadings with the lesson Key Concept.

Life Comes From Life Use a figure to summarize Redi's experiment.

Skills Lab *Please Pass the Bread!*

Targeted Print and Technology Resources

All in One Teaching Resources

L2 Guided Reading, pp. 47–50
L2 Transparencies A2, A3
L2 Skills Lab: *Please Pass the Bread!* pp. 53–54

www.PHSchool.com Web Code: cep-1011

Lab Activity Video/DVD
Skills Lab: *Please Pass the Bread!*

O **Student Edition on Audio CD**

Assess

Section Assessment Questions

 Have students use their completed Using Prior Knowledge graphic organizers to help them answer the questions.

Reteach

Use a concept map to identify characteristics of living things.

Targeted Print and Technology Resources

All in One Teaching Resources

• Section Summary, p. 46
L1 Review and Reinforce, p. 51
L3 Enrich, p. 52

Section 2 **Classifying Organisms**

 1–2 periods, 1/2–1 blocks

ABILITY LEVELS
L1 Basic to Average
L2 For All Students
L3 Average to Advanced

Objectives

A.1.2.1 Explain why biologists classify organisms.

A.1.2.2 Relate the levels of classification to the relationships between organisms.

A.1.2.3 Explain how taxonomic keys are useful.

A.1.2.4 Explain the relationship between classification and evolution.

Key Terms

• classification • taxonomy • binomial nomenclature • genus • species
• evolution

Local Standards

Preteach

Build Background Knowledge

Invite students to describe how libraries are organized.

 **Discover Activity** *Can You Organize a Junk Drawer?*

Targeted Print and Technology Resources

All in One Teaching Resources

L2 Reading Strategy Transparency A4: Asking Questions

O Presentation-Pro CD-ROM

Instruct

Why Do Scientists Classify? Use an imaginary fish to discuss classification.

The Naming System of Linnaeus Define *genus* and *species* and apply to an example.

Levels of Classification Use a drawing to discuss the levels of classification.

Taxonomic Keys Use a sample taxonomic key to discuss their usefulness.

Evolution and Classification Ask leading questions to help students relate evolution and classification.

 Skills Lab *Living Mysteries*

Targeted Print and Technology Resources

All in One Teaching Resources

L2 Guided Reading, pp. 57–60
L2 Transparencies A5, A6
L2 Skills Lab: *Living Mysteries,* pp. 63–65

Lab Activity Video/DVD
Skills Lab: *Living Mysteries*

www.PHSchool.com Web Code: ced-1012

O Student Edition on Audio CD

Assess

Section Assessment Questions

Have students use their completed Asking Questions graphic organizer to answer the questions.

Reteach

Have students list the levels of classification from broad to specific.

Targeted Print and Technology Resources

All in One Teaching Resources

• Section Summary, p. 56
L1 Review and Reinforce, p. 61
L3 Enrich, p. 62

Section 3 **Domains and Kingdoms**

 3–4 periods, 1 1/2–2 blocks

ABILITY LEVELS
- **L1** Basic to Average
- **L2** For All Students
- **L3** Average to Advanced

Objectives

A.1.3.1 List characteristics used to classify organisms.

A.1.3.2 Compare and contrast bacteria and archaea.

A.1.3.3 Name the kingdoms within Eukarya.

Key Terms

• prokayote • nucleus • eukaryote

Local Standards

Preteach

Build Background Knowledge

Have students name kinds of movies and discuss how the categories help them describe and compare organisms.

 **Discover Activity** *Which Organism Goes Where?*

Targeted Print and Technology Resources

 **Teaching Resources**

L2 Reading Strategy Transparency
A7: Comparing and Contrasting

⊙ **Presentation-Pro CD-ROM**

Instruct

Domain Bacteria Use a common example, a sore throat, to discuss bacteria.

Domain Archaea Use pictures to compare bacteria and Archaea.

Domain Eukarya Discuss characteristics of the kingdoms that make up Eukarya.

Targeted Print and Technology Resources

 **Teaching Resources**

L2 Guided Reading, pp. 68–69

www.SciLinks.org Web Code:
scn-0113

⊙ **Student Edition on Audio CD**

Assess

Section Assessment Questions

Have students use their Comparing and Contrasting graphic organizers to help answer the questions.

Reteach

As a class, summarize the characteristics of each domain and the kingdoms of Eukarya.

Targeted Print and Technology Resources

Teaching Resources

• Section Summary, p. 67

L1 Review and Reinforce, p. 70

L3 Enrich, p. 71

Section 4 The Origin of Life

 1–2 periods, 1/2–1 blocks

ABILITY LEVELS
L1 Basic to Average
L2 For All Students
L3 Average to Advanced

Objectives

A.1.4.1 Contrast the atmosphere of early Earth with today's atmosphere.

A.1.4.2 Describe some hypotheses about how life arose on Earth.

Key Terms

• fossil

Local Standards

Section Lesson Plans

Preteach

Build Background Knowledge

Discuss the gases found in air.

 **Discover Activity** *How Can the Composition of Air Change?*

Targeted Print and Technology Resources

All in One Teaching Resources

L2 Reading Strategy Transparency A8: Identifying Supporting Evidence

Presentation-Pro CD-ROM

Instruct

The Atmosphere of Early Earth Ask leading questions to help students understand that the composition of Earth's early atmosphere.

The First Cells Use a flow chart to discuss how the first cells formed and released oxygen into the atmosphere.

Targeted Print and Technology Resources

All in One Teaching Resources

L2 Guided Reading, pp. 74–76

www.SciLinks.org Web Code: scn-0114

Student Edition on Audio CD

Assess

Section Assessment Questions

Have students use their flowcharts sequencing the steps in protein synthesis to answer the questions.

Reteach

Use diagrams to summarize the structure of DNA and how cells make proteins.

Targeted Print and Technology Resources

All in One Teaching Resources

• Section Summary, p. 73
L1 Review and Reinforce, p. 77
L3 Enrich, p. 78

Chapter 1 Content Refresher

Go Online

NSTA-PDi LINKS

For: Professional development support
Visit: www.SciLinks.org/PDLinks
Web Code: scf-0110

Professional Development

Section 1 What Is Life?

Disproving Spontaneous Generation In 1651, an English physician, William Harvey, published a book describing his studies of reproduction. Harvey speculated that insects, worms, and frogs arise from seeds or eggs. Redi had read Harvey's book, so it may have inspired his experiments.

In 1860, the French Academy of Sciences offered a prize to anyone who could "throw new light" on spontaneous generation, and Pasteur responded. He had shown that organisms in air caused fermentation in milk and alcohol, and decided to investigate whether the organisms were always in the air or arose from spontaneous generation. Pasteur's conclusion that microorganisms develop from other microorganisms in the air was supported in 1876 by another Englishman, physicist John Tyndall. Tyndall was able to show that pure air did not contribute to the production of organisms as regular air did.

Homeostasis The concept of homeostasis was developed by a French scientist, Claude Bernard. Bernard was born in 1813, the son of an unsuccessful vineyard owner. His family could not afford to give him a formal science education. After an attempt at writing plays, Bernard enrolled in the Faculty of Medicine in Paris and became a research assistant, then a deputy for a famous physiologist. His experiments led Bernard to understand the role of the pancreas in digestion and the role of glycogen in liver function. He showed that glycogen serves as storage for carbohydrates, which could be broken down when needed. Bernard's discoveries illustrate homeostasis, how the body maintains a stable internal environment despite changes in the external environment.

Address Misconceptions

Students may think that plant food made by plants is the same as the plant food sold in flower shops and other stores. If this were true, we would not need plants. For more on this misconception, see **Address Misconceptions** in the section What Is Life?

Section 2 Classifying Organisms

Described Species To date, scientists have described around 1.8 million species of living organisms. Although the number of described species may seem large, scientists estimate that between 10 million and 100 million species actually exist. Also, millions of additional species have become extinct. Paleontologist Stephen Jay Gould estimated that 99 percent of all species that have lived on Earth no longer exist today. We know nothing of most of these species because they did not leave any fossil traces.

In 2000, an international group of scientists and other individuals established All Species Foundation. Its goal is to catalog every living species within 25 years. Currently the group is identifying about 15,000 species a year, but hopes to increase the pace to 60,000 annually.

Origins of Theory of Evolution When people think of evolution and natural selection, they usually think of Charles Darwin. However, it was another Englishman, Alfred Russel Wallace, who first introduced the term.

In 1848, Wallace went on an expedition to the Amazon. Most of the items he collected were lost on his return voyage when his ship sank. However, from 1854 to 1862, he traveled to the Malay Archipelago to gather more evidence to support his theory of evolution. In early 1858, he wrote, "There suddenly flashed before me the idea of the survival of the fittest."

Although Wallace came up with the idea of evolution through natural selection first, Darwin developed the theory further, provided more evidence, and was mainly responsible for the acceptance of the theory.

Section 3 Domains and Kingdoms

Classification The field of classification is always changing, as biologists identify new organisms and gain new understanding of genetic relationships and evolutionary histories. Before 1969, most scientists classified all organisms into two kingdoms—plants and animals. Starting around 1969, many scientists began using a five-kingdom classification system: Monera, Protista, Plantae, Fungi, and Animalia. In the five kindom system, all prokaryotes were included in kingdom Monera. Later, a distinction was made between organisms with nuclei and those without—giving rise to domains Prokarya and Eukarya. This was the predominant system until around 1990.

Starting in the 1970s, Carl Woese, a professor in the Department of Microbiology at the University of Illinois, and other scientists began finding evidence for a previously unknown group of prokaryotes—similar to, yet distinct from bacteria. Thus, prokaryotes were then divided into kingdoms Eubacteria and Archaebacteria, based on differences in structure, biochemistry, physiology, and evolutionary history.

Through extensive comparisons of the genetic sequences among prokaryotes, scientists found that the differences between archaebacteria and eubacteria are quite fundamental. Many systematicists therefore favor classifying prokaryotes into two different domains altogether—Archaea and Bacteria.

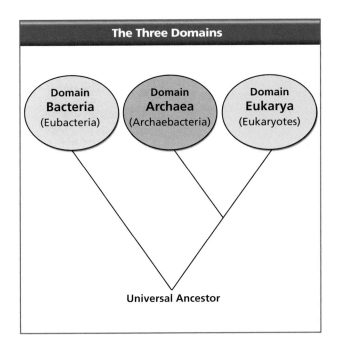

The Three Domains

Domain **Bacteria** (Eubacteria)

Domain **Archaea** (Archaebacteria)

Domain **Eukarya** (Eukaryotes)

Universal Ancestor

Section 4 The Origin of Life

Origin of Organic Building Blocks Some scientists have proposed that organic building blocks came from space. Two scientists, Jeffrey Bada and Luan Becker, studied the site of an ancient meteoroid crash in Ontario, Canada. They discovered a large quantity of buckyballs. Buckyballs, also called fullerenes, are microscopic spheres of 60 atoms of pure carbon in a structure similar to a geodesic dome. Buckyballs have a strange characteristic; the molecules have a cavity large enough to hold other elements or whole molecules. Once inside the cavity, an element cannot escape unless it is heated to a high temperature.

The buckyballs that Bada and Becker found in Ontario contained helium, which is rare on Earth but plentiful in space. The scientists reasoned that if the buckyballs came from outer space without burning up, other organic molecules could too.

Help Students Read

Sequencing

Ordering Events

Strategy Help students understand and visualize the steps in a process, or the order in which events occur. Sequences frequently involve cause-effect relationships. Readers can construct graphic organizers to help them visualize and comprehend a sequence. For most sequences, flowcharts are the graphic of choice. However, cycle diagrams are more appropriate for cycles. Before students begin, locate in the text a description of a several step process or a chain of cause and effects.

Example

1. Have students read the passage, thinking about what takes place first, second, third, and so on. Point out that the text will not always use order words such as *first, next, then,* and *finally*.
2. Review the passage, listing the steps or events in order.
3. If the passage describes a chain of steps or events, draw a flowchart on the board, having students tell the sequence of events, steps, or causes and effect. Write each part of the process in a separate box.
4. If the passage describes a cycle, use a cycle diagram to show the sequence.
5. Have students locate additional examples of sequential relationships in the text or visuals of the chapter. Students can depict the steps or events using graphic organizers.

Interactive Textbook
- Complete student edition
- Video and audio
- Simulations and activities
- Section and chapter activities

Chapter

1

Living Things

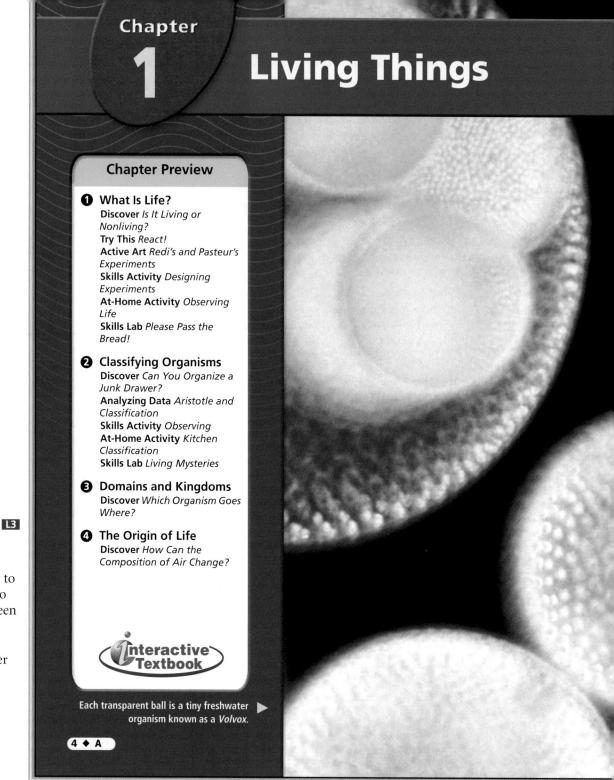

Interactive Textbook

Each transparent ball is a tiny freshwater organism known as a *Volvox.* ▶

4 ◆ A

Chapter Project   L3

Objectives
In this project, students observe an object to determine whether it is alive. Students also develop strategies for distinguishing between living and nonliving objects. After this Chapter Project, students will be able to
- observe characteristics of objects to infer whether they are alive
- carry out tests for signs of life
- classify living things into kingdoms

Skills Focus
Observing, inferring, classifying

Project Time Line 1 to 2 weeks

All in One Teaching Resources
- Chapter Project Teacher Notes
- Chapter Project Worksheet 1
- Chapter Project Worksheet 2
- Chapter Project Worksheet 3
- Chapter Project Scoring Rubric

Safety
 Review the Safety Guidelines in Appendix A.

Developing a Plan
During the first two days, students should observe their objects and record their observations. Allow at least three days for students to carry out tests for life characteristics. Students should make data tables and drawings during this stage. Finally, students should analyze their data, classify their objects, and plan a presentation.

Possible Materials
Provide students with living and nonliving objects and instructions on their care.
- Living objects may include brine shrimp, slime mold, bread mold, insect larvae, goldfish, plants, yeast (add one spoonful of baker's yeast and one spoonful of sugar to 250 mL warm water; observe under a microscope), and seeds (soak lentil seeds in water overnight then wrap in wet paper towel; place towel in a plastic bag and store in the dark; observe daily).

Video Preview

Lab zone™ Chapter **Project**

Mystery Object

It's not always easy to tell whether something is alive. In this chapter, you will learn the characteristics of living things. As you study this chapter, your challenge will be to determine whether or not a mystery object is alive.

Your Goal To study a mystery object for several days to determine whether or not it is alive

To complete the project, you must
- care for your object following your teacher's instructions
- observe your object each day, and record your data
- determine whether your object is alive, and if so, to which domain and kingdom it belongs
- follow the safety guidelines in Appendix A

Plan It! Before you get started, create a list of characteristics that living things share. Think about whether nonliving things also share these characteristics. Also, think about what kind of tests you can carry out to look for signs of life. Create data tables in which to record your observations.

Chapter 1 A ◆ 5

Living Things

Show the Video Preview to introduce the Chapter Project and overview the chapter content. Discussion questions: **What organism is the base of the food web found near a hydrothermal vent? What is the food source for this organism?** (*Bacteria, which use chemicals in the environment as food*)

Launching the Project

Show students living organisms, such as a plant and a snail. Ask: **What characteristics do these objects have in common?** (*Possible answer: They grow and respond to changes in the environment.*) **What tests could you design that would help you observe the characteristics of these living organisms?** (*Possible answers: Measure size over a period of time; observe under a microscope*) Explain to students that all tests must be approved so that living organisms are not injured.

Performance Assessment

The Chapter Project Scoring Rubric will help you evaluate how well students complete the Chapter Project. You may want to share the rubric with your students so that they will know what is expected. Students will be assessed on
- the detail of their observations
- how well they design tests to determine whether their object is alive and, if it is alive, if they are able to identify which domain and kingdom it belongs to
- the accuracy and organization of their testing and documentation, including how well they follow directions for the care of their objects
- whether they draw appropriate conclusions from their tests and present their results to the class in a clear and organized manner

- Nonliving objects may include pebbles, vermiculite, artificial plants (look real but do not grow or have a cellular structure), soluble salts in a saturated solution (so that "crystal gardens" appear to grow), hair (has cellular structure, but no longer living), and toys with microchips (can have complex responses).
- Plastic petri dishes and paper towels are useful for germinating seeds.

- BTB solution (bromthymol blue) can be used to test for presence of carbon dioxide in water.
- Provide equipment such as a microscope, glass slides, cover slips, scissors, a plastic dropper, a hand lens, and a ruler. Show students how to use a microscope and make a thin cross-section of material for observation under the microscope.

Portfolio

Objectives

After completing the lesson, students will be able to

A.1.1.1 List the characteristics all living things share.

A.1.1.2 Explain where living things come from.

A.1.1.3 Identify what all living things need to survive.

Target Reading Skill 🔄

Using Prior Knowledge Explain that using prior knowledge helps students connect what they already know to what they are about to read.

Answers

Possible answers include:

What You Know

1. Living things grow.

2. Living things are made of cells.

What You Learned

1. Unicellular organisms are composed of only one cell.

2. The cells of living things are composed of chemicals.

3. The cells of organisms use energy to do things they must do.

All in One Teaching Resources

• Transparency A1

Preteach

Build Background Knowledge 　　L2

Unusual Living Things

Ask students to describe the most unusual living thing they have seen. Ask: **What did it look like? Where did it live? What was so unusual about it?** Write the heading *Living Things* on the board and list the organisms as students identify them. Have students describe whether they thought the organism was a plant, an animal, or another life form.

Reading Preview

Key Concepts

• What characteristics do all living things share?

• Where do living things come from?

• What do living things need to survive?

Key Terms

• organism • cell • unicellular
• multicellular • stimulus
• response • development
• spontaneous generation
• controlled experiment
• autotroph • heterotroph
• homeostasis

🔄 Target Reading Skill

Using Prior Knowledge Look at the section headings and visuals to see what this section is about. Then write what you already know about living things in a graphic organizer like the one below. As you read, write what you learn.

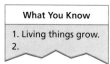

What You Know
1. Living things grow.
2.

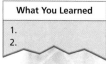

What You Learned
1.
2.

Lab zone Discover **Activity**

Is It Living or Nonliving?

1. Your teacher will give you and a partner a wind-up toy.

2. One of you will look for evidence that the toy is alive and the other will look for evidence that the toy is not alive.

3. Observe the wind-up toy. Record the characteristics of the toy that support your position about whether or not the toy is alive.

4. Share your lists of living and nonliving characteristics with your classmates.

Think It Over
Forming Operational Definitions Based on what you learned from the activity, create a list of characteristics that living things share.

It was an unusually damp summer for towns near Dallas, Texas. Bright yellow "blobs" began to appear everywhere. Looking like the slimy creatures in horror films, the blobs oozed slowly along the ground. Eventually, the glistening jelly-like masses overran people's yards and porches. Terrified homeowners didn't know what the blobs were. Some people thought that they were life forms from another planet.

People around Dallas were worried until biologists, scientists who study living things, put people's minds at ease. The blobs were slime molds—living things usually found on damp, decaying material on a forest floor. The unusually wet weather provided ideal conditions for the slime molds to grow.

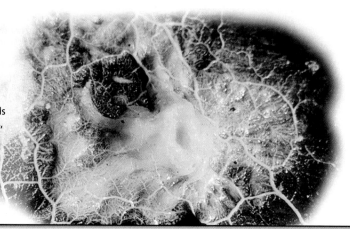

FIGURE 1
Slime Mold
Slime molds similar to these grew all over yards and porches near Dallas, Texas, one summer.

Lab zone Discover **Activity**

Skills Focus Forming operational definitions

Materials wind-up toys

Time 10 minutes

Tips Do not wind toys too tightly. Urge students to think of all living things, not just animals, as they make their lists.

L1 Expected Outcome Students could say that the toy is alive because it moves or that it is not alive because it does not eat, grow, or reproduce.

Think It Over All living things grow or change over time, while characteristics such as sleeping or talking are not shared among all organisms.

▲ Plant cells

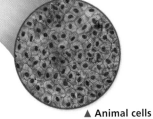

▲ Animal cells

FIGURE 2
Cellular Organization
Like all living things, the frog and plant are made of cells. Although the cells of different organisms are not identical, they share important characteristics.
Making Generalizations *In what ways are cells similar?*

The Characteristics of Living Things

If you were asked to name some living things, or **organisms,** you might name yourself, a pet, and maybe some insects or plants. You would probably not mention a moss growing in a shady spot, the mildew on bathroom tiles, or the slime molds that oozed across lawns. But all of these things are organisms that share important characteristics with all other living things. **All living things have a cellular organization, contain similar chemicals, use energy, respond to their surroundings, grow and develop, and reproduce.**

Cellular Organization All organisms are made of small building blocks called cells. A **cell** is the basic unit of structure and function in an organism. The smallest cells are so tiny that you could fit more than a million of them on the period at the end of this sentence. To see most cells, you need a microscope—a tool that uses lenses, like those in eyeglasses, to magnify small objects.

Organisms may be composed of only one cell or of many cells. **Unicellular,** or single-celled organisms, include bacteria (bak TIHR ee uh), the most numerous organisms on Earth. A bacterial cell carries out all of the functions necessary for the organism to stay alive.

Multicellular organisms are composed of many cells. In many multicellular organisms, the cells are specialized to do certain tasks. For example, you are made of trillions of cells. Specialized cells in your body, such as muscle and nerve cells, work together to keep you alive. Nerve cells carry messages about your surroundings to your brain. Other nerve cells then carry messages to your muscle cells, making your body move.

The Characteristics of Living Things

Teach Key Concepts `L2`
Characteristics of All Living Things

Focus Tell students that biologists organize living things into groups to make the organisms easier to study. Link this statement with the boldfaced subheadings that follow The Characteristics of Living Things.

Teach Define each characteristic and give an example that relates to humans.

Apply Ask: **Which characteristics apply to trees?** *(All of them)* **To dogs?** *(All)* **learning modality: logical/mathematical**

Use Visuals: Figure 2 `L2`
Cellular Organization

Focus Tell students that the images in the circles are cells that have been magnified.

Teach Help students identify individual cells in each image. Ask students to describe differences between the plant and animal cells in the figure. *(The frog's cells are round while the plant's cells are more rectangular. The plant cells have green structures inside them.)*

Apply Explain that mushrooms are neither plants nor animals. Ask: **What would you expect to see if you magnified a mushroom?** *(Cellular structures similar to yet distinct from plant and animal cells)* **learning modality: visual**

Independent Practice `L2`

All in One **Teaching Resources**

- Guided Reading and Study Worksheet: *What Is Life?*

⊙ **Student Edition on Audio CD**

Differentiated Instruction

English Learners/Beginning `L1`
Comprehension: Key Concept Write *Characteristics of Living Things* on the board. Direct students' attention to the boldfaced subheadings that follow it in the text. Explain each characteristic. Have students construct a concept circle by connecting each characteristic to the central concept with lines. **learning modality: logical/mathematical**

English Learners/Intermediate `L2`
Comprehension: Key Concept After students complete the Beginning activity, ask individuals to identify characteristics that all living things share. Then pair English learners with students who are proficient in English. Each pair should summarize the contents following one of the subheadings. **learning modality: verbal**

Monitor Progress _____ `L2`

Drawing Have students make drawings of a plant cell and an animal cell. Ask students to label each of their drawings.

Students can save their drawings in their portfolios. **Portfolio**

Answers
Figure 2 They are microscopic, carry out life activities, and have similar structures.

Integrating Chemistry L2

Tell students that all the chemicals in a human body cost only a few dollars. Show students the following materials: charcoal, chalk, a nail, a small sack of fertilizer, and a bottle of carbonated water. Challenge students to identify the chemicals in each item: charcoal *(carbon)*, chalk *(calcium)*, nail *(iron)*, fertilizer *(phosphorus, nitrogen, and potassium)*, carbonated water *(carbon dioxide and water)*. Explain that the body is made of nonliving chemicals. When arranged in one way, the chemicals make up living things. When arranged in other ways, they make up nonliving things. **learning modality: visual**

Help Students Read L2

What Is the Stimulus?

Sequence Refer to the Content Refresher, which provides guidelines for using sequence. Have students read the caption to Figure 3. Ask students to use the following words to describe the actions: *stimulus, response, cause, effect, first, second. (The opossum's arrival is the stimulus, cause, and first action. The kitten's baring its teeth is the response, effect, and second action.)*

Lab zone Try This **Activity**

React!

In this activity, you will test your responses to three different stimuli.

1. Have a partner clap his or her hands together about ten centimeters in front of your face. Describe how you react.

2. Look at one of your eyes in a mirror. Cover the eye with your hand for a minute. While looking in the mirror, remove your hand. Observe how the size of your pupil changes.

3. Bring a slice of lemon close to your nose and mouth. Describe what happens.

Classifying For each action performed, name the stimulus and the response.

The Chemicals of Life The cells of all living things are composed of chemicals. The most abundant chemical in cells is water. Other chemicals, called carbohydrates (kahr boh HY drayts), are a cell's main energy source. Two other chemicals, proteins (PROH teenz) and lipids, are the building materials of cells, much as wood and bricks are the building materials of houses. Finally, nucleic (noo KLEE ik) acids are the genetic material—the chemical instructions that direct the cell's activities.

Energy Use The cells of organisms use energy to do what living things must do, such as grow and repair injured parts. An organism's cells are always hard at work. For example, as you read this paragraph, not only are your eye and brain cells busy, but most of your other cells are working, too. The cells of your stomach and intestine are digesting food. Your blood cells are moving chemicals around your body. If you've hurt yourself, some of your cells are repairing the damage.

Response to Surroundings If you've ever seen a plant in a sunny window, you may have observed that the plant's stems have bent so that the leaves face the sun. Like a plant bending toward the light, all organisms react to changes in their environment. A change in an organism's surroundings that causes the organism to react is called a **stimulus** (plural *stimuli*). Stimuli include changes in temperature, light, sound, and other factors.

FIGURE 3
Stimulus and Response
All organisms respond to changes in their surroundings. When startled by the opossum, the kitten bares its teeth in response.

Lab zone Try This **Activity**

Skills Focus Classifying

Materials lemon slices, small mirrors

Time 10 minutes

Tips Remind students not to taste the lemon.

Expected Outcome clapping hands—sudden motion close to eyes/eyes blink; covering eyes, then uncover—change in

L1 light intensity/pupil contracts; lemon—smell/mouth puckers

Extend Challenge students to list 5 other stimulus/response actions of plants or animals. *(Possible answers: see a predator—run away; light source—plant stem turns toward)* **learning modality: kinesthetic**

An organism reacts to a stimulus with a **response**—an action or change in behavior. For example, has someone ever knocked over a glass of water by accident during dinner, causing you to jump? The sudden spilling of water was the stimulus that caused your startled response.

Growth and Development Another characteristic of living things is that they grow and develop. Growth is the process of becoming larger. **Development** is the process of change that occurs during an organism's life to produce a more complex organism. To grow and develop, organisms use energy to create new cells. Look at Figure 4 to see how a sunflower seed develops as it grows into a sunflower plant.

Reproduction Another characteristic of organisms is the ability to reproduce, or produce offspring that are similar to the parents. Robins lay eggs that develop into young robins that closely resemble their parents. Apples produce seeds that develop into apple trees, which in turn make more seeds. The mildew on your bathroom tiles will produce more mildew if you do not clean it off!

 Reading Checkpoint How do growth and development differ?

FIGURE 4
Sunflower Growth and Development

Over time, a tiny sunflower seed grows and develops into a tall sunflower plant. A great deal of energy is needed to produce the cells of a mature sunflower plant.
Comparing and Contrasting *How do the seedlings resemble the sunflower plant? How do they differ?*

▲ Tiny sunflower seedlings

▲ A mature sunflower

▲ Sunflower seeds

A ◆ 9

Construct a Crystal Garden

Materials crystal gardens

Time 3 days

Focus Tell students that they will grow a crystal garden and then determine whether it is living or nonliving.

Teach Have students construct a crystal garden and observe crystal growth. Then, have students list the characteristics of living things and state whether the crystals have each characteristic. Ask: **Are the crystals alive?** Have students write a short paragraph to support their conclusions.

Apply Ask students to list other objects that have some but not all of the characteristics of living things. *(One example is fire, which responds to wind, water, and air; uses energy; and can grow from a small fire to a large one. However, it is not made of cells, so it is not living.)* **learning modality: logical/ mathematical**

Monitor Progress L2

Skills Check Have each student choose one living thing and explain how he or she knows it is alive.

Answers

Figure 4 The seedling and the sunflower plant are both made of cells that contain complex chemicals; use energy, grow, and develop; respond to their environment; and can reproduce during some stage of their lives. Both have stems, roots, and leaves, and they are plants. They differ in their size and in the number of their cells.

 Reading Checkpoint Growth is the process of becoming larger. Development is the process of change that produces a more complex organism.

Life Comes From Life

Teach Key Concepts L2

Living Things Arise Through Reproduction

Focus Direct students' attention to Figure 5.

Teach Ask: **How many jars did Redi use?** *(2)* Ask: **How do they differ?** *(One is covered; the other is not.)* Ask: **What did Redi conclude from his experiment?** *(The meat did not make maggots; the maggots came from flies.)*

Apply Ask: **If you found a baby mouse, what could you conclude?** *(Possible answer: A mother mouse lives nearby.)* **learning modality: visual**

 **Teaching Resources**

• Transparencies A2, A3

 Teacher **Demo** L2

Compare Broth Samples

Materials beef broth that has been exposed to air for 2 to 3 days, beef broth from a freshly opened can

Time 10 minutes

Focus Show students the two cans of broth.

Teach Do not allow students to touch or taste the broth. Ask: **What is the difference between the two cans of broth?** *(The older broth will appear cloudier than the fresh one.)* **Why do you think Redi's and Pasteur's experiments used food?** *(Possible answer: People were concerned about food going bad.)*

Apply Ask: **How can you prevent the spread of germs through food?** *(Possible answers: wash hands before handling food, refrigerate food, cook food thoroughly)* Ask: **How do these behaviors prevent the spread of germs?** *(They kill some germs and prevent others from reproducing in the food.)*
learning modality: logical/mathematical

Go **Online**
active art

For: Redi's and Pasteur's Experiments activity
Visit: PHSchool.com
Web Code: cep-1011

Students can interact online with the art of Redi's and Pasteur's experiments.

FIGURE 5
Redi's Experiment

Francesco Redi designed one of the first controlled experiments. In his experiment, Redi showed that flies do not spontaneously arise from decaying meat. **Controlling Variables** *What is the manipulated variable in this experiment?*

▲ Maggots on meat

Go **Online**
active art

For: Redi's and Pasteur's Experiments activity
Visit: PHSchool.com
Web Code: cep-1011

Uncovered jar   Covered jar

1 Redi placed meat in two identical jars. He left one jar uncovered. He covered the other jar with a cloth that let in air.

2 After a few days, Redi saw maggots (young flies) on the decaying meat in the open jar. There were no maggots on the meat in the covered jar.

3 Redi reasoned that flies had laid eggs on the meat in the open jar. The eggs hatched into maggots. Because flies could not lay eggs on the meat in the covered jar, there were no maggots there. Redi concluded that decaying meat did not produce maggots.

Life Comes From Life

Today, when people observe moths flying out of closets or weeds poking out of cracks in the sidewalk, they know that these organisms are the result of reproduction. **Living things arise from living things through reproduction.**

Four hundred years ago, however, people believed that life could appear from nonliving material. For example, when people saw flies swarming around decaying meat, they concluded that flies could arise from rotting meat. The mistaken idea that living things can arise from nonliving sources is called **spontaneous generation.** It took hundreds of years of experiments to convince people that spontaneous generation does not occur.

Redi's Experiment In the 1600s, an Italian doctor named Francesco Redi helped to disprove spontaneous generation. Redi designed a controlled experiment to show that flies do not arise from decaying meat. In a **controlled experiment**, a scientist carries out two tests that are identical in every respect except for one factor. The one factor that a scientist changes is called the manipulated variable.

Boiled broth **Unboiled broth**

① Pasteur put clear broth into two flasks with curved necks. The necks would let in oxygen but keep out bacteria from the air. Pasteur boiled the broth in one flask to kill any bacteria in the broth. He did not boil the broth in the other flask.

② In a few days, the unboiled broth became cloudy, showing that new bacteria were growing. The boiled broth remained clear. Pasteur concluded that bacteria do not spontaneously arise from the broth. New bacteria appeared only when living bacteria were already present.

Later, Pasteur took the flask with the broth that had remained clear and broke its curved neck. Bacteria from the air could now enter the flask. In a few days, the broth became cloudy. This evidence confirmed that new bacteria arise only from existing bacteria.

FIGURE 6
Pasteur's Experiment
Louis Pasteur's carefully controlled experiment demonstrated that bacteria arise only from existing bacteria.

▲ Pasteur in his laboratory

In Redi's experiment, shown in Figure 5, the manipulated variable was whether or not the jar was covered. Flies were able to enter the uncovered jar and lay their eggs on the meat inside. These eggs hatched into maggots, which developed into new flies. The flies could not enter the covered jar, however. Therefore, no maggots formed on the meat in the covered jar. Through his experiment, Redi was able to conclude that rotting meat does not produce flies.

Pasteur's Experiment Even after Redi's work, many people continued to believe that spontaneous generation could occur. In the mid-1800s, the French chemist Louis Pasteur designed some controlled experiments that finally rejected spontaneous generation. As shown in Figure 6, he demonstrated that new bacteria in broth appeared only when they were produced by existing bacteria. The experiments of Redi and Pasteur helped to convince people that living things do not arise from nonliving material.

 Reading Checkpoint What is a controlled experiment?

 **Lab zone Build Inquiry** L3

Design a Poster

Materials markers, poster board

Time 30 minutes

Focus Tell students they will design posters to show how Redi's and Pasteur's experiments helped disprove the idea of spontaneous generation. Divide the class into small groups for this purpose.

Teach Have students review the two experiments and choose one to illustrate. Encourage students to brainstorm how they will illustrate the experiment. Posters might show a flowchart, comic strip, or illustrated story, for example. Display the posters and allow students to present them to the class.

Apply Remind students that controlled experiments have a manipulated or independent variable and a dependent variable. Ask: **Which variables in these two experiments are manipulated and which are dependent?** *(Redi's experiment: manipulated—whether or not there was a cover; dependent—whether or not maggots formed on the meat; Pasteur's experiment: independent—whether or not the broth was boiled; dependent—growth of bacteria)*
learning modality: visual

Differentiated Instruction

Less Proficient Readers L1
Recognizing Word Parts Students may not understand *variable*. Write the prefix *vari-* on the board. Explain that it means "diverse" or "having different characteristics." Have students look up words that begin with *vari*. Ask students to find synonyms that will help them identify *variables* in an experiment. **learning modality: verbal**

Gifted and Talented L3
Summarizing Ask students to explain how Pasteur's experiments led to the development of pasteurization. Students can summarize the process, its impact on society, and its link to Pasteur's experiments in a chart, poster, or report. **learning modality: verbal**

Monitor Progress _____ L2

Writing Ask students to write a short paragraph explaining how we know that spontaneous generation does not take place.

Students can save their paragraphs in their portfolios. **Portfolio**

Answers
Figure 5 Whether or not the jar was covered

 Reading Checkpoint An experiment in which two tests are identical except for one factor

The Needs of Living Things

Teach Key Concepts L2

Living Things Have Four Basic Needs

Focus Ask students to think of the things they need to live.

Teach Write the boldfaced concept statement on the board and read it aloud. Give students examples of each of the needs listed (food, water, living space, and stable internal conditions). Tell them that all of these things are needed by all living things.

Apply Ask students to choose a living thing and describe how it meets each of these needs. **learning modality: logical/ mathematical**

Address Misconceptions L2

"Plant Food" Is Not Food

Focus Students may be confused by the statement that plants make their own food and commercial "plant food." Show students the label from a plant-food package. Point out the ingredients (usually forms of nitrogen, phosphorus, and potassium).

Teach Tell students that these chemicals are not actually food because they are not a source of energy. They are nutrients that plants need to grow, develop, and make food. The "food" that plants make is sugar.

Apply Ask: **List some nutrients people need that do not provide energy.** (*Possible answers: water, vitamins, minerals*) **learning modality: logical/mathematical**

FIGURE 7
Food, Water, and Living Space

This environment meets the needs of the many animals that live there. **Inferring** *How do the trees and other plants meet their needs for food?*

The Needs of Living Things

Though it may seem surprising, flies, bacteria, and all other organisms have the same basic needs as you. **All living things must satisfy their basic needs for food, water, living space, and stable internal conditions.**

Food Recall that organisms need a source of energy to live. They use food as their energy source. Organisms differ in the ways they obtain energy. Some organisms, such as plants, capture the sun's energy and use it to make food. Organisms that make their own food are called **autotrophs** (AW toh trohfs). *Auto-* means "self" and *-troph* means "feeder." Autotrophs use the food they make to carry out their own life functions.

Organisms that cannot make their own food are called **heterotrophs** (HET uh roh trohfs). *Hetero-* means "other." Heterotrophs obtain their energy by feeding on others. Some heterotrophs eat autotrophs and use the energy in the autotroph's stored food. Other heterotrophs consume heterotrophs that eat autotrophs. Therefore, a heterotroph's energy source is also the sun—but in an indirect way. Animals, mushrooms, and slime molds are examples of heterotrophs.

The porcupine, a heterotroph, obtains its energy by feeding on green plants.

12 ◆ A

Water All living things need water to survive. In fact, most organisms can live for only a few days without water. Organisms need water to obtain chemicals from their surroundings, break down food, grow, move substances within their bodies, and reproduce.

One property of water that is vital to living things is its ability to dissolve more chemicals than any other substance on Earth. In fact, water makes up about 90 percent of the liquid part of your blood. The food that your cells need dissolves in blood and is transported to all parts of your body. Waste from cells dissolves in blood and is carried away. Your body's cells also provide a watery environment in which chemicals are dissolved.

Living Space All organisms need a place to live—a place to get food and water and find shelter. Whether an organism lives in the freezing Antarctic or the scorching desert, its surroundings must provide what it needs to survive.

Because there is a limited amount of space on Earth, some organisms must compete for space. Trees in a forest, for example, compete with other trees for sunlight above ground. Below ground, their roots compete for water and minerals.

Lab zone Skills Activity

Designing Experiments

Your teacher will give you a slice of potato. Predict what percentage of the potato's mass is water. Then come up with a plan to test your prediction. For materials, you will be given a hairdryer and a balance. Obtain your teacher's approval before carrying out your plan. How does your result compare with your prediction?

Integrating Chemistry L2

Materials 2 small beakers, salt, sugar, 60 mL vegetable oil, 60 mL water, wooden stirrers

Time 10 minutes

Safety
Review the Safety Guidelines in Appendix A.
Ask half the class to dissolve 10 g of salt in a beaker of water and 10 g in a beaker of oil. The other half of the class should try to dissolve 10 g of sugar in the water and oil. Remind students not to taste the materials and to clean up spills immediately. Ask: **What were your results?** *(The water dissolves both sugar and salt. The oil does not dissolve salt.)* Ask: **What makes water a good liquid for cells to live in?** *(It dissolves materials better than oil does.)* **learning modality: kinesthetic**

The stream fulfills the moose's need for water.

The owl finds a suitable living space in a tree hollow.

A ◆ 13

Monitor Progress _____ L2

Skills Check Have students choose one living thing and give examples of how it meets its basic needs.

Lab zone Skills Activity

Skills Focus Designing experiments L2
Materials balance, hair dryer, paper towels, thin potato slices, small mirrors
Time 30 minutes
Safety Review the Safety Guidelines in Appendix A.
Tips Before class, slice the potatoes thin (but not too thin or they will blow away).

Keep slices in a container of cold water. Tell students to thoroughly dry potato slices.

Expected Outcome Have students find the mass of the wet potato slices, use the hair dryer to dry the slices, find the mass of the dry slices, and subtract to find the mass of the water lost. Have students place the slices on a paper towel on a flat surface and

turn them frequently. The water content of the potato slices is about 40%.

Extend Ask students to find the water content of other fruits or vegetables (apples, carrots, peppers). Encourage students to predict the water content before they begin. **learning modality: kinesthetic**

Assess

Reviewing Key Concepts

1. a. Cellular organization, similar chemicals, energy use, response to surroundings, growth and development, and reproduction **b.** Response to surroundings **c.** It has all the characteristics of life. Movement is not a characteristic of life although many living things move.
2. a. The mistaken idea that living things can arise from nonliving things **b.** Spontaneous generation cannot occur, because living things can only arise from living things. Redi's and Pasteur's experiments help to disprove spontaneous generation. **c.** It showed that new bacteria in broth appeared only when there were existing bacteria.
3. a. A source of energy (food), water, living space, and stable internal conditions **b.** Getting energy by eating food **c.** It helps the fox keep it internal body temperature stable even though the temperature of the fox's surroundings changes.

Reteach **L1**

Have each student create a concept map that includes the characteristics and needs of living things.

Performance Assessment **L2**

Writing Have students invent a living thing that meets all the criteria in this section. Ask students to write a paragraph describing the characteristics of this new organism.

[Portfolio]

All in One Teaching Resources

• Section Summary: *What Is Life?*
• Review and Reinforcement: *What Is Life?*
• Enrich: *What Is Life?*

FIGURE 8
Homeostasis
Sweating helps your body maintain a steady body temperature. Your body produces sweat during periods of strenuous activity. As the sweat evaporates, it cools your body down.

Stable Internal Conditions Organisms must be able to keep the conditions inside their bodies stable, even when conditions in their surroundings change significantly. For example, your body temperature stays steady despite changes in the air temperature. The maintenance of stable internal conditions is called **homeostasis** (hoh mee oh STAY sis).

Homeostasis keeps internal conditions just right for cells to function. Think about your need for water after a hard workout. When water levels in your body decrease, chemicals in your body send signals to your brain, causing you to feel thirsty.

Other organisms have different mechanisms for maintaining homeostasis. Consider barnacles, which as adults are attached to rocks at the edge of the ocean. At high tide, they are covered by water. At low tide, however, the watery surroundings disappear, and barnacles are exposed to hours of sun and wind. Without a way to keep water in their cells, they would die. Fortunately, a barnacle can close up its hard outer plates, trapping some water inside. In this way, a barnacle can keep its body moist until the next high tide.

✓ **Reading Checkpoint** **What is homeostasis?**

Section **1** Assessment

🎯 **Target Reading Skill** Using Prior Knowledge Review your graphic organizer and revise it based on what you just learned in the section.

Reviewing Key Concepts

1. a. Reviewing List the six characteristics of living things.
  b. Inferring A bird sitting in a tree flies away as you walk by. Which of the life characteristics explains the bird's behavior?
  c. Applying Concepts Explain why the tree, which does not move away, is also considered a living thing.
2. a. Defining What was meant by the idea of *spontaneous generation*?
  b. Explaining Why is this idea incorrect?
  c. Summarizing How did Pasteur's experiment help show that spontaneous generation does not occur?

3. a. Identifying What four things do all organisms need to survive?
  b. Describing Which need is a fox meeting by feeding on berries?
  c. Applying Concepts The arctic fox has thick, dense fur in the winter and much shorter fur in the summer. How does this help the fox maintain homeostasis?

Lab zone **At-Home Activity**

Observing Life With a family member, observe a living thing, such as a family pet, a houseplant, or a bird outside your window. Record your observations as you study the organism. Prepare a chart that shows how the organism meets the four needs of living things discussed in this section.

Lab zone **At-Home Activity**

Observing Life **L1** Remind students to list the needs of living things and to include them in their charts. Ask students whether their family members agree with the information they recorded in their chart.

Lab zone **Chapter Project**

Keep Students on Track Have each student examine their mystery object, record observations, and develop a plan to test for different characteristics and predict how a living thing would respond to each test. Review plans. Work with students to revise plans that do not meet your approval.

Please Pass the Bread!

Problem

What factors are necessary for bread molds to grow?

Skills Focus

observing, controlling variables

Materials

- paper plates
- plastic dropper
- bread without preservatives
- sealable plastic bags
- tap water
- packing tape

Procedure

1. Brainstorm with others to predict which factors might affect the growth of bread mold. Record your ideas.

2. Place two slices of bread of the same size and thickness on separate, clean plates.

3. To test the effect of moisture on bread mold growth, add drops of tap water to one bread slice until the whole slice is moist. Keep the other slice dry. Expose both slices of bread to the air for one hour.

4. Put each slice into its own sealable bag. Press the outside of each bag to remove the air. Seal the bags. Then use packing tape to seal the bags again. Store the bags in a warm, dark place.

5. Copy the data table into your notebook.

6. Every day for at least five days, briefly remove the sealed bags from their storage place. Record whether any mold has grown. Estimate the area of the bread where mold is present. **CAUTION:** *Do not unseal the bags. At the end of the experiment, give the sealed bags to your teacher.*

Analyze and Conclude

1. **Observing** How did the appearance of the two slices of bread change over the course of the experiment?

2. **Inferring** How can you explain any differences in appearance between the two slices?

3. **Controlling Variables** What was the manipulated variable in this experiment? Why was it necessary to control all other variables except this one?

4. **Communicating** Suppose that you lived in Redi's time. A friend tells you that molds just suddenly appear on bread. How would you explain to your friend about Redi's experiment and how it applies to molds and bread?

Design an Experiment

Choose another factor that may affect mold growth, such as temperature or the amount of light. Set up an experiment to test the factor you choose. Remember to keep all conditions the same except for the one you are testing. *Obtain your teacher's permission before carrying out your investigation.*

Data Table				
	Moistened Bread Slice		Unmoistened Bread Slice	
Day	Mold Present?	Area With Mold	Mold Present?	Area With Mold
1				
2				

Chapter 1 A ◆ 15

Please Pass the Bread! L2

Prepare for Inquiry

Key Concept

Bread mold needs water to grow.

Skills Objective

After this lab, students will be able to

- control variables to determine the effect of different factors
- draw conclusions about how factors affect bread mold growth

Prep Time 20 minutes

Class Time 20 minutes the first day, then 5 minutes for each of the next 5 days

Advance Planning

Obtain bread without preservatives the day before

Safety

⚠️ Do not open sealed bags. Released mold spores could aggravate allergies, asthma, or other medical conditions. Review the safety guidelines in Appendix A.

All in One Teaching Resources

- Lab Worksheet: *Please Pass the Bread!*

Guide Inquiry

Introduce the Procedure

Show students how to slide the bread off the side of the plate and into the bag. Students can use a grid containing squares of equal size to record and estimate mold growth. A 5×5 grid contains 25 squares, so each represents 4% of the slice.

Expected Outcome

Mold should grow on the moistened bread, but not on the dry bread.

Analyze and Conclude

1. The moistened bread became moldy. The unmoistened bread remained almost the same.

2. Mold grew on the moistened bread because it had the right conditions to grow—water, food (the bread), and living space (a dark, warm place).

3. The manipulated variable was moisture. If the other variables are not controlled, experimenters cannot be sure which variable caused a specific change.

4. Redi showed that spontaneous generation does not occur. Mold is produced only by existing mold and grows when environmental conditions are suitable.

Extend Inquiry

Design an Experiment Students' designs should take account of the fact that bread mold spores are in the air.

Objectives

After completing the lesson, students will be able to

A.1.2.1 Explain why biologists classify organisms.

A.1.2.2 Relate the levels of classification to the relationships between organisms.

A.1.2.3 Explain how taxonomic keys are useful.

A.1.2.4 Explain the relationship between classification and evolution.

Target Reading Skill

Asking Questions Explain that changing a head into a question helps students anticipate the ideas, facts, and events they are about to read.

Answers

Possible questions and answers include: **Why do scientists classify?** (*Scientists classify because they want to organize living things into groups so they are easier to study.*) **What system did Linnaeus use to name organisms?** (*He used a system called binomial nomenclature.*) **What are the levels of classification?** (*Domain, kingdom, phylum, class, order, family, genus, species*)

All in One Teaching Resources
- Transparency A4

Preteach

Build Background Knowledge L2

How Libraries Are Organized

Ask: **How do libraries organize their books?** (*First by whether they are fiction or nonfiction, then by subject matter, then in alphabetical order by author's last name, first name, and finally title*) Discuss with students how difficult it would be to find a book in the library without an organizing system.

Reading Preview

Key Concepts
- Why do biologists organize living things into groups?
- What do the levels of classification indicate about the relationship between organisms?
- How are taxonomic keys useful?
- What is the relationship between classification and evolution?

Key Terms
- classification • taxonomy
- binomial nomenclature
- genus • species • evolution

Target Reading Skill

Asking Questions Before you read, preview the red headings. In a graphic organizer like the one below, ask a *what*, *why*, or *how* question for each heading. As you read, write the answers to your questions.

Classifying Organisms

Question	Answer
Why do scientists classify?	Scientists classify because . . .

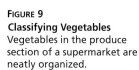

FIGURE 9
Classifying Vegetables
Vegetables in the produce section of a supermarket are neatly organized.

Lab zone Discover Activity

Can You Organize a Junk Drawer?

1. Your teacher will give you some items that you might find in the junk drawer of a desk. Your job is to organize the items.
2. Examine the objects and decide on three groups into which you can sort them.
3. Place each object into one of the groups, based on how the item's features match the characteristics of the group.
4. Compare your grouping system with those of your classmates.

Think It Over
Classifying Which of your classmates' grouping systems seemed most useful? Why?

Suppose you had only ten minutes to run into a supermarket to get what you needed—milk and tomatoes. Could you do it? In most supermarkets this would be an easy task. You'd probably find out where the dairy and produce sections are, and head straight to those areas. Now imagine if you had to shop for these same items in a market where things were randomly placed throughout the store. Where would you begin? You'd have to search through a lot of things before you found what you needed. You could be there for a long time!

Lab zone Discover Activity

Skills Focus Classifying

Materials items such as envelopes, erasers, paper, paper clips, pencils, rubber bands, stamps, tape

Time 15 minutes

Tips Avoid using sharp objects. Stress that items in a set must share at least one common trait.

L1

Expected Outcome Students may group the items in a number of ways, such as by function (items you write with) or by shape (round).

Think It Over Each grouping system will have strengths and weaknesses. Criteria for usefulness will vary. Possibilities include systems that emphasize similar functions or that allow objects to be found quickly.

Why Do Scientists Classify?

Just as shopping can be a problem in a disorganized store, finding information about a specific organism can also be a problem. So far, scientists have identified more than one million kinds of organisms on Earth. That's a large number, and it is continually growing as scientists discover new organisms. Imagine how difficult it would be to find information about one particular organism if you had no idea even where to begin. It would be a lot easier if similar organisms were placed into groups.

Organizing living things into groups is exactly what biologists have done. Biologists group organisms based on similarities, just as grocers group milk with dairy products and tomatoes with produce. **Classification** is the process of grouping things based on their similarities.

Biologists use classification to organize living things into groups so that the organisms are easier to study. The scientific study of how living things are classified is called **taxonomy** (tak SAHN uh mee). Taxonomy is useful because once an organism is classified, a scientist knows a lot about that organism. For example, if you know that a crow is classified as a bird, then you know that a crow has wings, feathers, and a beak.

 Reading Checkpoint What is the scientific study of how living things are classified called?

FIGURE 10
Classifying Beetles
These beetles belong to a large insect collection in a natural history museum. They have been classified according to characteristics they share. **Observing** *What characteristics may have been used to group these beetles?*

Living Things

Video Preview
▶ Video Field Trip
Video Assessment

Instruct

Why Do Scientists Classify?

Teach Key Concepts ▫L2▫
Organisms Are Organized into Groups

Focus Tell students that like organisms are grouped together. This makes it easier to study them.

Teach Write *kaz* on the board. Tell students this organism is a fish. Ask students to list what they know about *kaz* based on its classification.

Apply Ask: **How might you classify a sunflower, a robin, a lizard, a blue jay, and a tree?** *(Possible answers: sunflower and tree as plants; robin, lizard, and blue jay as animals; robin and blue jay as birds)* **learning modality: logical/mathematical**

Independent Practice ▫L2▫

▫All in One▫ **Teaching Resources**

• Guided Reading and Study Worksheet: *Classifying Organisms*

◉ **Student Edition on Audio CD**

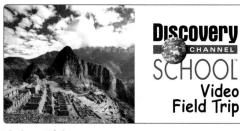

Living Things

Show the Video Field Trip to help students understand the classification of organisms. Discussion question: **What is the broadest level of classification?** *(Domain)*

Differentiated Instruction

Special Needs ▫L2▫
Classifying Help students understand the concept of classification by discussing classification of rocks. Give students samples of igneous, metamorphic, and sedimentary rocks. Display a sample of each rock type in front of a labeled box. Ask students to classify their rock samples. **learning modality: kinesthetic**

Monitor Progress ▫L2▫

Writing Have students describe the difference between classification and taxonomy.

Answer

 Taxonomy

The Naming System of Linnaeus

Teach Key Concepts L2
Scientific Names Have Two Parts

Focus Write these scientific names on the board: *Perognathus californicus, Perognathus nelsoni, Perognathus spinatus.*

Teach Explain that these animals are North American field pocket mice. Ask: **What genus/genera do these animals belong to?** *(Perognathus)* **What are the species of these mice?** *(Perognathus californicus, Perognathus nelsoni, and Perognathus spinatus)* Stress to students that both terms of the scientific name must be used to indicate an organism's species. The first term, the genus, can be used alone, while the second term (known as the specific epithet) cannot.

Extend Challenge students to see how much information they can infer about these animals from their names. *(Possible answers: They are different species, but all belong to the same genus. Mating among them would not produce fertile offspring. Students might infer that* P. nelsoni *was discovered by someone named Nelson,* P. californicus *is found in California, and* P. spinatus *has prickly fur.)* **learning modality: verbal**

Help Students Read L2
Analyze the Parts of Binomial
Word Part Analysis/Build Vocabulary
Write the term *binomial nomenclature* on the board. Tell students that *bi-* means "two" and *nomen* means "name." Ask: **What does the term *binomial* mean?** *(Two names)*

The Naming System of Linnaeus

Taxonomy also involves naming organisms. In the 1750s, the Swedish naturalist Carolus Linnaeus devised a system of naming organisms that is still used today. Linnaeus placed organisms in groups based on their observable features. Based on his observations, Linnaeus gave each organism a unique, two-part scientific name. This naming system Linnaeus used is called **binomial nomenclature** (by NOH mee ul NOH men klay chur). The word *binomial* means "two names."

Genus and Species The first word in an organism's scientific name is its genus. A **genus** (JEE nus) (plural *genera*) is a classification grouping that contains similar, closely related organisms. For example, pumas, marbled cats, and house cats are all classified in the genus *Felis*. Organisms that are classified in the genus *Felis* share characteristics such as sharp, retractable claws and behaviors such as hunting other animals.

The second word in a scientific name often describes a distinctive feature of an organism, such as where it lives or its appearance. Together, the two words indicate a unique species. A **species** (SPEE sheez) is a group of similar organisms that can mate with each other and produce offspring that can also mate and reproduce.

FIGURE 11
Binomial Nomenclature
These three different species of cats belong to the same genus. Their scientific names share the same first word, *Felis*. The second word of their names describes a feature of the animal.

Felis concolor
(Puma)
Concolor means "the same color" in Latin. Notice that this animal's coat is mostly the same color.

Felis marmorata
(Marbled cat)
Notice the marbled pattern of this animal's coat. *Marmorata* means "marble" in Latin.

Felis domesticus
(House cat)
Domesticus means "of the house" in Latin.

Aristotle and Classification

Many hundreds of years before Linnaeus, a Greek scholar named Aristotle developed a classification system for animals. Aristotle first divided animals into those he considered to have blood and those he did not. This graph shows Aristotle's classification system for "animals with blood."

1. **Reading Graphs** Into how many groups were these animals classified?

2. **Interpreting Data** Which group made up the largest percentage of animals?

3. **Calculating** What percentage of these animals either fly or swim?

4. **Inferring** In Aristotle's classification system, where would a cow be classified? A whale?

5. **Predicting** Would Aristotle's classification system be useful today? Explain.

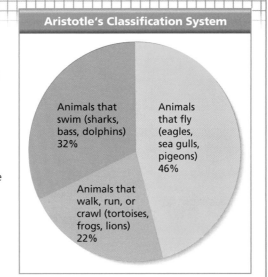

Aristotle's Classification System

Animals that swim (sharks, bass, dolphins) 32%

Animals that fly (eagles, sea gulls, pigeons) 46%

Animals that walk, run, or crawl (tortoises, frogs, lions) 22%

Using Binomial Nomenclature Notice in Figure 11 that a complete scientific name is written in italics. Only the first letter of the first word in a scientific name is capitalized. Notice also that scientific names contain Latin words. Linnaeus used Latin words in his naming system because Latin was the language that scientists used during that time.

Binomial nomenclature makes it easy for scientists to communicate about an organism because everyone uses the same scientific name for the same organism. Using different names for the same organism can get very confusing. For instance, look at the animal in Figure 12. People call it by a variety of names. Depending on where you live, you might call this animal a woodchuck, groundhog, or whistlepig. Fortunately, it has only one scientific name—*Marmota monax*.

Reading Checkpoint How is a scientific name written?

FIGURE 12
Marmota monax
Although there are many common names for this animal, it has only one scientific name, *Marmota monax*. **Making Generalizations** *What is the advantage of scientific names?*

Chapter 1 A ◆ 19

Math Skill Interpreting graphs

Focus Tell students that circle graphs show how the parts of a whole are related.

Teach Ask: **What does the whole circle represent?** *(All of the animals with blood classified by Aristotle's system)* **What does each wedge represent?** *(A smaller group of animals)*

Answers
1. 3
2. animals that fly
3. 78%
4. cow—animals that walk, run, or crawl; whale—animals that swim
5. Possible answer: This system includes only three categories, so it may not be very useful today. It also does not match that of modern scientists, who use characteristics other than movement to classify animals. For example, frogs and lions belong to very different groups.

Monitor Progress ⬛

Skills Check Have each student choose one living thing and explain how he or she knows it is alive.

Students can save their drawings in their portfolios. 💼 Portfolio

Answers
Figure 12 Using scientific names makes it easy for scientists to communicate about organisms because everyone uses the same name for the same organism.

Reading Checkpoint In italics

Differentiated Instruction

Less Proficient Readers **L1**
Communicating Have students use sketches, photographs, and short captions to create a visual display that compares common names and scientific names.

Students can stick to the general concept or use a specific example. A specific example would be a pill bug/wood louse/roly poly/ *Porcellio scaber*. **learning modality: visual**

Levels of Classification

Teach Key Concepts   L2

Organisms Are Grouped into General and Specific Groups

Focus Draw a series of eight concentric circles on the board. Label the outermost circle "Domain." Label the innermost circle "Species."

Teach Correlate the remaining circles with their corresponding classification level. Point out that the broadest group is the domain. Ask: **Which is the most specific group?** *(Species)*

Extend Ask: **Which animals will share the same innermost circle?** *(Only those of the same species)* **Which animals will share the circle around the species circle?** *(Those of the same genus)* **Which animals will share the same kingdom circle?** *(All animals)* **learning modality: logical/mathematical**

All in One Teaching Resources

• Transparency A5

Levels of Classification

The classification system that scientists use today is based on the contributions of Linnaeus. But today's classification system uses a series of many levels to classify organisms.

To help you understand the levels in classification, imagine a room filled with everybody who lives in your state. First, all of the people who live in your town raise their hands. Then, those who live in your neighborhood raise their hands. Then, those who live on your street raise their hands. Finally, those who live in your house raise their hands. Each time, fewer people raise their hands. But you'd be in all of the groups. The most general group you belong to is the state. The most specific group is the house. The more levels you share with others, the more you have in common with them.

The Major Levels of Classification Most biologists today classify organisms into the levels shown in Figure 13. Of course, organisms are not grouped by where they live, but rather by their shared characteristics. First, an organism is placed in a broad group, which in turn is divided into more specific groups.

As Figure 13 shows, a domain is the highest level of organization. Within a domain, there are kingdoms. Within kingdoms, there are phyla (FY luh) (singular *phylum*). Within phyla are classes. Within classes are orders. Within orders are families. Each family contains one or more genera. Finally, each genus contains one or more species. **The more classification levels that two organisms share, the more characteristics they have in common.**

Classifying an Owl Take a closer look at Figure 13 to see how the levels of classification apply to the great horned owl. Look at the top row of the figure. As you can see, a wide variety of other organisms also belong to the same domain as the horned owl.

Next, look at the kingdom, phylum, class, and order levels. Notice that as you move down the levels in the figure, there are fewer kinds of organisms in each group. More importantly, the organisms in each group have more in common with each other. For example, the class Aves includes all birds, while the order Strigiformes includes only owls. Different owls have more in common with each other than they do with other types of birds.

 Reading Checkpoint Which is a broader classification level—a kingdom or a family?

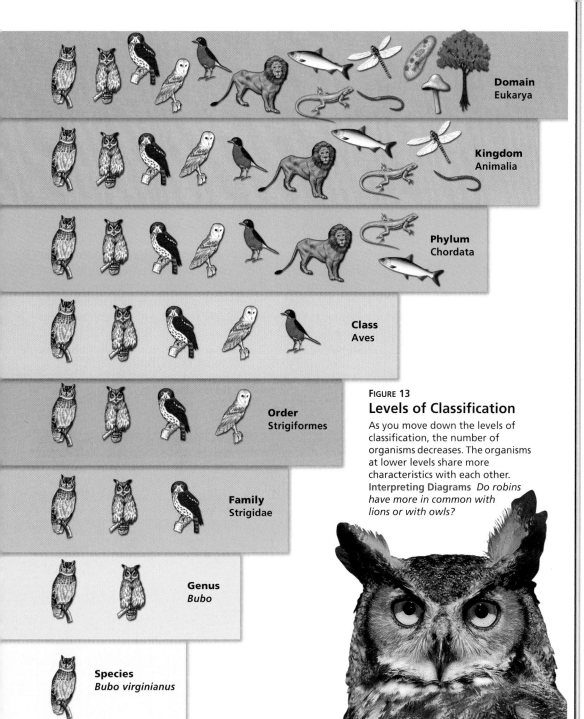

FIGURE 13
Levels of Classification

As you move down the levels of classification, the number of organisms decreases. The organisms at lower levels share more characteristics with each other.
Interpreting Diagrams *Do robins have more in common with lions or with owls?*

Domain
Eukarya

Kingdom
Animalia

Phylum
Chordata

Class
Aves

Order
Strigiformes

Family
Strigidae

Genus
Bubo

Species
Bubo virginianus

Make a Classification Chart

Materials colored pencils; dictionary; glue; list of class, order, and family of common pets; nature magazines; pen; poster board or heavyweight paper; ruler

Time 50 minutes

Focus Tell students to find the level in Figure 13 that would include a specific pet. Ask: **Which levels of Figure 13 would include a house cat?** (*Domain Eukarya; Kingdom Animalia; Phylum Chordata*)

Teach Direct students to create a model classification chart for a pet. Help students find the scientific name of their pet and determine its genus and species.

Apply Ask students how many classification levels the Magellan horned owl, *Bubo magellanicus* shares with *Bubo virginianus*. (*Seven*) **learning modality: visual**

Monitor Progress _____ L2

Skills Check Ask students to explain which classification level will always have the most different kinds of organisms and which level will always have the fewest different kinds of organisms. (*Domain, species; because domains include some kingdoms, many phyla, classes, orders, families, genera, and species, while a species includes only one specific kind of organism*)

Answers
Figure 13 *Owls; robins and owls are birds, and so robins share many more levels of classification with owls than they do with lions.*

 Reading Checkpoint) Kingdom

A ● 21

Taxonomic Keys

Teach Key Concepts **L2**
How to Identify Organisms

Focus Show students a photo of a tick.
Ask: **What is this organism called?**

Teach Show students how to read the
taxonomic key in Figure 14. Point out that
each step contains two statements. Find the
statement that is true for the organism you
are looking up and then follow the
instructions.

Extend Show students examples of field
guides. Ask students to find examples of
organisms that look similar. **learning
modality: visual**

Use Visuals: Figure 14 **L2**
Identifying Organisms

Focus Ask: **Which animals can you identify
using the key?** (*Centipede, millipede, mite,
tick, spider, scorpion, pseudoscorpion*)

Teach Have students draw a picture of each
organism in the key then compare drawings.

Apply Ask: **What other information did
you need to make the drawings?** (*Possible
answers: organisms' color, kind of legs, location
of eyes*) Ask: **Are these characteristics
necessary in the key?** (*No, but a key that
compares different animals might need this
information.*) **learning modality: visual**

 **Teaching Resources**

- Transparency A6

For: More on classifying living things
Visit: PHSchool.com
Web Code: ced-1012

FIGURE 14
Identifying Organisms
You can use a taxonomic key to
identify this organism. The six
paired statements in this key
describe physical characteristics of
different organisms.
Drawing Conclusions *What is this
creature?*

Taxonomic Keys

Why should you care about taxonomy? Suppose that you are
watching television and feel something tickling your foot.
Startled, you look down and see a tiny creature crawling across
your toes. Although it's only the size of a small melon seed, you
don't like the looks of its two claws waving at you. Then, in a
flash, it's gone.

How could you find out what the creature was? You could
use a field guide. Field guides are books with illustrations that
highlight differences between similar-looking organisms. You
could also use a taxonomic key. **Taxonomic keys are useful
tools for determining the identity of organisms.** A taxonomic
key consists of a series of paired statements that describe the
physical characteristics of different organisms.

The taxonomic key in Figure 14 can help you identify the
mysterious organism. To use the key, start by reading the pair of
statements numbered 1a and 1b. Notice that the two statements
are contrasting. Choose the one statement that applies to the
organism. Follow the direction at the end of that statement. For
example, if the organism has eight legs, follow the direction at
the end of statement 1a, which says "Go to Step 2." Continue this
process until the key leads you to the organism's identity.

✓ **Reading Checkpoint** **What are field guides?**

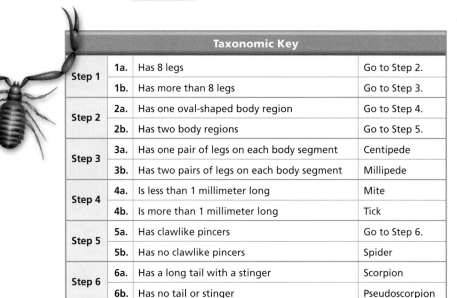

Taxonomic Key			
Step 1	1a.	Has 8 legs	Go to Step 2.
	1b.	Has more than 8 legs	Go to Step 3.
Step 2	2a.	Has one oval-shaped body region	Go to Step 4.
	2b.	Has two body regions	Go to Step 5.
Step 3	3a.	Has one pair of legs on each body segment	Centipede
	3b.	Has two pairs of legs on each body segment	Millipede
Step 4	4a.	Is less than 1 millimeter long	Mite
	4b.	Is more than 1 millimeter long	Tick
Step 5	5a.	Has clawlike pincers	Go to Step 6.
	5b.	Has no clawlike pincers	Spider
Step 6	6a.	Has a long tail with a stinger	Scorpion
	6b.	Has no tail or stinger	Pseudoscorpion

For: More on classifying
living things
Visit: PHSchool.com
Web Code: ced-1012

Students can review classifying in an online
interactivity.

Evolution and Classification

At the time that Linnaeus developed his classification system, people thought that species never change. In 1859, a British naturalist named Charles Darwin published a theory about how species can change over time. Darwin's theory has had a major impact on how species are classified.

Darwin's Theory Darwin collected data for his theory on the Galapagos Islands off the western coast of South America. As he studied the islands' finches, he observed that some species of finches were similar to each other but different from finches living in South America.

Darwin hypothesized that some members of a single species of finch flew from South America to the islands. Once on the islands, the species changed little by little over many generations until it was different from the species remaining in South America. After a while, the birds on the island could no longer mate and reproduce with those on the mainland. They had become a new species. In this way, two groups of a single species can accumulate enough differences over a very long time to become two separate species. This process by which species gradually change over time is called **evolution.**

Classification Today The theory of evolution has changed the way biologists think about classification. Scientists now understand that certain organisms are similar because they share a common ancestor. For example, Darwin hypothesized that the finches on the Galapagos Islands shared a common ancestor with the finches in South America. When organisms share a common ancestor, they share an evolutionary history. Today's system of classification considers the history of a species. **Species with similar evolutionary histories are classified more closely together.**

Determining Evolutionary History How do scientists determine the evolutionary history of a species? One way is to compare the structure of organisms. But today, scientists rely primarily on information about the chemical makeup of the organisms' cells. The more closely two species are related, the more similar the chemicals that make up their cells.

FIGURE 15
Galapagos Finches

These three species of finches that live on the Galapagos Islands may have arisen from a single species. Notice the differences in these birds' appearances, especially their beaks.

The large ground finch cracks open seeds with its strong, wide beak.

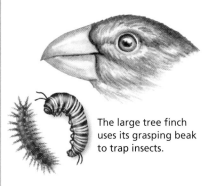

The large tree finch uses its grasping beak to trap insects.

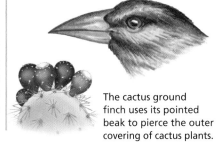

The cactus ground finch uses its pointed beak to pierce the outer covering of cactus plants.

Chapter 1   A ◆ 23

Evolution and Classification

Teach Key Concepts   L2
Species Change Over Time

Focus Point out the Galapagos Islands on a globe or a map.

Teach Say: Darwin found finches on the Galapagos Islands that were different from South American finches. Ask: **Why do you think the finches on the Galapagos Islands differ from South American finches?** *(Possible answer: They are isolated and live in different environments, so they evolved differently.)*

Extend Challenge students to sketch beaks that might be used to eat burrowing insects, mice, sunflower seeds, and fruit. **learning modality: visual**

Classification Today

Teach Key Concepts   L2
Classification is Based on Evolution

Focus Compare an organism's evolutionary history to a person's family tree. Ask: **How do you know who your ancestors are?** *(Possible answers: family records, family resemblance)*

Teach Ask: How can you figure out the ancestors of an organism? *(By studying their structures and chemical makeup)*

Extend Ask: **Why do we pay attention to theories about evolution when classifying organisms?** *(To group organisms that are related together)* **learning modality: verbal**

Monitor Progress _____   L2

Skills Check Ask students to explain how evolution and classification are linked. *(Classification is guided by information about evolutionary history.)*

Answers
Figure 14 A pseudoscorpion

✓ Reading Checkpoint Books with illustrations that highlight differences between similar-looking organisms

Answers

✓ Reading Checkpoint   Chemical makeup

Assess

Reviewing Key Concepts

1. a. To make studying organisms easier
b. Possible answers: Four legs, fur, sharp, retractable claws, hunts other animals
2. a. Domain, kingdom, phylum, class, order, family, genus, species **b.** Squirrels, because organisms in the same family are more similar to each other than to those in different families
3. a. A series of paired statements that describe the physical characteristics of different organisms; used for identifying organisms **b.** Sample answer:

Step 1	
1a. Red	Go to Step 2.
1b. Not red	Go to Step 3.
Step 2	
2a. Has smooth skin with seeds inside	Apple
2b. Has little seeds scattered all over the skin	Strawberry
Step 3	
3a. Yellow, elongated	Banana
3b. Orange, round	Orange

4. a. Change in a species over time
b. Organisms with similar evolutionary histories share a common ancestor and are therefore grouped together. **c.** They are similar.

Reteach **L1**

Have students list the levels of classification in order from broad to specific.

All in One Teaching Resources

• Section Summary: *Classifying Organisms*
• Review and Reinforcement: *Classifying Organisms*
• Enrich: *Classifying Organisms*

FIGURE 16

Classifying Skunks and Weasels
The skunk (bottom) and weasel (right) were once classified in the same family. Based on new chemical information, scientists reclassified skunks and weasels into different families.

New Information Sometimes, by studying the chemical makeup of organisms, scientists discover new information that changes what they had previously thought. For example, skunks and weasels were classified in the same family for 150 years. However, when scientists compared nucleic acids from the cells of skunks and weasels, they found many differences. These differences suggested that the two groups are not as closely related as previously thought. Some scientists proposed changing the classification of skunks. As a result, skunks were reclassified into their own family called Mephitidae, which means "noxious gas" in Latin.

✓ Reading Checkpoint   What kind of information do scientists mainly rely on to determine evolutionary history?

Section 2 Assessment

🎯 **Target Reading Skill** Asking Questions Use the answers to the questions you wrote about the headings to help you answer the questions below.

Reviewing Key Concepts

1. a. Reviewing Why do biologists classify?
b. Inferring Suppose someone tells you that a jaguarundi is classified in the same genus as house cats. What characteristics do you think a jaguarundi might have?
2. a. Listing List in order the levels of classification, beginning with domain.
b. Applying Concepts Woodchucks are classified in the same family as squirrels, but in a different family than mice. Do woodchucks have more characteristics in common with squirrels or mice? Explain.
3. a. Reviewing What is a taxonomic key?
b. Applying Concepts Create a taxonomic key that could help identify a piece of fruit as an apple, orange, strawberry, or banana.

4. a. Reviewing What is evolution?
b. Explaining How is knowing a species' evolutionary history important in its classification?
c. Predicting You discover a new organism that has a chemical makeup extremely similar to that of chickens. What is likely to be true about the evolutionary histories of your organism and chickens?

Lab zone At-Home **Activity**

Kitchen Classification With a family member, go on a "classification hunt" in the kitchen. Look in your refrigerator, cabinets, and drawers to discover what classification systems your family uses to organize items. Then explain to your family member the importance of classification in biology.

Lab zone At-Home **Activity**

Kitchen Classification **L1** Remind students to identify the criteria used to classify kitchen objects in their houses. Families may have organized items by size, function, or location. Ask students whether their family members agreed with their classification systems.

Lab zone Chapter **Project**

Keep Students on Track Encourage students to observe their object each day and record observations and drawings. If students seem bored because their object is not doing anything, encourage them to consider whether the inactivity shows that the object is not alive, or whether they should revise their methods of observation. For example, encourage students to explain how they could be sure that the object is not breathing or growing.

Living Mysteries

Problem
How can you create a taxonomic key to help identify tree leaves?

Skills Focus
observing, classifying, inferring

Materials
- a variety of leaves
- hand lens
- metric ruler

Procedure

1. Your teacher will give you five different tree leaves. Handle the leaves carefully.
2. Use a hand lens to examine each of the leaves. Look for characteristics such as those described in the table. Make a list of five or more identifying characteristics for each leaf.

Leaf Characteristics to Consider	
Characteristic	**Observations**
Overall Shape	Is the leaf needlelike and narrow, or is it flat and wide? For a flat leaf, is it rounded, oblong, heart-shaped, or some other shape?
Simple vs. Compound	Is the leaf a single unit, or is it made up of individual leaflets? If it is made up of leaflets, how are they arranged on the leaf stalk?
Pattern of Veins	Do the leaf's veins run parallel from a central vein, or do they form a branching pattern?
Leaf Edges	Are the edges of the leaf jagged or smooth?
Leaf Texture	Is the leaf's surface fuzzy, shiny, or another texture?

3. Use your observations to create a taxonomic key for the leaves. In creating your taxonomic key, use the characteristics you listed along with any others that you observe. Remember that your taxonomic key should consist of paired statements, similar to the one shown in Figure 14 in this chapter.
4. Exchange your leaves and taxonomic key with a partner. If your partner cannot identify all of the leaves using your key, revise your key as necessary.

Analyze and Conclude
1. **Observing** How are your leaves similar or different from one another?
2. **Classifying** How did you decide which characteristics to use in your taxonomic key?
3. **Inferring** Choose one of your leaves and look back over the list of characteristics you used to classify it. Do you think every single leaf of the same type would share those characteristics? Explain.
4. **Communicating** Explain in your own words why a taxonomic key is helpful. Include in your explanation why it is important that the paired statements in a taxonomic key be contrasting statements.

More to Explore
Suppose you are hiking through the woods and see many flowers of different colors, shapes, and sizes. You decide to create a taxonomic key to help identify the flowers. What characteristics would you include in the key?

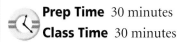

Living Mysteries   L2

Prepare for Inquiry

Skills Objective
After this lab, students will be able to
- observe and identify characteristics of leaves, such as pine, palm, cedar, maple, and orange
- classify organisms into one of the five leaf groups using a taxonomic key

Prep Time 30 minutes
Class Time 30 minutes

Advance Planning
Collect various leaves or photographs of leaves, such as pine, palm, cedar, maple, and orange.

Safety
Review the safety guidelines in Appendix A.

All in One Teaching Resources
- Lab Worksheet: *Living Mysteries*

Guide Inquiry

Introduce the Procedure
Suggest students try out the taxonomic key in Figure 14.

Expected Outcome
Student's keys will depend on the five leaves that they are given. The keys should follow the outline of the table of leaf characteristics provided, and lead to the correct identity of each leaf.

Analyze and Conclude
1. They differ in shape, number of leaves in a unit, pattern of veins, edges, and texture.
2. Answers will vary depending on leaves provided.
3. Yes, if they belong to the same species they share similar chacteristics.
4. The opposite statements are written so that organisms being classified match one choice or the other. Each pair is written to cover all possible choices and leads to either the correct name or the next step in the process.

Extend Inquiry

More to Explore Petal shape and arrangement, smell, number and size of flowers

Objectives

After completing the lesson, students will be able to

A.1.3.1 List characteristics used to classify organisms.

A.1.3.2 Compare and contrast bacteria and archaea.

A.1.3.3 Name the kingdoms within Eukarya.

Target Reading Skill 🔁

Comparing and Contrasting Explain that comparing and contrasting information shows how ideas, facts, and events are similar and different. The results of the comparison can have importance.

Answers

Bacteria: Prokaryotes; unicellular; Some are able to make food

Archaea: Prokaryotes; unicellular; Some are able to make food

Eukarya: *Protists*: Eukaryotes; unicellular or multicellular; Some are able to make food
Fungi: Eukaryotes; unicellular or multicellular; No
Plants: Eukaryotes; multicellular; Yes
Animals: Eukaryotes; multicellular; No

All in One Teaching Resources

• Transparency A7

Preteach

Build Background Knowledge   **L2**
Categorizing Movies

Ask: **How many different kinds of movies can you name?** Write appropriate suggestions on the board. (*Possible answers: action, mystery, romance, comedy, western, foreign*) Invite students to consider how using these categories helps them describe and compare movies.

Reading Preview

Key Concepts
• What characteristics are used to classify organisms?
• How do bacteria and archaea differ?
• What are the kingdoms within the domain Eukarya?

Key Terms
• prokaryote • nucleus
• eukaryote

🔁 Target Reading Skill
Comparing and Contrasting As you read, compare and contrast the characteristics of organisms in domains Bacteria, Archaea, and Eukarya, by completing a table like the one below.

Characteristics of Organisms

Domain or Kingdom	Cell Type and Number	Able to Make Food?
Bacteria	Prokaryote; unicellular	
Archaea		
Eukarya: Protists		
Fungi		
Plants		
Animals		

FIGURE 17
In the three-domain system of classification, all known organisms belong to one of three domains—Bacteria, Archaea, or Eukarya.

Lab zone Discover **Activity**

Which Organism Goes Where?
1. Your teacher will give you some organisms to observe. Two of the organisms are classified in the same kingdom.
2. Observe the organisms. Decide which organisms might belong in the same kingdom. Write the reasons for your decision. Wash your hands after handling the organisms.
3. Discuss your decision and reasoning with your classmates.

Think It Over
Forming Operational Definitions What characteristics do you think define the kingdom into which you placed the two organisms together?

Suppose you were an apprentice helping Linnaeus classify organisms. You probably would have identified every organism as either a plant or an animal. That's because over 200 years ago, people could not see the tiny organisms that are known to exist today. When microscopes, which make small objects look larger, were invented, a whole new world was revealed. As more and more powerful microscopes were developed, scientists discovered many new organisms and identified important differences among cells.

Today, a three-domain system of classification is commonly used. Shown in Figure 17, the three domains are Bacteria, Archaea, and Eukarya. Within the domains are kingdoms. **Organisms are placed into domains and kingdoms based on their cell type, their ability to make food, and the number of cells in their bodies.**

Three Domains of Life		
Bacteria	**Archaea**	**Eukarya**
		Protists Fungi Plants Animals

Lab zone Discover **Activity**

Skills Focus Forming operational definitions   **L1**

Materials green plant, insect or worm, mushroom, sea animal (tropical fish, starfish, or anemone)

Time 15 minutes

 Safety Caution students to be careful handling animals and to wash their hands immediately after the activity. Review the Safety Guidelines in Appendix A.

Tips Sea animals can be purchased at tropical fish stores.

Expected Outcome Some students may place the fish, starfish, or anemone in the same kingdom as the insect or worm. Fish, starfish, anemones, insects, and worms are all classified as animals.

Think It Over Students will likely focus on movement as a defining characteristic of this kingdom. Discuss other features biologists use to classify living things as animals, plants, or fungi, such as cell type, number of cells, and food-making ability.

Domain Bacteria

Although you may not know it, members of the domain Bacteria are all around you. You can find them in the yogurt you eat, on every surface you touch, and inside your body, both when you are healthy and sick.

Members of the domain Bacteria are prokaryotes (proh KA ree ohtz). **Prokaryotes** are organisms whose cells lack a nucleus. A **nucleus** (NOO klee us) (plural *nuclei*) is a dense area in a cell that contains nucleic acids—the chemical instructions that direct the cell's activities. In prokaryotes, nucleic acids are not contained within a nucleus.

Some bacteria are autotrophs, while others are heterotrophs. Bacteria may be harmful, such as those that cause strep throat. However, most bacteria are helpful. Some produce vitamins and foods like yogurt, and some recycle essential chemicals, such as nitrogen.

 Reading Checkpoint What is a nucleus?

Domain Archaea

Deep in the Pacific Ocean, hot gases and molten rock spew out from a vent in the ocean floor. It is hard to imagine that any living thing could exist in such harsh conditions. Surprisingly, a group of tiny organisms thrives in such places. They are members of the domain Archaea (ahr KEE uh), whose name comes from the Greek word for "ancient."

Archaea can be found in some of the most extreme environments on Earth, including hot springs, very salty water, swamps, and the intestines of cows! Scientists think that the harsh conditions in which archaea live are similar to those of ancient Earth.

Like bacteria, archaea are unicellular prokaryotes. And like bacteria, some archaea are autotrophs while others are heterotrophs. Archaea are classified in their own domain, however, because their chemical makeup differs from that of bacteria. **Although bacteria and archaea are similar in some ways, there are important differences in the structure and chemical makeup of their cells.**

 Reading Checkpoint Where can archaea be found?

FIGURE 18
Domain Bacteria
The bristles of a toothbrush (blue) scrub away at a film of bacteria (yellow) on a tooth. The bacteria in the inset are responsible for causing cavities.

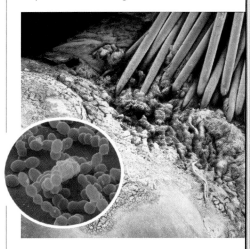

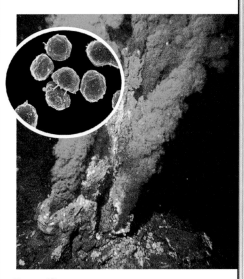

FIGURE 19
Domain Archaea
Heat-loving archaea (inset) thrive in deep-sea vents like these.
Classifying *What characteristics do archaea and bacteria share?*

Chapter 1 A ◆ 27

Domain Eukarya

Teach Key Concepts
Eukarya Are Eukaryotes

Focus List ten different plants, animals, protists, and fungi on the board and direct students' attention to the list. Tell students all these organisms are made of cells that have a nucleus (eukaryotes).

Teach List the kingdoms that make up Eukarya (Animals, Plants, Protists, Fungi). Review the main characteristics of each kingdom. Ask: **What do members of these kingdoms have in common?** *(They are eukaryotes.)*

Extend Have students classify the list of organisms from Focus into the four kingdoms. **learning modality: logical/mathematical**

Lab zone Teacher Demo L3

Staining Leaves

Materials alcohol, iodine, light green leaf, petri dish

Focus Tell students that iodine darkens when it touches starch.

Teach Soak the leaf in alcohol for 24 hours. Dry the leaf, place it in a glass dish, and cover it with iodine. Show the leaf to students. Ask: **What can you conclude?** *(The leaf contains starch.)* Explain to students that the food plants make is sugar, stored in the form of starch.

Apply Ask: **How did the starch get in the leaf?** *(The plant made it.)* **learning modality: visual**

Go Online
SciLINKS NSTA

For: Links on kingdoms
Visit: www.SciLinks.org
Web Code: scn-0113

Download a worksheet that will guide students' review of Internet resources on kingdoms.

▲ **Protists:** Paramecium

▲ **Fungi:** Mushrooms

FIGURE 20
Domain Eukarya
You can encounter organisms from all four kingdoms of Eukarya on a hike through the woods.
Making Generalizations *What characteristic do all Eukarya share?*

Go Online
SciLINKS NSTA

For: Links on kingdoms
Visit: www.SciLinks.org
Web Code: scn-0113

Domain Eukarya

What do seaweeds, mushrooms, tomatoes, and dogs have in common? They are all members of the domain Eukarya. Organisms in this domain are **eukaryotes** (yoo KA ree ohtz)—organisms with cells that contain nuclei. **Scientists classify organisms in the domain Eukarya into one of four kingdoms: protists, fungi, plants, or animals.**

Protists A protist (PROH tist) is any eukaryotic organism that cannot be classifed as an animal, plant, or fungus. Because its members are so different from one another, the protist kingdom is sometimes called the "odds and ends" kingdom. For example, some protists are autotrophs, while others are heterotrophs. Most protists are unicellular, but some, such as seaweeds, are large multicellular organisms.

Fungi If you have eaten mushrooms, then you have eaten fungi (FUN jy). Mushrooms, molds, and mildew are all fungi. Most fungi are multicellular eukaryotes. A few, such as the yeast you use for baking, are unicellular eukaryotes. Fungi are found almost everywhere on land, but only a few live in fresh water. All fungi are heterotrophs. Most fungi feed by absorbing nutrients from dead or decaying organisms.

Plants Dandelions on a lawn, mosses in a forest, and peas in a garden are familiar members of the plant kingdom. Plants are all multicellular eukaryotes and most live on land. In addition, plants are autotrophs that make their own food. Plants provide food for most of the heterotrophs on land.

The plant kingdom includes a great variety of organisms. Some plants produce flowers, while others do not. Some plants, such as giant redwood trees, can grow very tall. Others, like mosses, never grow taller than a few centimeters.

Differentiated Instruction

Less Proficient Readers L1
Compare and Contrast Have students work in small groups to prepare a compare and contrast table that shows similarities and differences among organisms in the six kingdoms. Suggest that students use these column headings: *Kingdom, Cell Type, Ability to Make Food, Number of Cells, Examples.* Have students list the kingdoms in the first column and fill in information from their reading for the remaining columns.

▲ **Plants:** Moss   ▲ **Animals:** Salamander

Animals A dog, a flea on the dog's ear, and a cat that the dog chases have much in common because all are animals. All animals are multicellular eukaryotes. In addition, all animals are heterotrophs. Animals have different adaptations that allow them to locate food, capture it, eat it, and digest it. Members of the animal kingdom live in diverse environments throughout Earth. Animals can be found from ocean depths to mountaintops, from hot, scalding deserts to cold, icy landscapes.

 Reading Checkpoint   Which two kingdoms consist only of heterotrophs?

Section 3 Assessment

Target Reading Skill Comparing and Contrasting Use the information in your table about Bacteria, Archaea, and Eukarya to help you answer the questions below.

Reviewing Key Concepts

1. **a. Listing** What are the three domains into which organisms are classified?
   b. Classifying What information do you need to know to determine the domain to which an organism belongs?
2. **a. Defining** What is a prokaryote?
   b. Classifying Which two domains include only organisms that are prokaryotes?
   c. Comparing and Contrasting How do the members of the two domains of prokaryotes differ?

3. **a. Reviewing** What do the cells of protists, fungi, plants, and animals have in common?
   b. Comparing and Contrasting How are protists and plants similar? How are they different?
   c. Inferring You learn that the Venus flytrap is in the same kingdom as pine trees. What characteristics do these organisms share?

Writing in Science

Detailed Observation Study a photo of an animal. Then write a detailed description of the animal without naming it. Describe the animal so that an artistic friend could paint it in detail without seeing it. Use adjectives that clearly and vividly describe the animal.

Objectives

After completing the lesson, students will be able to

A.1.4.1 Contrast the atmosphere of early Earth with today's atmosphere.

A.1.4.2 Describe some hypotheses about how life arose on Earth.

Target Reading Skill 🎯

Identifying Supporting Evidence Explain that identifying supporting evidence helps students understand the relationship between the facts and the hypothesis.

Answers

Possible evidence: Fossil evidence of archaea-like organisms; fossils dated to be between 3.4 and 3.5 billion years old.

All in One Teaching Resources

• Transparency A8

Preteach

Build Background Knowledge L2

Describe the Air Around Us

Tell students that the air around us is composed of gases in varying amounts. Ask: **What are some of the gases found in air?** (*Possible answers: Oxygen, nitrogen, carbon dioxide*) Tell students that in this section they will learn how the composition of gases in the atmosphere has changed over time.

The Origin of Life

Reading Preview

Key Concepts

• How was the atmosphere of early Earth different from today's atmosphere?

• How do scientists hypothesize that life arose on early Earth?

Key Term

• fossil

🎯 **Target Reading Skill**
Identifying Supporting Evidence As you read, identify the evidence that supports scientists' hypothesis of how life arose on Earth. Write the evidence in a graphic organizer like the one below.

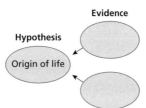

Hypothesis — Origin of life → Evidence

Lab zone Discover Activity

How Can the Composition of Air Change?

1.  Your teacher will give you two covered plastic jars. One contains a plant, and one contains an animal.
2. Observe the organisms in each jar. Talk with a partner about how you think each organism affects the composition of the air in its jar.
3. Predict how the amount of oxygen in each jar would change over time if left undisturbed.
4. Return the jars to your teacher.

Think It Over

Inferring Scientists hypothesize that Earth's early atmosphere was different from today's atmosphere. What role might early organisms have played in bringing about those changes?

You stare out the window of your time machine. You have traveled more than 3.5 billion years back in time, to an early point in Earth's history. The landscape is unfamiliar—rugged, with bare, jagged rocks and little soil. You search for a hint of green, but there is none. You see only blacks, browns, and grays. Lightning flashes all around you. You hear the rumble of thunder, howling winds, and waves pounding the shore.

You neither see nor hear any living things. However, you know that this is the time period when scientists hypothesize that early life forms arose on Earth. You decide to explore. To be safe, you put on your oxygen mask. Stepping outside, you wonder what kinds of organisms could ever live in such a place.

The Atmosphere of Early Earth

You were smart to put on your oxygen mask before exploring early Earth! You would not have been able to breathe because there was little oxygen in the air. Scientists think that conditions on early Earth were very different than they are today. **On ancient Earth, nitrogen, water vapor, carbon dioxide, and methane were probably the most abundant gases in the atmosphere.** In contrast, the major gases in the atmosphere today are nitrogen and oxygen.

Lab zone Discover Activity

Skills Focus Inferring L2

Materials two covered plastic jars; one containing a plant, the other, an animal

Time 10 minutes

 Safety Review the Safety Guidelines in Appendix A.

Tips Select animals such as snails, insects, or earthworms. Release animals immediately after students observe them.

Students may need help identifying facts such as respiration that will change the air inside containers.

Think It Over Because the animal consumes oxygen and the plant produces oxygen, students might suggest that early organisms either removed things from or released things into the air so that eventually the atmospheric composition changed.

Life on Early Earth Evidence suggests that the earliest forms of life appeared on Earth some time between 3.5 and 4.0 billion years ago. Because there was no oxygen, you, like most of today's organisms, could not have lived on Earth back then.

No one can ever be sure what the first life forms were like, but scientists have formed hypotheses about them. First, early life forms did not need oxygen to survive. Second, they were probably unicellular organisms. Third, they probably lived in the oceans. The first organisms probably resembled the archaea that live today in extreme environments, such as in polar ice caps, hot springs, and the mud of ocean bottoms.

Modeling Conditions on Early Earth One of the most intriguing questions that scientists face is explaining how early life forms arose. Although Redi and Pasteur showed that living things do not spontaneously arise on today's Earth, scientists reason that the first life forms probably did arise from nonliving materials.

In 1953, a young American graduate student, Stanley Miller, and his advisor, Harold Urey, provided the first clues as to how organisms might have arisen on Earth. They designed an experiment in which they recreated the conditions of early Earth in their laboratory. They placed water (to represent the ocean) and a mixture of the gases thought to compose Earth's early atmosphere into a flask. They were careful to keep oxygen and unicellular organisms out of the mixture. Then, they sent an electric current through the mixture to simulate lightning.

Within a week, the mixture darkened. In the dark fluid, Miller and Urey found some small chemical units that, if joined together, could form proteins—one of the building blocks of life.

 Reading Checkpoint What are the major gases in the atmosphere today?

FIGURE 21
Early Earth
The atmosphere of early Earth had little oxygen. There were frequent volcanic eruptions, earthquakes, and violent storms. **Inferring** *Could modern organisms have survived on ancient Earth? Why or why not?*

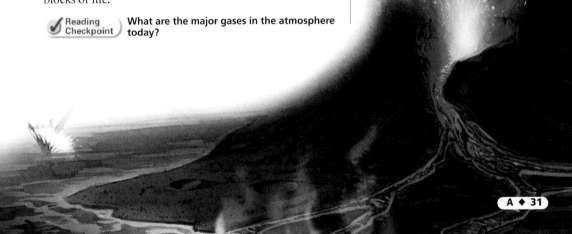

A ◆ 31

Instruct

Early Earth's Atmosphere

Teach Key Concepts L2
Early Earth Lacked Oxygen

Focus Tell students that early Earth had little oxygen.

Teach Ask: **Could you have lived on early Earth? Why or why not?** *(No, humans need oxygen.)* Most of today's organisms could not live on early Earth.

Extend Ask: **Why do scientists propose that archaea relatives might have been the first organisms on Earth?** *(They do not need oxygen. They can live in extreme environments. They are unicellular.)*
learning modality: logical/mathematical

Help Students Read L2
Sequence the Steps in the Experiment

Sequence Refer to the content Refresher, which provides guidelines for using sequence. Have students read the subsection *Modeling Conditions on Early Earth.* Have students sequence the steps in the experiment, including the results and conclusions drawn from them.

Independent Practice L2

All in One Teaching Resources

• Guided Reading and Study Worksheet: *The Origin of Life*

Student Edition on Audio CD

Monitor Progress _____ L2

Drawing Ask students to draw a picture of what early Earth might have looked like.

Students can save their drawings in their portfolios. **Portfolio**

Answers
Figure 21 No; there was little oxygen and the conditions were too extreme.

Reading Checkpoint Nitrogen and oxygen

The First Cells

Teach Key Concepts $L2$

How Cells Arose

Focus Experiments and fossils have led scientists to hypothesize how cells arose on Earth.

Teach Draw a flow chart on the board as follows: Chemical building blocks→Heterotrophs that did not need oxygen→Early autotrophs→Oxygen released into atmosphere. Discuss each step in the flow chart.

Extend Ask: **How does fossil evidence support the flow chart?** *(The 3.4–3.5 billion-year-old archaea-like fossils discovered were probably early heterotrophs that didn't need oxygen. Eventually, they gave rise to early autotrophs that produced oxygen.)* **learning modality: logical/mathematical**

Build Inquiry $L2$

Model Fossils

Materials almond, peanut, walnut, and pecan shells; clay; prepared plaster of Paris

Time 40 minutes

Focus Tell students that they will make models of two kinds of fossils: impressions and casts.

Teach Have students make impressions of each kind of shell in clay and compare them. Then have students fill their impressions with plaster to make casts. When the plaster dries, have students remove the clay and compare the casts with the shells.

Apply Ask: **What kind of fossil is shown in Figure 22?** *(Impressions)* Explain to students that fossils yield clues about organisms that lived a long time ago. **learning modality: kinesthetic**

The First Cells

In experiments similar to Miller and Urey's, other scientists succeeded in producing chemical units that make up carbohydrates and nucleic acids. The experimental results led scientists to formulate a hypothesis about how life arose on Earth.

Scientists hypothesize that the small chemical units of life formed gradually over millions of years in Earth's waters. Some of these chemical units joined to form the large chemical building blocks found in cells. Eventually, some of these large chemicals joined together and became the forerunners of the first cells.

Support From Fossil Evidence This hypothesis is consistent with fossil evidence. A **fossil** is a trace of an ancient organism that has been preserved in rock or another substance. Scientists have discovered fossils of what appear to have been archaea-like organisms. These ancient fossils have been dated to be between 3.4 and 3.5 billion years old. Therefore, these fossils support the idea that cells may have existed back then.

The first cells could not have needed oxygen to survive. They were probably heterotrophs that used the chemicals in their surroundings for energy. As the cells grew and reproduced, their numbers increased. In turn, the amount of chemicals available to them decreased.

At some point much later, some of the cells may have developed the ability to make their own food. These early ancestors of today's autotrophs had an important effect on the atmosphere. As they made their own food, they produced oxygen as a waste product. As the autotrophs thrived, oxygen accumulated in Earth's atmosphere. Over hundreds of millions of years, the amount of oxygen increased to its current level.

 Reading Checkpoint What is a fossil?

FIGURE 22
Fossil Evidence
These cell-like fossils were found in the rugged terrain of western Australia. They are the oldest fossils known—about 3.5 billion years old.

32 ◆ A

FIGURE 23
Unanswered Questions
Scientists continue to search for clues about the origin of life. *Applying Concepts What kind of evidence might be found in rocks?*

Unanswered Questions Many scientists today continue to explore the question of how and where life first arose on Earth. Laboratory experiments, like those by Miller and Urey, can never prove how life first appeared on Earth. Such experiments can only test hypotheses about how life forms could have arisen. No one will ever know for certain how and when life first appeared on Earth. However, scientists will continue to ask questions, test their models, and look for experimental and fossil evidence about the origin of life on Earth.

Section 4 Assessment

Target Reading Skill Identifying Supporting Evidence Refer to your graphic organizer as you answer the questions below.

Reviewing Key Concepts

1. a. Naming Which gases were probably most abundant in Earth's early atmosphere?
   b. Describing How did Miller and Urey model the conditions in Earth's early atmosphere?
   c. Inferring What can be inferred from the results of Miller and Urey's experiment?
2. a. Reviewing What experiments in addition to Miller and Urey's helped scientists hypothesize about how life arose on Earth?
   b. Sequencing Place these events in the proper sequence according to the hypothesis about how life arose on Earth: small chemical units form, cells make their own food, the first cells form, oxygen levels increase in the atmosphere, large chemical building blocks form.

c. Inferring How is the existence of organisms in hot springs today consistent with the scientific hypothesis of how life forms arose on Earth?

Writing in Science

Advertisement You are in charge of exhibits at a science museum. The museum is building an exhibit that models early Earth. Write an ad for the museum to attract visitors to see the new exhibit. Clearly describe to visitors what they will see and hear.

Chapter 1   A ◆ 33

A ● 33

Interactive Textbook
- Complete student edition
- Section and chapter self-assessments
- Assessment reports for teachers

Help Students Read

Developing Vocabulary

Vocabulary Rating Chart Have each student construct a chart with four columns labeled Term, Can Define or Use It, Have Heard or Seen It, and Don't Know. Have students copy the key terms from this chapter into the first column and rate their knowledge by putting a check in one of the other columns then have students read the parts that pertain to key term in question.

Word Forms Use the word *spontaneous* to help students understand the meaning of *spontaneous generation*. Explain that something that is spontaneous takes place without an external cause.

Connecting Concepts

Concept Maps Help students develop one way to show how the information in this chapter is related. All living things share certain characteristics and processes. Living things arise only from living things. Have students brainstorm to identify key concepts, key terms, details, and examples. Tell students to write each item on a sticky note and attach it at random to chart paper or to the board.

Tell students that this concept map will be organized in hierarchical order, and have them begin at the top with the key concepts. Ask students these questions to guide them in categorizing the information on the stickies: **What characteristics do all living things share? What are their needs? How are organisms classified?**

Prompt students by using connecting words or phrases such as "have," "for," and "based on" to indicate the basis for the organization of the map. The phrases should form a sentence between or among a set of concepts.

① What Is Life?

Key Concepts
- All living things have a cellular organization, contain similar chemicals, use energy, respond to their surroundings, grow and develop, and reproduce.
- Living things arise from living things through reproduction.
- All living things must satisfy their basic needs for food, water, living space, and stable internal conditions.

Key Terms

organism	development
cell	spontaneous generation
unicellular	controlled experiment
multicellular	autotroph
stimulus	heterotroph
response	homeostasis

② Classifying Organisms

Key Concepts
- Biologists use classification to organize living things into groups so that the organisms are easier to study.
- The more classification levels that two organisms share, the more characteristics they have in common.
- Taxonomic keys are useful tools for determining the identity of organisms.
- Species with similar evolutionary histories are classified more closely together.

Key Terms
classification
taxonomy
binomial
  nomenclature
genus
species
evolution

③ Domains and Kingdoms

Key Concepts
- Organisms are placed into domains and kingdoms based on their cell type, their ability to make food, and the number of cells in their bodies.
- Although bacteria and archaea are similar in some ways, there are important differences in the structure and chemical makeup of their cells.
- Scientists classify organisms in the domain Eukarya into one of four kingdoms: protists, fungi, plants, or animals.

Key Terms
prokaryote
nucleus
eukaryote

④ The Origin of Life

Key Concepts
- On ancient Earth, nitrogen, water vapor, carbon dioxide, and methane were probably the most abundant gases in the atmosphere.
- Scientists hypothesize that the small chemical units of life formed gradually over millions of years in Earth's waters. Some of these chemical units joined to form the large chemical building blocks found in cells. Eventually, some of these large chemicals joined together and became the forerunners of the first cells.

Key Term
fossil

Answer
Accept logical representations by students.

All in One Teaching Resources
- Key Terms Review: *Living Things*
- Connecting Concepts: *Living Things*

Review and Assessment

Go Online
PHSchool.com

For: Self-Assessment
Visit: PHSchool.com
Web Code: cea-1010

Organizing Information

Concept Mapping Copy the concept map about the needs of organisms onto a separate sheet of paper. Then complete it and add a title. (For more on Concept Mapping, see the Skills Handbook.)

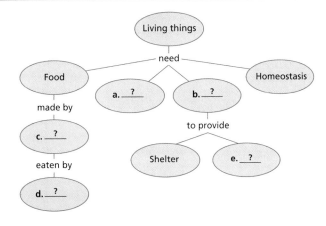

Reviewing Key Terms

Choose the letter of the best answer.

1. The idea that life could spring from nonliving matter is called
   a. development.
   b. spontaneous generation.
   c. homeostasis.
   d. evolution.

2. The scientific study of how living things are classified is called
   a. development. b. biology.
   c. taxonomy.   d. evolution.

3. A genus is divided into
   a. species. b. phyla.
   c. families. d. classes.

4. Which organisms have cells without nuclei?
   a. protists
   b. archaea
   c. plants
   d. fungi

5. Which gas was NOT a large part of Earth's early atmosphere?
   a. methane
   b. nitrogen
   c. oxygen
   d. water vapor

If the statement is true, write *true*. If it is false, change the underlined word or words to make the statement true.

6. Bacteria are <u>unicellular</u> organisms.

7. <u>Heterotrophs</u> can make their own food.

8. Linnaeus devised a system of naming organisms called <u>binomial nomenclature</u>.

9. The gray wolf, *Canis lupus,* and the red wolf, *Canis rufus,* belong to the same <u>species</u>.

10. The cells of a <u>prokaryote</u> lack a nucleus.

Letter You are an ocean scientist who has just discovered a new organism deep in the ocean. Write a letter to a colleague explaining how the organism should be classified and why.

DISCOVERY CHANNEL SCHOOL

Living Things
Video Preview
Video Field Trip
▶ Video Assessment

Review and Assessment

Concept Map
a. water
b. living space
c. autotrophs
d. heterotrophs
e. food and water

Reviewing Key Terms
1. b 2. c 3. a 4. b 5. c
6. true
7. autotrophs
8. true
9. genus
10. true

Writing in Science

Writing Mode Description

Scoring Rubric

4 Includes complete, accurate description of organism and uses logical reasoning for classification

3 Include all criteria but not may reasons

2 Includes accurate but brief description; few reasons

1 Includes brief or inaccurate description and illogical reasons

DISCOVERY CHANNEL SCHOOL
Video Assessment

Living Things

Show the Video Assessment to review chapter content and as a prompt for the writing assignment. Discussion question: **In what level of classification do organisms share the greatest number of characteristics?** *(At the species level)*

Go Online
PHSchool.com

For: Self-Assessment
Visit: PHSchool.com
Web Code: cea-1010

 **Teaching Resources**
- Transparency A9
- Chapter Test
- Performance Assessment Teacher Notes
- Performance Assessment Student Worksheet
- Performance Assessment Scoring Rubric

ExamView® Computer Test Bank CD-ROM

Checking Concepts

11. Students might point out that plants will bend toward sunlight and that plants grow, develop, and reproduce.

12. Sample answer: My dog gets energy from the food he eats and water from his water bowl. Our house is his living space.

13. A scientific name avoids confusion about the identity of the organism and gives information about an organism's characteristics.

14. The more closely two species are related, the more similar the chemicals that make up their cells.

15. Fungi are heterotrophs; plants are autotrophs.

16. The earliest organisms to live on Earth probably lived in the oceans. They were heterotrophs and took in chemicals from the waters around them for energy.

Thinking Critically

17. Although all robots use energy and some respond to their environments, they do not use energy to grow and develop. Living things are made of cells and are able to reproduce themselves.

18. This recipe may have worked because the grains attracted mice into the open pot. To disprove this, you could observe the pot to make sure mice did not enter or cover the pot so air could enter but mice could not.

19. *Entamoeba histolytica* and *Entamoeba coli*; they are in the same genus.

20. One domain (Eukarya); two kingdoms (animal and plant)

21. No, because the early atmosphere of Earth did not contain the right types of gases in the right amounts for humans to breathe safely.

Review and Assessment

Checking Concepts

11. Your friend thinks that plants are not alive because they do not move. How would you respond to your friend?

12. Describe how your pet, or a friend's pet, meets its needs as a living thing.

13. What are the advantages of identifying an organism by its scientific name?

14. What does the chemical makeup of the cells of an organism tell scientists about its evolutionary history?

15. What is the major difference between fungi and plants?

16. Describe where Earth's early organisms lived and how they obtained food.

Thinking Critically

17. Applying Concepts How do you know that a robot is not alive?

18. Relating Cause and Effect When people believed that spontaneous generation occurred, there was a recipe for making mice: Place a dirty shirt and a few wheat grains in an open pot; wait three weeks. List the reasons why this recipe might have worked. How could you demonstrate that spontaneous generation was not responsible for the appearance of mice?

19. Inferring Which two of the following organisms are most closely related: *Entamoeba histolytica, Escherichia coli, Entamoeba coli*? Explain your answer.

20. Classifying How many domains do the following organisms represent? Kingdoms?

21. Applying Concepts If you could travel to a planet with an atmosphere like that of early Earth, would you be able to survive? Explain.

Applying Skills

Refer to the illustrations below to answer Questions 22–25.

A student designed the experiment pictured below to test how light affects the growth of plants.

22. Controlling Variables Is this a controlled experiment? If so, identify the manipulated variable. If not, why not?

23. Developing Hypotheses What hypothesis might this experiment be testing?

24. Predicting Based on what you know about plants, predict how each plant will change in two weeks.

25. Designing Experiments Design a controlled experiment to determine whether the amount of water that a plant receives affects its growth.

Lab zone Chapter **Project**

Performance Assessment Prepare a display presenting your conclusion about your mystery object. Describe the observations that helped you to reach your conclusion. Compare your ideas with those of other students. If necessary, defend your work.

Lab zone Chapter **Project**   L3

Project Wrap-Up Students' displays should be well organized and describe how students tested their hypotheses. Have each student give a brief presentation to the class, describing how the results of their tests support their conclusions. Encourage students to talk about the results that they found surprising.

Reflect and Record Students may have trouble determining whether their object was alive if it was a fungus, a plant, or an animal such as coral that does not move.

Standardized Test Prep

Choose the letter of the best answer.

1. Which of the following statements about cells is *not* true?

   A Cells are the building blocks of living things.
   B Cells carry out the basic life functions of living things.
   C Some organisms are made up of only one cell.
   D Most cells can be seen with the naked eye.

2. Organisms that are autotrophs are classified in which of the following domains?

   F Bacteria
   G Archaea
   H Eukarya
   J all of the above

Use the table below and your knowledge of science to answer Questions 3–4.

Some Types of Trees			
Common Name of Tree	Kingdom	Family	Species
Bird cherry	Plants	Rosaceae	*Prunus avium*
Flowering cherry	Plants	Rosaceae	*Prunus serrula*
Smooth-leaved elm	Plants	Ulmaceae	*Ulmus minor*
Whitebeam	Plants	Rosaceae	*Sorbus aria*

3. In the system of binomial nomenclature, what is the name for the whitebeam tree?

   A Rosaceae
   B *Sorbus aria*
   C *Prunus serrula*
   D *Ulmus minor*

4. Which of the following organisms is most different from the other three?

   F *Prunus avium*
   G *Prunus serrula*
   H *Ulmus minor*
   J *Sorbus aria*

5. Pasteur's experiment in which he boiled broth in some flasks, but not in others, was a controlled experiment because

   A it showed that bacteria do not arise spontaneously.
   B the necks of both flasks were curved.
   C boiling or not boiling the broth was the only variable he changed.
   D the broth in both flasks remained clear.

Constructed Response

6. Name five characteristics that all living things share. Then describe each characteristic or give an example.

Applying Skills

22. Yes, the light is the manipulated variable.

23. Sample hypothesis: If plants do not have enough light, they will die.

24. In two weeks, the plant on the left might be dead, but the plant on the right will be healthy.

25. Sample experiment: Two plants receive the same amount and type of light. One receives one-fourth cup of water a day, and the other one-fourth cup every two days.

Standardized Test Prep

1. D   **2.** J   **3.** B   **4.** H   **5.** C

6. All organisms are made of cells, use energy, grow and develop, respond to their surroundings, and reproduce. Some organisms, such as bacteria, have only one cell, while others are composed of many cells. Animals use the energy from the food they eat to move, repair injured parts, and carry out other life processes. An acorn develops into an oak tree, which grows tall and strong. A person responds to cold temperatures by shivering. Finally, all living things reproduce, or produce offspring that are similar to themselves. Birds lay eggs that hatch into baby birds; bacteria divide to produce more bacteria.

Chapter at a Glance

PRENTICE HALL
TeacherEXPRESS™
Plan · Teach · Assess

 Chapter Project *Be a Disease Detective*

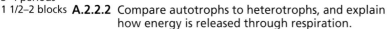 **Teaching Resources**
- Chapter Project Teacher Notes, pp. 100–101
- Chapter Project Student Overview, pp. 102–103
- Chapter Project Student Worksheets, pp. 104–105
- Chapter Project Scoring Rubric, p. 106

Technology

Local Standards

Discovery CHANNEL SCHOOL
Video Preview

Section 1 Viruses

2–3 periods
1–1 1/2 blocks

A.2.1.1 List characteristics of viruses and state reasons why viruses are considered to be nonliving.

A.2.1.2 Describe the components of the basic structure of a virus.

A.2.1.3 Explain how both active and hidden viruses multiply.

A.2.1.4 Discuss both positive and negative ways that viruses affect living things.

Go Online
active art

Section 2 Bacteria

3–4 periods
1 1/2–2 blocks

A.2.2.1 Name and describe structures, shapes, and sizes of a bacterial cell.

A.2.2.2 Compare autotrophs to heterotrophs, and explain how energy is released through respiration.

A.2.2.3 Contrast asexual and sexual methods of bacterial reproduction.

A.2.2.4 Explain the roles of bacteria in the production of oxygen and food, in environmental recycling and cleanup, and in health and medicine.

Go Online
PHSchool.com

Section 3 Viruses, Bacteria, and Your Health

2–3 periods
1–1 1/2 blocks

A.2.3.1 List four ways that infectious diseases can spread.

A.2.3.2 Describe treatments available for bacterial and viral diseases.

A.2.3.3 Describe how to protect themselves against infectious diseases.

Discovery CHANNEL SCHOOL
Video Field Trip

Go Online
SC*LINKS* NSTA

Review and Assessment

 Teaching Resources
- Key Terms Review, p. 134
- Transparency A17
- Performance Assessment Teacher Notes, p. 142
- Performance Assessment Scoring Rubric, p.143
- Performance Assessment Student Worksheet, p. 144
- Chapter Test, pp. 145–148

Discovery CHANNEL SCHOOL
Video Assessment

Go Online
PHSchool.com

Test Preparation

Test Preparation Blackline Masters

Lab zone Chapter Activities Planner

For more activities

LAB ZONE
Easy Planner
CD-ROM

Student Edition	Inquiry	Time	Materials	Skills	Resources
Chapter Project, p. 39	Open-Ended	3–4 weeks	**All in One** Teaching Resources See p. 100	Posing questions, interpreting data, drawing conclusions, communicating	**Lab zone Easy Planner** **All in One** Teaching Resources Support, pp. 100–102
Section 1					
Discover Activity, p. 40	Guided	10 minutes	1 key for each student or each group of students	Observing, inferring, predicting	**Lab zone Easy Planner**
Skills Lab, p. 47	Guided	Prep: 45 minutes Class: 40 minutes	Straight pin, meter stick, calculator (optional), long strips of paper, scissors, pencil, tape	Calculating, making models	**Lab zone Easy Planner Lab Activity Video** **All in One** Teaching Resources Skills Lab: *How Many Viruses Fit on a Pin?*, pp. 115–116
Section 2					
Discover Activity, p. 48	Guided	20 minutes	Paper cups; dried lima, kidney, or navy beans	Calculating, inferring	**Lab zone Easy Planner**
Try This, p. 50	Guided	20 minutes	Unpasteurized yogurt, plastic dropper, methylene blue, glass slide, cover slip, microscope, lab apron	Observing	**Lab zone Easy Planner**
Consumer Lab, pp. 58–59	Guided	Prep: 30 minutes Class: 1 hr, 15 minutes	Clock, wax pencil, transparent tape, 3 plastic petri dishes with sterile nutrient agar, 2 plastic droppers, 2 household disinfectants	Observing, controlling variables	**Lab zone Easy Planner Lab Activity Video** **All in One** Teaching Resources Consumer Lab: *Comparing Disinfectants*, pp.124–126
Section 3					
Discover Activity, p. 60	Guided	20 minutes	Aprons, plastic cups, eyedroppers, goggles, plastic gloves, distilled water, 0.01 M sodium hydroxide solution (enough for one student), phenol red solution (enough for every student)	Predicting	**Lab zone Easy Planner**

Section 1 Viruses

 *2–3 periods, 1–1 1/2 blocks*

ABILITY LEVELS
L1 Basic to Average
L2 For All Students
L3 Average to Advanced

Objectives

A.2.1.1 List characteristics of viruses and state reasons why viruses are considered to be nonliving.

A.2.1.2 Describe the components of the basic structure of a virus.

A.2.1.3 Explain how both active and hidden viruses multiply.

A.2.1.4 Discuss both positive and negative ways that viruses affect living things.

Local Standards

Key Terms

• virus • host • parasite • bacteriophage

Preteach

Build Background Knowledge

Invite students to name diseases, as you list them on the board. Ask them to identify any they know are caused by viruses. (*Sample: cold, flu, smallpox, measles, mumps, polio*)

 **Discover Activity** *Which Lock Does the Key Fit?*

Targeted Print and Technology Resources

All in One Teaching Resources

L2 Reading Strategy Transparency A10: Sequencing

O Presentation-Pro CD-ROM

Instruct

What Is a Virus? Students discuss the characteristics, shapes, and sizes of viruses. They learn how names are chosen for them.

The Structure of Viruses Students compare the similarities and differences in viral structures.

How Viruses Multiply Students learn how a virus takes over a host cell to reproduce viruses.

Viruses and the Living World Students learn both the diseases caused by some viruses and the usefulness of other viruses.

 Skills Lab *How Many Viruses Fit on a Pin?*

Targeted Print and Technology Resources

All in One Teaching Resources

L2 Guided Reading and Study Worksheet, pp. 109–112

L2 Transparencies, A11, A12, A13, A14

L2 Skills Lab: *How Many Viruses Fit on a Pin?*, pp. 115–116

Lab Activity Video/DVD
Skills Lab: *How Many Viruses Fit on a Pin?*

www.phschool.com Web Code: cep-1021

O Student Edition on Audio CD

Assess

Section Assessment Questions

 Have students use their Sequencing graphic organizers to answer questions.

Reteach

Students review flowchart about viruses with a partner, adding any necessary information.

Targeted Print and Technology Resources

All in One Teaching Resources

• Section Summary, p. 108

L1 Review and Reinforce, p. 113

L3 Enrich, p. 114

Section 2 **Bacteria**

 3–4 periods, 1 1/2–2 blocks

Objectives

A.2.2.1 Name and describe structures, shapes, and sizes of a bacterial cell.

A.2.2.2 Compare autotrophs to heterotrophs, and explain how energy is released through respiration.

A.2.2.3 Contrast asexual and sexual methods of bacterial reproduction.

A.2.2.4 Explain the roles of bacteria in the production of oxygen and food, in environmental recycling and cleanup, and in health and medicine.

Local Standards

Key Terms

- bacteria • cytoplasm • ribosome • flagellum • respiration • binary fission
- asexual reproduction • sexual reproduction • conjugation • endospore
- pasteurization • decomposer

Preteach

Build Background Knowledge

Students discuss samples of yogurt and Swiss cheese displayed in classroom. Students infer that they are all produced with the help of certain kinds of bacteria.

 **Discover Activity** *How Quickly Can Bacteria Multiply?*

Targeted Print and Technology Resources

All in One Teaching Resources

L2 Reading Strategy: Building Vocabulary

⦿ **Presentation-Pro CD-ROM**

Instruct

The Bacterial Cell Students discuss structures, shapes, and sizes of bacteria.

Obtaining Food and Energy Students compare autotrophs to heterotrophs and then discuss energy released through respiration.

Reproduction Students study the conditions needed for bacteria to reproduce, comparing and contrasting asexual and sexual methods of bacterial reproduction.

The Role of Bacteria in Nature Students discuss roles of bacteria in the production of oxygen and food, in health care, and in the manufacture of medicine.

 **Consumer Lab** *Comparing Disinfectants*

Targeted Print and Technology Resources

All in One Teaching Resources

L2 Guided Reading and Study Worksheet, pp. 119–121

L2 Transparency A15

L2 Consumer Lab: *Comparing Disinfectants*, p. 124–126

Lab Activity Video/DVD
Consumer Lab: *Comparing Disinfectants*

www.phschool.com Web Code: ced-1022

⦿ **Student Edition on Audio CD**

Assess

Section Assessment Questions

Have students use "Building Vocabulary" definitions to write sentences about key terms.

Reteach

Students answer the assessment questions using their "Building Vocabulary" definitions.

Targeted Print and Technology Resources

All in One Teaching Resources

- Section Summary, p. 118
L1 Review and Reinforce, p. 122
L3 Enrich, p. 123

Section 3 Viruses, Bacteria, and Your Health

ABILITY LEVELS
L1 Basic to Average
L2 For All Students
L3 Average to Advanced

 2–3 periods, 1–1 1/2 block

Objectives

A.2.3.1 List four ways that infectious diseases can spread.

A.2.3.2 Describe treatments available for bacterial and viral diseases.

A.2.3.3 Describe how students can protect themselves against infectious diseases.

Local Standards

Key Terms

• infectious disease • toxin • antibiotic • antibiotic resistance • vaccine

---

Preteach

Build Background Knowledge

Students recall a time when they were ill. They make inferences about how they think they contracted the disease. Write their responses on the board to use later in class period.

 **Discover Activity** *How Can You Become "Infected"?*

Targeted Print and Technology Resources

 **Teaching Resources**

L2 Reading Strategy Transparency A16: Using Prior Knowledge

⊙ **Presentation-Pro CD-ROM**

Instruct

How Infectious Diseases Spread Students learn about sources of infectious diseases. Students discuss that infectious diseases spread through contact with persons, contaminated objects, infected animals, and other environmental sources of disease.

Treating Infectious Diseases Students learn about antibiotics and antibiotic resistance. They learn that no medication exists that can cure viral infections.

Preventing Infectious Diseases Students learn how vaccines work and their role in preventing infectious diseases.

Targeted Print and Technology Resources

Teaching Resources

L2 Guided Reading and Study Worksheet, pp. 129–131

www.SciLinks.org Web Code: scn-0123

⊙ **Student Edition on Audio CD**

Assess

Section Assessment Questions

Students use their Using Prior Knowledge graphic organizers to answer assessment questions.

Reteach

Students review graphic organizers and revise them based on what they have learned.

Targeted Print and Technology Resources

Teaching Resources

• Section Summary, p. 128

L1 Review and Reinforce, p. 132

L3 Enrich, p. 133

Chapter 2 Content Refresher

Section 1 Viruses

Characteristics of Viruses Viruses vary widely in size and shape. However, all viruses share a similar structure. A virus particle consists of a protein capsid enclosing a nucleic acid core. Some viruses are also surrounded by a membrane envelope, which derives from its host but also contains viral proteins.

Viruses can be classified according to the type of nucleic acid they contain. The genetic material may be double-stranded DNA, single-stranded DNA, double-stranded RNA, or single-stranded RNA. Viruses are also classified according to their structure and the host organisms they infect. Viruses infect organisms from all three domains. However, because the interaction between a virus' proteins and the proteins on a host's cell is highly specific, a particular virus is able to infect only certain types of cells.

Section 2 Bacteria

Bacteria in the Body Bacteria are part of the normal flora of humans. Found on the skin, in the mouth, intestines, and other sites, these bacteria are part of the mixture of microorganisms that regularly live in or on the body without causing harm. The normal flora of humans consists of more than 200 species of bacteria. In normal health, the interaction between the bacteria and the human host are thought to be mutualistic. The host provides the bacteria with a stable shelter and temperature, and a supply of nutrients. In return, the bacteria provides the host with benefits including aid in digesting, production of certain vitamins, stimulation of the immune system, and competition against other pathogens.

Address Misconceptions

Some students may think that all organisms are either plants or animals. Bacteria are organisms but are not animals or plants. In fact, they are classified under a separate domain. For a thorough strategy for overcoming this misconception, see **Address Misconceptions** in the section Bacteria.

Section 3 Viruses, Bacteria, and Your Health

Vaccines Vaccines contain small amounts of dead or modified virus, bacteria, or other pathogen. Each type of pathogen has a particular kind of protein on its surface. When a vaccine is injected into the blood stream, B cells in the blood stream respond to the surface proteins by producing antibodies. The antibodies attach to the surface proteins to "neutralize" or inactivate it. In addition, "memory" cells are produced and remain in the blood for years, ready to mount a quick protective immune response against subsequent infection with the same disease-causing agent.

Help Students Read

Comparing and Contrasting
Identifying Similarities and Differences

Strategy Help students read and understand material that discusses two or more related topics or concepts. This strategy helps students identify similarities and differences, thus enabling them to link prior knowledge with new information.

Example
1. Have students compare two or more topics under a heading. Tell them that when they compare, they should focus on both similarities and differences. Remind them to look for signal words: similarities—*similar, also, just as, like, likewise, in the same way;* differences—*but, however, although, whereas, on the other hand, different, unlike.*
2. Have students contrast two or more topics or concepts. Remind them that when they contrast, they should focus only on differences.
3. Have students create a chart or diagram comparing or contrasting two or more topics or concepts they read about in this section. Suggest that they create either a compare/contrast table or a Venn diagram.

Chapter 2

Viruses and Bacteria

Chapter Preview

❶ Viruses
Discover *Which Lock Does the Key Fit?*
Math Skills *Diameter*
Active Art *Active and Hidden Viruses*
Skills Lab *How Many Viruses Fit on a Pin?*

❷ Bacteria
Discover *How Quickly Can Bacteria Multiply?*
Try This *Bacteria for Breakfast*
Analyzing Data *Population Explosion*
Science and History *Bacteria and Foods of the World*
At-Home Activity *Edible Bacteria*
Consumer Lab *Comparing Disinfectants*

❸ Viruses, Bacteria, and Your Health
Discover *How Can You Become "Infected"?*
Science and Society *Antibiotic Resistance—An Alarming Trend*

Interactive Textbook

Bacteria (blue and purple rods) and other microorganisms lurk in a kitchen sponge. ▶

Lab zone **Chapter Project** 〔L3〕

Objectives
This project will introduce students to viruses and bacteria and their importance in human health. Students will investigate childhood diseases by doing research and by preparing, conducting, and analyzing a survey. After this Chapter Project, students will be able to
- pose questions to research diseases
- prepare and conduct a survey
- interpret data collected in a survey
- draw conclusions about childhood diseases
- communicate the survey's results

Skills Focus
Posing questions, interpreting data, drawing conclusions, communicating

Project Time Line 3–4 weeks

All in One **Teaching Resources**
- Chapter Project Teacher Notes
- Chapter Project Worksheet 1
- Chapter Project Worksheet 2
- Chapter Project Worksheet 3
- Chapter Project Scoring Rubric

Developing a Plan
Before the project, check with the school librarian and nurse to see whether they are willing to help students during the research phase. During the first week, students will research a childhood disease. During the second and third weeks, students will write and conduct their surveys. In week four, students will analyze the results of their surveys and present their report to the class.

Possible Materials
- Students may need to use a library in their research.
- Access to computers will be necessary for Internet research.
- Students may talk to the school nurse about her experience concerning effects of disease.
- Students may talk to their doctors to research their diseases.

DISCOVERY CHANNEL SCHOOL

Viruses and Bacteria:
Bacteria
▶ Video Preview
Video Field Trip
Video Assessment

DISCOVERY CHANNEL SCHOOL
Video Preview

Viruses and Bacteria

Show the Video Preview to introduce the Chapter Project and overview the chapter content. Discussion question: **Describe one way that bacteria can be useful.** (*Bacteria can be used to control hazardous wastes.*)

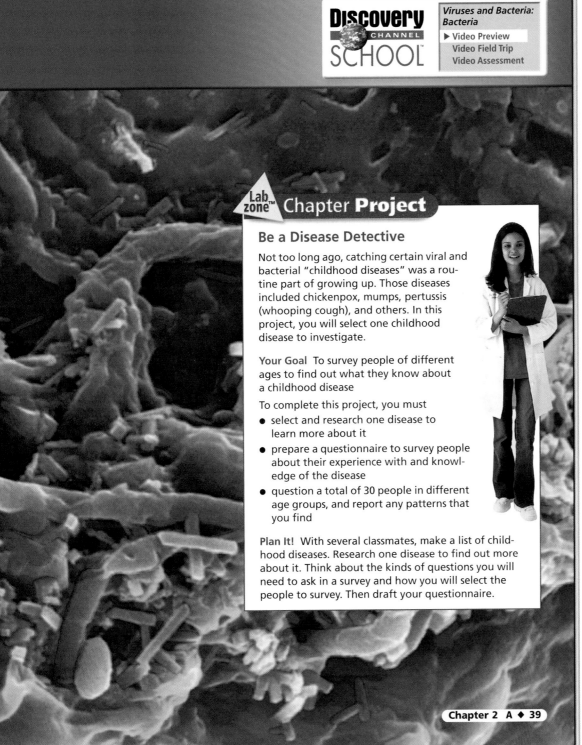

Lab zone™ Chapter Project

Be a Disease Detective

Not too long ago, catching certain viral and bacterial "childhood diseases" was a routine part of growing up. Those diseases included chickenpox, mumps, pertussis (whooping cough), and others. In this project, you will select one childhood disease to investigate.

Your Goal To survey people of different ages to find out what they know about a childhood disease

To complete this project, you must

- select and research one disease to learn more about it
- prepare a questionnaire to survey people about their experience with and knowledge of the disease
- question a total of 30 people in different age groups, and report any patterns that you find

Plan It! With several classmates, make a list of childhood diseases. Research one disease to find out more about it. Think about the kinds of questions you will need to ask in a survey and how you will select the people to survey. Then draft your questionnaire.

Chapter 2   A ◆ 39

Performance Assessment

The Chapter Project Scoring Rubric will help you evaluate how well students complete the Chapter Project. You may want to share the scoring rubric with your students so that they are clear about what will be expected of them. Students will be assessed on

- the thoroughness of their research on the disease
- how well-organized, complete, and informative the survey is
- the clarity, thoroughness, and organization of their survey analysis and written reports
- how well they use their results to explain any possible change in the occurrence of, or the knowledge about, the disease they researched
- their presentations and how well they convey their results and conclusions to the students in the class

Portfolio

Launching the Project

To introduce the project and to stimulate student interest, ask: **What vaccinations did you have when you were younger?** (*Sample: diphtheria, tetanus, measles, polio, mumps, rubella*) **What are the symptoms of these diseases?** (*Students may have difficulty describing the symptoms because these diseases are now quite rare, due in part to the use of vaccines.*) Tell students that the vaccinations for these diseases were introduced beginning in the 1930s with the development of vaccines for tetanus and diphtheria. Also, discuss the chickenpox (*Varicella*) vaccine, which was introduced in the United States in 1995. Some students in your class may have had chickenpox and will be able to describe the symptoms accurately. Ask: **Do you think students ten years from now will be able to describe the symptoms of chickenpox?** (*Probably not, since few will have had the disease growing up.*)

Objectives

After this lesson, students will be able to
A.2.1.1 List characteristics of viruses and state reasons why viruses are considered to be nonliving.
A.2.1.2 Describe the components of the basic structure of a virus.
A.2.1.3 Explain how both active and hidden viruses multiply.
A.2.1.4 Discuss both positive and negative ways that viruses affect living things.

Target Reading Skill

Sequencing Explain that organizing information from beginning to end helps students understand a step-by-step process.

Answer

One way students might organize the information is: How Active Viruses Multiply—1. Virus attaches to the surface of a living cell. 2. Virus injects genetic material into cell. 3. Cell produces viral proteins and genetic material. 4. Viruses assemble. 5. Cell bursts, releasing viruses. How Hidden Viruses Multiply—1. Virus attaches to cell. 2. Virus injects its genetic material. 3. Virus's genetic material becomes part of cell's genetic material. 4. Later, virus's genetic material becomes active. 5. Cell produces viral proteins and genetic material; viruses are assembled. 6. Cell bursts, releasing viruses.

All in One Teaching Resources

• Transparency A10

Preteach

Build Background Knowledge L2

Identifying Viral Diseases
Invite students to name diseases they are familiar with. List the diseases on the board. Tell students that viruses are the cause of some diseases. Encourage them to identify any diseases on the list that they know are caused by viruses. (*Sample: cold, flu, smallpox, measles, mumps, polio*)

Reading Preview

Key Concepts
• How do viruses differ from living things?
• What is the basic structure of a virus?
• How do viruses multiply?

Key Terms
• virus • host • parasite
• bacteriophage

Target Reading Skill

Sequencing As you read, make two flowcharts that show how active and hidden viruses multiply. Put the steps in the process in separate boxes in the flowchart in the order in which they occur.

How Active Viruses Multiply

| Virus attaches to the surface of a living cell |

↓

| Virus injects genetic material into cell |

↓

FIGURE 1
Virus Shapes
Viruses come in various shapes.

Lab zone — Discover **Activity**

Which Lock Does the Key Fit?
1. Your teacher will give you a key.
2. Study the key closely. Think about what shape the keyhole on its lock must have. On a piece of paper, draw the shape of the keyhole.
3. The lock for your key is contained in the group of locks your teacher will provide. Try to match your key to its lock without inserting the key into the keyhole.

Think It Over
Inferring Suppose that each type of cell had a unique "lock" on its surface. How might a unique lock help protect a cell from invading organisms?

It is a dark and quiet night. An enemy spy slips silently across the border. Invisible to the guards, the spy creeps cautiously along the edge of the road, heading toward the command center. Undetected, the spy sneaks by the center's security system and reaches the door. Breaking into the control room, the spy takes command of the central computer. The enemy is in control.

Moments later the command center's defenses finally activate. Depending on the enemy's strength and cunning, the defenses may squash the invasion before much damage is done. Otherwise the enemy will win and take over the territory.

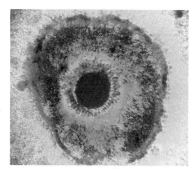

▲ The round chickenpox virus causes an itchy rash on human skin.

▼ This robotlike virus, called a bacteriophage, infects bacteria.

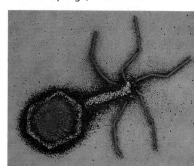

Lab zone — Discover **Activity**

Skills Focus Observing, inferring, predicting

Materials key for each group of students, locks that match the keys given to the students

Time 10 minutes

Tips This activity will create interest and anticipation for the concept of virus specificity.

L1

Expected Outcome Students will gain interest in and understanding of the lock-and-key concept and be ready to apply it to the fit between a virus's protein coat and its host cell.

Think It Over An invading organism would not be able to "enter" a cell unless it had a unique "key" that fits the "lock" on the cell's surface.

What Is a Virus?

Although this spy story may read like a movie script, it describes similar events that can occur in your body. The spy acts very much like a virus invading an organism. A **virus** is a tiny, non-living particle that enters and then reproduces inside a living cell. No organisms are safe from viruses. From the smallest bacterial cell to the tallest tree, from your pet cat to your younger brother, there is a virus able to invade that organism's cells.

Characteristics of Viruses Most biologists today consider viruses to be nonliving because viruses do not have all the characteristics essential for life. Viruses are not cells and do not use their own energy to grow or to respond to their surroundings. Viruses also cannot make food, take in food, or produce wastes. The only way in which viruses are like organisms is that they are able to multiply. **Although viruses can multiply, they do so differently than organisms. Viruses can multiply only when they are inside a living cell.**

The organism that a virus enters and multiplies inside is called a host. A **host** is an organism that provides a source of energy for a virus or another organism. A virus acts like a **parasite** (PA ruh syt), an organism that lives on or in a host and causes it harm. Almost all viruses destroy the cells in which they multiply.

Virus Shapes As you can see in Figure 1, viruses vary widely in shape. Some viruses are round, while some are rod-shaped. Other viruses are shaped like bricks, threads, or bullets. There are even viruses that have complex, robotlike shapes, such as the bacteriophage in Figure 1. A **bacteriophage** (bak TEER ee oh fayj) is a virus that infects bacteria. In fact, its name means "bacteria eater."

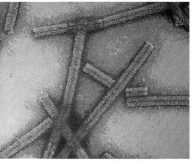

▲ Tube-shaped tobacco mosaic viruses infect tobacco plants.

▼ These round viruses are responsible for causing West Nile disease in animals.

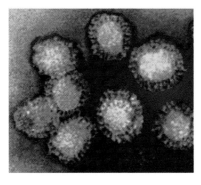

▲ The bullet-shaped rabies virus infects nerve cells in certain animals.

Chapter 2 A ◆ 41

Use Visuals: Figure 2 L1

Virus Sizes

Focus Remind students that viruses can reproduce only inside cells. Ask: **What can you conclude about the size of viruses from this information?** (*Viruses are much smaller than cells.*)

Teach Have students study Figure 2 and compare the sizes of the viruses and bacteria cells. Explain that bacteria are much smaller than most body cells. Explain also that viruses are even smaller than bacteria, which are the smallest living organisms.

Apply Ask: **How might the many different sizes and shapes of viruses influence their effect on the bodies of their hosts?** (*Sample answer: It may be hard for the body to recognize and fight viruses because they are so small and so different from one another.*)
learning modality: visual

 **Teaching Resources**

• Transparency A11

 Build Inquiry L2

Making Models of Viral Structures

Materials construction paper of different colors, glue, poster board, scissors

Time 30 minutes

Focus Review viral structure.

Teach Before class, cut out four large circles to represent four different types of cells. Use scissors to notch the edges of the circles so that each circle has a distinct pattern. Divide the class into four groups and give each group one cell model. Challenge groups to create model viruses to attach to their type of cell. When students have completed their models, each group can make a poster showing the cell and the viruses.

Apply Ask: **If each virus can attach to only one kind of cell, does that mean that each cell can be attacked by only one kind of virus?** (*No, viruses of different sizes with different structures can attach to the same type of cell.*) **learning modality: kinesthetic**

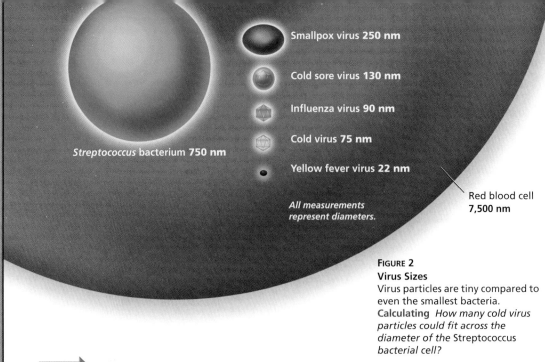

Smallpox virus **250 nm**

Cold sore virus **130 nm**

Influenza virus **90 nm**

Cold virus **75 nm**

Yellow fever virus **22 nm**

Streptococcus bacterium **750 nm**

All measurements represent diameters.

Red blood cell **7,500 nm**

FIGURE 2
Virus Sizes
Virus particles are tiny compared to even the smallest bacteria.
Calculating *How many cold virus particles could fit across the diameter of the* Streptococcus *bacterial cell?*

 **Skills**

Diameter

The diameter of a circle is a line that passes through the center of the circle and has both of its endpoints on the circle. To find the diameter, draw a line like the one shown below. Then, use a metric ruler to measure the length of the line. For example, the diameter of a penny is about 1.9 mm.

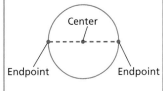

Center

Endpoint   Endpoint

Practice Problem Measure the diameter of a quarter and a CD.

Virus Sizes Just as viruses vary in shape, they also vary in size. Viruses are smaller than cells and cannot be seen with the microscopes you use in school. Viruses are so small that they are measured in units called nanometers (nm). One nanometer is one billionth of a meter (m). The smallest viruses are about 20 nanometers in diameter, while the largest viruses are more than 200 nanometers in diameter. The average virus is quite small when compared with even the smallest cells—those of bacteria.

Naming Viruses Because viruses are not considered organisms, scientists do not use traditional binomial nomenclature to name them. Currently, scientists name viruses in a variety of ways. Some viruses, such as the polio virus, are named after the disease they cause. Other viruses are named for the organisms they infect. The tobacco mosaic virus, for example, infects plants in the tobacco family. Scientists named the West Nile virus after the place in Africa where it was first found. Sometimes, scientists name viruses after people. The Epstein-Barr virus, for example, was named for the two scientists who first identified the virus that causes the disease known as mononucleosis, or mono.

Reading Checkpoint Which is larger—a virus or a bacterium?

42 ◆ A

Math Skills

Diameter 1. quarter—2.4cm; CD—12cm

The Structure of Viruses

Although viruses may look very different from one another, they all have a similar structure. **All viruses have two basic parts: a protein coat that protects the virus and an inner core made of genetic material.** A virus's genetic material contains the instructions for making new viruses. Some viruses are also surrounded by an additional outer membrane, or envelope.

The proteins on the surface of a virus play an important role during the invasion of a host cell. Each virus contains unique surface proteins. The shape of the surface proteins allows the virus to attach to certain cells in the host. Like keys, a virus's proteins fit only into certain "locks," or proteins, on the surface of a host's cells. Figure 3 shows how the lock-and-key action works.

Because the lock-and-key action of a virus is highly specific, a certain virus can attach only to one or a few types of cells. For example, most cold viruses infect cells only in the nose and throat of humans. These cells are the ones with proteins on their surface that complement or "fit" those on the virus. This explains why each virus has very specific host cells that it is able to infect.

 Reading Checkpoint What information does a virus's genetic material contain?

FIGURE 3
Virus Structure and Infection

All viruses consist of genetic material surrounded by a protein coat. Some viruses, like the ones shown here, are surrounded by an outer membrane envelope. A virus can attach to a cell only if the virus' surface proteins can fit those on the cell.

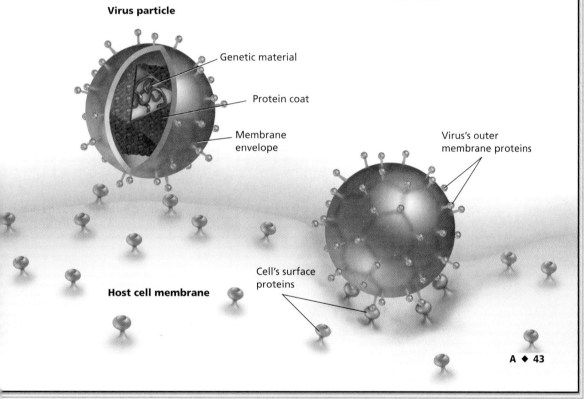

Virus particle

Genetic material

Protein coat

Membrane envelope

Virus's outer membrane proteins

Cell's surface proteins

Host cell membrane

A ◆ 43

The Structure of Viruses

Teach Key Concepts L2
Two Structural Components

Focus Tell students that every virus has two basic structural components.

Teach Ask: **What two structural components does every virus have?** (*A protein coat and an inner core of genetic material*) **How does a virus's protein coat relate to the host cells?** (*The proteins on the outer surface of the virus can attach to proteins on the surface of certain host cells.*)

Apply Ask: **How does this apply to the location where a virus is likely to be found?** (*A virus for a certain disease attaches itself to a specific type of cell, often found in a specific part of the body.*) **learning modality: visual**

 **Teaching Resources**
• Transparency A12

Predicting Fit of Virus and Cell L2

Materials clothing snaps or fasteners
Time 5 minutes

Focus Direct students' attention to Figure 3.

Teach Ask students to observe the way the clothing snaps attach to each other. Fasten and unfasten them as you allow all students to see. Ask: **Would one of these snaps fit other types of snaps or fastener?** (*No, it fits only the unique partner it was made to fit.*)

Apply Ask: **How does that relate to the viral protein coat and the host cell's surface?** (*The fit between the viral proteins and cell proteins is very specific, just as these kinds of snaps fit with only each other.*) **learning modality: visual**

Monitor Progress L2

Drawing Have students draw labeled diagrams of the viruses shown on this page. Ask them to indicate where the *viral protein* fits into the *cell's surface protein* by adding arrows. Students may keep their drawings in their portfolios.

Portfolio

Answers
Figure 2 Ten

Reading Checkpoint A bacterium

Reading Checkpoint Instructions for making new viruses

A ● 43

Differentiated Instruction

Gifted and Talented L3
Creating Displays Have students briefly research viruses to choose one aspect of viruses they would like to present to the class. You may want their presentations to include posters to make them more interesting and more informative. Give students a deadline for submitting their topics for approval before proceeding with the project. Try to have each student present a different aspect of viruses.

Challenge students to make their presentations very interesting for the class. You may choose to add some competition to the project by asking the class to vote on the presentations. The goal is to make this project especially valuable for the gifted and talented students but also beneficial for the rest of the class. **learning modality: verbal**

How Viruses Multiply

Teach Key Concepts L2
Viruses Take Over

Focus Ask students to look at the visuals under the heading *How Viruses Multiply*.

Teach Ask: **What are the similarities and the differences between the active and the hidden viruses?** *(Similarity: Both inject their genetic material into a host cell. Both burst open the cell after they multiply. Difference: An active virus multiplies immediately, while a hidden virus hides and later multiplies. The genetic material of a hidden virus becomes a part of the host cell's genetic material for a time while it hides.)*

Apply Ask: **What is the difference in the effects of the active and the hidden viruses?** *(The effects of an active virus infection are immediate; the effects of a hidden virus infection take a while to appear. Both eventually burst and kill the host cell.)*

learning modality: visual

 **Teaching Resources**

• Transparencies A13, A14

Go Online
active art

For: Active and Hidden Viruses activity
Visit: PHSchool.com
Web Code: cep-1021

Students explore the two methods viruses use to multiply.

Help Students Read

Relate Text and Visuals Refer to the Content Refresher, which provides the guidelines for relating text and visuals. Have students preview the text on these two pages, including Figure 4. After they preview, have students write two questions about the figures. Ask students to answer their questions as they read. Then, ask them each to compare their questions and answers with the questions and answers of a partner.

How Viruses Multiply

After a virus attaches to a host cell, it enters the cell. **Once inside a cell, a virus's genetic material takes over many of the cell's functions. It instructs the cell to produce the virus's proteins and genetic material. These proteins and genetic material then assemble into new viruses.** Some viruses take over cell functions immediately. Other viruses wait for a while.

Active Viruses After entering a cell, an active virus immediately goes into action. The virus's genetic material takes over cell functions, and the cell quickly begins to produce the virus's proteins and genetic material. Then these parts assemble into new viruses. Like a photocopy machine left in the "on" position, the invaded cell makes copy after copy of new viruses. When it is full of new viruses, the host cell bursts open, releasing hundreds of new viruses as it dies.

FIGURE 4
Active and Hidden Viruses

Active viruses enter cells and immediately begin to multiply, leading to the quick death of the invaded cells. Hidden viruses "hide" for a while inside host cells before becoming active.

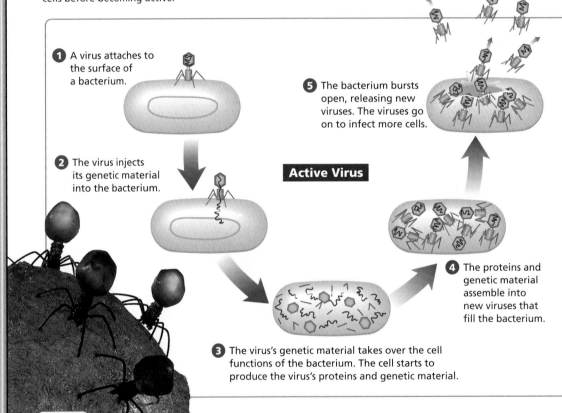

1. A virus attaches to the surface of a bacterium.

2. The virus injects its genetic material into the bacterium.

3. The virus's genetic material takes over the cell functions of the bacterium. The cell starts to produce the virus's proteins and genetic material.

4. The proteins and genetic material assemble into new viruses that fill the bacterium.

5. The bacterium bursts open, releasing new viruses. The viruses go on to infect more cells.

Active Virus

44 ◆ A

Hidden Viruses Other viruses do not immediately become active. Instead, they "hide" for a while. After a hidden virus enters a host cell, its genetic material becomes part of the cell's genetic material. The virus does not appear to affect the cell's functions and may stay in this inactive state for years. Each time the host cell divides, the virus's genetic material is copied along with the host's genetic material. Then, under certain conditions, the virus's genetic material suddenly becomes active. It takes over the cell's functions in much the same way that active viruses do. Soon, the cell is full of new viruses and bursts open.

The virus that causes cold sores is an example of a hidden virus. It can remain inactive for months or years inside nerve cells in the face. While hidden, the virus causes no symptoms. When it becomes active, the virus causes a swollen, painful sore to form near the mouth. Strong sunlight and stress are two factors that scientists believe may activate a cold sore virus. After an active period, the virus once again "hides" in the nerve cells until it becomes active again.

 Reading Checkpoint Where in a host cell does a hidden virus "hide" while it is inactive?

Go Online
active art

For: Active and Hidden Viruses activity
Visit: PHSchool.com
Web Code: cep-1021

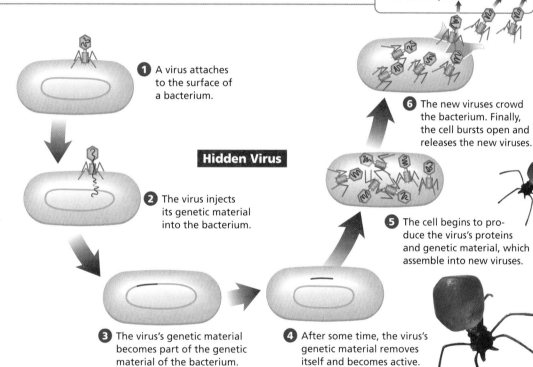

❶ A virus attaches to the surface of a bacterium.

❷ The virus injects its genetic material into the bacterium.

❸ The virus's genetic material becomes part of the genetic material of the bacterium.

Hidden Virus

❹ After some time, the virus's genetic material removes itself and becomes active.

❺ The cell begins to pro- duce the virus's proteins and genetic material, which assemble into new viruses.

❻ The new viruses crowd the bacterium. Finally, the cell bursts open and releases the new viruses.

A ◆ 45

Viruses and the Living World

Can a Virus Be Helpful?

Focus Ask students how they think viruses might be helpful.

Teach Ask: **What is gene therapy?** *(It is a medical technique where scientists can use a virus to treat certain disorders.)*

Apply Ask: **How does gene therapy work?** *(Scientists add needed genetic material to a virus and use the virus to deliver the genetic material to a patient's cells.)* **learning modality: verbal**

Monitor Progress
L2

Answer

 Reading Checkpoint
Scientists add important genetic material to a virus. Then the virus enters a host cell and inserts that genetic material.

Assess

Reviewing Key Concepts

1. a. A nonliving particle that invades a cell, using the cell's structures to reproduce **b.** Similarities: Both multiply. Differences: Viruses are nonliving; organisms are living. Viruses are not cells, can't make or take in food, produce wastes, and do not use their own energy to grow or respond to their surroundings. Viruses have two basic parts; organisms are more complex. To multiply, viruses use host's structures; organisms use their own structures. **c.** Viruses cannot exist without organisms.
2. a. All viruses have a protein coat that surrounds an inner core of genetic material **b.** They fit the proteins on the surface of the host cell. These proteins must fit together for the virus to be able to invade the host cell.
3. a. Virus attaches to cell, injects viral genetic material, makes viral proteins and genetic material. New viruses form. Cell bursts, releasing viruses. **b.** The viral genetic material becomes part of the cell's genetic material. Later, the virus's genetic material separates from the cell's genetic material and becomes active. **c.** The influenza virus is active. Soon after "catching" it from someone, the symptoms appear.

Viruses and the Living World

If you've ever had a cold sore or been sick with a cold or the flu, you know that viruses can cause disease. However, you might be surprised to learn that viruses can also be put to good use.

Viruses and Disease Some viral diseases, such as colds, are mild—people are sick for a short time but soon recover. Other viral diseases, such as acquired immunodeficiency syndrome, or AIDS, have much more serious effects on the body.

Viruses also cause diseases in organisms other than humans. For example, apple trees infected by the apple mosaic virus may produce less fruit. House pets, such as dogs and cats, can get deadly viral diseases, such as rabies and distemper.

Usefulness of Viruses The news about viruses isn't all bad. In a technique called gene therapy, scientists take advantage of a virus's ability to enter a host cell. They add genetic material to a virus and then use the virus as a "messenger service" to deliver the genetic material to cells that need it.

Gene therapy shows some promise as a medical treatment for disorders such as cystic fibrosis (SIS tik fy BRO sis). People with cystic fibrosis lack the genetic material they need to keep their lungs functioning properly. Gene therapy delivers the needed genetic material to their lung cells.

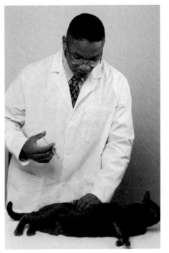
FIGURE 5
Viruses and Disease
Veterinarians can give pets injections that protect the animals against many viral diseases.

 Reading Checkpoint
How is a virus's ability to get inside a host cell useful to scientists?

Section 1 Assessment

Target Reading Skill **Sequencing** Refer to your flowcharts about how viruses multiply as you answer Question 3.

Reviewing Key Concepts

1. a. Defining What is a virus?
   b. Comparing and Contrasting How are viruses similar to organisms? How are they different?
   c. Inferring Scientists hypothesize that viruses could not have existed on Earth before organisms appeared. Use what you know about viruses to support this hypothesis.
2. a. Identifying What basic structure do all viruses share?
   b. Relating Cause and Effect What role do the proteins in a virus's outer coat play in the invasion of a host cell?

3. a. Reviewing Trace the steps by which an active virus multiplies, from when it first enters a host to when the host cell bursts open.
   b. Sequencing List the additional steps that occur when a hidden virus multiplies.
   c. Classifying Do you think that the influenza virus is an active virus or a hidden virus? Explain your reasoning.

Math Practice

Diameter Measure the diameter of a dime. Then, find a round object that you predict might have a diameter that is ten times the size of a dime. Measure the diameter of the object. How close was your prediction?

Reteach
L1

Have students draw tables to summarize the reproduction of active and hidden viruses, comparing the steps of each.

Performance Assessment
L2

Drawing Have students draw and label a sketch to identify different shapes of viruses.

All in One Teaching Resources

• Section Summary: *Viruses*
• Review and Reinforcement: *Viruses*
• Enrich: *Viruses*

Math Practice

Diameter Review with students how to measure diameter. A dime measures about 1.7 cm in diameter. After students complete the activity, discuss reasons that their predictions were not closer to the actual measurements.

How Many Viruses Fit on a Pin?

Problem

How can a model help you understand how small viruses are?

Skills Focus

calculating, making models

Materials

- straight pin • long strips of paper • pencil
- meter stick • scissors • tape
- calculator (optional)

Procedure

1. Examine the head of a straight pin. Write a prediction about the number of viruses that could fit on the pinhead. **CAUTION:** *Avoid pushing the pin against anyone's skin.*

2. Assume that the pinhead has a diameter of about 1 mm. If the pinhead were enlarged 10,000 times, then its diameter would measure 10 m. Create a model of the pinhead by cutting and taping together narrow strips of paper to make a strip that is 10 m long. The strip of paper represents the diameter of the enlarged pinhead.

3. Lay the 10-m strip of paper on the floor of your classroom or in the hall. Imagine creating a large circle that had the strip as its diameter. The circle would be the pinhead at the enlarged size. Calculate the area of the enlarged pinhead using this formula:

   Area $= \pi \times$ radius^2

   Remember that you can find the radius by dividing the diameter by 2.

4. A virus particle may measure 200 nm on each side (1 nm equals a billionth of a meter). If the virus were enlarged 10,000 times, each side would measure 0.002 m. Cut out a square 0.002 m by 0.002 m to serve as a model for a virus. (*Hint*: 0.002 m = 2 mm.)

5. Next, find the area in meters of one virus particle at the enlarged size. Remember that the area of a square equals side $\times$ side.

6. Now divide the area of the pinhead that you calculated in Step 3 by the area of one virus particle to find out how many viruses could fit on the pinhead.

7. Exchange your work with a partner, and check each other's calculations.

Analyze and Conclude

1. **Calculating** Approximately how many viruses can fit on the head of a pin?

2. **Predicting** How does your calculation compare with the prediction you made? If the two numbers are very different, explain why your prediction may have been inaccurate.

3. **Making Models** What did you learn about the size of viruses by magnifying both the viruses and pinhead to 10,000 times their actual size?

4. **Communicating** In a paragraph, explain why scientists sometimes make and use enlarged models of very small things such as viruses.

More to Explore

Think of another everyday object that you could use to model some other facts about viruses, such as their shapes or how they infect cells. Describe your model and explain why the object would be a good choice.

These papilloma viruses, ▶ which cause warts, are about 50 nm in diameter.

Analyze and Conclude

1. About 20 million

2. Have students explain whether their predictions were based on reasoning or whether they "just guessed."

3. When magnified, the pinhead was very large while the virus size was still very small.

4. The enlarged models help them to understand details of scale and structure.

Extend Inquiry

More to Explore Have students compare their models with what they know about viruses to determine models' strengths and weaknesses.

Safety

Remind students not to harm anyone with the pins. Caution students not to lose pins. Review the safety guidelines in Appendix A.

How Many Viruses Fit on a Pin? 【L2】

Prepare for Inquiry

Key Concept

To help appreciate the small size of viruses, people often compare them to known objects.

Skills Objectives

Students will be able to

- make a model showing a virus's size compared to the head of a pin
- calculate the number of viruses that could fit on a pin's head

Prep Time 45 minutes

Class Time 40 minutes

Alternative Materials

To make the 10-m strip, obtain long rolls of paper such as adding machine tape.

All in One Teaching Resources

- Lab Worksheet: *How Many Viruses Fit on a Pin*

Guide Inquiry

Invitation

Point out that referring to how many items fit on a pinhead often occurs when discussing things that are very small or very numerous.

Introduce the Procedure

Review metric measurements to ensure that students remember the metric units of measurement. Review the idea of scale. Remind students of everyday examples of the ways in which scale is used.

Troubleshooting the Experiment

Remind students that there are often different ways to solve specific calculation problems. Match up students who are using similar methods, then let different groups share their strategies.

Expected Outcome

Area of the enlarged pinhead: $\pi \times$ radius^2 = $3.1 \times 25 = 77.5$ m^2; area of enlarged virus: $0.002 \times 0.002 = 0.000004$ m^2; could fit $77.5/0.000004 = 19,375,000$ viruses on pinhead

Objectives

After this lesson, students will be able to

A.2.2.1 Name and describe structures, shapes, and sizes of a bacterial cell.

A.2.2.2 Compare autotrophs to heterotrophs, and explain how energy is released through respiration.

A.2.2.3 Contrast asexual and sexual methods of bacterial reproduction.

A.2.2.4 Explain the roles of bacteria in the production of oxygen and food, in environmental recycling and cleanup, and in health and medicine.

Target Reading Skill

Building Vocabulary Explain that knowing the definitions of key-concept words helps students understand what they read.

Answers

One way students might organize the information is: Students may write one or two descriptive phrases to help them remember the key term. Call on students to share their definitions.

Preteach

Build Background Knowledge   L1

Helpful Bacteria

Display samples of yogurt and Swiss cheese. Ask students what these foods have in common. Then, record their responses on the board. Tell students that these products are all produced with the help of certain kinds of bacteria. Ask: **What other foods can you think of that might be prepared with the aid of bacteria?** (*Accept all reasonable answers, such as buttermilk, sauerkraut, and sour cream.*)

Reading Preview

Key Concepts

- How do the cells of bacteria differ from those of eukaryotes?
- What do bacteria need to survive?
- Under what conditions do bacteria thrive and reproduce?
- What positive roles do bacteria play in people's lives?

Key Terms

- bacteria • cytoplasm
- ribosome • flagellum
- respiration • binary fission
- asexual reproduction
- sexual reproduction
- conjugation • endospore
- pasteurization • decomposer

Target Reading Skill

Building Vocabulary A definition states the meaning of a word or phrase by telling about its most important feature or function. After you read the section, reread the paragraphs that contain definitions of Key Terms. Use all the information you have learned to write a definition of each Key Term in your own words.

Lab zone Discover **Activity**

How Quickly Can Bacteria Multiply?

1. Your teacher will give you some beans and paper cups. Number the cups 1 through 8. Each bean will represent a bacterial cell.
2. Put one bean into cup 1 to represent the first generation of bacteria. Approximately every 20 minutes, a bacterial cell reproduces by dividing into two cells. Put two beans into cup 2 to represent the second generation of bacteria.
3. Calculate how many bacterial cells there would be in the third generation if each cell in cup 2 divided into two cells. Place the correct number of beans in cup 3.
4. Repeat Step 3 five more times. All the cups should now contain beans. How many cells are in the eighth generation? How much time has elapsed since the first generation?

Think It Over

Inferring Based on this activity, explain why the number of bacteria can increase rapidly in a short period of time.

They thrive in your container of yogurt. They lurk in your kitchen sponge. They coat your skin and swarm inside your nose. You cannot escape them because they live almost everywhere—under rocks, in the ocean, and all over your body. In fact, there are more of these organisms in your mouth than there are people on Earth! You don't notice them because they are very small. These organisms are bacteria.

The Bacterial Cell

Although there are billions of bacteria on Earth, they were not discovered until the late 1600s. A Dutch merchant named Anton van Leeuwenhoek (LAY vun hook) found them by accident. Leeuwenhoek made microscopes as a hobby. One day, while using one of his microscopes to look at scrapings from his teeth, he saw some tiny, wormlike organisms in the sample. However, Leeuwenhoek's microscopes were not powerful enough to see any details inside these organisms.

Lab zone Discover **Activity**

Skills Focus Calculating, inferring   L1

Materials dried beans; paper cups

Time 20 minutes

Tips Remind students to calculate the elapsed time based on the fact that it takes 20 minutes for bacteria to divide.

Expected Outcome Cup 1—1 bean; Cup 2—2 beans; Cup 3—4 beans;

Cup 4—8 beans; Cup 5—16 beans; Cup 6—32 beans; Cup 7—64 beans; Cup 8—128 beans. There are 128 cells in the eighth generation. Two hours and 20 minutes have passed since only 1 bacterium existed.

Think It Over Students will infer that the numbers increase rapidly because each bacterium can double every 20 minutes.

Cell Structures If Leeuwenhoek had owned one of the high-powered microscopes in use today, he would have seen the single-celled organisms known as **bacteria** (singular *bacterium*) in detail. **Bacteria are prokaryotes. The genetic material in their cells is not contained in a nucleus.** In addition to lacking a nucleus, the cells of bacteria also lack many other structures that are found in the cells of eukaryotes.

Most bacterial cells are surrounded by a rigid cell wall that protects the cell. Just inside the cell wall is the cell membrane, which controls what materials pass into and out of the cell. The region inside the cell membrane, called the **cytoplasm** (SY toh plaz um), contains a gel-like material. Located in the cytoplasm are tiny structures called **ribosomes** (RY buh sohmz), chemical factories where proteins are produced. The cell's genetic material, which looks like a tangled string, is also found in the cytoplasm. If you could untangle the genetic material, you would see that it forms a circular shape. The genetic material contains the instructions for all of the cell's functions.

A bacterial cell may also have a **flagellum** (fluh JEL um) (plural *flagella*), a long, whiplike structure that helps a cell to move. A flagellum moves the cell by spinning in place like a propeller. A bacterial cell can have many flagella, one, or none. Most bacteria that do not have flagella cannot move on their own. Instead, they are carried from place to place by the air, water currents, objects, or other methods.

Go Online
PHSchool.com

For: More on bacteria
Visit: PHSchool.com
Web Code: ced-1022

FIGURE 6
Bacterial Cell Structures
This model shows the structures found in a typical bacterial cell.
Relating Diagrams and Photos
What structures does the Salmonella *bacterium in the photograph use to move?*

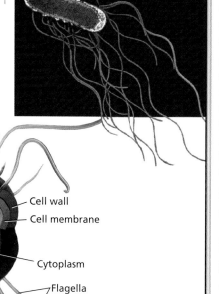

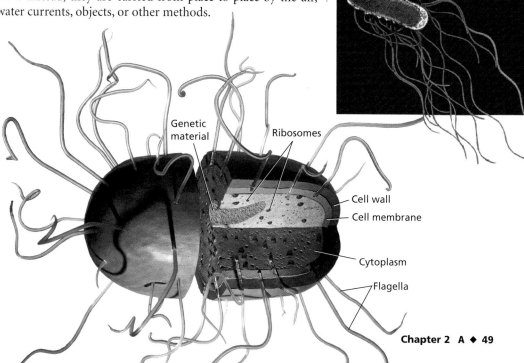

Genetic material

Ribosomes

Cell wall

Cell membrane

Cytoplasm

Flagella

Chapter 2 A ◆ 49

Differentiated Instruction

English Learners/Beginning L1
Vocabulary: Science Glossary
Pronounce and define aloud the vocabulary words. Have students start a glossary on index cards, with each term and its definition in English on one side and in the student's primary language on the other side. Students may want to draw and label diagrams on their cards.
learning modality: verbal

English Learners/Intermediate L2
Vocabulary: Science Glossary Students may expand on the activity described at left by adding other terms in this section. Have students write sentences using these words. Give students an opportunity to practice pronunciation by calling on individuals to read their sentences aloud. **learning modality: verbal**

Instruct

The Bacterial Cell

Teach Key Concepts L2

How Are Bacteria Recognized?

Focus Students learn structures, shapes, and sizes of bacteria.

Teach Write the terms *prokaryote* and *eukaryote* on the board, and invite students to recall their meanings. Ask: **What are the similarities and differences between prokaryotes and eukaryotes?** *(Both have genetic material and ribosomes and reproduce by cell division. Prokaryotes do not have a nucleus or other membrane-bound cell organelles; eukaryotes do.)* Use the photos in Figure 7 to teach the large variety of bacterial shapes. Ask: **What are the names of bacterial shapes shown in Figure 7?** *(Spherical, rod-shaped, spiral)* Ask: **How big are bacteria?** *(Bacteria are microscopic, but some are as big as a period at the end of a sentence.)*

Apply Cell appearance, shape, and size, as seen under very powerful microscopes in medical labs, help doctors identify bacteria that cause disease. See captions under the photos in Figure 7 for examples of cell shapes and the diseases caused by bacteria of these various shapes. **learning modality: visual**

All in One Teaching Resources
• Transparency A15

Independent Practice L2

All in One Teaching Resources
• Guided Reading and Study Worksheet: *Bacteria*

Student Edition on Audio CD

Go Online
PHSchool.com

For: More on bacteria
Visit: PHSchool.com
Web Code: ced-1022
Students can review bacteria in an online interactivity.

Monitor Progress L2

Answer
Figure 6 Flagella

A ● 49

Address Misconceptions L1

What Are Bacteria?

Focus Students who are accustomed to thinking of organisms as plants or animals may need extra help to understand that bacteria *are* organisms but *are not* animals or plants.

Teach Ask: **What do bacteria have in common with animals?** (*They are alive; some are heterotrophs.*) **How are they different?** (*Bacteria are simple one-celled organisms; animals have many cells that are highly organized. Bacteria are prokayotes; animals are eukaryotes.*)

Apply Tell students that, though bacteria are very small, they help sustain life on Earth. Bacteria aid in digestion, help make certain antibiotics, convert nitrogen in the roots of certain plants, and break down organic matter. In fact, they are more helpful than they are harmful. **learning modality: verbal**

Classifying Bacteria

Materials light microscope, prepared slides of bacterial species that exhibit these shapes: rodlike (*bacilli*), spherical (*cocci*), and spiral-shaped (*spirilla*)

Time 20 minutes

Focus Tell students that they are going to observe and identify the three main bacterial cell shapes.

Teach Caution students that glass slides are very fragile. Invite students to look at Figure 8 and to read the captions carefully, comparing and contrasting the appearance of the different bacteria. Then, as students view the various slides, have them sketch what they observe. Have pairs of students compare sketches and classify the bacteria as rod-shaped (*bacilli*), spherical (*cocci*), or spiral-shaped (*spirilla*).

Apply Tell students that the shapes they see are the same as those seen in medical labs. When a patient is sick, a health care provider might send a patient's tissue sample to a medical lab. There, the sample is examined under a microscope or a culture is grown to identify any harmful bacteria that are present. **learning modality: visual**

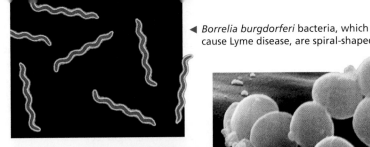

◀ *Borrelia burgdorferi* bacteria, which cause Lyme disease, are spiral-shaped.

FIGURE 7
Bacterial Cell Shapes
Most bacteria have one of three basic shapes.

Escherichia coli bacteria ▶ have rodlike shapes. These bacteria are found in your intestines.

▲ These *Staphylococcus aureus*, found on human skin, are spherical.

Lab zone **Try This Activity**

Bacteria for Breakfast
In this activity, you will observe helpful bacteria in a common food.

1. Put on your apron. Add water to plain yogurt to make a thin mixture.
2. With a plastic dropper, place a drop of the mixture on a glass slide.
3. Use another plastic dropper to add one drop of methylene blue dye to the slide. **CAUTION:** *This dye can stain your skin.*
4. Put a coverslip on the slide.
5. Observe the slide under both the low- and high-power lenses of a microscope.

Observing Draw a diagram of what you see under high power. Label any cell structures that you see.

Cell Shapes If you were to look at bacteria under a microscope, you would notice that most bacterial cells have one of three basic shapes: spherical, rodlike, or spiral. Figure 7 shows these different shapes. It is the chemical makeup of the cell wall that determines the shape of a bacterial cell. The shape of the cell helps scientists identify the type of bacteria. For example, bacteria that cause strep throat are spherical.

Cell Sizes Bacteria vary greatly in size. The largest known bacterium is about as big as the period at the end of this sentence. An average bacterium, however, is much smaller. For example, strep throat bacteria are about 0.5 to 1 micrometer in diameter. A micrometer is one millionth of a meter.

Obtaining Food and Energy

From the bacteria that live in soil to those that live in the pores of your skin, all bacteria need certain things to survive. **Bacteria must have a source of food and a way of breaking down the food to release its energy.**

Obtaining Food Some bacteria are autotrophs and make their own food. Autotrophic bacteria make food in one of two ways. Some capture and use the sun's energy as plants do. Others, such as bacteria that live deep in mud, do not use the sun's energy. Instead, these bacteria use the energy from chemical substances in their environment to make their food.

Lab zone **Try This Activity**

Skills Focus Observing L2
Materials unpasteurized yogurt, plastic dropper, methylene blue, glass slide, cover slip, microscope, lab apron
Time 20 minutes
Tips Students will need to use the highest powers of the microscope. As they observe the bacteria in yogurt, have students classify the bacteria according to their shape: spherical, rod, or spiral. Caution them to not drop the glass slides, and to avoid getting methylene blue on their skin or clothing.

Expected Outcome The bacteria appears as dark blue dots against a cloudy, pale blue background. Bacteria are so small that students will be unable to see them unless they are using high-powered microscopes.

Extend Challenge students to observe yogurt that contains added *Lactobacillus acidophilus* (the contents will be listed on the label) and to draw what they observe under the microscope. **learning modality: visual**

Some bacteria are heterotrophs and cannot make their own food. Instead, heterotrophic bacteria must consume other organisms or the food that other organisms make. Heterotrophic bacteria may consume a variety of foods—from milk and meat, which you might also eat, to the decaying leaves on a forest floor.

Respiration Like all organisms, bacteria need a constant supply of energy to carry out their functions. This energy comes from food. The process of breaking down food to release its energy is called **respiration.** Like many other organisms, most bacteria need oxygen to break down their food. But a few kinds of bacteria do not need oxygen for respiration. In fact, those bacteria die if oxygen is present in their surroundings. For them, oxygen is a poison that kills!

 Reading Checkpoint   **What are the two ways that autotrophic bacteria can make food?**

FIGURE 8
Obtaining Food
Bacteria can obtain food in several ways. **Comparing and Contrasting** *How do autotrophs and heterotrophs differ in the way they obtain food?*

◄ These autotrophic bacteria, which live in hot springs, use chemical energy from their environment to make food.

These heterotrophic ▶ bacteria, found in yogurt, break down the sugars in milk for food.

The autotrophic bacteria ▶ that cause the green, cloudy scum in this pond use the sun's energy to make food.

Chapter 2   A ◆ 51

Obtaining Food and Energy

Teach Key Concepts   L2
Food Becomes Energy

Focus Point out that bacteria, like all organisms, need a source of energy.

Teach Ask: **What are two sources of energy for autotrophic bacteria?** (*The sun is one source of energy. Chemical substances in the environment are another source.*) Ask: **What is a source of energy for heterotrophic bacteria?** (*Heterotrophic bacteria get nutrition from other organisms or from food that other organisms make.*)

Apply Ask: **What benefit is there in knowing how bacteria obtain and utilize their food?** (*Understanding how bacteria obtain and utilize food enables us to help useful bacteria and to kill harmful bacteria.*)
learning modality: verbal

Monitor Progress _____   L2

Drawing Have each student draw the three shapes of bacteria and label them without referring to the photos in Figure 7. Students can save their drawings in their portfolios.

Portfolio

Answers
Figure 8 Autotrophs make their own food; heterotrophs must consume other organisms for food or the food they make.

✓ Reading Checkpoint   Using (1) the sun's energy, or (2) chemical energy from substances in the environment

A ● 51

Reproduction

Teach Key Concepts L2

When Conditions Are Right

Focus Tell students that the conditions bacteria need to reproduce include sufficient food and the right temperature.

Teach Ask: **What are two types of reproduction in bacteria?** (*Asexual reproduction, sexual reproduction*) **How can bacteria survive when conditions are not good enough for reproduction?** (*Endospores, which contain genetic material, are produced by bacteria. Endospores can endure unfavorable conditions. Later, when conditions are favorable, endospores open up, and the bacteria can begin to grow and multiply.*)

Apply Ask: **What benefit is there in knowing how bacteria reproduce?** (*If we understand how bacteria reproduce, we can promote the growth of good bacteria and prevent the reproduction of harmful bacteria.*) **learning modality: verbal**

FIGURE 9
Asexual Reproduction
Bacteria such as *Escherichia coli* reproduce by binary fission. Each new cell is identical to the parent cell.

Reproduction

Under the right conditions, the number of bacteria can increase quite quickly. **When bacteria have plenty of food, the right temperature, and other suitable conditions, they thrive and reproduce frequently.** Under these ideal conditions, some bacteria can reproduce as often as once every 20 minutes. It's a good thing that growing conditions for bacteria are rarely ideal. Otherwise, there would soon be no room on Earth for other organisms!

Asexual Reproduction Bacteria reproduce by a process called **binary fission,** in which one cell divides to form two identical cells. Binary fission is a form of asexual reproduction. **Asexual reproduction** is a reproductive process that involves only one parent and produces offspring that are identical to the parent. During binary fission, a cell first duplicates its genetic material and then divides into two separate cells. Each new cell gets its own complete copy of the parent cell's genetic material as well as some of the parent's ribosomes and cytoplasm.

Sexual Reproduction Some bacteria may at times undergo a simple form of sexual reproduction. **Sexual reproduction** involves two parents who combine their genetic material to produce a new organism, which differs from both parents. During a process called **conjugation** (kahn juh GAY shun), one bacterium transfers some of its genetic material into another bacterium through a thin, threadlike bridge that joins the two cells. After the transfer, the cells separate. Conjugation, shown in Figure 10, results in bacteria with new combinations of genetic material. When these bacteria divide by binary fission, the new genetic material passes to the new cells. Conjugation does not increase the number of bacteria. However, it does result in new bacteria that are genetically different from the parent cells.

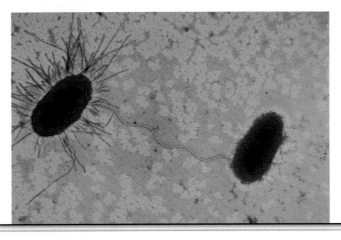

FIGURE 10
Sexual Reproduction
During conjugation, one bacterium transfers some of its genetic material into another bacterium.
Observing *What structure allows the cells to transfer genetic material?*

52 ◆ A

Math Analyzing Data

Population Explosion

Suppose a bacterium reproduces by binary fission every 20 minutes. The new cells survive and reproduce at the same rate. This graph shows how the bacterial population would grow from a single bacterium.

1. **Reading Graphs** What variable is being plotted on the horizontal axis? What is being plotted on the vertical axis?

2. **Interpreting Data** According to the graph, how many cells are there after 20 minutes? 1 hour? 2 hours?

3. **Drawing Conclusions** Describe the pattern you see in the way the bacterial population increases over 2 hours.

4. **Predicting** Do you think the bacterial population would continue to grow at the same rate? Why or why not?

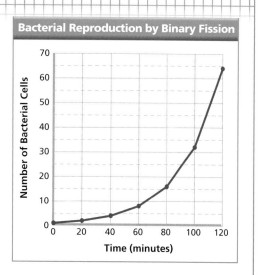

Bacterial Reproduction by Binary Fission

Vertical axis: Number of Bacterial Cells (0–70)
Horizontal axis: Time (minutes) (0–120)

Endospore Formation Sometimes, conditions in the environment become unfavorable for the growth of bacteria. For example, food sources can disappear, water can dry up, or the temperature can fall or rise dramatically. Some bacteria can survive harsh conditions by forming endospores like those in Figure 11. An **endospore** is a small, rounded, thick-walled, resting cell that forms inside a bacterial cell. It contains the cell's genetic material and some of its cytoplasm.

Because endospores can resist freezing, heating, and drying, they can survive for many years. For example, the bacteria that cause botulism, *Clostridium botulinum*, produce heat-resistant endospores that can survive in improperly canned foods. Endospores are also light—a breeze can lift and carry them to new places. If an endospore lands in a place where conditions are suitable, it opens up. Then the bacterium can begin to grow and multiply.

 Reading Checkpoint Under what conditions do endospores form?

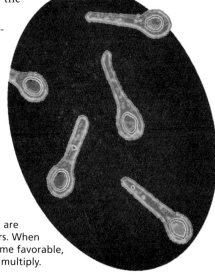

FIGURE 11
Endospore Formation
The red circles within these bacteria are endospores that can survive for years. When conditions in the environment become favorable, the bacteria can begin to grow and multiply.

Differentiated Instruction

Special Needs L1
Classifying Bacteria by Shape Have students title three poster boards *Spherical*, *Rod-shaped*, and *Spiral-shaped*. Then have them collect copies of photographs of these shapes of bacteria, and mount them on the appropriate poster boards. Have reference books (and/or Internet access), scissors, and poster board available. Use the boards to review bacterial shapes.
learning modality: visual

Gifted and Talented L3
Research Reproduction Have each gifted and talented student research a different aspect of bacterial reproduction and write a report summarizing their findings. They could choose from sexual reproduction or asexual reproduction. Reports could also include information on conjugation or endospore formation.
learning modality: verbal

Math Analyzing Data

Math Skill Interpreting graphs

Focus Tell students that line graphs can show change over time.

Teach Remind students that a graph is a way of visualizing numerical information. Ask: **How does the slope of the line after 100 minutes compare to its slope the first 20 minutes?** (*The slope is much steeper after 100 minutes than it is during the first 20 minutes.*) **What is the reason for the difference in the slope?** (*More bacteria are doubling in number with time. The number of bacteria dividing increases with each division.*)

Answers
1. Time (minutes); number of bacterial cells
2. 2 cells after 20 minutes; 8 cells after 1 hour; 64 cells after 2 hours
3. The number of cells doubles with each division.
4. Not likely. They will continue to reproduce at this rate only as long as the conditions are favorable.

Lab zone Build **Inquiry** L3

Designing Experiments

Materials beakers, dried beans, water
Time 20 minutes

Focus Ask: **What do bacteria need to survive?** (*Food, energy, favorable environment*)

Teach Tell students they will design an experiment to show the conditions that bacteria need in order to grow. Students should formulate a hypothesis, have a control, and design a method of observing and recording results. (*Designs will vary. When dried beans are placed in water, the water will become cloudy after about 48 hours because of the growth of bacteria.*)

Apply Have students design a test for the effects of environmental conditions such as temperature. **learning modality: verbal**

Monitor Progress L2

Oral Presentation Have students describe conditions bacteria need in order to survive and explain how some bacteria survive when the conditions are not present.

Answers
Figure 10 A thin, threadlike bridge.
 Reading Checkpoint Harsh conditions, such as extreme temperatures or lack of food

The Role of Bacteria in Nature

Teach Key Concepts   L2

The Value of Bacteria

Focus Tell students that bacteria can be both helpful and harmful.

Teach Ask: **What kind of bacteria help provide oxygen for breathing?** *(Autotrophic bacteria use the sun's energy to produce food, releasing oxygen.)* **What are some negative ways that bacteria affect food?** *(Some kinds of bacteria cause food to spoil.)*

Apply Ask: **How did Louis Pasteur help to prevent harmful bacteria from growing in food?** *(Louis Pasteur invented the process of pasteurization, heating food to a temperature high enough to kill most harmful bacteria.)* **How are bacteria beneficial as decomposers in the soil?** *(As decomposers, bacteria in soil break down dead organisms, returning basic chemicals to the environment for other living things to reuse.)* **learning modality: verbal**

Lab zone **Build Inquiry**   L3

Drawing Conclusions

Materials empty boil-in bags, bottles, cans, freezer packages, jars, vacuum-sealed packages, and other containers from a variety of prepared foods with labels included

Time 20 minutes

Focus Review various methods of food preparation and spoilage prevention with students.

Teach Prior to the activity, ask students to bring in various clean and empty food packages. Tell students they will examine some modern ways to preserve food. Organize students into groups; provide each group with two or three packages. **CAUTION:** *Be sure packaging materials are clean. Have students wash their hands with soap and water after handling packaging materials.* Challenge students to draw conclusions about food preparation and spoilage prevention.

Apply Ask students to infer how each spoilage-prevention method inhibits the growth of bacteria. Have a reporter from each group share findings with the class. **learning modality: verbal**

The Role of Bacteria in Nature

When you hear the word *bacteria*, you may think about getting sick. After all, strep throat, many ear infections, and other diseases are caused by bacteria. However, most bacteria are either harmless or helpful to people. In fact, in many ways, people depend on bacteria. **Bacteria are involved in oxygen and food production, environmental recycling and cleanup, and in health maintenance and medicine production.**

Oxygen Production Would it surprise you to learn that the air you breathe depends in part on bacteria? As autotrophic bacteria use the sun's energy to produce food, they also release oxygen into the air. As you learned in Chapter 1, there was little oxygen in Earth's atmosphere billions of years ago. Scientists think that autotrophic bacteria were responsible for first adding oxygen to Earth's atmosphere. Today, the distant offspring of those bacteria help keep oxygen levels in the air stable.

Science and History

Bacteria and Foods of the World

Ancient cultures lacked refrigeration and other modern methods of preventing food spoilage. People in these cultures developed ways to use bacteria to preserve foods. You may enjoy some of these foods today.

2300 B.C. Cheese
Ancient Egyptians made cheese from milk. Cheese-making begins when bacteria feed on the sugars in milk. The milk separates into solid curds and liquid whey. The curds are processed into cheeses, which keep longer than milk.

1000 B.C. Pickled Vegetables
The Chinese salted vegetables and packed them in containers. Naturally occurring bacteria fed on the vegetables and produced a sour taste. The salt pulled water out of the vegetables and left them crisp. These vegetables were part of the food rations given to workers who built the Great Wall of China.

500 B.C. Dried Meat
People who lived in the regions around the Mediterranean Sea chopped meat, seasoned it with salt and spices, rolled it, and hung it to dry. Bacteria in the drying meat gave unique flavors to the food. The rolled meat would keep for weeks in cool places.

2500 B.C.   **1500 B.C.**   **500 B.C.**

Food Production Do you like cheese, sauerkraut, or pickles? The activities of helpful bacteria produce all of these foods and more. For example, bacteria that grow in apple cider change the cider to vinegar. Bacteria that grow in milk produce dairy products such as buttermilk, yogurt, sour cream, and cheeses.

However, some bacteria cause food to spoil when they break down the food's chemicals. Spoiled food usually smells or tastes foul and can make you very sick. Refrigerating and heating foods are two ways to slow down food spoilage. Another method, called pasteurization, is most often used to treat beverages such as milk and juice. During **pasteurization,** the food is heated to a temperature that is high enough to kill most harmful bacteria without changing the taste of the food. As you might have guessed, this process was named after Louis Pasteur, its inventor.

Writing in Science

Research and Write Find out more about one of these ancient food-production methods and the culture that developed it. Write a report about the importance of the food to the culture.

A.D. 500
Soy Sauce
People in China crushed soybeans into mixtures of wheat, salt, bacteria, and other microorganisms. The microorganisms fed on the proteins in the wheat and soybeans. The salt pulled water out of the mixture. The protein-rich soy paste that remained was used to flavor foods. The soy sauce you may use today is made in a similar manner.

A.D. 1500
Chocolate Beverage
People in the West Indies mixed beans from the cocoa plant with bacteria and other microorganisms, then dried and roasted them. The roasted beans were then brewed to produce a beverage with a chocolate flavor. The drink was served cold with honey, spices, and vanilla.

A.D. 1850
Sourdough Bread
Gold prospectors in California ate sourdough bread. The *Lactobacillus sanfrancisco* bacteria gave the bread its sour taste. Each day before baking, cooks would set aside some dough that contained the bacteria to use in the next day's bread.

A.D. 500	A.D. 1500	A.D. 2500

Drawing Conclusions   L2

Materials several lettuce leaves, two plates

Time 5 minutes today; 10 minutes 4 days later

Focus Show students how bacteria act as decomposers.

Teach *First day:* Put several leaves of lettuce on each of two plates. Place one plate in a refrigerator. Place the other in a warm place. Allow the plates to sit for several days.

Four days later: Show the plates to students and give them time to observe the lettuce and describe what they see. *(The lettuce that was left out has become rotten and slimy.)* Ask: **What made the lettuce change as it did?** *(Bacteria)* **How does temperature affect the growth of some bacteria?** *(Lower temperatures may slow the rate of growth.)* Explain that bacteria broke down the components of the lettuce for food.

Apply Ask: **How are the bacteria in the lettuce similar to the bacteria that act as decomposers in the environment?** *(Like other decomposers, bacteria in the lettuce feed on dead matter and convert it into different forms.)* **learning modality: visual**

Use Visuals: Figure 13   L1

Environmental Cleanup

Focus Tell students that Figure 13 shows a substance that contains *Ochrobactrum anthropi,* bacteria that break down oil from oil spills, converting it to harmless substances.

Teach Explain that oil-eating bacteria have become very helpful in cleaning up oil and grease in many locations, such as those with major oil spills.

Apply Ask: **What are some other ways these bacteria might be useful?** *(Substances containing oil-eating or grease-eating bacteria are now sold for cleaning driveways, parking lots, and even drains.)* **learning modality: visual**

FIGURE 12
Environmental Recycling
Decomposing bacteria are at work recycling the chemicals in these leaves. **Predicting** *What might a forest be like if there were no decomposing bacteria in the soil?*

Environmental Recycling If you recycle glass or plastic, then you have something in common with some heterotrophic bacteria. These bacteria, which live in the soil, are **decomposers**—organisms that break down large chemicals in dead organisms into small chemicals.

Decomposers are "nature's recyclers." They return basic chemicals to the environment for other living things to reuse. For example, the leaves of many trees die in autumn and drop to the ground. Decomposing bacteria spend the next months breaking down the chemicals in the dead leaves. The broken-down chemicals mix with the soil and can then be absorbed by the roots of nearby plants.

Another type of recycling bacteria, called nitrogen-fixing bacteria, help plants survive. Nitrogen-fixing bacteria live in the soil and in swellings on the roots of certain plants, such as peanut, pea, and soybean. These helpful bacteria convert nitrogen gas from the air into nitrogen products that plants need to grow. On their own, plants cannot use nitrogen present in the air. Therefore, nitrogen-fixing bacteria are vital to the plants' survival.

Environmental Cleanup Some bacteria help to clean up Earth's land and water. Can you imagine having a bowl of oil for dinner instead of soup? Well, some bacteria prefer the oil. They convert the poisonous chemicals in oil into harmless substances. Scientists have put these bacteria to work cleaning up oil spills in oceans and gasoline leaks in the soil under gas stations.

✓ **Reading Checkpoint**   **What role do bacterial decomposers play in the environment?**

FIGURE 13
Environmental Cleanup
Scientists use bacteria such as these *Ochrobactrum anthropi* to help clean up oil spills.

56 ◆ A

Health and Medicine Did you know that many of the bacteria living in your body actually keep you healthy? In your digestive system, for example, your intestines teem with bacteria. Some help you digest your food. Some make vitamins that your body needs. Others compete for space with disease-causing organisms, preventing the harmful bacteria from attaching to your intestines and making you sick.

Scientists have put some bacteria to work making medicines and other substances. The first medicine-producing bacteria were made in the 1970s. By manipulating the bacteria's genetic material, scientists engineered bacteria to produce human insulin. Although healthy people can make their own insulin, those with some types of diabetes cannot. Many people with diabetes need to take insulin daily. Thanks to bacteria's fast rate of reproduction, large numbers of insulin-making bacteria can be grown in huge vats. The human insulin they produce is then purified and made into medicine.

FIGURE 14
Bacteria and Digestion
Bacteria living naturally in your intestines help you digest food.

Section 2 Assessment

Target Reading Skill Building Vocabulary
Use your definitions to help answer the questions below.

Reviewing Key Concepts

1. a. **Reviewing** Where is the genetic material located in a bacterial cell?
   b. **Summarizing** What is the role of each of these structures in a bacterial cell: cell wall, cell membrane, ribosomes, flagellum?

2. a. **Listing** What are the three ways in which bacteria obtain food?
   b. **Describing** How do bacteria obtain energy to carry out their functions?
   c. **Inferring** You have just discovered a new bacterium that lives inside sealed cans of food. How do you think these bacteria obtain food and energy?

3. a. **Defining** What is binary fission?
   b. **Explaining** Under what conditions do bacteria thrive and reproduce frequently by binary fission?

   c. **Inferring** Why might bacteria that undergo conjugation be better able to survive when conditions become less than ideal?

4. a. **Listing** A friend states that all bacteria are harmful to people. List three reasons why this statement is inaccurate.
   b. **Applying Concepts** In what ways might bacteria contribute to the success of a garden in which pea plants are growing?

Lab zone At-Home **Activity**

Edible Bacteria With a family member, look around your kitchen for foods that are made using bacteria. Read the food labels to see if bacteria is mentioned in the food's production. Discuss with your family member the helpful roles that bacteria play in people's lives.

Lab zone At-Home **Activity**

Edible Bacteria L2 Provide students with a list of keywords (for example, *cultures, live cultures, active cultures,* or *enzymes*) to look for on food labels to help them identify bacteria in products such as cheese, yogurt, buttermilk, or sour cream. You may also want them to further research the terms *cultures* and *enzymes*. Students will observe that bacteria play a large role in the foods they eat.

Lab zone Chapter **Project**

Keep Students on Track Make sure students' survey questions will elicit relevant information. Encourage them to ask questions requiring yes/no or numerical answers. For other questions, students should devise a tally system to record the most common responses. Encourage students to test and revise the questions.

Monitor Progress L2

Answers
Figure 12 Nothing would decay. Debris would accumulate deeper and deeper. Eventually nothing would be able to grow.

✓ **Reading Checkpoint** They break down dead organisms into basic chemicals that other organisms can reuse.

Assess

Reviewing Key Concepts

1. **a.** In the cytoplasm **b.** The cell wall protects the cell. The cell membrane controls what materials enter and leave the cell. The ribosomes (in the cytoplasm) are chemical factories where proteins are produced. The flagella are long, whiplike structures that help the cell move.
2. **a.** Making food from the sun's energy, using energy from chemicals in the environment, and consuming other organisms or food that other organisms make **b.** Bacteria obtain their energy from food, whether they are autotrophs or heterotrophs. **c.** They probably make food from the chemicals in the food in the can.
3. **a.** A form of asexual reproduction; one cell divides to form two identical cells **b.** When food is plentiful, temperatures are right, and other conditions are suitable **c.** These bacteria will contain new combinations of genetic material.
4. **a.** Many bacteria are helpful. Bacteria are involved in oxygen and food production, in environmental recycling and cleanup, and in health maintenance and medicine production. **b.** Bacteria that live on the roots of peas can convert nitrogen from the air into nitrogen that plants need to grow.

Reteach L1

List ways that bacteria are involved in oxygen and food production, in environmental cleanup, and in health maintenance and medicine production.

Performance Assessment L2

Writing Have students describe bacteria that are helpful or harmful to humans.

All in One Teaching Resources

- Section Summary: *Bacteria*
- Review and Reinforcement: *Bacteria*
- Enrich: *Bacteria*

Comparing Disinfectants L2

Prepare for Inquiry

Key Concept
The growth of bacteria can be controlled through the use of disinfectants.

Skills Objectives
Students will be able to
- observe bacterial growth
- infer how well a disinfectant controls bacterial growth
- draw conclusions regarding the best way to use disinfectants

Prep Time 30 min
Class Time 1 hr, 15 min

Advance Planning
Select disinfectants that contain different active ingredients, such as pine-scented cleaners or bleach. Before class, dilute disinfectants at least tenfold to reduce the possibility of injury to students. Pour enough disinfectant into a small container that students can fill droppers without inserting them into the main container of disinfectant. Make sure the room is well ventilated. Review the use of safety goggles and the eyewash apparatus in case disinfectant is accidentally splashed into the eye of a student. Because disinfectants may bleach or stain clothes, students should wear a lab apron. After opening a package of agar plates, use all of the plates right away or dispose of leftover plates, because they will not remain sterile.

Safety
 Dilute the disinfectants at least tenfold to reduce the chances of injury to students. Caution students to use care when working with the disinfectants. Keep an eyewash apparatus on hand in case disinfectant is accidentally splashed into a student's eye. Tell students to inform you immediately if a spill occurs. Review the safety guidelines in Appendix A. Dispose of the petri dishes and all other materials according to the proper procedures. Be sure to check your district's and state's guidelines for the proper disposal of bacterial cultures.

All in One Teaching Resources
- Lab Worksheet: *Comparing Disinfectants*

Comparing Disinfectants

Problem
How well do disinfectants control the growth of bacteria?

Skills Focus
observing, controlling variables

Materials
- clock
- wax pencil
- 2 plastic droppers
- transparent tape
- 2 household disinfectants
- 3 plastic petri dishes with sterile nutrient agar

Procedure

1. Copy the data table into your notebook.

2. Work with a partner. Obtain 3 petri dishes containing sterile nutrient agar. Without opening them, use a wax pencil to label the bottoms A, B, and C. Write your initials on each plate.

3. Wash your hands thoroughly with soap, and then run a fingertip across the surface of your worktable. Your partner should hold open the cover of petri dish A, while you run that fingertip gently across the agar in a zig-zag motion. Close the dish immediately.

4. Repeat Step 3 for dishes B and C.

5. Use a plastic dropper to transfer 2 drops of one disinfectant to the center of petri dish A. Open the cover just long enough to add the disinfectant to the dish. Close the cover immediately. Record the name of the disinfectant in your data table. **CAUTION:** *Do not inhale vapors from the disinfectant.*

6. Repeat Step 5 for dish B but add 2 drops of the other disinfectant. **CAUTION:** *Do not mix any disinfectants together.*

7. Do not add any disinfectant to dish C.

8. Tape down the covers of all 3 petri dishes so that they will remain tightly closed. Allow the 3 dishes to sit upright on your work surface for at least 5 minutes. **CAUTION:** *Do not open the petri dishes again. Wash your hands with soap and water.*

9. As directed by your teacher, store the petri dishes in a warm, dark place where they can remain for at least 3 days. Remove them only to make a brief examination each day.

10. After one day, observe the contents of each dish without removing the covers. Estimate the percentage of the agar surface that shows any changes. Record your observations. Return the dishes to their storage place when you have finished making your observations. Wash your hands with soap.

Data Table				
Petri Dish	Disinfectant	Day 1	Day 2	Day 3
A				
B				
C				

Guide Inquiry

Invitation
Ask students why some cleaning products contain disinfectants. Have students discuss the fact that bacteria are present everywhere around them. Controlling bacteria by using disinfectants helps prevent disease transmission and food spoilage.

Introduce the Procedure
Before students begin, review the growth needs of bacteria. Ask: **What do bacteria need to grow?** *(A source of food)* Explain to students that the agar is formulated to contain nutrients bacteria need to grow. Next, ask: **Where will the bacteria in these petri dishes get food?** *(From the nutrient agar)* Ask: **Why is it important to store all 3 petri dishes in the same place?** *(So that temperature and other conditions will be the same for all 3)* Have students store petri dishes upside down so condensed water will collect on the inside cover of the dish instead of dropping into the agar.

11. Repeat Step 10 after the second day and again after the third day.

12. After you and your partner have made your last observations, return the petri dishes to your teacher unopened.

Analyze and Conclude

1. **Observing** How did the appearance of dish C change during the lab?

2. **Comparing and Contrasting** How did the appearance of dishes A and B compare with dish C?

3. **Drawing Conclusions** How did the appearance of dishes A and B compare with each other? What can you conclude about the two disinfectants from your observations?

4. **Controlling Variables** Why was it important to set aside one petri dish that did not contain any disinfectant?

5. **Communicating** Based on the results of this lab, what recommendation would you make to your family about the use of disinfectants? Explain where in the house these products would be needed most and why.

Design an Experiment

Go to a store and look at soap products that claim to be "antibacterial" soaps. How do their ingredients differ from other soaps? Design an experiment to test how well these products control the growth of bacteria. *Obtain your teacher's permission before carrying out your investigation.*

A ◆ 59

Troubleshooting the Experiment

Stress the safety procedures associated with any lab dealing with bacteria. Emphasize that students must not open the petri dishes after the initial procedures. Remind students that differences may arise due to the fact that bacteria from random sources (such as classroom desktops) were used to inoculate each dish.

Expected Outcome

Several colonies of bacteria will grow on the control dish C. Dishes A and B will have fewer colonies and/or smaller colonies.

Analyze and Conclude

1. Answer will vary, but numerous bacterial colonies will be growing on the agar surface.

2. Dishes A and B will have fewer colonies, smaller colonies, or both.

3. Answers will vary depending on the disinfectants used. Any differences between A and B may be due to the relative effectiveness of the two disinfectants. They could also be due to other factors, such as the distribution of different kinds of bacteria picked up off the work surface.

4. The dish without disinfectant, dish C, was the control. It shows how bacteria grew when no disinfectant was applied.

5. Students may mention using disinfectants to clean locations and implements associated with food preparation, bathroom facilities, and children's rooms, especially during times of family illness.

Extend Inquiry

Design an Experiment Encourage students to compare the labels of antibacterial soaps with the labels of disinfectants to look for any common ingredients. Students' plans are to include clear and safe procedures and are to clearly identify the control and the variables to be tested.

Objectives

After this lesson, students will be able to

A.2.3.1 List four ways that infectious diseases can spread.

A.2.3.2 Describe treatments available for bacterial and viral diseases.

A.2.3.3 Describe how to protect themselves against infectious diseases.

Target Reading Skill 🔄

Using Prior Knowledge Explain that using prior knowledge helps students connect what they already know to what they are about to read.

Answers

Possible answers include:

What You Know

1. You can catch diseases from somebody who has one.

2. Some diseases can be treated with medicines.

What You Learned

1. You can catch diseases through contact with an infected person, a contaminated object, an infected animal, or an environmental source.

2. Antibiotic resistance results when some bacteria are able to survive in the presence of an antibiotic.

All in One Teaching Resources

• Transparency A16

Preteach

Build Background Knowledge L1

How Do Infectious Diseases Spread?

Invite students to recall the last time they were ill and make inferences as to how they may have gotten the disease. Write their responses on the board. *(Accept all reasonable responses.)*

Reading Preview

Key Concepts

• How do infectious diseases spread?

• What treatments are effective for bacterial and viral diseases?

• How can you protect yourself against infectious diseases?

Key Terms

• infectious disease
• toxin
• antibiotic
• antibiotic resistance
• vaccine

🔄 Target Reading Skill

Using Prior Knowledge Look at the section headings and visuals to see what this section is about. Then write what you already know about diseases caused by viruses and bacteria in a graphic organizer like the one below. As you read, write what you learn.

What You Know
1. You can catch a cold from somebody who has one. 2.

What You Learned
1. 2.

Lab zone Discover Activity

How Can You Become "Infected"?

1. Put on goggles and plastic gloves. Your teacher will give you a plastic dropper and a plastic cup half filled with a liquid. Do not taste, smell, or touch the liquid.

2. Your teacher will signal the start of a "talking" period. Choose a classmate to talk with briefly. As you talk, exchange a dropperful of the liquid in your cup with your classmate.

3. At your teacher's signal, talk to another classmate. Exchange a dropperful of liquid.

4. Repeat Step 3 two more times.

5. Your teacher will add a few drops of a liquid to each student's cup. If your fluid turns pink, it indicates that you have "contracted a disease" from one of your classmates. Wash your hands when you have finished the activity.

Think It Over

Predicting How many more rounds would it take for everyone in your class to "become infected"? Why do you think some diseases can spread quickly through a population?

One day you're feeling fine. The next day, you're achy, sneezy, and can hardly get out of bed. You've caught a cold—or more accurately, a cold has caught you!

How Infectious Diseases Spread

Have you ever wondered how you "catch" a cold, strep throat, or the chickenpox? These and many other diseases are called **infectious diseases**—illnesses that pass from one organism to another. **Infectious diseases can spread through contact with an infected person, a contaminated object, an infected animal, or an environmental source.** Once contact occurs, disease-causing agents, such as viruses and bacteria, may enter a person through breaks in the skin, or they may be inhaled or swallowed. Others may enter the body through the moist linings of the eyes, ears, nose, mouth, or other body openings.

Lab zone Discover Activity

Skills Focus Predicting L1

Materials aprons, distilled water, plastic cups, eyedroppers, phenol red solution, safety goggles, plastic gloves, 0.01 M sodium hydroxide solution

Time 20 minutes

Tips Give each student a cup of water. "Infect" one cup with sodium hydroxide, but do not inform the students. Tell them

that phenol red will stain clothing. It is an acid-base indicator that turns red in contact with the base sodium hydroxide.

Expected Outcome After 3 rounds, up to 8 students will be "infected".

Think It Over In a class of 30, all will be "infected" after 5 rounds. Some diseases spread in the same way that bacteria reproduce—quickly.

Contact With an Infected Person Direct contact such as touching, hugging, or kissing an infected person can spread some infectious diseases. For example, kissing an infected person can transmit cold sores. Contact can also occur indirectly. A common form of indirect contact is inhaling the tiny drops of moisture that an infected person sneezes or coughs into the air. These drops of moisture may contain disease-causing organisms, such as flu or cold viruses.

Contact With a Contaminated Object Certain viruses and bacteria can survive for a while outside a person's body. They can be spread via objects such as eating utensils. For example, drinking from a cup used by an infected person can spread diseases such as strep throat and mononucleosis. If you touch an object that an infected person has sneezed or coughed on, you may transfer some viruses or bacteria to yourself if you then touch your mouth or eyes. You may also get sick if you drink water or eat food that an infected person has contaminated.

Contact With an Infected Animal Animal bites can transmit some serious infectious diseases to humans. For example, the deadly disease rabies can be transferred through the bite of an infected dog, raccoon, or some other animals. Tick bites can transmit the bacteria that cause Lyme disease. Mosquito bites can spread the virus that causes encephalitis, a serious disease in which the brain tissues swell.

Contact With Environmental Sources Certain viruses and bacteria live naturally in food, soil, and water. These places can be environmental sources of disease. For example, poultry, eggs, and meat often contain salmonella bacteria. Eating foods that contain these bacteria can lead to one type of food poisoning. Cooking the foods thoroughly kills the bacteria. *Clostridium tetani,* a soil-dwelling bacterium, can enter a person's body through a wound. It produces a **toxin**, or poison, that causes the deadly disease tetanus.

 Reading Checkpoint What is one way you can prevent the spread of infectious diseases?

FIGURE 15
How Infectious Diseases Spread
Infectious diseases spread by contact with infected or contaminated sources.

▲ Sneezing releases disease-causing organisms into the air.

Sharing of ▶ contaminated objects can transfer organisms.

The bite of a ▶ *Culex nigripalpus* mosquito can transmit the virus that causes encephalitis.

▲ Raw eggs may contain salmonella bacteria that cause food poisoning.

Chapter 2 A ◆ 61

Treating Infectious Diseases

Teach Key Concepts   [L2]
Infectious Diseases

Focus Ask students to think of an example of a disease that can be treated with an antibiotic.

Teach Tell them that an antibiotic is a substance that can kill bacteria without harming the host cells. There are hundreds of antibiotics from which to choose. However, antibiotics do not fight a viral disease, and some antibiotics are not as effective against bacteria as they were in the past.

Apply Ask: **What is the reason that doctors do not prescribe antibiotics for a viral disease?** (*Antibiotics do not kill viruses.*) **Why are doctors cautious about over-prescribing antibiotics?** (*Too many antibiotics prescribed may result in antibiotic resistance.*) **learning modality: verbal**

Use Visuals: Figure 16   [L1]
Common Bacterial Diseases

Focus Students become familiar with symptoms and treatments listed for these bacterial diseases.

Teach Ask: **What advantage would there be in learning these symptoms?** (*If you had been exposed to any of these diseases, you would be able to watch for the symptoms of the disease.*) Ask: **What is the major treatment of these bacterial diseases?** (*Treatment is usually antibiotics. However, in the case of food poisoning, antitoxin medicines may be prescribed. In each case, a health care professional should be consulted.*)

Apply Call students' attention to the prevention of these diseases. Emphasize that prevention is better than cure. **learning modality: verbal**

Discovery CHANNEL SCHOOL™
Video Field Trip

Viruses and Bacteria
Show the Video Field Trip to help students understand how quickly an infectious

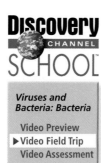

Discovery CHANNEL SCHOOL™

Viruses and Bacteria: Bacteria

Video Preview
▶ Video Field Trip
Video Assessment

Treating Infectious Diseases

There are thousands of infectious diseases, many of which are caused by bacteria and viruses. Others are caused by protists and fungi, which you will learn about in Chapter 3.

It's likely that at one point or another, you will come in contact with an infectious disease. Once you start to have symptoms of an infectious disease, your attention probably quickly turns to helping yourself feel better.

Bacterial Diseases **Fortunately, many bacterial diseases can be cured with medications known as antibiotics.** An **antibiotic** is a chemical that can kill bacteria without harming a person's cells. Antibiotics are made naturally by some bacteria and fungi. Today, antibiotics such as penicillin are made in large quantities in factories. Penicillin works by weakening the cell walls of some bacteria and causing the cells to burst.

FIGURE 16
Common Bacterial Diseases
Many common infectious diseases are caused by bacteria. Understanding how such diseases spread is useful in knowing how to prevent them.
Classifying *Which of these bacterial diseases are spread by contact with an infected person?*

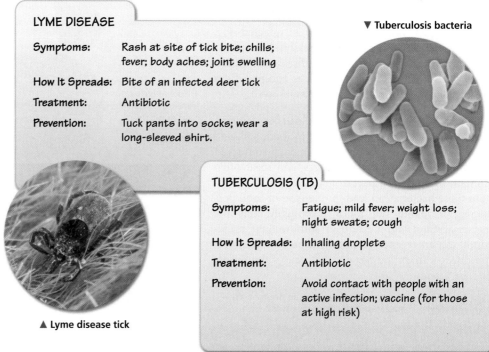

LYME DISEASE

Symptoms:	Rash at site of tick bite; chills; fever; body aches; joint swelling
How It Spreads:	Bite of an infected deer tick
Treatment:	Antibiotic
Prevention:	Tuck pants into socks; wear a long-sleeved shirt.

▲ Lyme disease tick

▼ Tuberculosis bacteria

TUBERCULOSIS (TB)

Symptoms:	Fatigue; mild fever; weight loss; night sweats; cough
How It Spreads:	Inhaling droplets
Treatment:	Antibiotic
Prevention:	Avoid contact with people with an active infection; vaccine (for those at high risk)

62 ◆ A

disease can spread. Discussion question: **How did the plague spread from rats to humans?** (*Through fleas; when fleas fed on the blood of infected rats and then bit people, the fleas transmitted the disease from rats to humans*)

If you have ever had a strep throat infection, you know that the infection makes swallowing feel like your throat is full of barbed wire. But soon after you begin taking the antibiotic that your doctor prescribes, your throat feels better. The antibiotic quickly kills the bacteria that cause strep throat.

Unfortunately, antibiotics are less effective today than they once were. Over the years, many bacteria have become resistant to antibiotics. **Antibiotic resistance** results when some bacteria are able to survive in the presence of an antibiotic.

The recent increase in tuberculosis cases demonstrates the impact of antibiotic resistance. As patients began to take antibiotics to treat tuberculosis in the 1940s, the number of tuberculosis cases dropped significantly. Unfortunately, there were always a few tuberculosis bacteria that were resistant to the antibiotics. As resistant bacteria survive and reproduce, the number of resistant bacteria increases. The number of tuberculosis cases has increased over the last 20 years. Today, antibiotic resistance is a serious problem and some bacterial diseases are becoming very difficult to treat.

Go Online

SciLINKS™ NSTA

For: Links on infectious diseases
Visit: www.SciLinks.org
Web Code: scn-0123

▼ Strep throat bacteria

TETANUS (Lockjaw)

Symptoms:	Stiff jaw and neck muscles; spasms; difficulty swallowing
How It Spreads:	Deep puncture wound
Treatment:	Antibiotic; opening and cleaning the wound
Prevention:	Vaccine

STREP THROAT

Symptoms:	Fever; sore throat; swollen glands
How It Spreads:	Inhaling droplets; contact with a contaminated object
Treatment:	Antibiotic
Prevention:	Avoid contact with infected people; do not share utensils, cups, or other objects.

FOOD POISONING

Symptoms:	Vomiting; cramps; diarrhea; fever
How It Spreads:	Eating foods containing the bacteria
Treatment:	Antitoxin medicines
Prevention:	Properly cook and store foods; avoid foods in rusted and swollen cans.

Chapter 2 A ◆ 63

Differentiated Instruction

English Learners/Beginning L1
Simplify the Explanation Speaking directly and succinctly, read aloud the information about the diseases given on the index cards in the figures on this spread. Then, repeat it in simple language. Be sure the students understand by asking them to repeat back to you in their own words the text you have just read. **learning modality: verbal**

English Learners/Intermediate L2
Thinking Skills Use the strategy given at left, but expect more from Intermediate students when repeating content back to you. Remember that English language learners may possess higher-order thinking skills even though they may not have mastered the English language. **learning modality: verbal**

Go Online

SciLINKS™ NSTA

For: Links on infectious diseases
Visit: www.SciLinks.org
Web Code: scn-0123

Download a worksheet that will guide students' review of Internet resources on viruses, bacteria, and health.

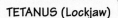

Lab zone Teacher **Demo** L2

Inferring How Diseases Spread

Materials disposable petri dishes with sterile nutrient agar, masking tape, wax marking pencil

Time 20 minutes for setup; 10 minutes on each of the next 2 days

Focus Ask: **Where do you think you might find bacteria?** (Sample answers: On door handle, in plant soil, on window shade rods, in sponge.)

Teach Tell students that nutrient agar contains a substance that feeds bacteria. Using objects in the classroom on which bacteria might be found, gently touch each object to the top of the agar in one petri dish. Have petri dish lids off for only a very short time, so that other microorganisms do not get into the dish. Mark the dish with the name of the object. **CAUTION:** Do not collect samples from humans or pets. Place a small piece of tape at each side of the dish to secure the lid. Place the dishes upside down in a warm, dark place. Allow students to observe the dishes after 24 and 48 hours. Have groups compare the results and make inferences about the sources of disease-causing bacteria. Ask: **What do you expect to see in two days?** (Colonies of bacteria.)

Apply Ask: **What effect could colonies of bacteria have on your health?** (Bacterial growth will mean that many of these bacteria can grow within humans as well, some possibly causing disease.) **learning modality: visual**

Monitor Progress L2

Skills Check Have students explain what antibiotics are and how they work.

Answer
Figure 16 Tuberculosis, strep throat

A ● 63

Predicting Effects of Antibiotics L2

Materials antibiotic disk of aureomycin, broth culture of *Escherichia coli*, disposable petri dish, sterile cotton swab, sterile nutrient agar, sterile tweezers

Time 20 minutes for setup; 10 minutes for observation after 48 hours

Focus This demonstration encourages students to predict and observe how an antibiotic might affect a common bacterium.

Teach Transfer two drops of the *E. coli* culture onto the sterile agar. Using a cotton swab, spread the culture evenly across the agar. Use sterile tweezers to place the aureomycin disk in the middle of the agar. Cover the petri dish, seal it with tape, and place it in a dark, warm spot for 48 hours. **CAUTION:** *Do not open the petri dish after it has been inoculated. Wash your hands thoroughly. Do not allow students to come into contact with the bacterial culture.* Have students predict what they will observe in the dish. Allow time to observe the culture after 48 hours. Light-colored cloudy areas will indicate the growth of bacteria. A clear area shows where the *E. coli* bacteria were killed or prevented from growing by the aureomycin.

Apply Challenge students to infer how effective the antibiotic was against bacterial growth. Dispose of the petri dishes and all other materials according to the proper procedures. Be sure to check your district's and state's guidelines for the proper disposal of bacterial cultures. **learning modality: visual**

Preventing Infectious Diseases

Teach Key Concepts L2
Prevention of Infectious Diseases

Focus Prevention IS better than cure.

Teach A vaccine stimulates the immune system to produce substances that fight a specific disease.

Apply Ask: **What are some ways to prevent infectious disease?** (*Eating right, getting enough sleep, drinking fluids, exercising, and getting recommended vaccines*) **learning modality: verbal**

Viral Diseases Unlike with bacterial diseases, there are currently **no medications that can cure viral infections.** However, many over-the-counter medications can help relieve symptoms of a viral infection. These medications are available without a prescription. While over-the-counter medications can make you feel better, they can also delay your recovery if you resume your normal routine while you are still sick. They can also hide symptoms that would normally prompt you to go to a doctor.

The best treatment for viral infections is often bed rest. Resting, drinking lots of fluids, and eating well-balanced meals may be all you can do while you recover from a viral disease.

✓ Reading Checkpoint **What are over-the-counter medications?**

FIGURE 17
Common Viral Diseases
Although there is currently no cure for viral diseases, there are ways to treat the symptoms and prevent their transmission.

INFLUENZA (Flu)

Symptoms:	High fever; sore throat; headache; cough
How It Spreads:	Contact with contaminated objects; inhaling droplets
Treatment:	Bed rest; fluids
Prevention:	Vaccine (mainly for the high-risk ill, elderly, and young)

HEPATITIS C

Symptoms:	Oftentimes no symptoms; jaundice (yellowing of the eyes and skin); fatigue
How It Spreads:	Contact with the blood of an infected person
Treatment:	Drugs to slow viral multiplication
Prevention:	Avoid contact with infected blood.

CHICKENPOX

Symptoms:	Fever; red, itchy rash
How It Spreads:	Contact with the rash; inhaling droplets
Treatment:	Antiviral drug (for adults)
Prevention:	Vaccine

ACQUIRED IMMUNO-DEFICIENCY SYNDROME (AIDS)

Symptoms:	Weight loss; chronic fatigue; fever; diarrhea; frequent infections
How It Spreads:	Sexual contact; contact with blood; pregnancy, birth, and breastfeeding
Treatment:	Drugs to slow viral multiplication
Prevention:	Avoid contact with infected body fluids.

◀ Chickenpox virus

64 ◆ A

Preventing Infectious Diseases

Of course, you would probably rather not get sick in the first place. **Vaccines are important tools that help prevent the spread of infectious diseases.** A vaccine is a substance introduced into the body to stimulate the production of chemicals that destroy specific viruses or bacteria. A vaccine may be made from dead or altered viruses or bacteria. Because they are dead or altered, the viruses or bacteria in the vaccine do not cause disease. Instead, they activate the body's natural defenses. In effect, the vaccine puts the body "on alert." If that virus or bacterium ever invades the body, it is destroyed before it can cause disease. You may have been vaccinated against diseases such as polio, measles, tetanus, and chickenpox.

Another important way to protect against infectious diseases is to keep your body healthy. You need to eat nutritious food, as well as get enough sleep, fluids, and exercise. You can also protect yourself by washing your hands often and by not sharing eating or drinking utensils. Storing food properly, keeping kitchen equipment and surfaces clean, and cooking meats well can prevent food poisoning.

Unfortunately, despite your best efforts, you'll probably get infectious diseases, such as colds, from time to time. When you do get ill, get plenty of rest and follow your doctor's recommendations. Also, it's very important to try not to infect others.

FIGURE 18
Preventing Infectious Diseases
Hand washing is a simple yet effective way to prevent the spread of many infectious diseases. *Applying Concepts How else can you prevent the spread of infectious diseases?*

 Reading Checkpoint Why don't vaccines cause disease themselves?

Section 3 Assessment

Target Reading Skill Using Prior Knowledge Review your graphic organizer and revise it based on what you just learned in the section.

Reviewing Key Concepts

1. a. Defining What is an infectious disease?
   b. Describing What are the four ways infectious diseases can spread?
   c. Developing Hypotheses Twenty people became sick after attending a strawberry festival. Describe a scenario that could explain how the people got sick.
2. a. Reviewing What is the best treatment for bacterial diseases? For viral diseases?
   b. Relating Cause and Effect Use what you know about how antibiotics work to explain why they are ineffective against viral diseases.

3. a. Reviewing What is a vaccine?
   b. Explaining How are vaccines important in keeping your body healthy?
   c. Predicting Suppose two people catch the flu. One person has been vaccinated against the flu while the other has not. Who will recover more quickly? Why?

 **Writing in Science**

Public Service Announcement Write a public service announcement for a radio show that teaches young children how to stay healthy and avoid diseases such as the flu. Include a list of do's and don'ts and other helpful advice.

Chapter 2 A ◆ 65

Writing in Science

Writing Mode Persuasion
Scoring Rubric
4 Includes complete and accurate persuasive writing at a child's level
3 Includes accurate persuasive writing but lacks some required criteria
2 Includes very brief but accurate persuasive writing
1 Includes poor persuasive writing

Lab zone Chapter Project

Keep Students on Track Make sure students have collected most of their survey results, and that they are keeping organized records of their data. Review with the class some of the ways (line graphs, bar charts) in which data can be visually presented.

Monitor Progress _____ L2

Answers

Figure 18 Sample answer: By keeping kitchen areas clean

 Reading Checkpoint Medicines that need no prescriptions

 Reading Checkpoint Because they are made from dead or altered viruses or bacteria

Assess

Reviewing Key Concepts

1. a. An illness that passes from one organism to another **b.** Contact with an infected person, a contaminated object, an infected animal, and environmental sources **c.** One or more persons attending the festival might have had an infectious disease, or a food that was eaten at the festival might have been contaminated with a bacterium that causes food poisoning.
2. a. Bacterial diseases: antibiotics; viral diseases: bed rest, drinking plenty of fluids, and eating well-balanced meals; over-the-counter medications may relieve symptoms **b.** Antibiotics are chemicals that kill bacteria. Antibiotics cannot kill viruses; viruses are nonliving.
3. a. A vaccine is a substance introduced into the body that stimulates production of chemicals that destroy specific disease-causing organisms. **b.** Vaccines activate the body's defenses against a specific bacterium or virus that could cause serious illness. **c.** The one who was vaccinated will recover faster. After a vaccine, if the organism invades the body, it is destroyed.

Reteach L1

Have students list ways that infectious diseases can be spread and describe preventative actions they can take.

Performance Assessment L2

Skills Check Have students collect photos that illustrate various bacteria.

All in One Teaching Resources

- Section Summary: *Viruses, Bacteria, and Your Health*
- Review and Reinforcement: *Viruses, Bacteria, and Your Health*
- Enrich: *Viruses, Bacteria, and Your Health*

Science and Society

Antibiotic Resistance— An Alarming Trend

Key Concept

Antibiotic resistance is an increasing problem resulting from the widespread use of antibiotics.

Build Background Knowledge

Treating Bacterial Diseases

Review with students what they know about the use of antibiotics to treat bacterial diseases. Ask: **What is an antibiotic?** (*A chemical that can kill bacteria without harming the host's cells*) **How do antibiotics work?** (*Some work by weakening the cell walls of the target bacteria.*)

Introduce the Debate

Encourage students to think about how antibiotics have altered everyday life. Before the early 1940s, any significant wound was potentially fatal because of bacterial infection. Today very few individuals die from bacterial infections obtained through cuts. Have students consider the implications of bacteria that are resistant to all known antibiotics. (*Resistant bacteria are difficult to kill.*)

Facilitate the Decision

- Be sure students understand how antibiotic-resistant populations of bacteria can evolve.
- Divide the class into three groups. Have one group research the question of over-prescribing antibiotics and the problems caused when patients do not take all of a prescribed medication. Have the second group research non-medical uses of antibiotics, and have the third group research the search for new antibiotics.
- Each group is to limit the information they want to share with the class to two or three main points, each point being well supported by facts. Have each group select two spokespersons to serve on the panel.

Science and Society

Antibiotic Resistance— An Alarming Trend

Penicillin, the first antibiotic, became available for use in 1943. Soon antibiotics became known as the "wonder drugs." Over the years, they have reduced the occurrence of many bacterial diseases and saved millions of lives. But each time an antibiotic is used, a few resistant bacteria may survive. They pass on their resistance to the next generation of bacteria. As more patients take antibiotics, the number of resistant bacteria increases.

In 1987, penicillin killed more than 99.9 percent of a type of ear infection bacteria. By 2000, about 30 percent of these bacteria were resistant to penicillin. Diseases such as tuberculosis are on the rise due in part to growing antibiotic resistance.

The Issues

What Can Doctors Do?

Each year, more than 20 billion dollars worth of antibiotics are sold to drugstores and hospitals worldwide. More than half of antibiotic prescriptions are unnecessary. They include those written for colds and other viral illnesses, which antibiotics are ineffective against. If doctors could better identify the cause of an infection, they could avoid prescribing unnecessary antibiotics.

Bacterial Meningitis Infection in the brain and spinal cord

Conjunctivitis Infection of the eyelids

Ear Infection

Strep Throat

Bacterial Pneumonia Inflammation of the lungs

Dental Cavities

Tuberculosis Infection of the lungs

Stomach Ulcer A break in the stomach lining

Background

Facts and Figures The problems of antibiotic resistance are often most dramatic in hospitals, where many patients are being treated with antibiotics. Because patients who are already ill are at higher risk because of weakened immune systems, many cases of bacterial infection are acquired in hospitals. One strain of the deadly bacteria *Staphylococcus aureus* was discovered in 1997 to be resistant to the antibiotic vancomycin. Fortunately, this particular strain could be treated with other antibiotics, but many forms of these bacteria have already developed resistance to all drugs except vancomycin.

What Can Patients Do?

If a doctor prescribes a ten-day course of antibiotics, the patient should take all of the prescription to make sure that all the bacteria have been killed. If a patient stops taking the antibiotic, resistant bacteria will survive and reproduce. Then, a second or third antibiotic may be necessary. Patients also need to learn that some illnesses are best treated with rest and not with antibiotics.

Limiting Nonmedical Uses of Antibiotics

About half of the antibiotics used each year are not given to people. Instead, the drugs are fed to food animals, such as cattle and poultry, to prevent illness and increase growth. Reducing this type of use would limit the amount of the drugs in food animals and in the people who eat them. But these actions might increase the risk of disease in animals and lead to higher meat prices.

Finding New Antibiotics

Scientists are trying to identify new antibiotics. By using new and different antibiotics, scientists hope that bacteria will not develop resistance as quickly. Scientists are also researching other ways to fight bacteria.

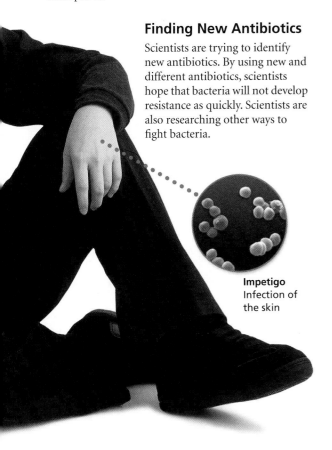

Impetigo
Infection of the skin

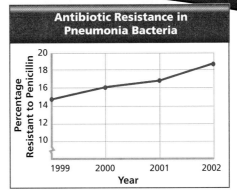

Antibiotic Resistance in Pneumonia Bacteria

The percentage of resistant bacteria has increased steadily over the years.

1. Identify the Problem
How can the use of antibiotics make these medicines less effective?

2. Analyze the Options
List all the ways to fight the development of antibiotic resistance in bacteria. Mention any costs or drawbacks.

3. Find a Solution
Make a persuasive poster about one way to deal with antibiotic resistance. Support your viewpoint with sound reasons.

Go Online
PHSchool.com

For: More on bacterial resistance
Visit: PHSchool.com
Web Code: ceh-1020

- On the second day, organize a panel discussion. Allow the spokespersons to present the results of their research (8–10 minutes each), and allow time for the class to ask questions of the panel.
- On the third day, the students make posters to place in selected places within the school. Have students make posters using information collected during the research and panel discussion as well as information from their textbook. Provide students with samples of persuasive or informative posters.

You Decide

1. Each time an antibiotic is used, some bacteria may be resistant and thus survive. With time, the number and kinds of resistant bacteria have increased.

2. To fight the development of antibiotic resistance in bacteria, doctors can avoid prescribing unnecessary antibiotics. When an antibiotic is prescribed, patients should take the full course of the antibiotic. The widespread use of antibiotics in cattle and chickens can be reduced, even though more animals might die of disease and meat prices might rise.

3. Posters should be informative and accurate, supporting a clearly stated viewpoint with logical reasoning.

Go Online
PHSchool.com

For: More on bacterial resistance
Visit: PHSchool.com
Web Code: ceh-1020

Students can research this issue online.

Extend

Have the groups prepare a community health bulletin on this issue. Encourage them to list the problems and to identify solutions that individuals can implement to prevent antibiotic resistance.

Differentiated Instruction

Less Proficient Readers **L1**
Finding the Main Idea Teach students that identifying the main idea of a paragraph is a key step in reading. Tell them that each paragraph is usually about a specific topic. The most important thing that the author says about the topic is called the main idea of the paragraph. Finding the main idea usually involves these three steps: (1) Previewing the paragraph by skimming the sentences to find the main topic. (2) Carefully reading the paragraph to see what supporting details about the topic are included. (3) Identifying the main idea by asking yourself, "What point is the author making by presenting these details?" **learning modality: verbal**

i̇nteractive Textbook

- Complete student edition
- Section and chapter self-assessments
- Assessment reports for teachers

Help Students Read

Building Vocabulary

Vocabulary Rating Chart Have each student construct a chart with four columns labeled *Term, Can Define or Use It, Have Heard or Seen It*, and *Don't Know*. Tell students to copy the Key Terms from this chapter into the first column and rate their knowledge by putting a check in one of the other columns. Then have them reread the parts that pertain to Key Terms in question.

Words in Context Help students learn the meaning of new words or phrases by examining context. Tell students to look for familiar words or phrases that surround a new term; these are clues to the new term's meaning.

Connecting Concepts

Concept Maps Help students develop one way to show how the information in the chapter is related. A virus is a nonliving particle that enters a cell and then reproduces; a bacterium is a unicellular organism whose cell does not contain a nucleus. Have students brainstorm to identify the key concepts, key terms, details, and examples. Then write each one on a sticky note and attach it at random to chart paper or to the board.

Tell students that this concept map will be organized in hierarchical order and to begin at the top with the key concepts. Ask students these questions to guide them to categorize the information on the stickies: **What are some characteristics of viruses? Describe the basic structure of a virus. What structures can be found in a bacterial cell?**

① Viruses

Key Concepts

- Although viruses can multiply, they do so differently than organisms. Viruses can multiply only when they are inside a living cell.
- All viruses have two basic parts: an outer coat that protects the virus and an inner core made of genetic material.
- Once inside a cell, a virus's genetic material takes over many of the cell's functions. The genetic material instructs the cell to produce the virus's proteins and genetic material. These proteins and genetic material then assemble into new viruses.

Key Terms
virus
host
parasite
bacteriophage

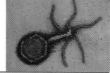

② Bacteria

Key Concepts

- Bacteria are prokaryotes. The genetic material in their cells is not contained in a nucleus.
- Bacteria must have a source of food and a way of breaking down the food to release its energy.
- When bacteria have plenty of food, the right temperature, and other suitable conditions, they thrive and reproduce frequently.
- Bacteria are involved in oxygen and food production, environmental recycling and cleanup, and in health maintenance and medicine production.

Key Terms

bacteria	asexual reproduction
cytoplasm	sexual reproduction
ribosome	conjugation
flagellum	endospore
respiration	pasteurization
binary fission	decomposer

③ Viruses, Bacteria, and Your Health

Key Concepts

- Infectious diseases can spread through contact with an infected person, a contaminated object, an infected animal, or an environmental source.
- Fortunately, many bacterial diseases can be cured with medications known as antibiotics.
- Unlike with bacterial diseases, there are currently no medications that can cure viral infections.
- Vaccines are important tools that help prevent the spread of infectious diseases.

Key Terms
infectious disease
toxin
antibiotic
antibiotic resistance
vaccine

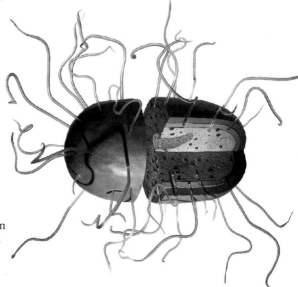

68 ◆ A

Prompt students by using connecting words or phrases, such as "is composed of," "reproduces by," and "can cause" to indicate the basis for the organization of the map. The phrases should form a sentence between or among a set of concepts.

Answer
Accept all logical presentations by students.

All in One Teaching Resources

- Key Terms Review: *Viruses and Bacteria*
- Connecting Concepts: *Viruses and Bacteria*

Go Online
PHSchool.com
For: Self-Assessment
Visit: PHSchool.com
Web Code: cea-1020

Organizing Information

Comparing and Contrasting Copy the Venn diagram comparing viruses and bacteria onto a separate sheet of paper. Then complete it and add a title. (For more information on Comparing and Contrasting, see the Skills Handbook.)

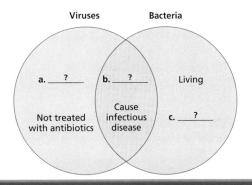

Viruses   Bacteria

a. ___?___   b. ___?___   Living

Not treated with antibiotics

Cause infectious disease

c. ___?___

Organizing Information
a. Nonliving
b. Can be useful
c. Treated with antibiotics
Possible title: Comparing Viruses and Bacteria

Reviewing Key Terms

Choose the letter of the best answer.

1. Bacteriophages are viruses that attack and destroy
   a. other viruses.   **b.** bacteria.
   c. plants.   **d.** humans.

2. Which part of a virus determines which host cells it can infect?
   a. nucleus
   b. ribosomes
   c. flagellum
   d. surface proteins

3. Viruses multiply
   a. by conjugation.
   b. by binary fission.
   c. by taking over a cell's functions.
   d. both asexually and sexually.

4. Most bacteria are surrounded by a rigid protective structure called the
   a. cell wall.
   b. cell membrane.
   c. protein coat.
   d. flagellum.

5. Which of the following help prevent the spread of infectious diseases?
   a. toxins
   b. vaccines
   c. parasites
   d. endospores

If the statement is true, write *true*. If it is false, change the underlined word or words to make the statement true.

6. <u>Active viruses</u> enter a cell and immediately begin to multiply.

7. During <u>conjugation</u>, one bacterium transfers genetic material to another bacterial cell.

8. <u>Binary fission</u> is the process of breaking down food to release energy.

9. Bacteria form <u>endospores</u> to survive unfavorable conditions in their surroundings.

10. A <u>vaccine</u> is a chemical that can kill bacteria without harming a person's cells.

Reviewing Key Terms
1. b   **2.** d   **3.** c   **4.** a   **5.** b
6. True
7. True
8. False; Respiration
9. True
10. False; An antibiotic

Writing in Science

 **Writing in Science**

Debate Suppose you are preparing for a debate about whether bacteria are beneficial or harmful. Select one side of the argument and write a paragraph defending your position. Be sure to give an example to support your argument.

Discovery CHANNEL SCHOOL

Viruses and Bacteria: Bacteria
Video Preview
Video Field Trip
▶ Video Assessment

Writing Mode Persuasion
Scoring Rubric
4 Exceeds criteria
3 Meets criteria; develops sound argument supported by facts and an example
2 Includes clear position but weak support
1 Incomplete; argument not supported by facts

Discovery CHANNEL SCHOOL Video Assessment

Viruses and Bacteria

Show the Video Assessment to review chapter content and as a prompt for the writing assignment. Discussion questions: **Besides through flea bites, how else was the plague spread?** (*Rats; one form of the plague spread through the air contaminated by infected people*) **What might have brought the plague to an end?** (*The population that survived had a natural immunity to the bacteria. The rats that were carrying the plague themselves died.*)

Go Online
PHSchool.com   For: Self-Assessment
Visit: PHSchool.com
Web Code: cea-1020

Students can take a practice test that is automatically scored.

All in One Teaching Resources
- Transparency A17
- Chapter Test
- Performance Assessment Teacher Notes
- Performance Assessment Student Worksheet
- Performance Assessment Scoring Rubric

ExamView® Computer Test Bank CD-ROM

Checking Concepts

11. Viruses are not cells; do not carry on the functions of cells; cannot reproduce on their own.

12. The proteins in the coat of the virus will fit only with certain proteins on the surface of a cell.

13. After a hidden virus enters a host cell, its genetic material becomes part of the cell's genetic material. When the host cell divides, the virus's genetic material is copied along with the host's genetic material. When certain conditions cause the virus's genetic material to become active, it takes over the cell's functions.

14. Cell wall—protects the cell; cell membrane—controls what materials enter and leave the cell; cytoplasm—contains ribosomes and genetic material; ribosomes—produce protein; genetic material—contains instructions for the cell's functions; flagellum—helps cell to move

15. Most bacteria reproduce asexually by binary fission, especially when conditions are favorable. Some bacteria can reproduce sexually by conjugation.

16. They help you digest food, make vitamins for you, and keep harmful bacteria from living in your tissues.

17. Antibiotics kill bacteria without harming body cells. For example, penicillin weakens the cell walls of some bacteria and causes them to burst.

18. Vaccines stimulate the body to produce chemicals that fight off specific invading viruses and bacteria.

Thinking Critically

19. A—rodlike; B—spiral

20. Both invade the host cell and cause it to start producing new viruses. With an active virus, the takeover occurs immediately after entry into the cell. With hidden viruses, the genetic material of the virus is incorporated into the cell's genetic material and it can be years before the virus actively takes over the cell.

21. A substance that includes living cells because viruses need to infect living cells in order to multiply

22. The bacteria may develop antibiotic resistance. Not all the bacteria will be killed if the antibiotic course is stopped early. Any resistant bacteria will survive and reproduce. A second or third antibiotic might then be necessary.

Checking Concepts

11. List three ways that viruses differ from cells.

12. Explain why a certain virus will attach to only one or a few types of cells.

13. Describe how a hidden virus multiplies.

14. What are the parts of a bacterial cell? Explain the role of each part.

15. Describe how bacteria reproduce.

16. How do the bacteria that live in your intestines help you?

17. Explain how antibiotics kill bacteria.

18. How do vaccines prevent the spread of some infectious diseases?

Thinking Critically

19. **Classifying** Classify the bacteria in each photo according to their shape.

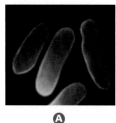 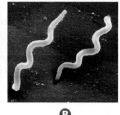

Ⓐ **Ⓑ**

20. **Comparing and Contrasting** Describe the similarities and differences between active and hidden viruses.

21. **Problem Solving** Bacteria will grow in the laboratory on a gelatin-like substance called agar. Viruses will not grow on agar. If you needed to grow viruses in the laboratory, what kind of substance would you have to use? Explain your reasoning.

22. **Predicting** A friend has been prescribed a ten-day course of antibiotics for a bacterial infection. Your friend feels much better after three days and decides to stop taking the medication. What do you think might happen and why?

Math Practice

23. **Diameter** How much greater is the diameter of a penny than the diameter of a dime?

Applying Skills

Use the graph to answer Questions 24–27.

The graph shows how the number of bacteria that grow on a food source changes over time.

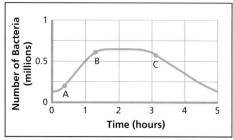

A Bacterial Population Over Time

24. **Reading Graphs** What do the numbers on the vertical axis represent?

25. **Interpreting Data** Explain what is happening between points A and B.

26. **Developing Hypotheses** Develop a hypothesis to explain why the number of bacteria appears to stay constant between points B and C.

27. **Designing Experiments** How could you test the hypothesis you developed in Question 26? What would your results show?

 Lab zone **Chapter Project**

Performance Assessment Present your project to your class. Explain why you chose the questions and survey group that you did. Use graphs or other visual displays to highlight any patterns that you found. Be sure to support your conclusions with data.

Lab zone **Chapter Project**   **L3**

Project Wrap-Up Have students present their projects while their classmates take notes. Students' conclusions must be drawn from the results of their own surveys. Encourage students to compare their data with other sources.

Choose the letter of the best answer.

1. If you know that an organism is a prokaryote, you know that
   A its cell does not contain a nucleus.
   B its cell does not contain ribosomes.
   C the organism is a heterotroph.
   D the organism cannot move on its own.

2. Which of these statements about the sizes of bacteria and viruses is true?
   F Viruses can be seen with a hand lens but bacteria cannot.
   G Both bacteria and viruses can be seen with a hand lens.
   H Bacteria can be seen with a light microscope but viruses cannot.
   J Neither bacteria nor viruses can be seen with a light microscope.

3. What will most likely happen after the virus in the diagram attaches to the bacterial cell?

   A The virus will inject its proteins into the bacterial cell.
   B The virus will inject its genetic material into the bacterial cell.
   C The bacterial cell will inject its proteins into the virus.
   D The bacterial cell will inject its genetic material into the virus.

4. Which of the following statements about viruses is *not* true?
   F Viruses can multiply only inside a living cell.
   G Viruses have genetic material.
   H Virus particles are smaller than bacterial cells.
   J Diseases caused by viruses can be cured by antibiotics.

5. Paola grew a new culture of bacteria and measured the population's growth over time. The number of bacteria increased sharply over the first few hours but then tapered off. Which of the following statements about these observations is true?
   A The initial conditions for bacterial growth were favorable.
   B The number of bacteria increased as the bacteria reproduced asexually.
   C After a period of time, the bacteria started to run out of food, space, and other resources.
   D all of the above

Constructed Response

6. Compare and contrast viruses and bacteria with respect to their sizes, structures, and methods of reproduction.

Chapter 2 A ◆ 71

23. The diameter of a penny is 1.9 cm. The diameter of a dime is 1.7 cm. The diameter of a penny is 0.2 cm greater than the diameter of a dime.

Applying Skills

24. Numbers of bacteria in millions

25. Bacteria are rapidly reproducing because they have plenty of food available.

26. Sample: The number of bacteria stays constant between points B and C because the amount of food available to the bacteria can support only this number of bacteria.

27. Students might suggest preparing petri dishes with different amounts of food and graphing the growth patterns of the bacteria.

Standardized Test Prep

1. A **2.** H **3.** B **4.** J **5.** D
6. Size: Viruses are very small and are measured in nanometers. Bacteria vary in size, but are larger than viruses and can be seen by a light microscope.

Structure: Viruses have two parts, a protein coat that protects the virus, and an inner core made of genetic material. Bacteria have a cell wall, a cell membrane, cytoplasm with ribosomes in it and with genetic material, and may have a flagellum.

Methods of reproduction: Viruses enter a host cell and the virus's genetic material takes over many of the cell's functions. It instructs the cell to produce the virus's proteins and genetic material. Bacteria may reproduce by asexual or sexual reproduction, or the formation of endospores.

Chapter at a Glance

Chapter at a Glance

PRENTICE HALL
Teacher**EXPRESS**™
Plan • Teach • Assess

 Chapter **Project** *A Mushroom Farm*

All in One Teaching Resources

- Chapter Project Teacher Notes, pp. 156–157
- Chapter Project Student Overview, pp. 158–159
- Chapter Project Student Worksheets, pp. 160–161
- Chapter Project Scoring Rubric, p. 162

DISCOVERY
CHANNEL
SCHOOL
Video Preview

 Section 1

Protists

A.3.1.1 Describe the characteristics of animal-like protists and give examples.

3–4 periods
1 1/2–2 blocks **A.3.1.2** Describe the characteristics of plantlike protists and give examples.

A.3.1.3 Describe the characteristics of funguslike protists and give examples.

Go **Online**
active art

 Section 2

Algal Blooms

A.3.2.1 Describe the causes and effects of red tides.

2–3 periods **A.3.2.2** Describe the causes and effects of eutrophication
1–1 1/2 blocks
.

Go **Online**
SCi**LINKS**™
NSTA

Section 3

Fungi

A.3.3.1 Name the characteristics fungi share.

1–2 periods **A.3.3.2** Explain how fungi reproduce.
1/2–1 block **A.3.3.3** Describe the roles fungi play in nature.

Go **Online**
SCi**LINKS**™
NSTA

DISCOVERY
CHANNEL
SCHOOL
Video Field Trip

Review and Assessment

All in One Teaching Resources

- Key Terms Review, p. 189
- Transparency A26
- Performance Assessment Teacher Notes, p. 196
- Performance Assessment Scoring Rubric, p. 197
- Performance Assessment Student Worksheet, p. 198
- Chapter Test, pp. 199–202

DISCOVERY
CHANNEL
SCHOOL

Go **Online**
PHSchool.com

Test Preparation

**Test Preparation
Blackline Masters**

Chapter Activities Planner

For more activities

LAB ZONE Easy Planner CD-ROM

Student Edition	Inquiry	Time	Materials	Skills	Resources
Chapter Project, p. 73	Open-Ended	4–5 weeks	**All in One Teaching Resources** See p. 156	Developing hypotheses, designing experiments, drawing conclusions, communicating	**Lab zone Easy Planner** **All in One Teaching Resources** Support pp. 156–157
Section 1					
Discover Activity, p. 74	Guided	25 minutes	plastic dropper, pond water, microscope slide, coverslip, microscope	Observing	**Lab zone Easy Planner**
Try This, p. 79	Directed	15 minutes	paramecium culture, *Chlorella* culture, plastic dropper, microscope and slide, cotton fibers,	Inferring	**Lab zone Easy Planner**
Skills Activity, p. 80	Guided	20 minutes	euglena culture, plastic petri dish, aluminum foil, compound microscope	Predicting	**Lab zone Easy Planner**
Section 2					
Discover Activity, p. 84	Directed	15 minutes	clear plastic container, water, green paper punches, spoons	Predicting	**Lab zone Easy Planner**
Skills Lab, p. 87	Directed	Day 1: 30 minutes; 10 minutes a day follow-up	4 glass jars with lids, aged tap water, graduated cylinder, marking pen, aquarium water, liquid fertilizer	Controlling variables, drawing conclusions, predicting	**Lab zone Easy Planner** **Lab Activity Video** **All in One Teaching Resources** Skills Lab: *An Explosion of Life*, pp. 177–178
Section 3					
Discover Activity, p. 88	Guided	15 minutes	self-seal bags, tape, hand lens, old bread, fruit	Observing	**Lab zone Easy Planner**
Try This, p. 92	Directed	25 minutes	round balloon, cotton balls, tape, stick or ruler about 30 cm long, modeling clay, pin	Making models	**Lab zone Easy Planner**
Skills Lab, pp. 96–97	Directed	45 minutes	5 plastic narrow-necked bottles, 5 round balloons, 5 plastic straws, dry powered yeast, sugar, salt, warm water, marking pen, beaker, graduated cylinder, metric ruler, string	Measuring, inferring, drawing conclusions	**Lab zone Easy Planner** **Lab Activity Video** **All in One Teaching Resources** Skills Lab: *What's for Lunch?*, pp. 186–188

Section 1 **Protists**

 3–4 periods, 1–1 1/2 blocks

Objectives

A.3.1.1 Describe the characteristics of animal-like protists and give examples.
A.3.1.2 Describe the characteristics of plantlike protists and give examples.
A.3.1.3 Describe the characteristics of funguslike protists and give examples.

Local Standards

Key Terms

• protozoan • pseudopod • contractile vacuole • cilia • symbiosis
• mutualism • algae • pigment • spore

Preteach

Build Background Knowledge

Students discuss which characteristics must be considered to determine whether or not "blobs" in a dish are alive.

 **Discover Activity** *What Lives in a Drop of Pond Water?*

Targeted Print and Technology Resources

All in One Teaching Resources
L2 Reading Strategy Transparency A18: Outlining

Presentation-Pro CD-ROM

Instruct

What Is a Protist? Students explore the shared characteristics and tremendous diversity of organisms in the protist kingdom

Animal-Like Protists Students discuss the general traits of animal-like protists and the differences that divide them into four distinct groups.

Plantlike Protists Students identify traits of plantlike protists, called algae, and distinguish the various types, exploring differences in pigments, size, structures, habitats, and functions.

Funguslike Protists Students determine shared characteristics among and differences between the three groups of funguslike protists.

Targeted Print and Technology Resources

All in One Teaching Resources
L2 Guided Reading, pp. 165–168
L2 Transparencies A19, A20, A21, A22

www.phschool.com Web Code: cep-1031

Student Edition on Audio CD

Assess

Section Assessment Questions

Have students use their completed Outlining graphic organizer to help answer the questions.

Reteach

Students name features shared by protists and identify the many differences that make the group so diverse.

Targeted Print and Technology Resources

All in One Teaching Resources
• Section Summary, p. 164
L1 Review and Reinforce, p. 169
L3 Enrich, p. 170

Section 2 Algal Blooms

 2–3 periods, 1–1 1/2 blocks

Objectives

A.3.2.1 Describe the causes and effects of red tides.

A.3.2.2 Describe the causes and effects of eutrophication.

Key Terms

• algal bloom • red tide • eutrophication

Local Standards

Preteach

Build Background Knowledge

Students recall that algae live on the surface of water bodies and consider the scenario of algae growing so abundant as to block sunlight from the water.

 **Discover Activity** *How Can Algal Growth Affect Pond Life?*

Targeted Print and Technology Resources

All in One Teaching Resources

L2 Reading Strategy Transparency A23: Comparing and Contrasting

⊙ **Presentation-Pro CD-ROM**

Instruct

Saltwater Blooms Students explore causes and effects of saltwater algal blooms, called red tides.

Freshwater Blooms Students consider the causes and effects of eutrophication, the process by which algae growth increases in a pond or lake over time.

 Skills Lab *An Explosion of Life*

Targeted Print and Technology Resources

All in One Teaching Resources

L2 Guided Reading, pp. 173–174

L2 Skills Lab: *An Explosion of Life,* pp. 177–178

▬ **Lab Activity Video/DVD**
Skills Lab: *An Explosion of Life*

www.SciLinks.org Web Code: scn-0132

⊙ **Student Edition on Audio CD**

Assess

Section Assessment Questions

↺ Have students use their completed Comparing and Contrasting graphic organizer to help answer the questions.

Reteach

Students describe the processes that lead to algal blooms in saltwater and freshwater, then compare the two types of blooms.

Targeted Print and Technology Resources

All in One Teaching Resources

• Section Summary, p. 172

L1 Review and Reinforce, p. 175

L3 Enrich, p. 176

Section Lesson Plans

Section 3 Fungi

 1–2 periods, 1/2–1 block

ABILITY LEVELS
L1 Basic to Average
L2 For All Students
L3 Average to Advanced

Objectives

A.3.3.1 Name the characteristics that all fungi share.
A.3.3.2 Describe the ways that fungi reproduce.
A.3.3.3 List the roles fungi play in nature.

Key Terms

• fruiting body • hyphae • budding • lichen

Local Standards

Preteach

Build Background Knowledge

Students discuss what they know about mushrooms, both those cultivated and those in natural habitats, and begin to consider their similarities to plants.

Lab zone Discover Activity *Do All Molds Look Alike?*

Targeted Print and Technology Resources

All in One Teaching Resources

L2 Reading Strategy Transparency A24: Using Prior Knowledge

⊙ **Presentation-Pro CD-ROM**

Instruct

What Are Fungi? Students consider traits shared by fungi and examine their habitats, cell structure, and means of obtaining food.

Reproduction in Fungi Students discuss fungal spores and the fruiting bodies that release them, and determine when and how fungi reproduce either sexually or asexually, and how fungi are characterized this way.

The Role of Fungi in Nature Students explore the many roles of fungi on Earth: decomposers, recyclers, disease agents, disease fighters, and organisms living in symbiosis with other organisms.

Targeted Print and Technology Resources

All in One Teaching Resources

L2 Guided Reading, pp. 181–183
L2 Transparency A25
L2 Skills Lab: *What's for Lunch?*, pp. 186–188

📼 **Lab Activity Video/DVD**
Skills Lab: *What's for Lunch?*

www.SciLinks.org Web Code: scn-0133

⊙ **Student Edition on Audio CD**

Assess

Section Assessment Questions

↻ Have students use their Using Prior Knowledge graphic organizers to help answer the questions.

Reteach

Students produce a chart or diagram illustrating basic characteristics of fungi, how they reproduce and obtain food, and the roles they play in nature.

Targeted Print and Technology Resources

All in One Teaching Resources

• Section Summary, p. 180
L1 Review and Reinforce, p. 184
L3 Enrich, p. 185

Chapter 3 Content Refresher

Section 1 Protists

Algae as a Food Source Many people worldwide consume large amounts of algae as a food source. The algae harvested every year are worth billions of dollars. The most widely farmed alga is *Porphyra,* a red alga. The green algae *Monostroma* and *Ulva,* also known as sea lettuce, are eaten in salads, soups, and other dishes. *Chlorella,* a green alga known for its high protein content, is considered a potentially efficient source of nutrition for astronauts on long space journeys.

Address Misconceptions

Students may think that all red algae look red. Green, red, and brown algae all contain various pigments, so they don't always appear the color they are named. For more on this misconception, see **Address Misconceptions** in the section Protists.

Section 2 Algal Blooms

Saltwater Dead Zones Coastal areas lacking strong winds or tides to mix the sea water, such as bays and gulfs, are at most risk for red tides. In these areas, freshwater runoff tends to float on top of the denser sea water. Bottom layers fill with dead plant matter, which decomposes and rapidly consumes oxygen. Entire bays can suffocate below the surface. In the Gulf of Mexico, an area approximately the size of New Jersey (18,000 sq km) goes through this deadly process every summer, mostly as a result of the input of fertilizer and sewage runoff from the massive watershed of the Mississippi River. This lifeless region is known as the "Dead Zone."

Saltwater Dead Zones

Mississippi River Basin

Dead Zone

Section 3 Fungi

Indoor Air Pollution One group of fungi, molds, is widely associated with issues of indoor air quality. Mold spores grow quickly on any damp surface, including wood, paper, and carpet. The potential health effects of molds in homes, schools, and offices are debated, but they probably represent at least moderate health risks. Airborne toxins released by molds can irritate eyes, noses, and throats, or—more seriously—lungs. Many asthmatics react to mold allergens, and individuals with weak immune systems are particularly sensitive to infection from mold pathogens. Keeping a building mold-free is impossible, but health risks can be reduced by controlling interior moisture.

Help Students Read

Previewing Visuals

Improve Understanding Through Visual Images

Strategy Show students that, before they read a chapter, figures and tables can be previewed to activate students' prior knowledge and allow them to predict what they are about to read. Have students locate and read over figures and tables. Ask them to predict what the text in that section will discuss.

Example

1. Select a section of the chapter, such as *The Role of Fungi in Nature.*
2. Instruct students to view the figures and write questions that they have about the visuals.
3. After reading, have students share their questions and answers.

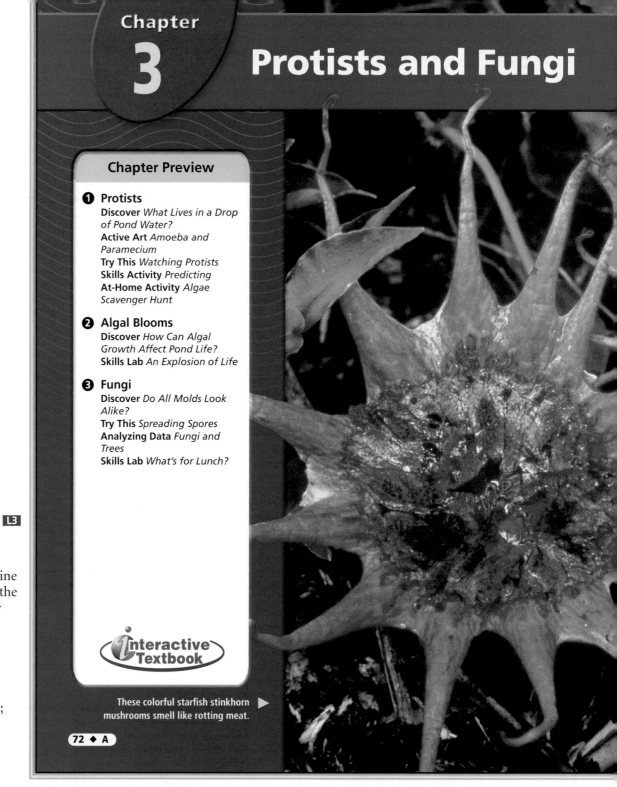

Chapter

3

Protists and Fungi

Chapter Preview

❶ Protists
Discover *What Lives in a Drop of Pond Water?*
Active Art *Amoeba and Paramecium*
Try This *Watching Protists*
Skills Activity *Predicting*
At-Home Activity *Algae Scavenger Hunt*

❷ Algal Blooms
Discover *How Can Algal Growth Affect Pond Life?*
Skills Lab *An Explosion of Life*

❸ Fungi
Discover *Do All Molds Look Alike?*
Try This *Spreading Spores*
Analyzing Data *Fungi and Trees*
Skills Lab *What's for Lunch?*

interactive
Textbook

These colorful starfish stinkhorn ▶
mushrooms smell like rotting meat.

72 ◆ A

Chapter Project   L3

Objectives

This project will allow students to determine the effect of changing a single variable on the growth of mushrooms. After this Chapter Project, students will be able to

- develop a hypothesis concerning how a variable affects mushroom growth;
- design and perform an experiment to test their hypotheses;
- draw conclusions based on their results;
- communicate their results in the form of a poster.

Skills Focus

Developing hypotheses, designing experiments, drawing conclusions, communicating

Project Time Line   4–5 weeks

All in One **Teaching Resources**

- Chapter Project Teacher Notes
- Chapter Project Worksheet 1
- Chapter Project Worksheet 2
- Chapter Project Worksheet 3
- Chapter Project Scoring Rubric

Developing a Plan

Students first discuss mushrooms, decide which variable to test, and develop experimental designs to test their variables. Depending on conditions tested, the experiment will take 2–3 weeks. Allow one week following the end of the project for data analysis and poster preparation.

Possible Materials

It is difficult to grow mushrooms from spores you collect yourself. Mushroom growing kits, available from most biological supply companies, provide all the materials necessary to complete this project. You may need additional pots and peat moss. You can use milk cartons, two-liter plastic bottle bottoms, or other such containers with holes cut in the bottom. A spray bottle works

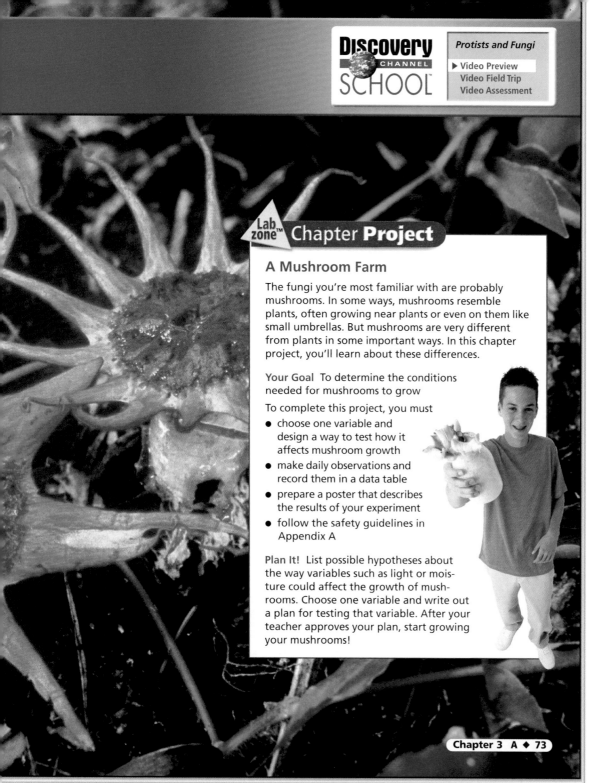

Lab zone™ Chapter **Project**

A Mushroom Farm

The fungi you're most familiar with are probably mushrooms. In some ways, mushrooms resemble plants, often growing near plants or even on them like small umbrellas. But mushrooms are very different from plants in some important ways. In this chapter project, you'll learn about these differences.

Your Goal To determine the conditions needed for mushrooms to grow

To complete this project, you must

- choose one variable and design a way to test how it affects mushroom growth
- make daily observations and record them in a data table
- prepare a poster that describes the results of your experiment
- follow the safety guidelines in Appendix A

Plan It! List possible hypotheses about the way variables such as light or moisture could affect the growth of mushrooms. Choose one variable and write out a plan for testing that variable. After your teacher approves your plan, start growing your mushrooms!

Chapter 3 A ◆ 73

Protists and Fungi

Show the Video Preview to introduce the Chapter Project and overview the chapter content. Discussion question: **How do epiphytes and lichen contribute to the tree canopy ecosystem?** (*When epiphytes and lichen die, they decompose and form a rich humus soil within the canopy where other organisms can live*)

Discuss experimental design; emphasize the difference between manipulated and responding variables, and why other variables must be controlled. Have students form groups, choose variables, and develop hypotheses about how mushroom growth will be affected by their variable. Check that some groups choose different variables.

Performance Assessment

The Chapter Project Scoring Rubric will help you evaluate how well students complete the Chapter Project. You may wish to share the scoring rubric with your students so they are clear about what will be expected of them. Students will be assessed on

- how well they define and control the variables in their experiment;
- how well their experimental design tests their hypotheses, and the thoroughness of their data collection;
- their analysis of the results, and the clarity and organization of their poster;
- their ability to work cooperatively as a group.

Students can save their posters in their portfolios.

Portfolio

---

well for watering the containers. For testing variables you will need

- a dark location and a light source (to test light);
- a thermometer and a warm and a cool location (to test temperature);
- substrate lacking nutrients and some fertilizer (to test nutrients).

Launching the Project

To introduce the project, ask: **How do you think mushrooms grow?** (*In damp and warm places, such as in the forest after a rain.*) **Are they like plants?** Students may know that mushrooms are fungi but may also think of them as plants. Encourage students to discuss similarities and differences between mushrooms and plants. Have students read the project description above.

Objectives

After completing the lesson, students will be able to

A.3.1.1 Describe the characteristics of animal-like protists and give examples.

A.3.1.2 Describe the characteristics of plantlike protists and give examples.

A.3.1.3 Describe the characteristics of funguslike protists and give examples.

Target Reading Skill 🔄

Outlining Explain that using an outline format helps organize information by main topic, subtopic, and details.

Answers

Protists
I. What is a Protist?
II. Animal-Like Protists
   A. Protozoans With Pseudopods
   B. Protozoans With Cilia
   C. Protozoans With Flagella
   D. Protozoans That Are Parasites
III. Plantlike Protists
   A. Diatoms
   B. Dinoflagellates
   C. Euglenoids
   D. Red Algae
   E. Green Algae
   F. Brown Algae
IV. Funguslike Protists
   A. Slime Molds
   B. Water Molds
   C. Downy Mildews

All in One Teaching Resources

• Transparency A18

Preteach

Build Background Knowledge   L2

Characterizing Living Organisms
Review characteristics of living things. Before class, place several drops of vegetable oil in a small dish of water. Add a few drops of green food coloring to the water. Place the dish on an overhead projector. Ask students: **How can you tell whether the blobs you see are alive?** (*Sample answer: Check for reaction to stimuli, taking in food, breathing, and movement.*)

Section 1 Protists

Reading Preview

Key Concept
• What are the characteristics of animal-like, plantlike, and funguslike protists?

Key Terms
• protist • protozoan
• pseudopod
• contractile vacuole • cilia
• symbiosis • mutualism
• algae • pigment • spore

🔄 Target Reading Skill

Outlining As you read, make an outline about protists that you can use for review. Use the red section headings for the main topics and the blue headings for the subtopics.

Protists
I. What is a protist?
II. Animal-like protists
A. Protozoans with pseudopods
B.
C.

Lab zone Discover **Activity**

What Lives in a Drop of Pond Water?

1. Use a plastic dropper to place a drop of pond water on a microscope slide.
2. Put the slide under your microscope's low-power lens. Focus on the objects you see.
3. Find at least three different objects that you think might be organisms. Observe them for a few minutes.
4. Draw the three organisms in your notebook. Below each sketch, describe the movements or behaviors of the organism. Wash your hands thoroughly when you have finished.

Think It Over
Observing What characteristics did you observe that made you think that each organism was alive?

Look at the objects in Figure 1. What do they look like to you? Jewels? Beads? Stained glass ornaments? You might be surprised to learn that these beautiful, delicate structures are the walls of unicellular organisms called diatoms. Diatoms live in both fresh water and salt water and are an important food source for many marine organisms. They have been called the "jewels of the sea."

FIGURE 1
Diatoms
These glasslike organisms are classified as protists.

Lab zone Discover **Activity**

Skills Focus Observing   L1

Materials plastic dropper, pond water, microscope slide, cover slip, microscope

Time 25 minutes

Tips Have students predict what they might observe in the water. Suggest students use their high-power objective lenses if they have them.

Expected Outcome Both algae and protozoans should be visible. Green algae have a greenish tint, but most organisms appear colorless. Organisms with flagella or pseudopods could be either protozoans or algae.

Think It Over Students will probably associate movement with life.

FIGURE 2
Protists
Protists include animal-like, plantlike, and funguslike organisms.
Comparing and Contrasting *In what ways do protists differ from one another?*

▲ These shells are the remains of unicellular, animal-like protists called foraminifera.

What Is a Protist?

Diatoms are only one of the vast varieties of protists. **Protists** are eukaryotes that cannot be classified as animals, plants, or fungi. Because protists are so different from one another, you can think of them as the "odds and ends" kingdom. However, protists do share some characteristics. In addition to being eukaryotes, all protists live in moist surroundings.

The word that best describes protists is *diversity*. For example, most protists are unicellular, but some are multicellular. Some are heterotrophs, some are autotrophs, and others are both. Some protists cannot move, while others zoom around their moist surroundings.

Because of the great variety of protists, scientists have proposed several ways of grouping these organisms. One useful way of grouping protists is to divide them into three categories, based on characteristics they share with organisms in other kingdoms: animal-like protists, plantlike protists, and funguslike protists.

 Reading Checkpoint In what kind of environment do all protists live?

Animal-Like Protists

What image pops into your head when you think of an animal? A tiger chasing its prey? A snake slithering onto a rock? Most people immediately associate animals with movement. In fact, movement is often involved with an important characteristic of animals—obtaining food. All animals are heterotrophs that must obtain food by eating other organisms.

Like animals, animal-like protists are heterotrophs, and most are able to move from place to place to obtain food. But unlike animals, animal-like protists, or **protozoans** (proh tuh ZOH unz), are unicellular. Protozoans can be classified into four groups, based on the way they move and live.

▲ This red alga is a multicellular, plantlike protist found on ocean floors.

▲ The yellow slime mold oozing off the leaf is a funguslike protist.

Chapter 3 A ◆ 75

What Is a Protist?

Teach Key Concepts L2
Describing Protist Characteristics

Focus Emphasize that protists are highly diverse but do share some traits.

Teach Ask: **Which traits are shared by all protists?** *(They are eukaryotes that live in moist environments.)* **Name the diverse protist categories.** *(Animal-like, plantlike, funguslike)*

Apply Ask: **What characteristic would a plantlike protist have?** *(The ability to make its own food)* **learning modality: verbal**

Independent Practice L2

All in One Teaching Resources

• Guided Reading and Study Worksheet: *Protists*

⊙ **Student Edition on Audio CD**

Animal-Like Protists

Teach Key Concepts
Comparing Protists and Animals

Focus Ask: **What are some animal traits?** *(Sample answers: They are consumers; most can move about to obtain food.).*

Teach Explain that animal-like protists are heterotrophs and that most can move about to obtain food. Ask: **What name is given to animal-like protists?** *(Protozoans)* **How do protozoans differ from animals?** *(Protozoans are unicellular; animals are multicellular.)*

Apply Ask: **What characteristic can be used to classify protozoans?** *(How they move)* **learning modality: verbal**

Differentiated Instruction

**English Learners/Beginning L1
Comprehension: Modified Cloze**
Distribute a simple paragraph about protists, leaving some strategic words blank. For example, "Animal-like protists are called ____. They can be grouped by how they ____ and ____." Provide students a list of the correct answers, and have them fill in each blank with one of those words. **learning modality: verbal**

**English Learners/Intermediate L2
Comprehension: Modified Cloze**
Distribute the cloze paragraph designed for Beginning Level, but add some incorrect answers to the list of correct answers. Students can work in pairs to correct each other's answers, and to collaborate in writing a definition, in English, of the words that they filled in. **learning modality: verbal**

Monitor Progress L2

Answers
Figure 2 Structure, unicellular or multicellular; habitat

 Reading Checkpoint Moist environment

A ● 75

Help Students Read

Previewing Visuals Refer to the Content Refresher, which provides guidelines for Previewing Visuals. Before students read the section on protozoans with pseudopods and protozoans with cilia, have them study Figures 3 and 4 and read the labels. Call on student volunteers to name protozoan structures used for locomotion (*Cilia, pseudopods*), feeding (*Food vacuole, oral groove*), and reproduction (*Nucleus*). Have students read the text in this section, then together discuss the functions of the structures observed prior to reading.

Observing Pseudopod Movement

Materials plastic dropper, amoeba culture, microscope slide, cover slip, microscope

Time 20 minutes

Focus Review with students the function of an amoeba's pseudopods.

Teach Have students place a drop of the amoeba culture on a slide, carefully add a cover slip, and then observe the organisms under low and high power.

Apply Ask: **Can you tell when the amoeba is using its pseudopods to eat and when it is using them to move?** (*Students may say that when the amoeba is eating, it wraps two pseudopods around the food; when it is moving, it puts out a pseudopod and flows into it.*) Students can sketch what they observe and label the parts of the amoeba. Observations should include the organism's shape, size, and motion. **learning modality: visual**

For: Amoeba and Paramecium activity
Visit: PHSchool.com
Web Code: cep-1031

Students learn about two types of protozoans, the amoeba and the paramecium.

FIGURE 3
Amoeba

Amoebas are sarcodines that live in either water or soil. They feed on bacteria and smaller protists.

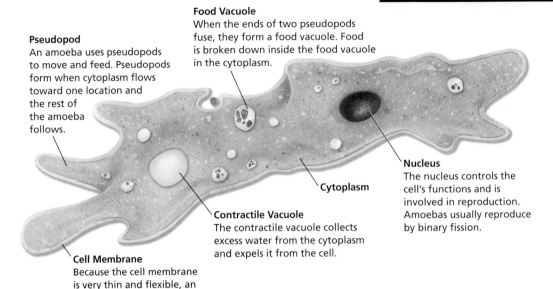

Food Vacuole
When the ends of two pseudopods fuse, they form a food vacuole. Food is broken down inside the food vacuole in the cytoplasm.

Pseudopod
An amoeba uses pseudopods to move and feed. Pseudopods form when cytoplasm flows toward one location and the rest of the amoeba follows.

Nucleus
The nucleus controls the cell's functions and is involved in reproduction. Amoebas usually reproduce by binary fission.

Cytoplasm

Contractile Vacuole
The contractile vacuole collects excess water from the cytoplasm and expels it from the cell.

Cell Membrane
Because the cell membrane is very thin and flexible, an amoeba's shape changes constantly.

For: Amoeba and Paramecium activity
Visit: PHSchool.com
Web Code: cep-1031

Protozoans With Pseudopods The amoeba in Figure 3 belongs to the group of protozoans called sarcodines. Sarcodines move and feed by forming **pseudopods** (SOO duh pahdz)—temporary bulges of the cell. The word *pseudopod* means "false foot." Pseudopods form when cytoplasm flows toward one location and the rest of the organism follows. Pseudopods enable sarcodines to move. For example, amoebas use pseudopods to move away from bright light. Sarcodines also use pseudopods to trap food. The organism extends a pseudopod on each side of the food particle. The two pseudopods then join together, trapping the particle inside.

Protozoans that live in fresh water, such as amoebas, have a problem. Small particles, like those of water, pass easily through the cell membrane into the cytoplasm. If excess water were to build up inside the cell, the amoeba would burst. Fortunately, amoebas have a **contractile vacuole** (kun TRAK til VAK yoo ohl), a structure that collects the extra water and then expels it from the cell.

76 ◆ A

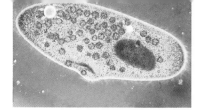

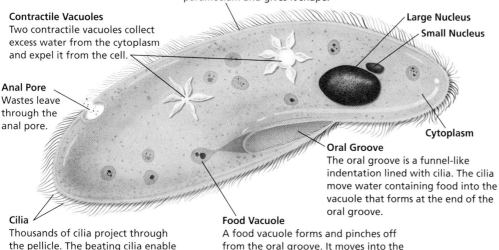

Pellicle
A stiff but flexible covering, called the pellicle, surrounds a paramecium and gives it shape.

FIGURE 4
Paramecium
Paramecia are ciliates that live mostly in fresh water. Like amoebas, paramecia feed on bacteria and smaller protists.

Contractile Vacuoles
Two contractile vacuoles collect excess water from the cytoplasm and expel it from the cell.

Anal Pore
Wastes leave through the anal pore.

Large Nucleus

Small Nucleus

Cytoplasm

Oral Groove
The oral groove is a funnel-like indentation lined with cilia. The cilia move water containing food into the vacuole that forms at the end of the oral groove.

Cilia
Thousands of cilia project through the pellicle. The beating cilia enable a paramecium to move smoothly in one direction.

Food Vacuole
A food vacuole forms and pinches off from the oral groove. It moves into the cytoplasm. Inside the vacuole, the food is broken down and then distributed.

Protozoans With Cilia The second group of animal-like protists are the ciliates. Ciliates have structures called **cilia** (SIL ee uh), which are hairlike projections from cells that move with a wavelike motion. Ciliates use their cilia to move and obtain food. Cilia act something like tiny oars to move a ciliate. Their movement sweeps food into the organism.

The cells of ciliates, like the paramecium in Figure 4, are complex. Notice that the paramecium has two contractile vacuoles that expel water from the cell. It also has more than one nucleus. The large nucleus controls the everyday tasks of the cell. The small nucleus functions in reproduction.

Paramecia usually reproduce asexually by binary fission. Sometimes, however, paramecia reproduce by conjugation. This occurs when two paramecia join together and exchange some of their genetic material.

 **Reading Checkpoint** What are cilia?

Use Visuals: Figures 3 and 4 [L1]
Amoeba and Paramecium

Focus Have students observe the figures.

Teach Ask: **What do these two protists have in common?** (*They eat the same things, and they both have nuclei, cytoplasm, food vacuoles, and contractile vacuoles.*) Ask: **What is different about them?** (*Amoebas live in soil and water, paramecia only in water; paramecia move with cilia, amoebas move with pseudopods; paramecia ingest food into an oral groove, amoebas surround food with pseudopods; amoebas have one nucleus, paramecia have two.*)

Apply Ask: **What characteristics make the amoeba suited to life in either soil or water?** (*Sample answer: It can change its shape and flow easily through different substances. The contractile vacuole allows excess water to be expelled.*) **What characteristics make the paramecium suited to living only in water?** (*Sample answer: Its two contractile vacuoles remove excess water from the cell. Their cilia, which move the paramecium through water and sweep food into the oral groove, may not be as effective in a solid environment such as soil. Their rigid shape may hinder movement through compact soil.*) **learning modality: visual**

All in One Teaching Resources
• Transparencies A19, A20

Differentiated Instruction

Gifted and Talented [L3]
Investigating Protozoan Groups
Provide books or online sources on ciliate and sarcodine (amoeba) protozoans. Have students prepare and present a visual display that highlights the features of one of the two groups: the variety of protozoans in the group, what they eat, whether any cause disease to humans, and so forth. **learning modality: visual**

Less Proficient Readers [L1]
Identifying Protozoan Structures
Provide students with a list of amoeba and paramecium structures presented in Figures 3 and 4, and an accompanying list of their descriptions. Have students match structures with descriptions as they observe Figures 3 and 4 or the relevant transparencies. **learning modality: visual**

Monitor Progress [L2]

Oral Presentation Have students compare and contrast the characteristics of an amoeba and a paramecium.
Answers

 Reading Checkpoint Hairlike projections from cells that move with a wavelike motion

Modeling Animal-Like Protists

Materials clay, paint, string, pipe cleaners, cardboard, and other materials of students' choice

Time 30 minutes

Focus Challenge small groups to design models of one of the four kinds of animal-like protists.

Teach Have students consult photos in the text or in reference materials. Models should include unique details for each organism, with labels. Have students compare and contrast the models, explaining similarities and differences. They should note the structures, shapes, and methods of movement of the various animal-like protozoans.

Apply Challenge groups to use their models to demonstrate how these organisms move or feed. **learning modality: kinesthetic**

Integrating Health   L1

Avoiding Health Threats of Parasites in Water

Ask students to describe ways that hikers can avoid ingesting *Giardia.* (*Sample answers: Carry enough water, use water purifying treatments, boil water before using.*) Inform students that the safest way to purify water of organisms is to boil it for at least three minutes. This will kill the organisms, but it will not necessarily make the water safe if the water also contains chemical pollutants. **learning modality: verbal**

FIGURE 5
Giardia
When people drink from freshwater streams and lakes, they can get hiker's disease. *Giardia intestinalis* (inset) is the protozoan responsible for this disease. *Inferring Why is it important for hikers to filter stream water?*

FIGURE 6
Malaria Mosquito
Anopheles mosquitoes can carry the parasitic protozoan *Plasmodium,* which causes malaria in people.

78 ◆ A

Protozoans With Flagella The third group of protozoans are flagellates (FLAJ uh lits), protists that use long, whiplike flagella to move. A flagellate may have one or more flagella.

Some of these protozoans live inside the bodies of other organisms. For example, one type of flagellate lives in the intestines of termites. There, they digest the wood that the termites eat, producing sugars for themselves and for the termites. In turn, the termites protect the protozoans. The interaction between these two species is an example of **symbiosis** (sim bee OH sis)—a close relationship in which at least one of the species benefits. When both partners benefit from living together, the relationship is a type of symbiosis called **mutualism.**

Sometimes, however, a protozoan harms its host. For example, *Giardia* is a parasite in humans. Wild animals, such as beavers, deposit *Giardia* in freshwater streams, rivers, and lakes. When a person drinks water containing *Giardia,* these protozoans attach to the person's intestine, where they feed and reproduce. The person develops a serious intestinal condition commonly called hiker's disease.

Protozoans That Are Parasites The fourth type of protozoans are characterized more by the way they live than by the way they move. They are all parasites that feed on the cells and body fluids of their hosts. These protozoans move in a variety of ways. Some have flagella, and some depend on hosts for transport. One even produces a layer of slime that allows it to slide from place to place!

Many of these parasites have more than one host. For example, *Plasmodium* is a protozoan that causes malaria, a disease of the blood. Two hosts are involved in *Plasmodium's* life cycle—humans and a species of mosquitoes found in tropical areas. The disease spreads when a healthy mosquito bites a person with malaria, becomes infected, and then bites a healthy person. Symptoms of malaria include high fevers that alternate with severe chills. These symptoms can last for weeks, then disappear, only to reappear a few months later.

✓ **Reading Checkpoint** **What is symbiosis?**

Plantlike Protists

Plantlike protists, which are commonly called **algae** (AL jee), are extremely diverse. **Like plants, algae are autotrophs.** Most are able to use the sun's energy to make their own food.

Algae play a significant role in many environments. For example, algae that live near the surface of ponds, lakes, and oceans are an important food source for other organisms in the water. In addition, much of the oxygen in Earth's atmosphere is made by these algae.

Algae vary greatly in size. Some algae are unicellular, while others are multicellular. Still others are groups of unicellular organisms that live together in colonies. Colonies can contain from a few cells up to thousands of cells. In a colony, most cells carry out all functions. But, some cells may become specialized to perform certain functions, such as reproduction.

Algae exist in a wide variety of colors because they contain many types of **pigments**—chemicals that produce color. Depending on their pigments, algae can be green, yellow, red, brown, orange, or even black.

Diatoms Diatoms are unicellular protists with beautiful glasslike cell walls. Some float near the surface of lakes or oceans. Others attach to objects such as rocks in shallow water. Diatoms are a food source for heterotrophs in the water. Many diatoms can move by oozing chemicals out of slits in their cell walls. They then glide in the slime.

When diatoms die, their cell walls collect on the bottoms of oceans and lakes. Over time, they form layers of a coarse substance called diatomaceous (dy uh tuh MAY shus) earth. Diatomaceous earth makes a good polishing agent and is used in household scouring products. It is even used as an insecticide—the diatoms' sharp cell walls puncture the bodies of insects.

Dinoflagellates Dinoflagellates (dy noh FLAJ uh lits) are unicellular algae surrounded by stiff plates that look like a suit of armor. Because they have different amounts of green, orange, and other pigments, dinoflagellates exist in a variety of colors.

All dinoflagellates have two flagella held in grooves between their plates. When the flagella beat, the dinoflagellates twirl like toy tops as they move through the water. Many glow in the dark. They light up the ocean's surface when disturbed by a passing boat or swimmer.

Flagella

FIGURE 7
Dinoflagellates
Dinoflagellates whirl through the water with their flagella.

Chapter 3 A ◆ 79

Build **Inquiry**

L2

Building Models of Algae

Materials none

Time 15 minutes

Focus Direct students to make a "living" model of how algae of various sizes take in food and eliminate waste.

Teach Divide the class into three groups: unicellular algae, multicellular algae, and a colony of algae. Have each student act out the role of an individual algae cell. Give each group a deck of cards to use as a food source, and encourage the "cells" to act out how each organism accomplishes food intake and waste elimination.

Apply Have students describe food intake and waste elimination in terms of whether they are individual or cooperative processes. (*Sample answers: unicellular: individual students pick up and put down cards without interacting; multicellular: cooperative model—one student picks up a card and passes it on, another puts it down; colony: both individual and cooperative.* **learning modality: kinesthetic**

Help Students Read

Summarizing Summarizing the information presented in the text will help students to focus on main ideas and remember what they read. Have students read the paragraphs describing the types of plantlike protists and summarize them by restating the main ideas in their own words.

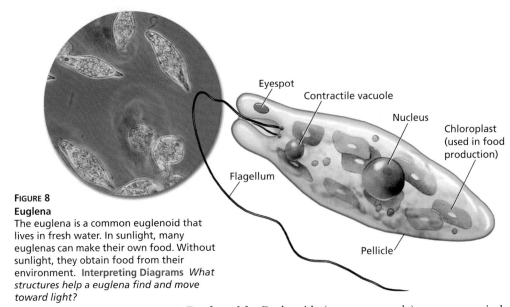

FIGURE 8
Euglena
The euglena is a common euglenoid that lives in fresh water. In sunlight, many euglenas can make their own food. Without sunlight, they obtain food from their environment. **Interpreting Diagrams** *What structures help a euglena find and move toward light?*

Skills **Activity**

Predicting

Predict what will happen when you pour a culture of euglena into a petri dish, and then cover half the dish with aluminum foil. Give a reason for your prediction.

Then carry out the experiment with a culture of euglena in a plastic petri dish. Cover half the dish with aluminum foil. After 10 minutes, uncover the dish. What do you observe? Was your prediction correct? Explain why euglena behave this way.

Euglenoids Euglenoids (yoo GLEE noydz) are green, unicellular algae that are found mostly in fresh water. Unlike other algae, euglenoids have one animal-like characteristic—they can be heterotrophs under certain conditions. When sunlight is available, most euglenoids are autotrophs that produce their own food. However, when sunlight is not available, euglenoids will act like heterotrophs by obtaining food from their environment. Some euglenoids live entirely as heterotrophs.

In Figure 8, you see a euglena, which is a common euglenoid. Notice the long, whiplike flagellum that helps the organism move. Locate the eyespot near the flagellum. Although the eyespot is not really an eye, it contains pigments. These pigments are sensitive to light and help the euglena recognize the direction of a light source. You can imagine how important this response is to an organism that needs light to make food.

Red Algae Almost all red algae are multicellular seaweeds. Divers have found red algae growing more than 260 meters below the ocean's surface. Their red pigments are especially good at absorbing the small amount of light that is able to reach deep ocean waters.

People use red algae in a variety of ways. Carrageenan (ka ruh JEE nun) and agar, substances extracted from red algae, are used in products such as ice cream and hair conditioner. For people in many Asian cultures, red algae is a nutrient-rich food that is eaten fresh, dried, or toasted.

80 ◆ A

Skills **Activity**

Skills Focus Predicting   L2

Materials euglena culture, plastic petri dish, aluminum foil, compound microscope

Time 20 minutes

Tips Tell students to record their predictions and the reasons for them.

Expected Outcome Students will probably predict that the euglena will move toward the light because it needs light to make food. The result of the experiment will confirm this prediction. The covered area will no longer be green, because the euglena have moved to the uncovered area and the light.

Extend Ask students to identify the source of the green tint of the euglena culture. (*Chloroplasts*) **learning modality: visual**

FIGURE 9
Green Algae
Green algae range in size from unicellular organisms to multicellular seaweeds. This multicellular sea lettuce, *Ulva*, lives in oceans.

Green Algae Green algae, which contain green pigments, are quite diverse. Most green algae are unicellular. Some, however, form colonies, and a few are multicellular. Most green algae live in either fresh water or salt water. The few that live on land are found on rocks, in the crevices of tree bark, or in moist soils.

Green algae are actually very closely related to plants that live on land. Green algae and plants contain the same type of green pigment and share other important similarities. In fact, some scientists think that green algae belong in the plant kingdom.

Brown Algae Many of the organisms that are commonly called seaweeds are brown algae. In addition to their brown pigment, brown algae also contain green, yellow, and orange pigments. As you can see in Figure 10, a typical brown alga has many plantlike structures. Holdfasts anchor the alga to rocks. Stalks support the blades, which are the leaflike structures of the alga. Many brown algae also have gas-filled sacs called bladders that allow the algae to float upright in the water.

Brown algae flourish in cool, rocky waters. Brown algae called rockweed live along the Atlantic coast of North America. Giant kelps, which can grow as long as 100 meters, live in some Pacific coastal waters. The giant kelps form large underwater "forests" where many organisms, including sea otters and abalone, live.

Some people eat brown algae. In addition, substances called algins are extracted from brown algae and used as thickeners in puddings and other foods.

 Reading Checkpoint What color pigments can brown algae contain?

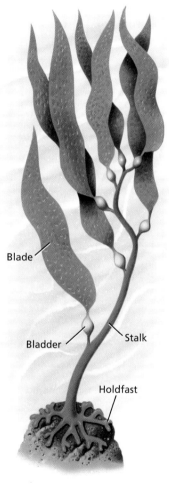

Blade

Bladder

Stalk

Holdfast

FIGURE 10
Brown Algae
Giant kelps are brown algae that have many plantlike structures.
Interpreting Diagrams *What plant structures do the kelp's holdfasts and blades resemble?*

Use Visuals: Figure 8 L1
Euglena

Focus Emphasize that a unicellular organism can have functional structures.

Teach Ask: **How many cells does a euglena have?** *(One)* Point out that structures such as flagella, the eyespot, and the chloroplast are all part of the same cell. Some students may be confused that a unicellular organism has so many parts. Explain that a cell is the smallest structure capable of performing all the functions required for life.

Apply Ask: **Is the cell shown in the figure specialized to do certain tasks?** *(No, it performs all the functions necessary to maintain the euglena's life.)* **learning modality: visual**

Address Misconceptions
Red Algae Are Not Always Red

Focus Explain that algae contain other pigments in addition to the dominant pigment. The combination of pigments creates a great variety of colors.

Teach Students may think that all green algae look green, all red algae look red, and all brown algae look brown. Inform them that although these algae contain the pigment in their names, they also contain other pigments, sometimes in such concentrations that, for example, a red alga may actually look pink or purple.

Apply Remind students that plant leaves also contain pigments. Ask: **What is the function of the pigments in algae and in plant leaves?** *(They absorb light needed for the algae and plants to make food.)* **learning modality: verbal**

Monitor Progress L2

Writing Ask students to describe the characteristics of diatoms, euglenoids, or red algae. Students can save their descriptions in their portfolios.

 Portfolio

Answers
Figure 8 The eyespot helps the euglena find light, and the flagellum helps the euglena move toward light.
Figure 10 The holdfasts resemble roots and the blades resemble leaves.

 Reading Checkpoint Brown, green, yellow, and orange.

Differentiated Instruction

Special Needs L1
Identifying Protists Display in stations around the room pictures of various protists, such as slime molds, paramecia, euglenoids, diatoms, and algae. Have small groups list on index cards the characteristics they observe in the pictures. Next display three headings on the board: animal-like protists, plantlike protists, and funguslike protists. Have students attach under the appropriate headings the index cards containing the protist traits observed in the pictures. Discuss any overlap of traits among the protist groups, and ask students if it is possible to create an operational definition of a protist. **learning modality: visual**

Funguslike Protists

Teach Key Concepts

Exploring Funguslike Protists

Focus Review with students the characteristics of fungi: heterotrophs, have cell walls, use spores to reproduce.

Teach With students, prepare a chart or start a Venn diagram to show basic characteristics of plants, animals, and fungi. Illustrate your answers: **How are funguslike protists like animals?** (*They are heterotrophs.*) **How are they like plants?** (*Their cells have cell walls; they use spores to reproduce.*) **Which of these traits do fungi also exhibit?** (*They have cell walls, are heterotrophs, and, reproduce with spores*)

Apply Ask: **How have funguslike protists caused human deaths?** (*Water molds destroyed the Irish potato crops in 1845 and 1846, triggering starvation.*) **learning modality: visual**

Observing Slime Mold

Materials compound microscope, slime mold culture, plastic petri dish with cover, oatmeal

Time 15 minutes for setup, 10 minutes for observation after 24 hours

Focus Tell students that individual slime mold cells can join together and respond to stimuli as a giant mass.

Teach Pair students; give each pair a covered petri dish containing slime mold culture to observe under the microscope. Ask students to predict how slime molds will react when oatmeal is placed in the dish. Students can test predictions by uncovering the dish, putting a few flakes about 1 mm from a branch of the slime mold, and putting the cover back on. After 24 hours in a cool, dark place, the slime mold should increase in size, spread across, and engulf the oatmeal.

Apply Ask: **What did you observe that suggests the slime mold is alive?** (*It moved toward the oatmeal and engulfed it.*) **learning modality: visual**

Funguslike Protists

The third group of protists are the funguslike protists. Recall from Chapter 1 that fungi include organisms such as mushrooms and yeast. Until you learn more about fungi in Section 3, you can think of fungi as the "sort of like" organisms. Fungi are "sort of like" animals because they are heterotrophs. They are "sort of like" plants because their cells have cell walls. In addition, most fungi use spores to reproduce. A **spore** is a tiny cell that is able to grow into a new organism.

Like fungi, funguslike protists are heterotrophs, have cell walls, and use spores to reproduce. All funguslike protists are able to move at some point in their lives. The three types of funguslike protists are slime molds, water molds, and downy mildews.

Slime Molds Slime molds are often brilliantly colored. They live on forest floors and other moist, shady places. They ooze along the surfaces of decaying materials, feeding on bacteria and other microorganisms. Some slime molds are so small that you need a microscope to see them. Others may cover an area of several meters!

Slime molds begin their life cycle as tiny, individual amoeba-like cells. The cells use pseudopods to feed and creep around. Later, the cells grow bigger or join together to form a giant, jellylike mass. In some species, the giant mass is multicellular and forms when food is scarce. In others, the giant mass is actually a giant cell with many nuclei.

The mass oozes along as a single unit. When environmental conditions become harsh, spore-producing structures grow out of the mass and release spores. Eventually the spores develop into a new generation of slime molds.

Figure 11
Slime Molds
The chocolate tube slime mold first forms a tapioca-like mass (top). When conditions become harsh, the mass grows spore-producing stalks (right). The stalks, or "chocolate tubes," are covered with millions of brown spores.

Water Molds and Downy Mildews Most water molds and downy mildews live in water or moist places. These organisms often grow as tiny threads that look like fuzz. Figure 12 shows a fish attacked by a water mold and a leaf covered by downy mildew.

Water molds and downy mildews attack many food crops, such as potatoes, corn, and grapes. A water mold impacted history when it destroyed the Irish potato crops in 1845 and 1846. The loss of these crops led to a famine. More than one million people in Ireland died, and many others moved to the United States and other countries.

▲ Water mold on fish

▼ Downy mildew on grape leaf

 Reading Checkpoint In what environments are water molds found?

FIGURE 12
Water Molds and Downy Mildews
Many water molds are decomposers of dead aquatic organisms. Others are parasites of fish and other animals. Downy mildews are parasites of many food crops.

Section 1 Assessment

Target Reading Skill Outlining Use your outline about protists to help you answer the questions below.

Reviewing Key Concepts

1. **a. Listing** List the four types of animal-like protists. How does each type move or live?
   b. Comparing and Contrasting How are these four types of protists similar to animals? How are they different?
   c. Classifying You observe an animal-like protist under the microscope. It has no hairlike or whiplike structures. It moves by forming temporary bulges of cytoplasm. How would you classify this protist?

2. **a. Reviewing** In what way are diatoms, dinoflagellates, and other plantlike protists similar to plants?
   b. Making Generalizations Why is sunlight important to plantlike protists?
   c. Making Judgments Would you classify euglena as an animal-like protist or as a plantlike protist? Explain.

3. **a. Listing** What are the three types of funguslike protists?
   b. Describing In what ways are funguslike protists similar to fungi?

Lab zone At-Home Activity

Algae Scavenger Hunt Look around your house with a family member to find products that contain substances made from algae. Look at both food and nonfood items. Before you begin, tell your family member that substances such as diatomaceous earth, algin, and carrageenan are products that come from algae. Make a list of the products and the algae-based ingredient they contain. Share your list with the class.

Answers

Reading Checkpoint In water or moist places

Assess

Reviewing Key Concepts

1. a. Protozoans with pseudopods, protozoans with cilia, protozoans with flagella, protozoans that are parasites **b.** Similar to animals: they are heterotrophs that can move from place to place; different: they are unicellular. **c.** As a protozoan with pseudopods.
2. a. They are autotrophs. **b.** Their pigments absorb the sunlight, which they need to make food. **c.** Possible answer: Although euglena have animal-like and plantlike characteristics, they should probably be classified as plantlike protists because they have the unique ability to make thier own food.
3. a. Slime molds, water molds, downy mildews **b.** They are heterotrophs, have cell walls, and use spores to reproduce.

Reteach L1
Discuss the characteristics shared by all protists, then use a "quiz bowl" format to classify protists by animal-like, plantlike, and funguslike traits.

Performance Assessment L2
Writing Ask students to imagine they are a paramecium. Have them write a short story of their encounters with other microscopic life forms such as amoebas, euglenoids, slime molds, and other protists. Encourage students to describe how these organisms behave and how to identify them.

Students can save their stories in their portfolios.

All in One Teaching Resources
• Section Summary: *Protists*
• Review and Reinforce: *Protists*
• Enrich: *Protists*

Lab zone At-Home Activity

Algae Scavenger Hunt L1 Encourage students to explain to family members that algae can be found in many products such as ice cream, hair conditioners, toothpaste, and scouring products. Students may wish to see who can find the most products containing algae.

2 Algal Blooms

Objectives

After completing the lesson, students will be able to

A.3.2.1 Describe the causes and effects of red tides.

A.3.2.2 Describe the causes and effects of eutrophication.

Target Reading Skill

Comparing and Contrasting Explain that comparing and contrasting information shows how ideas, facts, and events are similar and different. The results of the comparison can have importance.

Answers

Saltwater blooms—Effects: Toxins concentrated in fish and shellfish that eat algae can cause illness to people and other large organisms when they consume the fish or shellfish. Freshwater blooms—Causes: Nutrients build up, causing a rapid increase in algae growth; Effect: Fishes and other organisms in the water die.

All in One Teaching Resources

• Transparency A23

Preteach

Build Background Knowledge L2

Visualizing Abundant Algae

Remind students that algae live on the surface of ponds, lakes, and oceans. Ask: **What do you think would happen if there were so many algae on the water's surface that they blocked sunlight from getting into the water?** (*Sample: The organisms in the water that need sunlight to make food would die.*)

Reading Preview

Key Concept

• What are the causes and effects of saltwater and freshwater algal blooms?

Key Terms

• algal bloom
• red tide
• eutrophication

Target Reading Skill

Comparing and Contrasting As you read, compare and contrast the two types of algal blooms in a table like the one below.

Algal Blooms

Properties	Saltwater Blooms	Freshwater Blooms
Causes	Increase in nutrients or temperature	
Effects		

Lab zone Discover Activity

How Can Algal Growth Affect Pond Life?

1. Pour water into a plastic petri dish until the dish is half full. The petri dish will represent a pond.
2. Sprinkle a spoonful of green paper punches into the water to represent green algae growing in a pond.
3. Sprinkle two more spoonfuls of paper punches into the water to represent one cycle of algae reproduction.
4. Sprinkle four more spoonfuls of paper punches into the water to represent the next reproduction cycle of the algae.

Think It Over

Predicting How might algae growing near the surface affect organisms living deep in a pond?

Over a five week period one year, the bodies of 14 humpback whales washed up along beaches on Cape Cod, Massachusetts. The whales showed no outward signs of sickness. Their stomachs were full of food. Their bodies contained plenty of blubber to insulate them from changes in water temperature. What caused such seemingly healthy animals to die?

When biologists examined the dead whales' tissues, they identified the cause of the puzzling deaths. The whales' cells contained a deadly toxin produced by a dinoflagellate called *Alexandrium tamarense*. The population of these algae had grown rapidly in the ocean waters through which the whales were migrating. When the whales fed on the toxin-producing algae or on fishes that had eaten the algae, the toxins reached a deadly level and killed the whales.

Algae are common in oceans, lakes, and ponds. They float near the surface of the waters and use sunlight to make food. The rapid growth of a population of algae is called an **algal bloom.** Algal blooms can occur in both saltwater and freshwater environments. **In general, algal blooms occur when nutrients increase in the water.**

◀ A humpback whale

84 ◆ A

Lab zone Discover Activity

Skills Focus Predicting L1

Materials clear plastic container, water, green paper punches, spoons

Time 15 minutes

Tips Use a hole punch to make green paper punches. After students complete their models, ask: **What does your model show about how algae can grow on a** pond? (*How rapidly the number of algae can increase*)

Expected Outcome The green paper punches will eventually cover the surface of the water.

Think It Over If algae cover the pond's surface, less light and air will reach the bottom, and organisms deep in the pond will die.

Saltwater Blooms

In Figure 13, you see an algal bloom in ocean water. Saltwater algal blooms are commonly called **red tides** because the algae that grow rapidly often contain red pigments and turn the color of the water red. But red tides do not always look red. Some red tides are brown, green, or even colorless, depending on the species of algae that blooms. Dinoflagellates and diatoms are two algae that frequently bloom in red tides.

Causes of Red Tides Scientists are not sure why some populations of saltwater algae increase rapidly at times. But red tides occur most often when there is an increase in nutrients in the water. Some red tides occur regularly in certain seasons. For example, the cold bottom layers of the ocean contain a lot of nutrients. When this cold water mixes with the surface waters, more nutrients become available to surface organisms. With greater concentrations of nutrients present in the surface waters, blooms of algae occur. Increases in ocean temperature due to climate changes also affect the occurrence of red tides.

Effects of Red Tides Red tides are dangerous when the toxins that the algae produce become concentrated in the bodies of organisms that consume the algae. Shellfish, such as clams and mussels, feed on large numbers of the algae and store the toxins in their cells. Fishes may also feed on the algae and store the toxins. When people or other large organisms eat these shellfish and fishes, it may lead to severe illness or even death. Public health officials close beaches in areas of red tides to prevent people from fishing or gathering shellfish.

 Reading Checkpoint What determines the color of saltwater blooms?

FIGURE 13
Red Tide
Rapid algae growth has caused a red tide in this small bay off the coast of California. Blooms of toxic dinoflagellates such as *Gymnodinium* (inset) can have serious consequences.
Relating Cause and Effect *What organisms are affected by red tides?*

Go Online
SciLINKS
For: Links on algae
Visit: www.SciLinks.org
Web Code: scn-0132

Saltwater Blooms

Teach Key Concepts   L2
Exploring Algal Blooms in Salt Water

Focus Explain that scientists know only general causes of red tides.

Teach Ask: **Why are saltwater algal blooms called "red tides"?** (*Because the algae that form them often contain red pigments that turn the water red*) **Under what water conditions are red tides most likely to occur?** (*When nutrients in the water increase; sometimes seasonally, or when water temperatures increase with changes in climate conditions*) **When and how can red tides prove dangerous to humans?** (*Algae that form red tides may produce toxins harmful to people; these toxins build up in shellfish and fish that eat the algae. People that eat organisms containing the toxins can die or become seriously ill.*)

Apply Ask: **What function does the red pigment provide the algae in red tides?** (*The ability to absorb sunlight so that the algae can make their own food*) **learning modality: verbal**

Independent Practice   L2

All in One Teaching Resources

• Guided Reading and Study Worksheet: *Algal Blooms*

⊙ **Student Edition on Audio CD**

Go Online
SciLINKS
For: Links on algae
Visit: www.SciLinks.org
Web Code: scn-0132

Download a worksheet that will guide students' review of Internet resources on algae.

Differentiated Instruction

Gifted and Talented   L3
Flowcharts Have small groups of students create large flowcharts that show the processes that cause red tides and eutrophication. Tell them to include pictures that they draw or get from magazines or the Internet. Remind them to include both natural events and human activities that affect each process. **learning modality: logical/mathematical**

Special Needs   L1
Describing Red Tides Allow students needing extra instruction to work with those completing the Gifted and Talented exercise. Students can assist in gathering pictures and organizing them for the display. **learning modality: visual**

Monitor Progress _____ L2

Answers
Figure 13 Fish, other organisms in the water, and people

 Reading Checkpoint Pigments contained by the species of algae that bloom

A ● 85

Freshwater Blooms

Teach Key Concepts L2

Examining Freshwater Blooms

Focus Ask students to observe the thick layer of algae in Figure 14.

Teach Define *eutrophication* and discuss how it can be harmful to bodies of water. Ask: **When does eutrophication occur?** *(When excess nutrients build up, causing algae to grow)* **What human sources increase eutrophication?** *(Fertilizer runoff; sewage treatment wastewater)* **Why do pond organisms die with eutrophication?** *(Plants and algae beneath the surface can't make food; they die and their decomposers use up oxygen needed by other organisms, such as fish.)*

Apply Ask: **How are saltwater and freshwater blooms similar?** *(Both occur when nutrients in water increase.)* **learning modality: verbal**

Monitor Progress L2

Answer

 Eutrophication

Assess

Reviewing Key Concepts

1. a. Rapid growth of a population of algae **b.** Ocean: increased nutrients, change in water temperatures; organisms that eat algae build up toxins harmful to organisms that eat them. Lake: increased nutrients from natural and human activities (fertilizer, sewage); organisms die from lack of food and oxygen. **c.** Freshwater blooms—smaller areas, easier to identify nutrient sources and measure effects.

Reteach L1

Sketch flow charts illustrating the processes that occur in both types of algal blooms.

 **Teaching Resources**

- Section Summary: *Algal Blooms*
- Review and Reinforce: *Algal Blooms*
- Enrich: *Algal Blooms*

FIGURE 14
Eutrophication
The thick layer of algae on the surface of a pond can threaten other organisms in the water.

Freshwater Blooms

Have you ever seen a pond or lake that looked as if it was coated with a layer of green paint or scum? The green layer usually consists of huge numbers of green algae.

Lakes and ponds undergo natural processes of change over time. **Eutrophication** (yoo troh fih KAY shun) is a process in which nutrients, such as nitrogen and phosphorus, build up in a lake or pond over time, causing an increase in algae growth.

Causes of Eutrophication Certain natural events and human activities can increase the rate of eutrophication. For example, when farmers and homeowners spread fertilizers on fields and lawns, some of the nutrients can run off into nearby lakes and ponds. Sewage treatment plants can leak wastewater into the soil. The nutrients in the wastewater make their way from the soil into water that leads into lakes and ponds. These events cause a rapid increase in algae growth. If the nutrient sources can be eliminated and the nutrients used up, eutrophication slows to its natural rate.

Effects of Eutrophication Eutrophication triggers a series of events with serious consequences. First, the layer of algae prevents sunlight from reaching plants and other algae beneath the surface. Those organisms die and sink to the bottom. Then decomposers, such as bacteria, which break down the bodies of the dead organisms, increase in number. Soon the bacteria use up the oxygen in the water. Without oxygen, fishes and other organisms in the water die. About the only organisms that survive are the algae on the surface.

Reading Checkpoint What natural process of change occurs over time in a pond or a lake?

Section 2 Assessment

Target Reading Skill Comparing and Contrasting Use the information in your table about algal blooms to help you answer the questions below.

Reviewing Key Concepts

1. a. Defining What is an algal bloom?
b. Comparing and Contrasting What might cause an algal bloom to occur in an ocean? In a lake? How would the algal bloom affect organisms living in each?
c. Predicting Would it be easier to control saltwater or freshwater blooms? Explain.

Writing in Science

News Report Something strange has happened to the local pond. It is covered with green scum and dead fish are floating on the surface. You have interviewed scientists about possible causes. Write a news report explaining to the public what has happened.

 Chapter Project

Keep Students on Track By now, your teacher should have approved your plan, and you should have started growing your mushrooms. Make careful observations of growth daily, including appropriate sketches and measurements. Use a table to organize the data you collect. (*Hint:* As you make your observations, be careful not to disturb the experiment or introduce any new variables.)

Writing in Science

Writing Mode Description
Scoring Rubric
4 Includes definition of *eutrophication*, explains causes and effects; tone is clear and engaging.
3 Includes all criteria; writing not engaging
2 Minimally covers criteria
1 Includes inaccurate or incomplete information

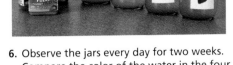

Lab zone Skills Lab

An Explosion of Life

Problem
How does the amount of fertilizer affect algae growth?

Skills Focus
controlling variables, drawing conclusions, predicting

Materials
- 4 glass jars with lids
- marking pen
- aged tap water
- aquarium water
- graduated cylinder
- liquid fertilizer

Procedure

1. Read through the steps in the procedure. Then write a prediction describing what you think will happen in each of the four jars.
2. Copy the data table into your notebook. Be sure to allow enough lines to make entries for a two-week period.
3. Label four jars A, B, C, and D. Fill each jar half full with aged tap water.
4. Add aquarium water to each jar until the jar is three-fourths full.
5. Add 3 mL of liquid fertilizer to jar B, 6 mL to jar C, and 12 mL to jar D. Do not add any fertilizer to jar A. Loosely screw the lid on each jar. Place all the jars in a sunny location where they will receive the same amount of direct sunlight.

6. Observe the jars every day for two weeks. Compare the color of the water in the four jars. Record your observations.

Analyze and Conclude

1. **Observing** How did the color in the four jars compare at the end of the two-week period? Did your observations match your prediction?
2. **Controlling Variables** What was the purpose of jar A? Explain.
3. **Drawing Conclusions** How can you account for any color differences among the four jars? What process and organisms were responsible for causing that color change?
4. **Predicting** Predict what would have happened if you placed the four jars in a dark location instead of in sunlight. Explain your prediction.
5. **Communicating** Write a warning label to be placed on a bag of fertilizer. On the label, explain what might happen to fish and other organisms if the fertilizer gets into a body of fresh water. Also, outline steps consumers can take to prevent these problems.

Design an Experiment
Some detergents contain phosphates, which are also found in many kinds of fertilizer. Design an experiment to compare how regular detergent and low-phosphate detergent affect the growth of algae. *Obtain your teacher's permission before carrying out your investigation.*

Data Table				
	Observations			
Day	Jar A (no fertilizer)	Jar B (3 mL of fertilizer)	Jar C (6 mL of fertilizer)	Jar D (12 mL of fertilizer)
Day 1				
Day 2				

Analyze and Conclude

1. Jar D was the darkest green, with jars C and B increasingly lighter, and jar A the lightest. Answers regarding predictions will vary.

2. Jar A served as the control.

3. The difference: fertilizer input. Eutrophication—increased nutrients causing rapid algal growth—caused the color changes.

4. Without light for algae to make food, jars would stay the same as the first day.

5. Labels should explain that fertilizer runoff speeds up algal growth, which eventually kills pond plants and animals. Consumers can prevent fertilizer runoff by using appropriate amounts, applying according to directions, and ensuring runoff is contained.

Lab zone Skills Lab L2

An Explosion of Life

Prepare for Inquiry

Skills Objectives
After this lab, students will be able to
- control variables;
- predict relative algae growth;
- draw conclusions about nutrient use.

🕐 **Prep Time** 30 minutes
Class Time 30 minutes first day; 10 minutes per day on subsequent days

Advance Planning
The tap water should stand for 3 days before the lab.

Safety
Review the safety guidelines in Appendix A. Dispose of the algae and all other materials according to the proper procedures. Be sure to check your district's and state's guidelines for the proper disposal of algal cultures.

All in One Teaching Resources
- Lab Worksheet: *An Explosion of Life*

Guide Inquiry

Invitation
Ask students what agricultural runoff after a rainstorm might contain. *(Soil, fertilizers)* Students will test the effect of fertilizer on algal growth.

Introduce the Procedure
Provide a display of the four labeled jars, filled to the appropriate levels, and the correct measures of fertilizer.

Extend Inquiry

Design an Experiment Use regular detergent in one set of jars and low-phosphate detergent in another.

Expected Outcome
Algae will grow fastest in jar D and slowest in jar A.

Objectives

After completing the lesson, students will be able to

A.3.3.1 Name the characteristics fungi share.

A.3.3.2 Explain how fungi reproduce.

A.3.3.3 Describe the roles fungi play in nature.

Target Reading Skill

Asking Questions Explain that changing a head into a question helps students anticipate the ideas, facts, and events they are about to read.

Answers

Possible questions and answers are:
What are fungi? *(Fungi are eukaryotes that have cell walls, are heterotrophs that feed by absorbing their food, and use spores to reproduce.)* **How do fungi reproduce?** *(Fungi usually reproduce by making spores.)* **What is the role of fungi in nature?** *(Fungi are important decomposers and recyclers.)*

All in One Teaching Resources

• Transparency A24

Preteach

Build Background Knowledge L2

Considering Mushroom Habitat

Ask students to describe what they know about how mushrooms grow. Some students may have seen mushrooms growing in the woods, while others may have seen cultivated mushrooms. Encourage students to think about how mushrooms are similar to plants.

Section 3 — Fungi

Reading Preview

Key Concepts
• What characteristics do fungi share?
• How do fungi reproduce?
• What roles do fungi play in nature?

Key Terms
• fungi • hyphae
• fruiting body • budding
• lichen

Target Reading Skill

Asking Questions Before you read, preview the red headings. In a graphic organizer like the one below, ask a *what* or *how* question for each heading. As you read, write answers to your questions.

Fungi

Question	Answer
What are fungi?	Fungi are . . .

Lab zone — Discover Activity

Do All Molds Look Alike?

1. Your teacher will give you two sealed, clear plastic bags—one containing moldy bread and another containing moldy fruit. **CAUTION:** *Do not open the sealed bags at any time.*
2. In your notebook, describe what you see.
3. Next, use a hand lens to examine each mold. Sketch each mold in your notebook and list its characteristics.
4. Return the sealed bags to your teacher. Wash your hands.

Think It Over
Observing How are the molds similar? How do they differ?

Unnoticed, a speck of dust lands on a cricket's back. But this is no ordinary dust—it is alive! Tiny glistening threads emerge from the dust and begin to grow into the cricket's moist body. As they grow, the threads release chemicals that slowly dissolve the cricket's tissues. Within a few days, the cricket's body is little more than a hollow shell filled with a tangle of the deadly threads. Then the threads begin to grow up and out of the dead cricket. They produce long stalks with knobs at their tips. When one of the knobs breaks open, it will release thousands of dustlike specks, which the wind can carry to new victims.

What Are Fungi?

The strange cricket-killing organism is a member of the fungi kingdom. Although you may not have heard of a cricket-killing fungus before, you are probably familiar with other kinds of fungi. For example, the molds that grow on stale bread and the mushrooms that sprout in yards are all fungi.

▶ A bush cricket attacked by a killer fungus.

Lab zone — Discover Activity

Skills Focus Observing **L1**

Materials Self-seal bags, tape, hand lens, old bread, fruit

Time 15 minutes

Tips At least one week before the activity, place pieces of moist bread and fruit in separate self-seal bags. Seal the bags, then make an extra seal with tape. Keep bags in a dark place at room temperature. Make sure students do not open the bags. Dispose of the sealed bags and all other materials according to proper procedures; check your district's and state's guidelines for proper disposal.

Expected Outcome Observations will depend on the kinds of fungi that grow.

Think It Over The molds will probably have similar threadlike appearances and fruiting bodies but will probably be of different colors.

Most **fungi** share several important characteristics. **Fungi are eukaryotes that have cell walls, are heterotrophs that feed by absorbing their food, and use spores to reproduce.** In addition, fungi need moist, warm places in which to grow. They thrive on moist foods, damp tree barks, lawns coated with dew, damp forest floors, and even wet bathroom tiles.

Cell Structure Fungi range in size from tiny unicellular yeasts to large multicellular fungi. The largest known organism on Earth is actually an underground fungus that covers an area as large as a thousand football fields!

The cells of all fungi are surrounded by cell walls. Except for the simplest fungi, such as unicellular yeasts, the cells of most fungi are arranged in structures called hyphae. **Hyphae** (HY fee) (singular hypha) are the branching, thread-like tubes that make up the bodies of multicellular fungi. The hyphae of some fungi are continuous threads of cytoplasm that contain many nuclei. Substances move quickly and freely through the hyphae.

What a fungus looks like depends on how its hyphae are arranged. In some fungi, the threadlike hyphae are loosely tangled. Fuzzy-looking molds that grow on old foods have loosely tangled hyphae. In other fungi, hyphae are packed tightly together. For example, the stalks and caps of the mushrooms shown in Figure 15 are made of hyphae packed so tightly that they appear solid. Underground, however, a mushroom's hyphae form a loose, threadlike maze in the soil.

 Reading Checkpoint **What do the bodies of multicellular fungi consist of?**

FIGURE 15
Structure of a Mushroom
The hyphae in the stalk and cap of a mushroom are packed tightly to form very firm structures. Underground hyphae, are arranged loosely. *Inferring What function might the underground hyphae perform?*

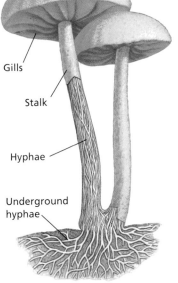

Cap

Gills

Stalk

Hyphae

Underground hyphae

Protists and Fungi

Show the Video Field Trip to help students understand the relationships that fungi have with other organisms. Discussion question: **How do leaf cutter ants build a fungus garden?** *(By crushing pieces of leaves and mixing them with digestive juices, creating a paste. The fungi grow and feed on the paste.)*

Instruct

What are Fungi?

Teach Key Concepts   L2

Identifying Fungi

Focus Ask students what bread mold has in common with the killer fungus shown attacking the bush cricket. *(Possible answer: Both grow on other organisms.)*

Teach Ask: **Which traits are shared by all fungi?** *(Eukaryotic, with cell walls; heterotrophs with similar means of feeding; spores for reproduction)* **Which fungi are unicellular?** *(Yeasts)* **What are hyphae?** *(Branching, threadlike tubes that form the body of multicellular fungi)*

Apply Explain that in most fungi, cytoplasm flows freely through the hyphae because the walls separating cells have a "hole" in them. Ask: **How do hyphae help a fungus in its life processes?** *(By allowing essential materials to move quickly throughout the fungus)* **learning modality: verbal**

All in One Teaching Resources
• Transparency A25

Independent Practice   L2

All in One Teaching Resources
• Guided Reading and Study Worksheet: *Fungi*

⊙ **Student Edition on Audio CD**

Monitor Progress _____   L2

Answers
Figure 15 Anchoring; absorbing materials

 Reading Checkpoint Hyphae

Differentiated Instruction

English Learners/Beginning   L1
Vocabulary: Science Glossary
Pronounce and define aloud for students the Key Terms for this section. Suggest that students start a personal glossary of vocabulary terms, with each term and its definition in English on one side of an index card and in the student's primary language on the other side. To help remember the meanings of the words,

students might draw and label diagrams. **learning modality: verbal**

Less Proficient Readers   L1
Vocabulary: Science Glossary Have students copy section Key Terms, then find and write the definitions as they read the section. Provide an unlabeled copy of Figure 15, and encourage students to add the labels. **learning modality: visual**

Reproduction in Fungi

FIGURE 16
How Fungi Obtain Food
The mold *Penicillium* often grows on old fruits such as oranges. Notice that some hyphae grow deep inside the orange.

Hyphae

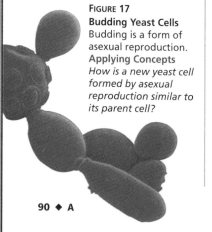

FIGURE 17
Budding Yeast Cells
Budding is a form of asexual reproduction. **Applying Concepts** *How is a new yeast cell formed by asexual reproduction similar to its parent cell?*

90 ◆ A

Obtaining Food Although fungi are heterotrophs, they do not take food into their bodies as you do. Instead, fungi absorb food through hyphae that grow into the food source. Figure 16 shows a mold feeding on an orange.

First, the fungus grows hyphae into a food source. Then digestive chemicals ooze from the hyphae into the food. The chemicals break down the food into small substances that can be absorbed by the hyphae.

As an analogy, imagine sinking your fingers down into a chocolate cake and dripping digestive chemicals out of your fingertips. Then imagine your fingers absorbing the digested cake particles!

Some fungi feed on dead organisms. Other fungi are parasites that break down the chemicals in living organisms.

Reproduction in Fungi

Like it or not, fungi are everywhere. The way they reproduce guarantees their survival and spread. **Fungi usually reproduce by making spores. The lightweight spores are surrounded by a protective covering and can be carried easily through air or water to new sites.** Fungi produce millions of spores, more than can ever survive. Only a few spores will fall where conditions are right for them to grow.

Fungi produce spores in reproductive structures called **fruiting bodies.** The appearances of fruiting bodies vary from one type of fungus to another. For some fungi, such as mushrooms and puffballs, the part of the fungus that you see is the fruiting body. In other fungi, such as bread molds, the fruiting bodies are tiny, stalklike hyphae that grow upward from the rest of the hyphae. A knoblike spore case at the tip of each stalk contains the spores.

Asexual Reproduction Most fungi reproduce both asexually and sexually. When there is adequate moisture and food, the fungi make spores asexually. Cells at the tips of their hyphae divide to form spores. The spores grow into fungi that are genetically identical to the parent.

Unicellular yeast cells undergo a form of asexual reproduction called **budding.** In budding, no spores are produced. Instead, a small yeast cell grows from the body of a parent cell somewhat similar to the way a bud forms on a tree branch. The new cell then breaks away and lives on its own.

Sexual Reproduction Most fungi can also reproduce sexually, especially when growing conditions become unfavorable. In sexual reproduction, the hyphae of two fungi grow together and genetic material is exchanged. Eventually, a new reproductive structure grows from the joined hyphae and produces spores. The spores develop into fungi that differ genetically from either parent.

Classification of Fungi Figure 18 shows three major groups of fungi. The groups are named for the appearance of their reproductive structures. Additional groups include water species that produce spores with flagella and those that form tight associations with plant roots.

 Reading Checkpoint **What is budding?**

FIGURE 18
Classification of Fungi

Three major groups of fungi include sac fungi, club fungi, and zygote fungi. **Comparing and Contrasting** *How do the spore-producing structures of sac fungi and club fungi compare?*

Sac Fungi ▶
Sac fungi produce spores in structures that look like long sacs, such as those at the tips of these hyphae. This group is the largest group of fungi and includes yeasts, morels, truffles, and some fungi that cause plant diseases. Sac fungi also include fungi that make up lichens.

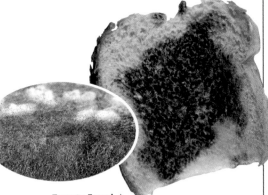

Club Fungi ▲
Club fungi produce spores in microscopic structures that look like clubs. This group includes mushrooms, bracket fungi, and rusts. Club fungi also include puffballs such as these, one of which is releasing its spores. The most poisonous fungi are club fungi.

Zygote Fungi ▲
Zygote fungi produce very resistant spores that can survive harsh environmental conditions. This group contains many common fruit and bread molds, such as this *Rhizopus*, and molds that attack and kill insects.

⌐ Differentiated Instruction

Special Needs L1
Observing Fungi Group students to allow those with differing proficiencies to work together. Give groups a selection of mushrooms from the grocery store, and a hand lens to use to observe them. Challenge students to identify mushroom structures. Have students gently twist off

the cap of one mushroom and break open the stalk from end to end. Ask: **Can you pull threadlike structures from the stalk?** (*Answers may vary depending on the mushroom.*) Tell students that these structures are hyphae. Make sure students wash their hands immediately after the activity. **learning modality: kinesthetic**

Observing Mushroom Spores

Materials mushroom spores in water, eyedropper, microscope, slide, cover slip

Time 15 minutes

Focus Remind students that spores result from reproduction.

Teach Have students use a dropper to place a drop of water with spores on a microscope slide, and cover it with a cover slip. Students can observe the spores under a microscope, and sketch their observations, including the color and shape of the spores.

Apply Ask: **How will the fungi that grow from spores produced sexually differ from the parent plants that produced them?** (*They will be genetically different.*) **learning modality: visual**

Use Visuals: Figure 18 L1
Classification of Fungi

Focus Have students look at the photos as a volunteer reads each caption.

Teach Students may be confused when they look at the puffball, because it does not resemble a club. Inform them that the club-shaped spore cases are microscopic and located inside the puffball. **learning modality: logical/mathematical**

Monitor Progress _____ L2

Writing Have students explain how fungi reproduce sexually and asexually.

Answers
Figure 17 It is genetically identical to its parent.
Figure 18 Sac fungi produce spores in saclike structures; club fungi produce spores on structures that look like clubs.

✔ Reading Checkpoint) A form of asexual reproduction; it does not produce spores.

The Role of Fungi in Nature

Teach Key Concepts

Examining the Diverse Roles of Fungi

Focus Tell students that fungi play many important roles in nature, both helpful and harmful.

Teach Ask: **How are fungi recyclers?** *(They are decomposers, breaking down chemicals in dead organisms and returning them to the soil.)* **How are they eaten as food?** *(Yeasts are used for making breads and wine, molds for making cheeses; many mushrooms are edible, truffles are delicacies.)* **Which types of fungi cause diseases?** *(Parasites in crop plants; athlete's foot and ringworm in humans)* **Which are disease fighters?** *(Those that produce antibiotics, such as* Penicillium*)* **How do fungi live associated with other organisms?** *(In mutualistic relationships with plant roots, or, in lichens, with an alga or bacterium)*

Apply Ask: **Fungi most often share their roles as decomposers, disease agents, and disease fighters with which organisms?** *(Bacteria)* **learning modality: logical/ mathematical**

Help Students Read

Reciprocal Teaching Have students read the section with a partner. One partner reads a paragraph aloud. Then the other partner summarizes the paragraph's contents and explains the main concepts. The partners continue to switch roles with each new paragraph until they have finished the section.

FIGURE 19
Truffles
Pigs are often used to hunt for truffles, a highly prized delicacy. Truffles (inset) are the round fruiting bodies of fungi that grow underground among the roots of certain trees. Some truffles are quite rare and can sell for several thousand dollars per kilogram!

Lab zone Try This **Activity**

Spreading Spores
In this activity, you will make a model of a fruiting body.

1. Break a cotton ball into five equal pieces. Roll each piece into a tiny ball.
2. Insert the cotton balls into a balloon.
3. Repeat Steps 1 and 2 until the balloon is almost full.
4. Inflate the balloon. Tie a knot in its neck. Tape the knotted end of the balloon to a stick.
5. Stand the stick upright in a mound of modeling clay.
6. ✂ Pop the balloon with a pin. Observe what happens.

Making Models Draw a diagram of the model you made. Label the stalk, the spore case, and the spores. Use your model to explain why fungi are found just about everywhere.

92 ◆ A

The Role of Fungi in Nature

Fungi affect humans and other organisms in many ways. **Fungi play important roles as decomposers and recyclers on Earth. Many fungi provide foods for people. Some fungi cause disease while others fight disease. Still other fungi live in symbiosis with other organisms.**

Environmental Recycling Like bacteria, many fungi are decomposers—organisms that break down the chemicals in dead organisms. For example, many fungi live in the soil and break down the chemicals in dead plant matter. This process returns important nutrients to the soil. Without fungi and bacteria, Earth would be buried under dead plants and animals!

Food and Fungi When you eat a slice of bread, you benefit from the work of yeast. Bakers add yeast to bread dough to make it rise. Yeast cells use the sugar in the dough for food and produce carbon dioxide gas as they feed. The gas forms bubbles, which cause the dough to rise. You see these bubbles as holes in a slice of bread. Without yeast, bread would be flat and solid. Yeast is also used to make wine from grapes. Yeast cells feed on the sugar in the grapes and produce carbon dioxide and alcohol.

Other fungi are also important sources of foods. Molds are used in the production of foods. The blue streaks in blue cheese, for example, are actually growths of the mold *Penicillium roqueforti*. People enjoy eating mushrooms in salads and soups and on pizza. Because some mushrooms are extremely poisonous, however, you should never pick or eat wild mushrooms.

Lab zone Try This **Activity**

Skills Focus Making models

Materials round balloon, cotton balls, tape, stick or ruler about 30 cm long, modeling clay, pin

Time 25 minutes

Tips If possible, blow up the balloons with a pump or compressed air so that the cotton balls do not get wet. Suggest

L2 students make the cotton balls as small as possible.

Expected Outcome The "spores" should fly out from the balloons and land in many directions, fairly far from the balloons. Students should explain that, just as air scattered the cotton balls, air currents catch and carry spores far and wide.
learning modality: kinesthetic

Disease-Fighting Fungi In 1928, a Scottish biologist named Alexander Fleming was examining petri dishes in which he was growing bacteria. To his surprise, Fleming noticed a spot of a bluish-green mold growing in one dish. Curiously, no bacteria were growing near the mold. Fleming hypothesized that the mold, a fungus named *Penicillium*, produced a substance that killed the bacteria near it.

Fleming's work contributed to the development of the first antibiotic, penicillin. It has saved the lives of millions of people with bacterial infections. Since the discovery of penicillin, many additional antibiotics have been isolated from both fungi and bacteria.

Disease-Causing Fungi Many fungi are parasites that cause serious diseases in plants. The sac fungus that causes Dutch elm disease is responsible for killing millions of elm trees in North America and Europe. Corn smut and wheat rust are two club fungi that cause diseases in important food crops. Fungal plant diseases also affect other crops, including rice, cotton, and soybeans, resulting in huge crop losses every year.

Some fungi cause diseases in humans as well. Athlete's foot causes an itchy irritation in the damp places between toes. Ringworm, another fungal disease, causes an itchy, circular rash on the skin. Because the fungi that cause these diseases produce spores at the site of infection, the diseases can spread easily from person to person. Both diseases can be treated with antifungal medications.

 Reading Checkpoint   What is one way fungi help fight diseases?

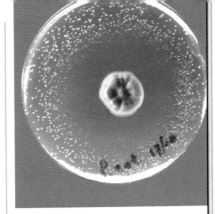

FIGURE 20
Penicillin
A *Penicillium* mold grows in the center of this petri dish. The mold produces the antibiotic penicillin, which prevents the tiny white colonies of bacteria from growing in the area around it.

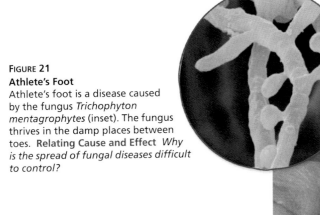

FIGURE 21
Athlete's Foot
Athlete's foot is a disease caused by the fungus *Trichophyton mentagrophytes* (inset). The fungus thrives in the damp places between toes. **Relating Cause and Effect** *Why is the spread of fungal diseases difficult to control?*

 A ◆ 93

Math Skill Interpreting graphs

Focus Have students study the graph. Ask: **What does this graph show?** *(The effect of root-associated fungi on the height of trees)*

What information do the two colors of bars represent? *(One represents trees with root-associated fungi; the other represents trees without root-associated fungi.)*

Teach Ask: **Which group of trees is the control group?** *(Those grown without fungi)*

Answers

1. By measuring average height in meters
2. Those grown with root-associated fungi
3. About 5 meters; about 1.5 meters
4. Root-associated fungi improve or enhance tree growth.

Integrating Earth Science L1

Examining Lichens

Provide students with hand lenses and samples of lichens on rocks or tree bark. As students observe the lichens, challenge them to infer why lichens are sensitive to environmental pollution. *(Lichens rapidly absorb substances directly from rainwater, so they are very susceptible to airborne pollutants.)* **learning modality: visual**

Fungi and Trees

A biologist conducted an experiment to see how root-associated fungi affect the growth of four different tree species. Each species was divided into two groups—trees grown with root-associated fungi and trees grown without the fungi.

1. **Reading Graphs** How did the biologist measure tree growth?

2. **Interpreting Data** For each species, which group of trees showed more growth?

3. **Calculating** What is the average height difference between sour orange trees that grew with root-associated fungi and those that grew without fungi? What is the height difference between avocado trees with and without the fungi?

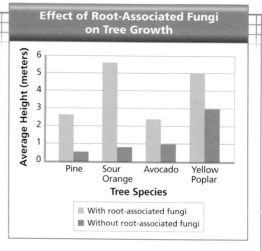

Effect of Root-Associated Fungi on Tree Growth

Average Height (meters) vs. Tree Species (Pine, Sour Orange, Avocado, Yellow Poplar)

- ☐ With root-associated fungi
- ■ Without root-associated fungi

4. **Drawing Conclusions** Based on this experiment, how do root-associated fungi affect tree growth?

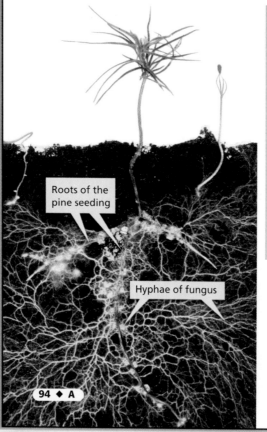

Roots of the pine seeding

Hyphae of fungus

94 ◆ A

Fungus–Plant Root Associations Some fungi help plants grow larger and healthier when their hyphae grow into, or on, the plant's roots. The hyphae spread out underground and absorb water and nutrients from the soil for the plant. With more water and nutrients, the plant grows larger than it would have grown without its fungal partner. The plant is not the only partner that benefits. The fungi get to feed on the extra food that the plant makes and stores. You can see the partnership between a fungus and a pine seedling in Figure 22.

Most plants have fungal partners. Many plants are so dependent on the fungi that they cannot survive without them. For example, orchid seeds cannot develop without their fungal partners.

 Reading Checkpoint How do fungi help plants grow?

FIGURE 22
Fungus–Plant Root Associations
An extensive system of fungal hyphae has grown in association with the roots of the pine seedling in the middle.
Classifying *What type of symbiosis do these two organisms exhibit?*

FIGURE 23
Lichens
The British soldier lichen consists of a fungus and an alga. The inset shows how entwined the alga is among the fungus's hyphae.

Alga
Fungus

Lichens A **lichen** (LY kun) consists of a fungus and either algae or autotrophic bacteria that live together in a mutualistic relationship. You have probably seen some familiar lichens—irregular, flat, crusty patches that grow on tree barks or rocks. The fungus benefits from the food produced by the algae or bacteria. The algae or bacteria, in turn, obtain shelter, water, and minerals from the fungus.

Lichens are often called "pioneer" organisms because they are the first organisms to appear on the bare rocks in an area after a volcanic eruption, fire, or rock slide has occurred. Over time, the lichens break down the rock into soil in which other organisms can grow. Lichens are also useful as indicators of air pollution. Many species of lichens are very sensitive to pollutants and die when pollution levels rise. By monitoring the growth of lichens, scientists can assess the air quality in an area.

 Reading Checkpoint What two organisms make up a lichen?

Go Online
SCiLINKS
For: Links on fungi
Visit: www.SciLinks.org
Web Code: scn-0133

Section 3 Assessment

Target Reading Skill Asking Questions Use the answers to the questions you wrote about the headings to help you answer the questions below.

Reviewing Key Concepts

1. a. Listing List three characteristics that a bread mold shares with a mushroom.
   b. Comparing and Contrasting How are the cells of a bread mold arranged? How are the cells of a mushroom arranged?
   c. Summarizing How does the cell structure of a fungus help it obtain food?

2. a. Reviewing What role do spores play in the reproduction of fungi?
   b. Sequencing Outline the steps by which fungi produce spores by sexual reproduction.
   c. Inferring Why is it advantageous to a fungus to produce millions of spores?

3. a. Identifying Name six roles that fungi play in nature.
   b. Predicting Suppose all the fungi in a forest disappeared. What do you think the forest would be like without fungi?

Writing in Science

Wanted Poster Design a "Wanted" poster for a mold that has been ruining food in your kitchen. Present the mold as a "criminal of the kitchen." Include detailed descriptions of the mold's physical characteristics, what it needs to grow, how it grows, and any other details that will help your family identify this mold. Propose ways to prevent new molds from growing in your kitchen.

Chapter 3 A ◆ 95

What's for Lunch? □L2

Prepare for Inquiry

Key Concept
The activity of yeast varies, depending on the amount of available food.

Skills Objectives
After this lab, students will be able to
• draw conclusions about whether sugar and salt act as food sources for yeast.

Prep Time 20 minutes
Class Time 45 minutes

Advance Planning
Before the lab, check a sample of yeast that is dissolved in warm water with sugar for 20 minutes, to make sure the yeasts are alive.

Safety
Students should wear safety goggles in case a balloon pops off a bottle or a bottle is accidentally dropped. Review the safety guidelines in Appendix A.

All in One Teaching Resources
• Lab Worksheet: *What's for Lunch?*

Guide Inquiry

Invitation
Tell students that yeasts produce carbon dioxide when they break down food. Carbon dioxide production can be measured to determine whether yeasts are feeding. Have students explain how carbon dioxide production will be measured in this lab.

Introduce the Procedure
Help students understand that when carbon dioxide gas forms in water, much of it will escape from the water's surface.

What's for Lunch?

Problem
How does the presence of sugar or salt affect the activity of yeast?

Skills Focus
measuring, inferring, drawing conclusions

Materials
• 5 small plastic narrow-necked bottles
• 5 round balloons • 5 plastic straws
• dry powdered yeast • sugar • salt
• warm water (40°–45°C) • marking pen
• beaker • graduated cylinder • metric ruler
• string

Procedure

1. Copy the data table into your notebook. Then read over the entire procedure to see how you will test the activity of the yeast cells in bottles A through E. Write a prediction about what will happen in each bottle.

2. Gently stretch each of the balloons so that they will inflate easily.

3. Using the marking pen, label the bottles A, B, C, D, and E.

4. Use a beaker to fill each bottle with the same amount of warm water. **CAUTION:** *Glass is fragile. Handle the beaker gently to avoid breakage. Do not touch broken glass.*

5. Put 25 mL of salt into bottle B.

6. Put 25 mL of sugar into bottles C and E.

7. Put 50 mL of sugar into bottle D.

8. Put 6 mL of powdered yeast into bottle A, and stir the mixture with a clean straw. Remove the straw and discard it.

9. Immediately place a balloon over the opening of bottle A. Make sure that the balloon opening fits very tightly around the neck of the bottle.

10. Repeat Steps 8 and 9 for bottle B, bottle C, and bottle D.

Troubleshooting the Experiment
• Do not let students overfill the bottles.
• Balloons may pop off the bottles during the lab.
• Caution students to use a fresh straw for each mixing. This is particularly important when mixing bottle E, because students must not introduce yeast by accident.

Expected Outcome
Balloon D should inflate the most. Balloon C should also inflate but noticeably less than balloon D. Balloons A, B, and E should not inflate.

Data Table

Bottle	Prediction	Observations	Circumference			
			10 min	20 min	30 min	40 min
A (Yeast alone)						
B (Yeast and 25 mL of salt)						
C (Yeast and 25 mL of sugar)						
D (Yeast and 50 mL of sugar)						
E (No yeast and 25 mL of sugar)						

11. Place a balloon over bottle E without adding yeast to the bottle.

12. Place the five bottles in a warm spot away from drafts. Every ten minutes for 40 minutes, measure the circumference of each balloon by placing a string around the balloon at its widest point. Include your measurements in the data table.

Analyze and Conclude

1. **Measuring** Which balloons changed in size during this lab? How did they change?

2. **Inferring** Explain why the balloon changed size in some bottles and not in others. What caused that change in size?

3. **Interpreting Data** What did the results from bottle C show, compared with the results from bottle D? Why was it important to include bottle E in this investigation?

4. **Drawing Conclusions** Do yeast use salt or sugar as a food source? How do you know?

5. **Communicating** In a paragraph, summarize what you learned about yeast from this investigation. Be sure to support each of your conclusions with the evidence you gathered.

Design an Experiment

Develop a hypothesis about whether temperature affects the activity of yeast cells. Then design an experiment to test your hypothesis. *Obtain your teacher's permission before carrying out your investigation.*

Go Online
PHSchool.com

For: Data sharing
Visit: PHSchool.com
Web Code: ced-1033

Analyze and Conclude

1. Balloons C and D changed during the lab. Balloon C filled up a little, and balloon D filled up a lot.

2. Some balloons were inflated by carbon dioxide gas. Other balloons remained unchanged because no carbon dioxide gas was produced by the yeast.

3. The balloon on bottle C did not inflate as much as the balloon on bottle D. When less sugar was available to the yeast (25 mL in bottle C versus 50 mL in bottle D), the yeast gave off less carbon dioxide. Without bottle E, there would be no way of knowing whether the gas was being produced by the sugar alone as it dissolved in the water.

4. They use sugar. Bottle B, which contained salt, produced no gas, indicating that the yeast was not active.

5. Student answers should explain that yeast cells use sugar as a food source, and they produce carbon dioxide as they break down food. Their feeding and production of carbon dioxide were proven by the inflation of balloons in bottles containing sugar, particularly in the bottle with the most sugar.

Extend Inquiry

Design an Experiment Students could prepare another bottle D and place it in a refrigerator. They would find that yeasts require warm environments to carry out their basic life processes.

Go Online
PHSchool.com

For: Data sharing
Visit: PHSchool.com
Web Code: cep-1033

Students can review data sharing in an online interactivity.

interactive Textbook

- Complete student edition
- Section and chapter self-assessments
- Assessment reports for teachers

Help Students Read

Building Vocabulary

Word-Part Analysis Tell students that the suffix *-sis* means *process* or *action,* the prefix *sym* means *along with* or *together,* and *bio* refers to life and living organisms. Thus *symbiosis* describes the close relationship between two species that benefits at least one of the species. The suffix *-ism* also means *act* or *process,* and the word *mutual* means *directed by each toward the other* or *shared in common.* Thus *mutualism* is a type of symbiosis in which each of two species benefit.

Word Forms Ask students to write their own definitions of *bloom* and *vacuole,* using the dictionary for help. Have students explain how the definitions relate to the terms *algal bloom* and *contractile vacuole.*

Connecting Concepts

Concept Maps Help students develop one way to show how the information in this chapter is related. Protists are a diverse group of organisms that include traits shared with animals, plants, and fungi. Algae are protists that can bloom dramatically when nutrients in water increase. Fungi, heterotrophs that reproduce with spores, vary in their reproductive structures and in the roles they play in nature. Have students brainstorm to identify the key concepts, key terms, details, and examples from this chapter, then write each one on a sticky note and attach it at random on chart paper or on the board. Tell students that this concept map will be organized in hierarchical order and to begin at the top with the key concepts. Ask students these questions to guide them to categorize the information on the sticky notes: **What traits do protists share and how do they differ? How are fungi similar to protists? Why do algal blooms occur?**

① Protists

Key Concepts

- Like animals, animal-like protists are heterotrophs, and most are able to move from place to place to obtain food.
- Like plants, algae are autotrophs.
- Like fungi, funguslike protists are heterotrophs, have cell walls, and use spores to reproduce.

Key Terms

protist
protozoan
pseudopod
contractile vacuole
cilia
symbiosis
mutualism
algae
pigment
spore

② Algal Blooms

Key Concepts

- In general, algal blooms occur when nutrients increase in the water.
- Red tides are dangerous when the toxins that the algae produce become concentrated in the bodies of organisms that consume the algae.
- Eutrophication triggers a series of events with serious consequences.

Key Terms

algal bloom
red tide
eutrophication

③ Fungi

Key Concepts

- Fungi are eukaryotes that have cell walls, are heterotrophs that feed by absorbing their food, and use spores to reproduce.
- Fungi usually reproduce by making spores. The lightweight spores are surrounded by a protective covering and can be carried easily through air or water to new sites.
- Fungi play important roles as decomposers and recyclers on Earth. Many fungi provide foods for people. Some fungi cause disease while others fight disease. Still other fungi live in symbiosis with other organisms.

Key Terms

fungi
hyphae
fruiting body
budding
lichen

What are the traits and roles of fungi?
Prompt students by using connecting words or phrases, such as "adapted to," "classified by," and "result in" to indicate the basis for the organization of the map. The phrases should form a sentence between or among a set of concepts.

Answer
Accept all logical presentations by students.

All in One Teaching Resources

- Key Terms Review: *Protists and Fungi*
- Connecting Concepts: *Protists and Fungi*

Go Online
PHSchool.com
For: Self-Assessment
Visit: PHSchool.com
Web Code: cea-1030

Organizing Information

Sequencing Copy the flowchart about changes in a lake onto a separate sheet of paper. Then complete it and add a title. (For more on Sequencing, see the Skills Handbook.)

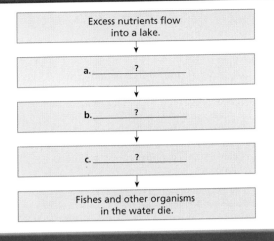

```
Excess nutrients flow
into a lake.
        ↓
a. _____?_____
        ↓
b. _____?_____
        ↓
c. _____?_____
        ↓
Fishes and other organisms
in the water die.
```

Reviewing Key Terms

Choose the letter of the best answer.

1. Which of the following characteristics describes all protists?
   a. They are unicellular.
   b. They can be seen with the unaided eye.
   c. Their cells have nuclei.
   d. They are unable to move on their own.

2. A protist structure that collects water and expels it from the cell is called a
   a. pseudopod.
   b. contractile vacuole.
   c. cilia.
   d. spore.

3. The interaction between two species in which at least one of the species benefits is called
   a. eutrophication.   b. hyphae.
   c. symbiosis.   d. budding.

4. An overpopulation of saltwater algae is called a(n)
   a. pigment.   b. lichen.
   c. red tide.   d. eutrophication.

5. A lichen is a symbiotic association between
   a. fungi and plant roots.
   b. algae and fungi.
   c. algae and bacteria.
   d. protozoans and algae.

If the statement is true, write *true*. If it is false, change the underlined word or words to make the statement true.

6. Ciliates use <u>flagella</u> to move.
7. Plantlike protists are called <u>protozoans</u>.
8. <u>Eutrophication</u> is the process by which nutrients in a lake build up over time.
9. Most fungi are made up of threadlike structures called <u>spores</u>.
10. Fungi produce spores in structures called <u>fruiting bodies</u>.

Writing in Science

Informational Pamphlet Create a pamphlet to teach young children about fungi. Explain where fungi live, how they feed, and the roles they play. Include illustrations as well.

Discovery CHANNEL SCHOOL

Protists and Fungi
Video Preview
Video Field Trip
► Video Assessment

Go Online
PHSchool.com
For: Self-assessment
Visit: PHSchool.com
Web Code: cea-1030

Students can take a practice test online that is automatically scored.

All in One Teaching Resources
- Transparency A26
- Chapter Test
- Performance Assessment Teacher Notes
- Performance Assessment Student Worksheet
- Performance Assessment Scoring Rubric

ExamView® Computer Test Bank CD-ROM

Review and Assessment

Organizing Information
a. Algal growth increases.
b. Layer of algae prevents sunlight from reaching plants and other algae beneath. These plants and algae die.
c. Decomposers increase in number and use up oxygen in the water.

Reviewing Key Terms
1. c 2. b 3. c 4. c 5. b
6. false; cilia
7. false; algae
8. true
9. false; hyphae
10. true

Writing in Science

Writing Mode Description
Scoring Rubric
4 Includes detailed, accurate information for all criteria and illustrations; art is neat and supports text
3 Includes all criteria; art somewhat extraneous
2 Minimally meets all criteria
1 Includes inaccurate or incomplete information

Discovery CHANNEL SCHOOL Video Assessment

Protists and Fungi

Show the Video Assessment to review chapter content and as a prompt for the writing assignment. Discussion questions: **Describe the relationship between fungi and algae in lichens.** (*In a lichen, the alga provides food for the fungus, while the fungus provides water and shelter for the alga; both organisms benefit.*) **What important role do fungi play in the ecosystem in which they live?** (*They act as decomposers and provide food.*)

Checking Concepts

11. An amoeba extends pseudopods around a food particle to engulf it.

12. Algae range from unicellular to huge multicellular individuals, as well as unicellular forms living in colonies.

13. Animal-like and funguslike protists are heterotrophs. Plantlike protists are autotrophs, but some can also be heterotrophs.

14. An algal bloom is a rapid increase in a population of algae. In the ocean, an algal bloom can cause a red tide to occur, which is dangerous because the toxins that the algae produce can become concentrated in the bodies of organisms that consume the algae. An algal bloom in a lake can increase the rate of eutrophication, blocking sunlight and depleting oxygen, thus killing organisms in the lake.

15. In sexual reproduction, two hyphae grow together, exchange genetic material, and produce a fruiting body.

16. The fungus benefits from food produced by the algae or bacteria, which obtain shelter, water, and minerals from the fungus.

Thinking Critically

17. Organism A is an amoeba, which engulfs its food with pseudopods. Organism B is a paramecium, which uses cilia to push food-containing water into its oral groove.

18. Most other life forms would probably disappear also. Algae provide food and oxygen for water animals and help maintain the oxygen in the atmosphere.

19. Fungi play many beneficial roles, especially that of decomposer. Killing fungi could allow the accumulation of dead plants and animals. Fungi also help many plants to survive.

20. There could be excess nutrients in the water, or it may be old and need to be changed. The scum could be from eutrophication, a natural process that occurs over time.

21. Keep it aired out, dry, and cool. Molds thrive in warm, moist environments.

Checking Concepts

11. Describe the process by which an amoeba obtains its food.
12. Describe the differences among algae in terms of their sizes.
13. Compare how animal-like, plantlike, and funguslike protists obtain food.
14. What are algal blooms? What problems can they cause in Earth's waters?
15. How does sexual reproduction occur in fungi?
16. Explain how the two organisms that make up a lichen both benefit from their symbiotic relationship.

Thinking Critically

17. Comparing and Contrasting Identify the organisms below. Describe the method by which each obtains food. What structures are involved?

18. Predicting If all algae suddenly disappeared from Earth's waters, what would happen to living things on Earth? Explain your answer.
19. Making Judgments You see an advertisement for a new, powerful fungicide guaranteed to kill most fungi on contact. What should people take into consideration before choosing to buy this fungicide?
20. Relating Cause and Effect You see some green scumlike material growing on the walls of your freshwater aquarium at home. List some possible reasons why this growth has occurred.
21. Problem Solving What are some actions that homeowners can take to discourage the growth of mold in their basements? Explain why these actions might help solve the problem.

Applying Skills

Use the graph to answer Questions 22–25.

When yeast is added to bread dough, the yeast cells produce carbon dioxide, which causes the dough to rise. The graph below shows how temperature affects the amount of carbon dioxide that is produced.

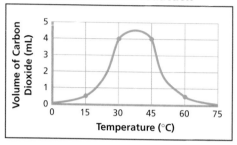

Temperature and Carbon Dioxide Production

22. Interpreting Data Based on the graph, at what temperature does yeast produce the most carbon dioxide?
23. Inferring Use the graph to explain why yeast is dissolved in warm water, rather than in cold water, when it is used to make bread.
24. Predicting Based on the graph, would you expect bread dough to rise if it were placed in a refrigerator (which is kept at about 2° to 5°C)? Explain.
25. Drawing Conclusions Explain how temperature affects the amount of carbon dioxide that the yeast cells produce.

Lab zone Chapter **Project**

Performance Assessment Create a poster that summarizes your experiment for the class. In your poster, include your hypothesis and describe the conditions that produced the best mushroom growth. Use diagrams and graphs to display your results. Did the project raise any new questions about mushrooms for you? If so, how could you answer those questions?

Lab zone Chapter **Project**   **L3**

Project Wrap-Up Provide students with materials for making the posters. Set aside time for them to work on posters during class, and allow them to look at each other's posters for ideas. Students should organize information on their posters in a clear manner.

Reflect and Record Some students may have found it difficult to organize their results because they changed the variables too often or were not confident of their results. Students may propose another experiment or talking to an expert as a way of answering their questions.

Standardized Test Prep

Choose the letter of the best answer.

1. Roberto fills a petri dish with pond water containing a mixture of protozoans and algae. He covers half the dish with aluminum foil and places it on a sunny windowsill. Predict what Roberto might observe after several days.
   A The protozoans and algae would be evenly distributed throughout the dish.
   B The protozoans and algae would be found only in the covered half of the petri dish.
   C More algae would be found in the uncovered half of the dish.
   D The protozoans can now make their own food.

2. Which of the following statements about fungus reproduction is true?
   F Fungi reproduce sexually by budding.
   G Fungi reproduce by making spores.
   H Fungi reproduce asexually when two hyphae join together and exchange genetic material.
   J Fungi do not reproduce sexually.

3. Which of the following statements about a paramecium is correct?
   A It has two contractile vacuoles that remove excess water from the cytoplasm.
   B It uses cilia to move.
   C It has two nuclei.
   D all of the above

4. Which structure tells you that the euglena shown below is an autotroph?

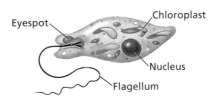

Eyespot · Chloroplast · Nucleus · Flagellum

   F eyespot
   G flagellum
   H nucleus
   J chloroplast

5. Which of the following is true of algal blooms?
   A They occur only in fresh water.
   B They occur only in salt water.
   C They occur when nutrients in the water increase.
   D They are caused by animal-like protists.

Constructed Response

6. During a hike in a state park, you notice some mushrooms growing on a log. Describe how the mushrooms use the log as a food source. Include information on what mushroom structures play a role in the process and the sequence of events that occur.

Applying Skills

22. At about 38°C

23. Yeast must be active and produce carbon dioxide so the dough will rise, and it is more active in warm water.

24. No. For the most part the dough would not continue to rise because yeast are usually inactive at that temperature.

25. The optimal temperature range for yeast activity is between 30°C and 45°C. Above or below this range, the amount of carbon dioxide produced decreases sharply.

Standardized Test Prep

1. C **2.** G **3.** D **4.** J **5.** C
6. The hyphae of the mushrooms grow into the log, which is a food source. Digestive chemicals from the hyphae ooze into the log and break it down into small substances that the hyphae can absorb.

Chapter at a Glance

PRENTICE HALL

Plan · Teach · Assess

 Chapter Project *Design and Build an Interactive Exhibit* **Technology** **Local Standards**

All in One Teaching Resources

- Chapter Project Teacher Notes, pp. 210–211
- Chapter Project Student Overview , pp. 212–213
- Chapter Project Student Worksheets , pp. 214–215
- Chapter Project Scoring Rubric, p. 216

Video Preview

Section 1 **The Plant Kingdom**

2–3 periods
1–1 1/2 blocks

A.4.1.1 Identify the characteristics all plants share.

A.4.1.2 Name all the things that a plant needs to live successfully on land.

A.4.1.3 Compare vascular and nonvascular plants.

A.4.1.4 Describe the stages of a plant's life cycle.

Video Field Trip

Section 2 **Photosynthesis and Light**

2–3 periods
1–1 1/2 blocks

A.4.2.1 Explain what happens when light strikes a green leaf.

A.4.2.2 Describe the overall process of photosynthesis.

Section 3 **Mosses, Liverworts, and Hornworts**

2–3 periods
1–1 1/2 blocks

A.4.3.1 Name some nonvascular plants and list the characteristics they share.

A.4.3.2 Describe the structure of a moss plant.

Section 4 **Ferns, Club Mosses, and Horsetails**

2–3 periods
1–1 1/2 blocks

A.4.4.1 Name some seedless vascular plants and list the characteristics they share.

A.4.4.2 Describe the structure of a fern plant and how it reproduces.

Review and Assessment

All in One Teaching Resources

- Key Terms Review, p. 251
- Transparency A36
- Performance Assessment Teacher Notes, p. 258
- Performance Assessment Scoring Rubric, p. 259
- Performance Assessment Student Worksheet, p. 260
- Chapter Test, pp. 261–264

Video Assessment

PHSchool.com

Test Preparation

**Test Preparation
Blackline Masters**

Chapter Activities Planner

For more activities

LAB ZONE Easy Planner CD-ROM

Student Edition	Inquiry	Time	Materials	Skills	Resources
Chapter Project, p. 103	Open-Ended	3–4 weeks	**All in One Teaching Resources** See p. 210	Observing, making models, communicating	**Lab zone Easy Planner** **All in One Teaching Resources** Support pp. 210–211
Section 1					
Discover Activity, p. 104	Guided	10 minutes	hand lens, leaf from plant with thick, fleshy leaves such as a jade, yucca, or aloe plant; leaf of a temperate climate plant such as a maple, oak, or common garden plant	Inferring	**Lab zone Easy Planner**
Section 2					
Discover Activity, p. 114	Guided	10 minutes	glue, hand mirror, prism, shoebox, white paper	Observing	**Lab zone Easy Planner**
Design Your Own Lab, pp. 120–121	Open-Ended	45 minutes	Elodea plants, water, wide-mouth container, sodium bicarbonate solution, 2 test tubes, wax pencil, lamp (optional)	Observing, controlling variables, designing experiments	**Lab zone Easy Planner** **All in One Teaching Resources** Design Your Own Lab: *Eye on Photosynthesis*, pp. 232–234
Section 3					
Discover Activity, p. 122	Directed	15 minutes	3 plastic graduated cylinders, dropper, 20 mL peat moss, 20 mL sand, stopwatch, water	Predicting	**Lab zone Easy Planner**
Skills Lab, p. 125	Guided	45 minutes	clump of moss, hand lens, metric ruler, toothpicks, plastic dropper, water	Observing, measuring	**Lab zone Easy Planner** **All in One Teaching Resources** Skills Lab: *Masses of Mosses*, pp. 242–243
Section 4					
Discover Activity, p. 126	Directed	10 minutes	dropper, food coloring, goggles, narrow glass tube, plastic petri dish, water	Inferring	**Lab zone Easy Planner**
Try This Activity, p. 128	Guided	20 minutes	fern plant, hand lens, plastic dropper, water	Inferring	**Lab zone Easy Planner**

Section 1 **The Plant Kingdom**

🕐 *2–3 days, 1–1 1/2 blocks*

ABILITY LEVELS
L1 Basic to Average
L2 For All Students
L3 Average to Advanced

Objectives

A.4.1.1 Identify characteristics that all plants share.

A.4.1.2 Name all the things that a plant needs to live successfully on land.

A.4.1.3 Compare vascular and nonvascular plants.

A.4.1.4 Describe the plant life cycle.

Local Standards

Key Terms

• photosynthesis • tissue • chloroplast • vacuole • cuticle • vascular tissue
• fertilization • zygote • nonvascular plant • vascular plant • chlorophyll
• sporophyte • gametophyte

Preteach

Build Background Knowledge

Ask students to explain how plants and animals are different.

 **Discover Activity** *What Do Leaves Reveal About Plants?*

Targeted Print and Technology Resources

All in One **Teaching Resources**

L2 Reading Strategy: Building Vocabulary

⊙ **Presentation-Pro CD-ROM**

Instruct

What Is a Plant? Use discussion to emphasize that all plants are autotrophs, that is, they produce their own food, and that all plants are eukaryotes that contain many cells.

Adaptations for Living on Land Help students understand that, to live on land, all plants need a way to get water and nutrients from their surroundings, transport water and nutrients within their bodies, support their bodies, and reproduce.

Classification of Plants Assist students in discerning two major categories of plants: plants with vascular tissue and plants without.

Complex Life Cycles Help students recognize that a plant's life cycle consists of two stages: the sporophyte stage and the gametophyte stage.

Targeted Print and Technology Resources

All in One **Teaching Resources**

L2 Guided Reading, pp. 219–222

L2 Transparencies A27, A28

www.phschool.com Web Code: cep-1041

⊙ **Student Edition on Audio CD**

Assess

Section Assessment Questions

🎯 Have students use their own definitions to help them answer questions.

Reteach

Direct students to make a chart listing the adaptations plants need to live on land and identify the adaptations as belonging to vascular plants.

Targeted Print and Technology Resources

All in One **Teaching Resources**

• Section Summary, p. 218

L1 Review and Assessment, p. 223

L3 Enrich, p. 224

Section 2 Photosynthesis and Light

 2–3 days, 1–1 1/2 blocks

Objectives

A.4.2.1 Explain what happens when light strikes a green leaf.
A.4.2.2 Describe the overall process of photosynthesis.

Key Terms

• transmission • reflection • absorption • accessory pigment

Local Standards

Preteach

Build Background Knowledge

Prompt students to describe how colored light affects the way we see colored objects.

 **Discover Activity** *What Colors Make Up Sunlight?*

Targeted Print and Technology Resources

 Teaching Resources

L2 Reading Strategy Transparency A29: Previewing Visuals

🔘 **Presentation-Pro CD-ROM**

Instruct

The Nature of Light Lead students through this subsection that addresses the topics of visible light, what happens when light strikes an object, plants and light, and the relationship between light and plant pigments.

The Photosynthesis Process Explain the equation for photosynthesis and discuss light's participation in the process.

Targeted Print and Technology Resources

Teaching Resources

L2 Guided Reading, pp. 227–229
L2 Transparencies A30, A31
L3 Design Your Own Lab: *Eye on Photosynthesis*, pp. 232–234

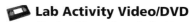 Web Code: cep-1042

📼 **Lab Activity Video/DVD**
Design Your Own Lab: *Eye on Photosynthesis*

🔘 **Student Edition on Audio CD**

Assess

Section Assessment Questions

Have students use their Preview Visuals graphic organizer to answer the questions.

Reteach

Provide an illustration showing photosynthesis, and direct students to label the components of the process: carbon dioxide, water, light energy, sugar, and water.

Targeted Print and Technology Resources

Teaching Resources

• Section Summary, p. 226
L1 Review and Assessment, p. 230
L3 Enrich, p. 231

Section 3 Mosses, Liverworts, and Hornworts

ABILITY LEVELS
- **L1** Basic to Average
- **L2** For All Students
- **L3** Average to Advanced

 2–3 days, 1–1/2 blocks

Objectives

A.4.3.1 Name some nonvascular plants and list the characteristics they all share.

A.4.3.2 Describe the structure of a moss plant.

Key Terms

• rhizoid • bog • peat

Local Standards

Preteach

Build Background Knowledge

Invite students to describe any mosses with which they are familiar.

 Lab zone Discover Activity *Will Mosses Absorb Water?*

Targeted Print and Technology Resources

All in One Teaching Resources

L2 Reading Strategy Transparency A32: Identifying Main Ideas

⊙ **Presentation-Pro CD-ROM**

Instruct

Mosses Help students recognize the simple plant parts of a moss plant—their stemlike, leaflike, and rootlike structures—as well as their importance.

Liverworts and Hornworts Assist students as they learn how to distinguish two remaining groups of nonvascular plants—liverworts and hornworts.

Targeted Print and Technology Resources

All in One Teaching Resources

L2 Guided Reading, pp. 237–239
L2 Transparency A33
L2 Skills Lab: *Masses of Mosses*, pp. 242–243

📼 **Lab Activity Video/DVD**
Skills Lab: *Masses of Mosses*

www.SciLinks.org Web Code: scn-0143

⊙ **Student Edition on Audio CD**

Assess

Section Assessment Questions

⟲ Have students use their Identifying Main Ideas graphic organizers as they answer the questions.

Reteach

Ask students to describe the life cycle of moss, describing how the sporophyte is formed and its function.

Targeted Print and Technology Resources

All in One Teaching Resources

• Section Summary, p. 236
L1 Review and Assessment, p. 240
L3 Enrich, p. 241

Section 4 Ferns, Club Mosses, and Horsetails

 2–3 days, 1–1/2 blocks

ABILITY LEVELS
L1 Basic to Average
L2 For All Students
L3 Average to Advanced

Objectives

A.4.4.1 Name some seedless vascular plants and list the characteristics they all share.

A.4.4.2 Describe the structure of a fern and how it reproduces.

Key Terms

• frond

Local Standards

Preteach

Build Background Knowledge

Have students draw what they think a fern looks like and then describe its characteristics.

Lab zone Discover Activity *How Quickly Can Water Move Upward?*

Targeted Print and Technology Resources

All in One Teaching Resources

L2 Reading Strategy Transparency A34: Asking Questions

⊙ **Presentation-Pro CD-ROM**

Instruct

Characteristics of Seedless Vascular Plants Stress that plants with vascular tissue can grow taller than nonvascular plants but that, without seeds, the plants must still live in moist areas to complete reproduction.

Ferns Have students study the structure of ferns and their reproduction through spores.

Club Mosses and Horsetails Have students read about the characteristics of club mosses and horsetails.

Targeted Print and Technology Resources

All in One Teaching Resources

L2 Guided Reading, pp. 246–248

L2 Transparency A35

⊙ **Student Edition on Audio CD**

Assess

Section Assessment Questions

Have students use their Asking Questions graphic organizers to answer the questions.

Reteach

Have students write brief paragraphs to describe the life cycle of ferns.

Targeted Print and Technology Resources

All in One Teaching Resources

• Section Summary, p. 245

L1 Review and Assessment, p. 249

L3 Enrich, p. 250

Chapter 4 Content Refresher

Section 1 The Plant Kingdom

Plant Traits and Diversity Plants are defined by a combination of traits. Plants are multicellular eukaryotes, with cell walls that contain cellulose. The great majority of plants are autotrophs—they capture the sun's energy and photosynthesize, thus making their own food. However, some plant species are entirely or partly heterotrophic. For example, dodder is a nonphotosynthetic parasite that depends completely on its host plant (such as buckwheat and sage), on which it grows, for food. Other plants, such as mistletoe, are only partially parasitic, with some photosynthetic parts. Some plants are "carnivorous"—they attract, trap, digest, and absorb insects to obtain an additional source of nutrients.

There is great diversity within the plant kingdom. Carnivorous plants represent only one example. Land plants in particular have developed successful adaptations that enable them to live in a wide variety of environments. One important adaptation of land plants is the production of lignin, a chemical that stiffens cell walls. Lignin provides strength and support, allowing a plant to grow large and tall.

Plants play critical roles in the ecosystems in which they are found. They are primary producers and form the foundation of many food webs. Plants also release oxygen gas, a product of photosynthesis essential for other organisms.

Section 2 Photosynthesis and Light

Plant's Use of Light Energy Photosynthesis requires raw materials including carbon dioxide and water; the products are sugar and oxygen. In addition, photosynthesis requires energy in the form of light to proceed.

Light moves in tiny packets of electromagnetic energy called photons. When a photon strikes—and is absorbed by—the green pigment chlorophyll in a plant's cell, the energy excites an electron in the chlorophyll molecule. The electron initially moves from a lower-energy state to one of higher energy. When the electron returns to its original state, it releases energy that initiates a chemical change. The chemical energy from this change is then stored, usually in the form of carbohydrates or sugar, in the plant's cells. The plant uses the energy stored in the sugar to carry out its life functions.

Address Misconceptions

Many students may think that plants need only soil and water to survive. However, carbon dioxide and light energy are essential for photosynthesis to occur. For a strategy overcoming this misconception, see **Address Misconceptions** in the section Photosynthesis and Light.

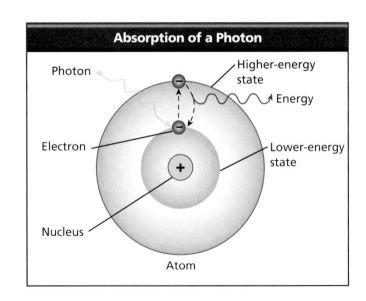

Absorption of a Photon

Photon — Higher-energy state — Energy — Electron — Lower-energy state — Nucleus — Atom

Section 3 Mosses, Liverworts, and Hornworts

Nonvascular Plants Mosses, liverworts, and hornworts are commonly referred to as nonvascular plants. Note, however, that some mosses do contain water-conducting tissues, though these tissues are not strong enough to provide efficient support or transport for the plant. Nonvascular plants have only their cell walls to provide support. (In vascular plants, the walls of the water-conducting tubes of true vascular plants contain a substance called lignin, which makes them stiff and strong.) Without efficient support and transport, nonvascular plants are small and restricted to moist environments.

Section 4 Ferns, Club Mosses, and Horsetails

Vascular Tissue and Water Transport Ferns, although more complex than mosses, are among the simplest of the vascular plants. Vascular tissue is responsible for delivering water and nutrients to parts of the plant distant from the roots. This allows plants to live at a distance from water and grow taller than their mossy relatives.

Dye travels up a plant stalk, such as celery, showing that vascular tissues accomplish their task. But how? How does a plant "suck up" water? Capillary action alone moves an insignificant amount of water upwards, especially in tall trees. The secret lies in the loss of water through a plant's leaves—transpiration.

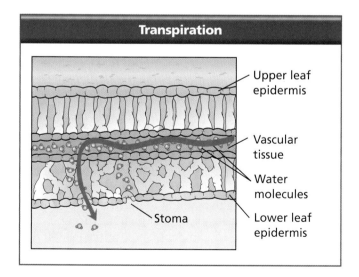

Transpiration

- Upper leaf epidermis
- Vascular tissue
- Water molecules
- Stoma
- Lower leaf epidermis

Transpiration subjects water in the xylem to tension, reaching from leaves to stems to roots. Water molecules are pulled upward, like links in a chain, partly due to capillary action but mostly due to the attraction of one water molecule to the next. The three-dimensional geometry of water's hydrogen bonds makes the bonds strong enough to link water molecules one to another in the xylem, but weak enough to allow molecules to escape from a leaf's surface. As one water molecule escapes from the leaf surface, another is pulled up to replace it. With this process, water can move at a rate of about 60 centimeters per minute in most plants. Of the water that moves through the leaf, 90 percent is lost by transpiration; only about 2 percent is used during photosynthesis.

Help Students Read

Relating Cause and Effect

Strategy Help students read and understand relationships between events. Cause-effect relationships are integral to science, so it is very important that students understand the cause-effect relationships developed in the text. Before students begin, assign a passage from this chapter.

Example

1. Remind students that a cause is what makes something happen and the effect is what happens as a result. Point out that in science, many actions cause an effect to occur.

2. Have students identify cause-effect relationships in the passage. Remind them that the text does not always directly state the cause-effect relationship, but in many cases clue words or phrases point out such a connection: *because, so, since, results, therefore, cause, lead to*. For example, rain is always slightly acidic *because* carbon dioxide dissolves in water droplets and forms carbonic acid.

3. Then explain that causes and effects often occur in chains with effects becoming causes of later effects. Have students find a cause-effect chain and show it in the form of a flowchart (insufficient oxygen for complete combustion → carbon monoxide produced → inhaled and absorbed by blood → hemoglobin cannot carry oxygen to cells).

Chapter 4
Introduction to Plants

Chapter Preview

❶ The Plant Kingdom
Discover *What Do Leaves Reveal About Plants?*
Active Art *Plant Cell Structures*
Analyzing Data *Water Loss in Plants*

❷ Photosynthesis and Light
Discover *What Colors Make Up Sunlight?*
Science and History *Unraveling the Mysteries of Photosynthesis*
Active Art *The Photosynthesis Process*
At-Home Activity *Reflecting on Light*
Design Your Own Lab *Eye on Photosynthesis*

❸ Mosses, Liverworts, and Hornworts
Discover *Will Mosses Absorb Water?*
At-Home Activity *Moss Hunt*
Skills Lab *Masses of Mosses*

❹ Ferns, Club Mosses, and Horsetails
Discover *How Quickly Can Water Move Upward?*
Try This *Examining a Fern*

ℹ️ **interactive Textbook**

▶ Ferns and other plants grow along a woodland stream.

Lab zone Chapter Project 〔L3〕

Objectives
During this project, students will produce an interactive exhibit describing how a specific product is derived from plants. Students will choose a single item, find its plant origin, and build an exhibit to present or explain the production or manufacturing processes surrounding the chosen product. After this Chapter Project, students will be able to
- identify materials and other products made from plants
- describe, and if feasible model, the production process from plant to finished item
- create an interactive exhibit
- adjust or redesign the exhibit based on initial feedback

Skills Focus
Observing, making models, communicating

Project Time Line 3 to 4 weeks

All in One Teaching Resources
- Chapter Project Teacher Notes
- Chapter Project Worksheet 1
- Chapter Project Worksheet 2
- Chapter Project Worksheet 3
- Chapter Project Worksheet 4
- Chapter Project Scoring Rubric

Developing a Plan
During the first week, students select a food-, clothing-, shelter-, or industry-related item, and begin researching where the plant needed to produce the item is grown and harvested. During the second week, students can research the processes used to turn the plant into the final product. In week three, students concentrate on designing an interactive exhibit to illustrate the plant growth and product manufacturing processes. Students show initial exhibit to young children and solicit feedback. Finally, students revise their interactive exhibit as needed and present revised exhibit to class.

DISCOVERY CHANNEL SCHOOL

Introduction to
Plants
▶ Video Preview
Video Field Trip
Video Assessment

Introduction to Plants

Show the Video Preview to introduce the Chapter Project and preview the chapter content. Discussion question: **How do some species of plants obtain nutrients in habitats with poor soil?** *(They capture and feed on insects.)*

Lab zone™ Chapter Project

Design and Build an Interactive Exhibit

Cotton, medicines, and paper are just some of the products that come from plants. Which plants are the sources of these products, and how are the products made? In this project, you will build an exhibit to teach young children how a plant becomes a useful product.

Your Goal To build an interactive exhibit showing how a particular plant is transformed into a useful product

To complete this project successfully, you must

- choose one plant product and research where it comes from
- design an interactive exhibit that shows how the product is made
- build your exhibit and ask some children to critique it
- use the children's feedback to redesign your exhibit
- follow the safety guidelines in Appendix A

Plan It! Think of a creative way to teach children about the plant product you chose. Then sketch out your exhibit design and obtain your teacher's approval to build it. Also, identify a few children who can provide you with useful feedback.

Possible Materials

- To begin research, students will need access to reference books, encyclopedia, and, if feasible, the Internet.
- Students will need art supplies to prepare their interactive exhibits. Access to computer would be helpful if students wish to develop a virtual interactive exhibit.

Launching the Project

With the class, make a list of products that come from plants. Have students identify the plant that each product comes from.

Indicate to students they may choose one of these products for their chapter project, or research a product of their own choosing. If a number of students are interested in the same product, allow them to work together to design and present the exhibit.

Performance Assessment

The Chapter Project Scoring Rubric will help you evaluate how well students complete the Chapter Project. You may want to share the scoring rubric with your students so they know what will be expected of them. Students will be assessed on

- thoroughness of research of the plant cultivation, harvest, and processing as plant is made into final product
- completeness of interactive exhibit, inclusion of major harvesting and processing steps
- revision or redesign of exhibit to accommodate initial feedback

Portfolio

Objectives

After this lesson, students will be able to
A.4.1.1 Identify the characteristics that all plants share.
A.4.1.2 Name all the things that a plant needs to live successfully on land.
A.4.1.3 Compare vascular and nonvascular plants.
A.4.1.4 Describe the stages of a plant's life cycle.

Target Reading Skill

Building Vocabulary Explain that knowing the definitions of key-concept words helps students understand what they read.

Answers

Students' definitions will vary. Check to see that definitions are appropriate or call on volunteers to share their definitions.

Preteach

Build Background Knowledge   L2

How are Plants Different From Animals?

Present students with a potted plant and ask them to identify at least two ways in which the plant is different from an animal. *(Sample answers: Plants cannot make noise; a plant does not move around.)*

---

1 The Plant Kingdom

Reading Preview

Key Concepts

- What characteristics do all plants share?
- What do plants need to live successfully on land?
- How do nonvascular plants and vascular plants differ?
- What are the different stages of a plant's life cycle?

Key Terms

- photosynthesis • tissue
- chloroplast • vacuole
- cuticle • vascular tissue
- fertilization • zygote
- nonvascular plant
- vascular plant • chlorophyll
- sporophyte • gametophyte

Target Reading Skill

Building Vocabulary A definition states the meaning of a word or phrase by telling about its most important feature or function. After you read the section, reread the paragraphs that contain definitions of Key Terms. Use all the information you have learned to write a definition of each Key Term in your own words.

Lab zone — Discover **Activity**

What Do Leaves Reveal About Plants?

1. Your teacher will give you two leaves from plants that grow in two very different environments: a desert and an area with average rainfall.
2. Carefully observe the color, size, shape, and texture of the leaves. Touch the surfaces of each leaf. Examine each leaf with a hand lens. Record your observations in your notebook.
3. When you have finished, wash your hands thoroughly with soap and water.

Think It Over
Inferring Use your observations to determine which plant lives in the desert and which does not. Give at least one reason to support your inference.

There are some very strange plants in the world. There are plants that trap animals, plants that bloom only once every thirty years, and plants with flowers that smell like rotting meat. You probably don't see such unusual plants every day. But you probably do see plants every day. You encounter plants whenever you see moss on a tree trunk, run across a lawn, or pick ripe tomatoes from a garden. And all plants, both the unfamiliar and the familiar, have a lot in common.

What Is a Plant?

Members of the plant kingdom share several characteristics. **Nearly all plants are autotrophs, organisms that produce their own food. All plants are eukaryotes that contain many cells. In addition, all plant cells are surrounded by cell walls.**

Plants Are Autotrophs You can think of a typical plant as a sun-powered, food-making factory. Sunlight provides the energy for this food-making process, called **photosynthesis**. During photosynthesis, a plant uses carbon dioxide gas and water to make food and oxygen. You will learn more about photosynthesis in Section 2.

Lab zone — Discover **Activity**

Skills Focus Inferring   L1

Materials hand lens, leaf from plant with thick, fleshy leaves, such as a jade, yucca, or aloe plant; leaf of a temperate climate plant, such as a maple, oak, or common garden plant

Time 10 minutes

Tips Select leaves that display adaptations easily associated with protection from bright sun and dry weather. Both leaves should be green.

Expected Outcome Students should observe a difference in leaf thickness, texture, and size.

Think It Over Students should infer that the plant with the small, thick, fleshy leaf lives in the desert or other hot, sunny climate, and that the plant with the larger, thinner, flatter leaf lives in an area of sufficient rainfall. Students will probably say that the thick leaf looks as if it has water in it.

▼ Plant cells

Plants Are Multicellular You don't need a microscope to see plants because they are multicellular. Plants vary greatly in size, of course. Both the tiniest moss and the tallest redwood tree are plants.

No matter how large or small a plant is, its cells are organized into **tissues**—groups of similar cells that perform a specific function in an organism. For example, most plants that live on land have tissues that transport materials throughout their bodies.

Plant Cells If you were to look at a plant's cells under a microscope, you would see that plants are eukaryotes. But unlike the cells of some other eukaryotes, a plant's cells are enclosed by a cell wall. The cell wall surrounds the cell membrane and separates the cell from the environment. Plant cell walls contain cellulose, a material that makes the walls rigid. Cell walls are what makes apples and carrots crunchy. Because their cell walls are rigid, plant cells look like small boxes.

Plant cells also contain many other structures, as shown in Figure 1. **Chloroplasts** (KLAWR uh plasts), which look something like green jelly beans, are the structures in which food is made. The Greek word *chloro* means "green." A **vacuole** is a large storage sac that can expand and shrink like a balloon. The vacuole stores many substances, including water, wastes, and food. A plant wilts when too much water has left its vacuoles.

Reading Checkpoint What is the function of the vacuole in a plant cell?

Chloroplast

Nucleus

Cell wall

Vacuole

Cell membrane

▲ Single plant cell

FIGURE 1
Plant Cell Structures
Like all plants, this maple tree is multicellular. Plants have eukaryotic cells that are enclosed by a cell wall. **Relating Diagrams and Photos** *Which cell structures can you see in the inset photograph of plant cells?*

Go Online
active art

For: Plant Cell Structures activity
Visit: PHSchool.com
Web Code: cep-1041

Chapter 4   A ◆ 105

A • 105

Adaptations for Living on Land

Teach Key Concepts L2
Plants Need Water

Focus Tell students that algae live in water and, as a result, they can obtain water and nutrients directly from the water.

Teach Ask: **What do plants need to survive on land?** *(A way to get water and then to transport it to all plant parts. Also, they need a way to reproduce without water.)* **Where do plants get water and nutrients?** *(From the soil)* **What plant adaptation reduces water loss?** *(Cuticle)* **What is vascular tissue?** *(A system of tubelike structures for transporting water, minerals, and food)* **learning modality: logical/mathematical**

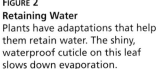

Math — Analyzing Data

Math Skill Interpreting graphs

Focus Tell students that a line graph shows how two variables are related.

Teach Direct students' attention to the graph. Ask: **What is this graph showing?** *(The amount of water loss in a plant at different times of the day)* **How can you tell how much water the plant lost at 6 P.M.?** *(Find 6 P.M. on the horizontal axis. Follow the vertical line extending up from the 6 P.M. mark until it hits the graph line. Read across to the vertical axis value—210 g.)* Point out that the water loss is measured in grams. Ask: **Why is water loss measured in grams rather than milliliters?** *(It is easier to measure the mass of a plant than the volume of water lost from a plant every hour. The mass of the plant is measured every hour; then the mass is subtracted from the measurement made an hour before.)*

Adaptations for Living on Land

Most plants live on land. How is living on land different from living in water? Imagine multicellular algae floating in the ocean. The algae obtain water and other materials directly from the water around them. Their bodies are held up toward the sunlight by the water. The water also aids in reproduction, allowing sperm cells to swim to egg cells.

Now imagine plants living on land. What adaptations would help them meet their needs without water all around them? **For plants to survive on land, they must have ways to obtain water and other nutrients from their surroundings, retain water, transport materials in their bodies, support their bodies, and reproduce.**

Obtaining Water and Other Nutrients Recall that all organisms need water to survive. Obtaining water is easy for algae because water surrounds them. To live on land, though, plants need adaptations for obtaining water from the soil. Plants must also have ways of obtaining other nutrients from the soil.

Retaining Water Plants must have ways of holding onto the water they obtain. Otherwise, they could easily dry out due to evaporation. When there is more water in plant cells than in the air, the water leaves the plant and enters the air. One adaptation that helps a plant reduce water loss is a waxy, waterproof layer called the **cuticle** that covers the leaves of most plants.

FIGURE 2
Retaining Water
Plants have adaptations that help them retain water. The shiny, waterproof cuticle on this leaf slows down evaporation.

Math — Analyzing Data

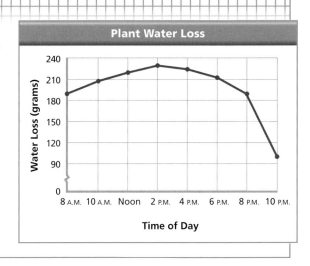

Water Loss in Plants
The graph shows how much water a certain plant loses during the hours shown.

1. **Reading Graphs** What variable is plotted along each axis?

2. **Interpreting Data** According to the graph, during what part of the day did the plant lose the most water? The least water?

3. **Drawing Conclusions** What could account for the pattern of water loss shown?

4. **Predicting** How would you expect the graph to look from 10 P.M. to 8 A.M.? Explain your reasoning.

Plant Water Loss graph: Water Loss (grams) on vertical axis (0 to 240); Time of Day on horizontal axis (8 A.M., 10 A.M., Noon, 2 P.M., 4 P.M., 6 P.M., 8 P.M., 10 P.M.)

Answers
1. Horizontal axis—time of day; vertical axis—water loss
2. Most—midday; least—in the evening.
3. The plant seemed to lose the most water during the sunniest or warmest parts of the day.
4. The line graph would descend during the night and then rise again in the morning hours, because the water loss is less during the night when there is no sun.

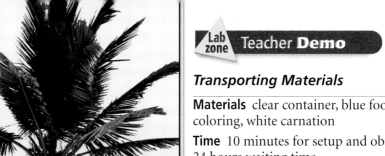

FIGURE 3
Transport and Support
For this tall coconut palm to survive, it must transport water, minerals, and food over long distances. It must also support its body so its leaves are exposed to sunlight.
Relating Cause and Effect *What structures allow plants to transport materials?*

Transporting Materials A plant needs to transport water, minerals, food, and other materials from one part of its body to another. In general, water and minerals are taken up by the bottom part of the plant, while food is made in the top part. But all of the plant's cells need water, minerals, and food.

In small plants, materials can simply move from one cell to the next. But larger plants need a more efficient way to transport materials farther, from one part of the plant to another. These plants have transporting tissue called vascular tissue. **Vascular tissue** is a system of tubelike structures inside a plant through which water, minerals, and food move.

Support A plant on land must support its own body. Support is not an issue for small plants that grow low to the ground. But for larger plants to survive, the plant's food-making parts must be exposed to as much sunlight as possible. Rigid cell walls and vascular tissue strengthen and support the large bodies of these plants.

Reproduction All plants undergo sexual reproduction that involves fertilization. **Fertilization** occurs when a sperm cell unites with an egg cell. The fertilized egg is called a **zygote.** For algae and some plants, fertilization can only occur if there is water in the environment. This is because the sperm cells of these plants swim through the water to the egg cells. Other plants, however, have an adaptation that makes it possible for fertilization to occur in dry environments. You will learn more about this adaptation in Chapter 5.

 Why do plants need adaptations to prevent water loss?

Water and minerals

Food

A ◆ 107

Lab zone **Teacher Demo** ⌊2⌋

Transporting Materials

Materials clear container, blue food coloring, white carnation

Time 10 minutes for setup and observation, 24 hours waiting time

Focus Tell students that this demonstration will help them see a plant's vascular system at work.

Teach Fill the vase with water and add 10 drops of the food coloring. Trim the carnation stem and place the carnation in the vase. The next day, ask: **What changes have occurred in the carnation?** *(The carnation now has blue streaks on the leaves.)* Allow students to observe the carnation. Ask: **What do you notice about the flower's petals?** *(There are thin streaks of color in the white petals.)*

Apply Ask: **How did the coloring reach the flower?** *(The blue water must have moved up the stem of the flower, through the vascular system.)* **learning modality: visual**

Help Students Read
Active Comprehension Have students read the first paragraph of *Transporting Materials.* Then ask: **What would you like to know about the kinds of things plants need to transport water?** *(Sample: How do they get water? Why can they stand upright?)* Write student responses on the board and have students read the remainder of the selection. After students are finished reading, ask them to respond to each question on the board.

Differentiated Instruction

Less Proficient Readers ⌊1⌋
Plant Cell Structure Pair less proficient readers with more able readers. Have the partners draw a large illustration of a cell. Then have them make several sticky labels for each cell feature: 1 for nucleus, 2 for cytoplasm, 1 for cell wall, 1 for vacuole, and 3 for chloroplast. Have students take turns placing a sticky in the appropriate portion of the illustration as they say a sentence describing the cell part. For example, "A plant cell has many chloroplasts."

Monitor Progress ⌊2⌋

Oral Presentation Have students briefly describe several ways that an oak tree is adapted to live on land.

Answers
Figure 3 Vascular tissues

 Because they need water to survive, and could easily dry up on land

Classification of Plants

Teach Key Concepts L2

Vascular and Nonvascular Plants

Focus Point out to students that scientists classify plants so that they are easier to study.

Teach Ask: **What are the two major groups of plants?** (*Vascular and nonvascular*) **Why are nonvascular plants short and low to the ground?** (*They have no tissue to provide support or to transport materials.*) **Why do nonvascular plants live in damp, shady places?** (*Materials must pass directly from the environment into cells, and then from one cell to the next. This process is slow, so materials do not travel far or quickly.*)

Apply Ask: **Why can vascular plants survive in a greater variety of environments than nonvascular plants?** (*Because vascular plants have a system to transport materials to every part of the plant, they can live in dry as well as damp environments.*) **How do angiosperms differ from gymnosperms?** (*Angiosperms are flowering vascular plants. Gymnosperms are also vascular plants but do not form fruits or flowers.*)

Discovery CHANNEL SCHOOL Video Field Trip

Introduction to Plants

Show the Video Field Trip to introduce students to the ways in which plants are adapted to live in many different environments. Discussion question: **How does phototropism help a plant to survive?** (*By enabling the plant to receive as much light as possible for photosynthesis*)

FIGURE 4

Plant Classification

The hundreds of thousands of plants that exist today can be classified as either nonvascular plants or vascular plants. Nonvascular plants are small and live in moist environments. Vascular plants can grow tall and live in diverse habitats. **Classifying** *What are the three groups of vascular plants?*

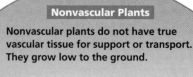

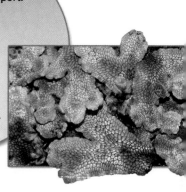

Nonvascular Plants

Nonvascular plants do not have true vascular tissue for support or transport. They grow low to the ground.

◄ Mosses grow in damp, shady places.

Liverworts grow on moist soil and rocks. ►

Discovery CHANNEL SCHOOL

Introduction to Plants

Video Preview
▶ Video Field Trip
Video Assessment

Classification of Plants

Scientists informally group plants into two major groups—nonvascular plants and vascular plants.

Nonvascular Plants Plants that lack a well-developed system of tubes for transporting water and other materials are known as **nonvascular plants.** Nonvascular plants are low-growing and do not have roots for absorbing water from the ground. Instead, they obtain water and materials directly from their surroundings. The materials then simply pass from one cell to the next. This means that materials do not travel very far or very quickly. This slow method of transport helps explain why most nonvascular plants live in damp, shady places.

Most nonvascular plants have only thin cell walls to provide support. This is one reason why these plants cannot grow more than a few centimeters tall.

Vascular Plants Plants with true vascular tissue are called **vascular plants.** Vascular plants are better suited to life in dry areas than are nonvascular plants. Their well-developed vascular tissue solves the problem of transport, moving materials quickly and efficiently throughout the plant's body.

Vascular tissue also provides strength, stability, and support to a plant. Thus, vascular plants are able to grow quite tall.

Vascular Plants

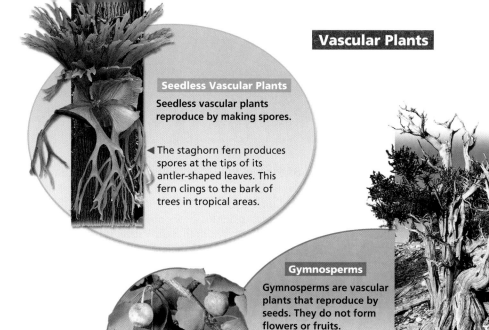

Seedless Vascular Plants

Seedless vascular plants reproduce by making spores.

◄ The staghorn fern produces spores at the tips of its antler-shaped leaves. This fern clings to the bark of trees in tropical areas.

Gymnosperms

Gymnosperms are vascular plants that reproduce by seeds. They do not form flowers or fruits.

◄ Ginkgo trees produce fleshy seeds that resemble fruits but are not. The seeds smell like vomit!

▲ The bristlecone pine can live for more than 4,000 years.

Angiosperms

Angiosperms are vascular plants that flower, and produce seeds that are surrounded by fruit.

The beavertail cactus produces brilliantly colored flowers. ▼

Wheat has been an important food crop for thousands of years. The grains, or fruits, are ground to make flour. ▶

A ◆ 109

Differentiated Instruction

English Learners/Beginning L1
Vocabulary: Word Analysis Contrast the meanings of *vascular* and *nonvascular*. Point out that the prefix *non-* sometimes means "not" and that words without this prefix may mean the opposite of words with the prefix. Explore the meanings of *sense/nonsense* and *essential/nonessential*.
learning modality: verbal

English Learners/Intermediate L2
Vocabulary: Word Analysis Repeat the activity at left, but have students speak or write sentences using the terms.
learning modality: verbal

Lab zone ▸ Build **Inquiry** L2

Local Plant Diversity

Focus Ask students how many different kinds of plants they think they could find around the school in 15 minutes.

Teach Take students on a walk around the school and have them record a description of as many different plant species they can find in 15 minutes. Each description should include where the plant was found, the plant's estimated size, any distinguishing characteristics, and a quick sketch of the plant. Allow students to work in pairs. One student can sketch while the partner records the description.

Apply Have students use their descriptions and the information in Figure 4 to classify the plants they recorded. **learning modality: visual**

Monitor Progress _____ L2

Skills Check Ask students to explain the difference between vascular plants and nonvascular plants.

Answers
Figure 4 Seedless vascular plants, gymnosperms, and angiosperms

A ● 109

Lab zone Build Inquiry L2

Algae and Plants

Materials microscope, samples of green algae, plant leaves, glass slides, tweezers, water, cover slips, dropper

Time 30 minutes

Focus Have students observe the algae and plant leaves without magnification. Ask: **How are the algae and plant leaves alike?** *(Both are green.)*

Teach Caution students that glass slides and cover slips are fragile. Have students place a drop of water containing the algae on a glass slide and cover it with a cover slip. Students should look at the algae slide and plant cross section under the microscope. Have students draw what they see and ask them to compare the cells in each. Ask: **What evidence did you see to support the idea that plants are descended from green algae?** *(Sample answer: Both types of cells contain chlorophyll.)* Encourage students to speculate on how scientists determined that the chlorophyll in the algae and the leaf was the same. *(Sample: They performed chemical tests to find the chemical structure.)* **learning modality: visual**

Complex Life Cycles

Teach Key Concepts
Sporophyte and Gametophyte

Focus Have students study Figure 6 and note that the plant life cycle alternates between two phases.

Teach Have students follow the diagram as you explain what is happening at each stage.

Apply Ask: **Which stage involves sexual reproduction? How can you tell?** *(The gametophyte stage; because the plant produces sperm cells and egg cells that join to become a zygote)* **learning modality: logical/ mathematical**

All in One Teaching Resources
• Transparency A28

Rock containing two plant fossils ▶

FIGURE 5
Ancient and Modern Plants
Fossils of ancient plants help scientists understand the origin of plants. These fossils are of two plants that lived about 300 million years ago. Notice the similarities between the fossils and modern-day ferns and horsetails.

Origin of Plants Which organisms were the ancestors of today's plants? In search of answers, biologists studied fossils, the traces of ancient life forms preserved in rock and other substances. The oldest plant fossils are about 400 million years old. The fossils show that even at that early date, plants already had many adaptations for life on land, including vascular tissue.

Better clues to the origin of plants came from comparing the chemicals in modern plants to those in other organisms. In particular, biologists studied a green pigment called **chlorophyll** (KLAWR uh fil), found in the chloroplasts of plants, algae, and some bacteria. Land plants and green algae contain the same forms of chlorophyll. This evidence led biologists to infer that ancient green algae were the ancestors of today's land plants. Further comparisons of genetic material clearly showed that plants and green algae are very closely related. In fact, some scientists think that green algae should be classified in the plant kingdom.

✓ Reading Checkpoint What is chlorophyll?

Complex Life Cycles

Plants have complex life cycles that include two different stages, the sporophyte stage and the gametophyte stage. In the **sporophyte** (SPOH ruh fyt) stage, the plant produces spores, tiny cells that can grow into new organisms. A spore develops into the plant's other stage, called the gametophyte. In the **gametophyte** (guh MEE tuh fyt) stage, the plant produces two kinds of sex cells: sperm cells and egg cells.

Figure 6 shows a typical plant life cycle. A sperm cell and egg cell join to form a zygote. The zygote then develops into a sporophyte. The sporophyte produces spores, which develop into the gametophyte. Then the gametophyte produces sperm cells and egg cells, and the cycle starts again. The sporophyte of a plant usually looks quite different from the gametophyte.

✓ Reading Checkpoint During which stage does a plant produce spores?

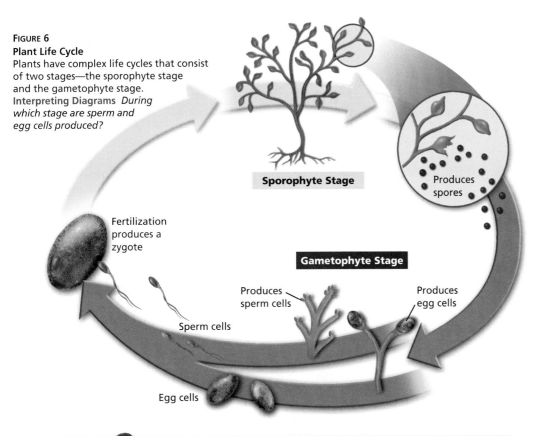

FIGURE 6
Plant Life Cycle
Plants have complex life cycles that consist of two stages—the sporophyte stage and the gametophyte stage.
Interpreting Diagrams During which stage are sperm and egg cells produced?

Sporophyte Stage

Fertilization produces a zygote

Produces spores

Gametophyte Stage

Produces sperm cells

Produces egg cells

Sperm cells

Egg cells

Section 1 Assessment

🎯 **Target Reading Skill** Building Vocabulary
Use your sentences to help you answer the questions below.

Reviewing Key Concepts

1. a. **Listing** List three characteristics of plants.
   b. **Comparing and Contrasting** Describe three ways that plant cells differ from the cells of some other eukaryotes.
   c. **Predicting** How might a plant cell be affected if it lacked chloroplasts?
2. a. **Identifying** What are five adaptations that plants need to survive on land?
   b. **Inferring** Why is a cuticle a useful adaptation in plants but not in algae?
3. a. **Reviewing** How do vascular plants differ from nonvascular plants?

b. **Explaining** Explain why vascular plants are better suited to life in dry areas.
c. **Classifying** Would you expect a tall desert plant to be a vascular plant? Explain.
4. a. **Describing** What are the two major stages of a plant's life cycle?
   b. **Sequencing** Describe in order the major events in the life cycle of a plant, starting with a zygote.

Writing in Science

Video Script You are narrating a video called *Living on Land*, which is written from the perspective of a plant. Write a one-page script for your narration. Be sure to discuss the challenges that life on land poses for plants and how they meet their needs.

Lab zone **Chapter Project**

Keep Students on Track Check to see that students have chosen their interactive exhibit item. Caution students who may have chosen an item whose production process is complicated and perhaps beyond students' limits. Meet with students and ask them to explain the next steps they plan to complete and what research tools they plan to use.

Writing in Science

Writing Mode Video Script
Scoring Rubric
4 Script includes accurate details about plant challenges and how plants meet them; writing is engaging
3 Includes all criteria; writing is unimaginative
2 Includes a few details
1 Includes inaccurate or irrelevant information

Monitor Progress _____ L2

Answers
Figure 6 The gametophyte stage

✓ **Reading Checkpoint** A green pigment found in the chloroplasts of plants, algae, and some bacteria.

✓ **Reading Checkpoint** The sporophyte stage

Assess

Reviewing Key Concepts

1. a. multicellular, autotrophic eukaryotes with cell walls **b.** Plant cells have a cell wall, chloroplasts, and vacuoles. **c.** Sample answer: It would not be able to produce food.
2. a. They must be able to obtain water and other materials from their environment, retain moisture, support their bodies, transport materials throughout their bodies, and reproduce. **b.** Because algae live in water, they have less problem with water loss.
3. a. Vascular plants have tissues for moving water and other materials throughout the entire plant; nonvascular plants do not.
b. Vascular plants can move water and food through the plant body quickly. **c.** Yes, because of the scarcity of water in the desert, a tall plant must have vascular tissue to supply its cells with water. Nonvascular plants are low-growing with no roots for absorbing water.
4. a. sporophyte and gametophyte **b.** A zygote develops into a sporophyte. The sporophyte produces spores that develop into the gametophyte. The gametophyte produces egg and sperm cells. A sperm cell and egg cell unite to form a zygote and the cycle continues.

Reteach L1
Have students make a chart listing the adaptations plants need to live on land and identify the adaptations as belonging to vascular plants.

Performance Assessment L2
Writing Have each student write paragraphs identifying several ways that an oak tree is adapted to live on land.

All in One Teaching Resources
• Section Summary: *The Plant Kingdom*
• Review and Reinforce: *The Plant Kingdom*
• Enrich: *The Plant Kingdom*

Technology and Society

Paper

Key Concept
Evaluate the benefits of using electronic paper versus traditional paper.

Build Background Knowledge
Have students look around the classroom and name all the products they can that are made of paper. Point out that educating students at all levels has been made possible for centuries through printed books. Ask a student volunteer to read the steps in making paper. Have the class identify the resources that are used to make paper. (*Trees, energy in the form of heat, chemicals, and water*) Remind students that even though paper can be recycled, it still remains the single largest component of waste in solid landfills. Explain that paper can be recycled only so many times.

Introduce the Debate
Have a student volunteer read the paragraphs *The Benefits of Paper* and *Paper and the Environment*. Ask: **What are some advantages and disadvantages of using paper?** (*The advantages are that many everyday items are made of paper, paper is inexpensive, and many people are employed in the paper industry. Disadvantages are that resources are used, making paper creates wastes—including dioxins—and paper creates a lot of garbage in landfills.*) **What is the chief advantage of e-paper?** (*It does not have the same environmental costs as paper.*)

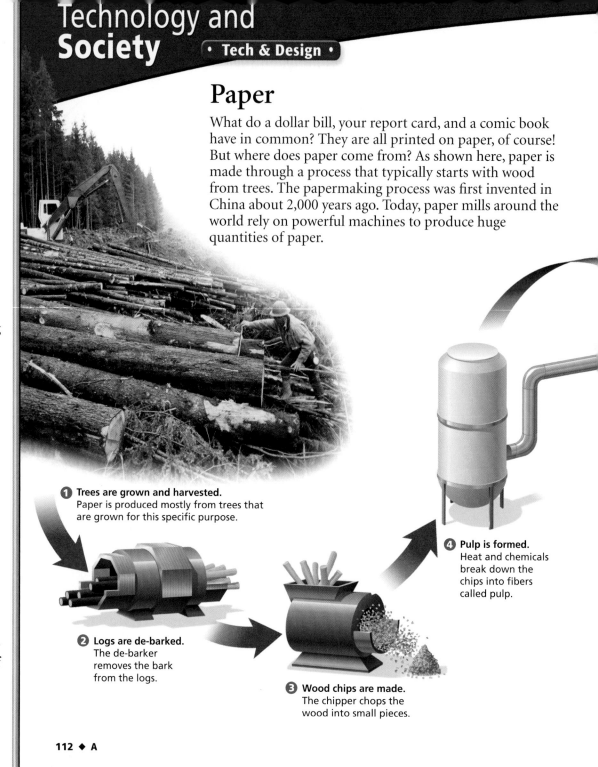

Paper

What do a dollar bill, your report card, and a comic book have in common? They are all printed on paper, of course! But where does paper come from? As shown here, paper is made through a process that typically starts with wood from trees. The papermaking process was first invented in China about 2,000 years ago. Today, paper mills around the world rely on powerful machines to produce huge quantities of paper.

1 Trees are grown and harvested.
Paper is produced mostly from trees that are grown for this specific purpose.

2 Logs are de-barked.
The de-barker removes the bark from the logs.

3 Wood chips are made.
The chipper chops the wood into small pieces.

4 Pulp is formed.
Heat and chemicals break down the chips into fibers called pulp.

112 ◆ A

Background

History of Science The first recorded effort to make paper was in A.D. 105 by a man in China named Ts'ai Lun. He mashed rags, bamboo, and mulberry wood into a liquid pulp, filtered the pulp on a screen, lifted out a sheet, and let it dry. Over the past 2,000 years, the basic process of making paper has not changed, though the techniques have changed, for example, using different chemicals in the pulping process. E-paper is a major departure from traditional paper. E-paper contains a layer of black and white ink and a layer of tiny electronic circuits. When different voltages are applied to the paper, different patterns of the white and black inks form to produce words and images.

The Benefits of Paper

Paper benefits society in so many ways. Many everyday items are made out of paper—tissues, paper cups, and cardboard packaging. Perhaps most important, paper is used as a portable, inexpensive way to print words and images. Throughout time, paper has allowed people to express their thoughts, record history, and share knowledge. In addition, the paper industry employs many people, and generates income for the economy.

Paper and the Environment

Paper has negative impacts on the environment. Each step in the papermaking process requires energy and produces wastes. Some of these wastes, such as dioxins, are toxic. Dioxins form when water is used to flush chemicals from the paper. Paper products also make up a lot of the garbage in landfills. Because of the environmental costs, engineers are working to create a new type of "paper" called electronic paper, or e-paper. Someday soon, you might use flexible, ultra-thin, digital screens instead of paper.

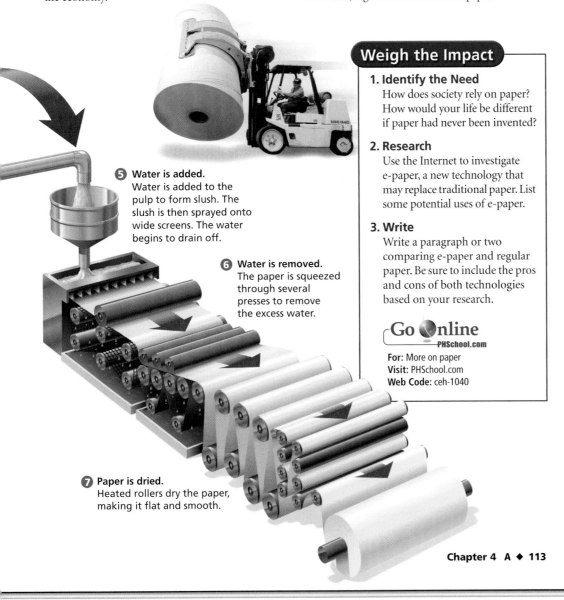

⑤ **Water is added.**
Water is added to the pulp to form slush. The slush is then sprayed onto wide screens. The water begins to drain off.

⑥ **Water is removed.**
The paper is squeezed through several presses to remove the excess water.

⑦ **Paper is dried.**
Heated rollers dry the paper, making it flat and smooth.

Weigh the Impact

1. Identify the Need
How does society rely on paper? How would your life be different if paper had never been invented?

2. Research
Use the Internet to investigate e-paper, a new technology that may replace traditional paper. List some potential uses of e-paper.

3. Write
Write a paragraph or two comparing e-paper and regular paper. Be sure to include the pros and cons of both technologies based on your research.

For: More on paper
Visit: PHSchool.com
Web Code: ceh-1040

Chapter 4 A ◆ 113

Facilitate the Debate

- Divide the class into small groups, and have each group member represent a different viewpoint on whether e-paper should replace traditional paper. Students might represent a person who works for the paper industry, a person whose business relies on paper (such as a bookstore), an ecologist or conservationist, and a citizen. Provide time for the groups to discuss the pros and cons of the widespread use of e-paper.
- After the group discussions, bring the class together to share some of the points discussed in the groups.

Weigh the Impact

1. Society relies on paper for printed words and images, and for everyday items, such as paper cups and cardboard packaging. Possible answer: My life would be different because I would not have had books, magazines, or newspapers to read, and writing would be limited.

2. Possible uses of e-paper include electronic billboards, downloading entire texts of books, downloading daily news instead of getting a paper newspaper, and downloading e-mails from the Internet.

3. Paragraphs should include the factors mentioned in the feature as well as others learned through research. Most students will recognize that e-paper is designed to replace only paper with text and images, not all uses of traditional paper.

Go Online
PHSchool.com
For: More on paper
Visit: PHSchool.com
Web Code: ceh-1040

Students can research this issue online.

Extend

Encourage students to research the following on newspapers: 1) the amount of landfill space they take up; 2) the number of trees used to print them; and 3) the amount of energy used to produce them. Explain that these numbers represent resources saved if e-paper is used instead of newspapers.

2 Photosynthesis and Light

Objectives

After this lesson, students will be able to
A.4.2.1 Explain what happens when light strikes a green leaf.
A.4.2.2 Describe the overall process of photosynthesis.

Target Reading Skill

Previewing Visuals Explain that looking at visuals before they read helps students activate prior knowledge and predict what they are about to read.

Answers

Possible questions and answers include: **How is sunlight involved in photosynthesis?** *(The energy in sunlight is used to make sugar.)* **Why does a plant need sugar?** *(The plant uses energy from the sugar to carry out life functions.)* **How does the plant use the water its roots take in?** *(Water molecules combine with carbon dioxide to form sugar and oxygen during photosynthesis.)*

All in One Teaching Resources

• Transparency A29

Preteach

Build Background Knowledge　L1

Colored Light, Colored Object

Ask students to describe how colored light affects the appearance of colored objects. Encourage students to think about neon lights holiday lights, and even the difference between artificial lighting at night and natural daylight. *(Students should recognize that colors appear different under different lights.)*

Reading Preview

Key Concepts

• What happens when light strikes a green leaf?
• How do scientists summarize the process of photosynthesis?

Key Terms

• transmission　• reflection
• absorption　• accessory pigment

Target Reading Skill

Previewing Visuals Preview Figure 9. Then write two questions that you have about the diagram in a graphic organizer like the one below. As you read, answer your questions.

The Photosynthesis Process

Q.	How is sunlight involved in photosynthesis?
A.	
Q.	

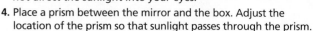

What Colors Make Up Sunlight?

1. Glue a piece of white paper onto the inside bottom of a shoe box.
2. Place the box on its side near a window or outside in a sunny area.
3. Hold a mirror in front of the open side of the box. Adjust the mirror until it reflects sunlight onto the paper in the box. **CAUTION:** *Do not direct the sunlight into your eyes.*
4. Place a prism between the mirror and the box. Adjust the location of the prism so that sunlight passes through the prism.
5. Describe what you see on the paper in the box.

Think It Over
Observing What did you learn about light from this activity?

The year was 1883. T. W. Engelmann, a German biologist, was at work in his laboratory. He peered into the microscope at some algae on a slide. The microscope had a prism located between the light source and the algae. As Engelmann watched the algae, he saw gas bubbles forming in the water around some of the cells. Curiously, no gas bubbles formed around other cells. Although Engelmann did not know it at the time, his experiment provided a clue about how light is involved in photosynthesis. To understand what Engelmann observed, you need to know more about the nature of light.

FIGURE 7
The Visible Spectrum
When white light passes through a prism, you can see that it is made up of the colors of the rainbow.

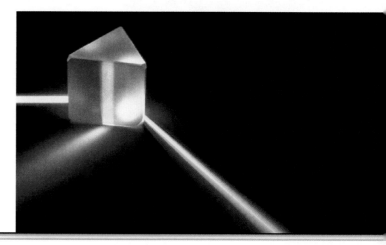

114 ◆ A

Skills Focus Observing　L1
Time 10 minutes
Materials glue, hand mirror, prism, shoe box, white paper
Tips If a sunny window or bright outside area is not available, students can use bright, narrow-beam flashlights to complete the activity. You may wish to

demonstrate how to hold the prism so that it projects a rainbow.

Expected Outcome When students reflect sunlight into the shoe box with a mirror, they should see white light on the paper in the shape of the mirror. When the light passes through the prism, they should see a spectrum (rainbow-like band of colors) on the paper.

Think It Over White light is made up of different colors.

Extend Challenge students to use different colors of paper inside the shoe box and describe what they see.

Green light is reflected by the leaf. You see the leaf as green.

Yellow light is reflected by the lemon. You see the lemon as yellow.

The Nature of Light

The sun is the source of energy on Earth. If you take a walk outside on a sunny day, you feel the sun's energy as it warms your skin. You see the energy in the form of light on objects around you. The light that you see is called white light. But when white light passes through a prism like the one in Figure 7, you can see that it is made up of the colors of the rainbow. Scientists refer to these colors—red, orange, yellow, green, blue, and violet—as the visible spectrum.

When Light Strikes Objects In addition to prisms, white light strikes many other objects. Some objects such as glass and other transparent materials allow light to pass through them. This process is called **transmission.** When light hits a shiny surface such as a mirror, the light bounces back. This process is called **reflection.** When dark objects, such as street pavements, take in light, it is called **absorption.**

Most objects, however, reflect some colors of the visible spectrum while they absorb other colors. When white light strikes the lemon in Figure 8, the lemon absorbs most of the light's colors. However, the lemon reflects yellow light. The lemon looks yellow because your eyes see the reflected color.

Plants and Light Like yellow lemons and most other objects, plants absorb some colors of the visible spectrum and reflect others. **When light strikes the green leaves of a plant, most of the green part of the spectrum is reflected. Most of the other colors of light are absorbed.**

FIGURE 8
When Light Strikes Objects
When white light strikes the lemon and the leaf, different colors of light are reflected by the two objects. Because of the reflected light, we see the lemon as yellow and the leaf as green.
Inferring What happens to the colors of light that are not reflected off the lemon and the leaf?

Chapter 4 A ◆ 115

Instruct

The Nature of Light

Teach Key Concepts **L2**
Reflected Colors

Focus Ask: **What colors are in white light?** *(Red, orange, yellow, green, blue, violet)*

Teach Have students compare the colors that are reflected in Figure 8. Ask: **What happens to the green in the sunlight when it reaches a plant's leaves?** *(It is reflected.)* **How does that affect what we see?** *(We see the leaf as green.)* **What happens to red and yellow in sunlight when they reach a plant leaf? How do you know?** *(They are absorbed; we do not see yellow or red, so they must be absorbed.)* **learning modality: visual**

All in One Teaching Resources
• Transparency A30

Bouncing light **L2**

Materials flashlight, 2 hand mirrors

Time 15 minutes

Focus Remind students that light travels in a straight line.

Teach Dim classroom lights and allow groups of four students to work together to arrange mirrors and flashlight so that the light beam goes around a corner. Ask: **What do you observe about the path of the light?** *(It bounces off the mirrors.)*

Apply Have two pairs challenge each other. Tell them to hold the flashlight in place so that the beam shines in a straight line. Have one pair choose a point that is not on that line and challenge the other pair to direct the light to that point. Then have pairs switch roles. **learning modality: kinesthetic**

All in One Teaching Resources
• Guided Reading and Study Worksheet: *Photosynthesis and Light*

Student Edition on Audio CD

Monitor Progress **L2**
Answer
Figure 8 They are absorbed.

Focus Have students study the timeline. Ask: **What does the timeline show?** *(Key dates when scientists put the pieces of the photosynthesis puzzle together)*

Teach As students read each segment of the timeline, challenge them to state the experimental question that the scientist was investigating. *(Van Helmont—What must be added to a tree for it to grow? Priestley— What happens to a burning candle sealed in a jar, with a plant and without a plant? Ingenhousz—Do leaves need sunlight to produce oxygen? Sachs—Do plants produce carbohydrates? Englemann—What colors of light are needed for photosynthesis? Calvin— What happens to the carbon in carbon dioxide during photosynthesis?)* After students have analyzed the timeline, ask: **Based on the findings of Van Helmont and Ingenhousz, what do plants need for photosynthesis?** *(Water and sunlight)* **Based on the findings of Priestley, Ingenhousz, and Sachs, what are the products of photosynthesis?** *(Oxygen and carbohydrates)*

Writing Mode Dialogue
Scoring Rubric
4 Information is accurate and gives details about the scientist's contribution; dialogue is interesting and lively
3 Includes all criteria; writing is uninteresting
2 Includes most criteria
1 Includes inaccurate or incomplete information

Portfolio

Plant Pigments When light strikes a leaf, it is absorbed by pigments found in the leaf's cells. Chlorophyll, the most abundant pigment in leaves, absorbs most of the blue and red light. Most of the green light, on the other hand, is reflected rather than absorbed. This explains why chlorophyll appears green in color, and why leaves usually appear green.

Other pigments, called **accessory pigments,** are also found in leaves. These pigments, which include orange and yellow pigments, absorb different colors of light than chlorophyll does. Most accessory pigments are not visible in plants because they are masked by chlorophyll.

Reading Checkpoint **What is the most abundant pigment in leaves?**

Science and **History**

Unraveling the Mysteries of Photosynthesis
What do plants need to make their own food? What substances do plants produce in the process of photosynthesis? Over time, the work of many scientists has provided answers to these questions.

1771
Joseph Priestley
When Joseph Priestley, an English scientist, placed a burning candle in a covered jar, the flame went out. When he placed both a plant and a candle in a covered jar, the candle kept burning. Priestley concluded that the plant released something into the air that kept the candle burning. Today, we know that plants produce oxygen, a product of photosynthesis.

1779
Jan Ingenhousz
Jan Ingenhousz, a Dutch scientist, placed branches with leaves in water. In sunlight, the leaves produced oxygen bubbles. In the dark, the leaves produced no oxygen. Ingenhousz concluded that plants need sunlight to produce oxygen, a product of photosynthesis.

1643
Jean-Baptiste Van Helmont
A Dutch scientist, Jean-Baptiste Van Helmont, planted a willow tree in a tub of soil. After five years of adding only water, the tree gained 74 kilograms. Van Helmont concluded that trees need only water to grow. Today, we know that water is one of the raw materials of photosynthesis.

| 1650 | 1700 | 1750 |

116 ◆ **A**

The Photosynthesis Process

When light strikes a plant's leaves, it sets in motion the process known as photosynthesis. You can think of photosynthesis as a two-part process. First, the plant captures energy from the sun. Then, it uses that energy to produce food.

Capturing Energy Because light is one form of energy, a substance that absorbs light absorbs energy. Just as a car requires the energy in gasoline to move, plants require energy in the form of light to power photosynthesis. Photosynthesis begins when light strikes the chlorophyll in a plant's chloroplasts. The light energy that is absorbed powers the next stage of the photosynthesis process.

Writing in Science

Research and Write Find out more about one of the scientists discussed in this timeline. Write a dialogue you might have had with the scientist. Discuss how the scientist's work contributed to our current understanding of photosynthesis.

1883
T. W. Engelmann
Building on the work of Jan Ingenhousz, T. W. Engelmann studied how different colors of light affect photosynthesis in green algae. He found that cells bathed in blue and red light had the fastest rates of photosynthesis. Today, scientists know that the chlorophyll in green algae and plants absorbs mostly blue and red light.

1948
Melvin Calvin
The American scientist Melvin Calvin traced the chemical path that the carbon from carbon dioxide follows during photosynthesis. By doing this, Calvin learned about the complex chemical reactions of photosynthesis.

1864
Julius Sachs
A German biologist, Julius Sachs, observed living leaf cells under a microscope. As he watched, he tested the cells for the presence of carbohydrates. Sachs discovered that plants produce carbohydrates during photosynthesis.

1850	1900	1950

The Photosynthesis Process

Teach Key Concepts   L2
The Role of Light

Focus Remind students that sunlight is a form of energy.

Teach Ask: **What are the two stages in photosynthesis?** *(First, the plant captures energy from the sun; then the plant uses the energy to power a series of chemical reactions that produce sugar and oxygen.)* **What raw materials are needed for photosynthesis?** *(Water and carbon dioxide)*

Apply Ask: **What happens to the food produced in plants that is not used?** *(It is stored.)* **How do organisms that eat plants benefit from photosynthesis?** *(When they eat plants, the organisms get the energy stored in the plants. They can use the energy for their own life processes.)* **learning modality: verbal**

All in One Teaching Resources
• Transparency A31

Help Students Read
Identifying Cause and Effect Refer to the Content Refresher, which provides guidelines for Relating Cause and Effect. Have students use a cause and effect graphic organizer to identify the causes and effect in the process of photosynthesis. Have them begin with light hitting the plant's leaf and end with the production of sugar.

Monitor Progress _____ L2

Writing Have students write a paragraph that summarizes the process of photosynthesis. Students can save their paragraph in their portfolios.

Answer

✓ Reading Checkpoint   Chlorophyll

A ● 117

Address Misconceptions L2
What do plants need?

Focus Students may know that water is a key ingredient for plant growth, but they may not realize the importance of light and carbon dioxide, since these are less tangible.

Teach Ask: **What is a unique ability of most plants, not shared by animals?** (*They can make their own food through photosynthesis.*) Emphasize that the "food" plants make is sugar, $C_6H_{12}O_6$. The carbon and oxygen atoms in the sugar molecule both come from carbon dioxide in the air. The hydrogen atoms in the sugar come from water. Light energy is what initiates and powers the chemical process.

Apply Ask: **What would happen if a plant did not receive enough carbon dioxide or light?** (*It wouldn't be able to make sugar.*)
learning modality: logical/mathematical

For: The Photosynthesis Process activity
Visit: PHSchool.com
Web Code: cep-1042

Students investigate the process of photosynthesis.

Use Visuals: Figure 9
The Photosynthesis Process

Focus Remind students that the purpose of photosynthesis is to capture the energy of sunlight and change it into a form that the plant can use for life processes.

Teach Write the equation for photosynthesis on the board. Then direct students' attention to Figure 9. As a volunteer reads the word equation, have students find the appropriate parts in the figure. Emphasize that the parts of the equation to the left of arrow are materials entering the plant before photosynthesis takes place. Those to the right are the products of photosynthesis.

Apply Ask: **Where does the plant obtain carbon dioxide for photosynthesis?** (*From the air*)

For: The Photosynthesis Process activity
Visit: PHSchool.com
Web Code: cep-1042

The Chemistry of Photosynthesis Light energy is just one of the things that plants need to carry out photosynthesis. Just as you need flour and eggs to make cookies, a plant also needs raw materials to make its own food. Plants use carbon dioxide gas and water as raw materials for photosynthesis.

During this stage of photosynthesis, plants use the energy absorbed by chlorophyll to power a series of complex chemical reactions. In these reactions, carbon dioxide from the air and water from the soil combine to produce sugar, a type of carbohydrate. Another product, oxygen gas, is also produced. The events of photosynthesis are pictured in Figure 9.

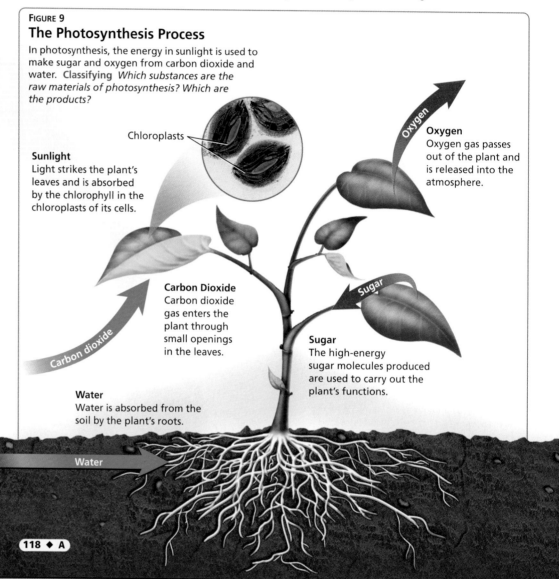

FIGURE 9
The Photosynthesis Process

In photosynthesis, the energy in sunlight is used to make sugar and oxygen from carbon dioxide and water. **Classifying** *Which substances are the raw materials of photosynthesis? Which are the products?*

Chloroplasts

Sunlight
Light strikes the plant's leaves and is absorbed by the chlorophyll in the chloroplasts of its cells.

Oxygen
Oxygen gas passes out of the plant and is released into the atmosphere.

Carbon Dioxide
Carbon dioxide gas enters the plant through small openings in the leaves.

Sugar
The high-energy sugar molecules produced are used to carry out the plant's functions.

Water
Water is absorbed from the soil by the plant's roots.

Water

Differentiated Instruction

Gifted and Talented L3

Students with good math skills may be interested in balancing the chemical equation for photosynthesis. Tell students that the chemical equation is balanced when the same number of each kind of atom is accounted for both before and after the reaction. Be sure students understand that they cannot break up molecules as they try to balance the equation. The balanced equation for photosynthesis is
$$6(CO_2) + 6(H_2O) \xrightarrow{\text{light energy}} C_6H_{12}O_6 + 6(O_2).$$
learning modality: logical/mathematical

The Photosynthesis Equation Scientists write equations to describe chemical reactions. A chemical equation shows raw materials and products. **The many chemical reactions of photosynthesis can be summarized by this equation:**

$$\text{carbon dioxide} + \text{water} \xrightarrow{\text{light energy}} \text{sugar} + \text{oxygen}$$
$$(CO_2) \quad + \quad (H_2O) \quad\quad\quad (C_6H_{12}O_6) + (O_2)$$

You can read this equation as, "carbon dioxide and water combine in the presence of light to produce sugar and oxygen." Photosynthesis takes place in the parts of a plant that contain chlorophyll.

Like all organisms, plants need a steady supply of energy to grow and develop, respond, and reproduce. The food made by plants during photosynthesis supplies energy for these processes. Any excess food made by plants is stored in their roots, stems, leaves, or fruits. Carrot plants, for example, store excess food in their roots. When you eat a carrot, you are eating the plant's stored food.

The other product of photosynthesis is oxygen. Most of the oxygen produced during photosynthesis passes out of the plant and into the air. It can then be used by other organisms for their body processes.

 Reading Checkpoint What are the products of photosynthesis?

FIGURE 10
Food Made by Plants
You can enjoy the results of photosynthesis in a salad. When you eat cucumbers, tomatoes, and other plant products, you are eating food made and stored by plants.

Section 2 Assessment

Target Reading Skill Previewing Visuals Refer to your questions and answers about photosynthesis to help you answer Question 2.

Reviewing Key Concepts

1. a. **Listing** What are three things that might happen to light when it strikes an object?
   b. **Relating Cause and Effect** What happens when light strikes a green leaf? How does this explain why leaves appear green?
   c. **Predicting** Predict whether a plant would grow better when exposed to green light or to blue light. Explain.
2. a. **Reviewing** What is the overall equation for photosynthesis?
   b. **Summarizing** In a sentence, summarize what happens during each of the two stages of photosynthesis.

c. **Applying Concepts** Explain how each of these conditions could affect photosynthesis in a plant: (a) cloudy weather, (b) drought, (c) bright sunlight.

Lab zone At-Home **Activity**

Reflecting on Light With a family member, look around your kitchen for objects that transmit, reflect, and absorb white light. Explain to your family member what happens to white light when it strikes each object. Then, choose one of the objects and explain why you see it as the color you do.

Chapter 4 A ◆ 119

A ● 119

Eye on Photosynthesis L3

Prepare for Inquiry

Key Concept
Plants require several factors to be present before photosynthesis can occur.

Skills Objectives
After this lab, students will be able to
- design experiments to determine what substances and conditions are necessary for photosynthesis
- perform tests on several variables
- analyze the results of their tests and draw conclusions

 Class Time 45 minutes

Advance Planning
Obtain *Elodea* plants. Prepare the sodium bicarbonate solution by using 0.5 g of sodium bicarbonate for each 100 mL of water. Boil water for Part 2 and let it cool.

Alternate Materials
If *Elodea* plants are not available, you may be able to find appropriate small water plants at a tropical fish supply store.

Safety
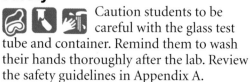 Caution students to be careful with the glass test tube and container. Remind them to wash their hands thoroughly after the lab. Review the safety guidelines in Appendix A.

- Skills Lab: *Eye on Photosynthesis*

Guide Inquiry

Invitation
Ask students to describe what might happen to a plant to make it turn brown instead of staying green. (*Sample: Too much sun, not enough water, disease, pests, change of seasons, poor soil*) Then have them describe the things plants need in order to be green and healthy.

Introduce the Procedure
- Have students use water to perfect their techniques of immersing a filled test tube before they use the sodium bicarbonate solution or boiled water.
- As students read through Steps 3 and 4, make certain they refer to the photograph on page 120.

Eye on Photosynthesis

Problem
What raw materials and conditions are involved in photosynthesis?

Skills Focus
observing, controlling variables, designing experiments

Materials
- *Elodea* plants
- water (boiled, then cooled)
- wide-mouthed container
- sodium bicarbonate solution
- 2 test tubes
- wax pencil
- lamp (optional)

Procedure

PART 1 Observing Photosynthesis

1. Use a wax pencil to label two test tubes *1* and *2*. Fill test tube 1 with sodium bicarbonate solution. Sodium bicarbonate provides a source of carbon dioxide for photosynthesis.

2. Fill the wide-mouthed container about three-fourths full of sodium bicarbonate solution.

3. Hold your thumb over the mouth of test tube 1. Turn the test tube over, and lower it to the bottom of the container. Do not let in any air. If necessary, repeat this step so that test tube 1 contains no air pockets. **CAUTION:** *Glass test tubes are fragile. Handle the test tubes carefully. Do not touch broken glass.*

4. Fill test tube 2 with sodium bicarbonate solution. Place an *Elodea* plant in the tube with the cut stem at the bottom. Put your thumb over the mouth of the test tube, and lower it into the container without letting in any air. Wash your hands.

5. Place the container with the two test tubes in bright light. After a few minutes, examine both test tubes for bubbles.

6. If bubbles form in test tube 2, observe the *Elodea* stem to see if it is producing the bubbles. The bubbles are oxygen bubbles. The production of oxygen signals that photosynthesis is taking place.

7. Leave the setup in bright light for 30 minutes. Observe what happens to any bubbles that form. Record your observations.

Troubleshooting the Experiment
- Make sure students do not grip the test tubes too tightly. Remind students to tell you immediately if anything breaks.
- Tell students not to expect dramatic results. Have them look for small bubbles of oxygen.
- Remind students to move on to the next procedure while they are waiting for results.

Expected Outcome
Students should observe tiny bubbles forming along the stems or leaves of the plant in Part 1. These bubbles will grow larger with time. If no bubbles are present, review the variables and make a fresh cut in the *Elodea* stem. Make sure all variables, such as sunlight, are at their maximum. Observations will support or reject students' hypotheses on whether a particular variable is important in photosynthesis.

PART 2 Is Carbon Dioxide Needed for Photosynthesis?

8. Your teacher will provide a supply of water that has been boiled and then cooled. Boiling removes gases that are dissolved in the water, including carbon dioxide.

9. Based on what you learned in Part 1, design an experiment to show whether or not carbon dioxide is needed for photosynthesis. Obtain your teacher's approval before carrying out your experiment. Record all your observations.

PART 3 What Other Conditions Are Needed for Photosynthesis?

10. Make a list of other conditions that may affect photosynthesis. For example, think about factors such as light, the size of the plant, and the number of leaves.

11. Choose one factor from your list. Then design an experiment to show how the factor affects photosynthesis. Obtain your teacher's approval before carrying out your experiment. Record all your observations.

Analyze and Conclude

1. **Observing** What process produced the bubbles you observed in Part 1?

2. **Controlling Variables** In Part 1, what was the purpose of test tube 1?

3. **Designing Experiments** For the experiments you carried out in Parts 2 and 3, identify the manipulated variable and the responding variable. Explain whether or not your experiments were controlled experiments.

4. **Drawing Conclusions** Based on your results in Part 2, is carbon dioxide necessary for photosynthesis?

5. **Posing Questions** What question about photosynthesis did you explore in Part 3? What did you learn?

6. **Communicating** In a paragraph, summarize what you learned about photosynthesis from this investigation. Be sure to support each of your conclusions with evidence from your experiments.

More to Explore

A small animal in a closed container will die, even if it has enough water and food. A small animal in a closed container with a plant, water, and food will not die. Use what you have learned from this experiment to explain these facts.

A ◆ 121

Analyze and Conclude

1. Photosynthesis

2. It was a control, to show whether the bubbles were truly related to the plant.

3. Sample answer: The manipulated variable was the presence or absence of sunlight. The responding variable was the production of oxygen. My experiment was controlled because I kept all the other variables the same for both test tubes.

4. Yes. Students' answers should reveal that no bubbles were formed when the plant was not exposed to a source of carbon dioxide.

5. Answers will depend on students' procedures, but students should realize that the most important factors for photosynthesis are light and the presence of carbon dioxide and water.

6. Students' paragraphs will vary, but each should conclude that carbon dioxide, water, and sunlight are needed for photosynthesis. Students should support their claims by citing their own observations from parts 1, 2, and 3 of the lab.

Extend Inquiry

More to Explore A small animal in a closed container will die once all the oxygen in the air has been used up, even if it has enough food and water. In a closed container with a plant, food, and water, a small animal can survive because the plant produces oxygen from photosynthesis. In this case, the small animal will have the oxygen, food, and water it needs.

Objectives

After this lesson, students will be able to
A.4.3.1 Name some nonvascular plants and list the characteristics they share.
A.4.3.2 Describe the structure of a moss plant.

Target Reading Skill

Identifying Main Ideas Explain that identifying main ideas and details helps students sort the facts from the information into groups. Each group can have a main topic, subtopics, and details.

Answers

Details include: Mosses, liverworts, and hornworts

All in One Teaching Resources

• Transparency A32

Preteach

Build Background Knowledge L2

Moss Descriptions

Ask students to describe any mosses with which they are familiar. *(Some may know about peat moss, sphagnum moss, or have seen moss growing on rocks or in wooded areas. Most students will describe them as green, spongy, soft, and moist.)* Explain to students that not everything people identify as mosses are actually classified as mosses. Point out that in this section students will learn the characteristics of mosses.

---

3 Mosses, Liverworts, and Hornworts

Reading Preview

Key Concept

• What characteristics do the three groups of nonvascular plants share?

Key Terms

• rhizoid • bog • peat

Target Reading Skill

Identifying Main Ideas As you read this section, write the main idea—the biggest or most important idea—in a graphic organizer like the one below. Then write three supporting details that give examples of the main idea.

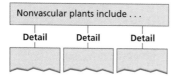

Main Idea

Nonvascular plants include . . .

| Detail | Detail | Detail |

Lab zone Discover Activity

Will Mosses Absorb Water?

1. Place 20 mL of sand into a plastic graduated cylinder. Place 20 mL of peat moss into a second plastic graduated cylinder.
2. Predict what would happen if you were to pour 10 mL of water slowly into each of the two graduated cylinders and then wait five minutes.
3. To test your prediction, use a third graduated cylinder to add 10 mL of water slowly to the sand. Then add 10 mL of water to the moss. After five minutes, record your observations.

Think It Over

Predicting How did your prediction compare with your results? What did you learn about moss from this investigation?

You pause from your hike to look at the forest around you. As far as you can see, you are surrounded by a living carpet of mosses. They are growing everywhere—up tree trunks, on rocks along the banks of the stream, and on the forest floor. Mosses make up one group of nonvascular plants. **The three major groups of nonvascular plants are mosses, liverworts, and hornworts. These low-growing plants live in moist environments where they can absorb water and other nutrients directly from their environment.** The watery surroundings also enable sperm cells to swim to egg cells during reproduction.

122 ◆ A

Lab zone Discover Activity

Skills Focus Predicting L1

Materials 3 plastic graduated cylinders, dropper, 20 mL peat moss, 20 mL sand, stopwatch, water

Time 15 minutes

Tips Suggest that students use a dropper to slowly add water to the sand and the peat moss. The peat moss absorbs water more readily if it is already damp.

Expected Outcome Students should find that the peat moss absorbs much more water than the sand.

Think It Over Some students will predict that the peat moss will absorb more water, others will predict that the sand will absorb more water. Students should observe that peat moss absorbs water well, and better than sand does.

Mosses

Have you ever seen mosses growing in the cracks of a sidewalk or in a shady spot? With more than 10,000 species, mosses are by far the most diverse group of nonvascular plants.

The Structure of a Moss If you were to look closely at a moss, you would see a plant that looks something like the one in Figure 11. The familiar green, fuzzy moss is the gametophyte generation of the plant. Structures that look like tiny leaves grow off a small, stemlike structure. Thin, rootlike structures called **rhizoids** anchor the moss and absorb water and nutrients. The sporophyte generation grows out of the gametophyte. The sporophyte grows a long, slender stalk with a capsule at the end. The capsule contains spores.

The Importance of Mosses Many people use peat moss in agriculture and gardening. The peat moss that gardeners use contains sphagnum (SFAG num) moss. Sphagnum moss grows in a type of wetland called a **bog**. The still water in a bog is so acidic that decomposers cannot live in the water. Thus when the plants die, they do not decay. Instead, the dead plants accumulate at the bottom of the bog. Over time, the mosses become compressed into layers and form a blackish-brown material called **peat**. Large deposits of peat exist in North America, Europe, and Asia. In Europe and Asia, people use peat as a fuel to heat homes and to cook food.

✓ **Reading Checkpoint** How does peat form?

FIGURE 11
A Moss Plant
A moss gametophyte is low-growing and has structures that look like roots, stems, and leaves. The stalklike sporophyte generation remains attached to the gametophyte.
Interpreting Diagrams
What structures anchor the gametophyte?

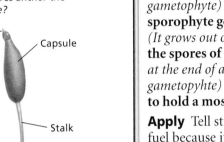

- Capsule
- Stalk
- Sporophyte
- Stemlike structure
- Leaflike structure
- Gametophyte
- Rhizoid

A ◆ 123

Instruct

Mosses

Teach Key Concepts ☐L2
Structure of Mosses

Focus Prompt students to think about any mosses they may have seen growing in the cracks of shaded sidewalks or on the north side of tree trunks. Have students match their recalled image with Figure 11.

Teach Ask: **Which generation of the moss plant is green and fuzzy and looks like leaves growing from a stalk?** (*The gametophyte*) **Where will you find the sporophyte generation of a moss plant?** (*It grows out of the gametophyte.*) **Where are the spores of the sporophyte?** (*In a capsule at the end of a stalk that grows from the gametopyhte*) **What structure acts like roots to hold a moss in place?** (*Rhizoid*)

Apply Tell students that peat can be used as fuel because it contains stored energy from dead plants. Ask: **Where did the plants get this energy?** (*They used the energy in sunlight to make food, which they stored.*)
learning modality: visual

Independent Practice ☐L2

☒ **Teaching Resources**
- Guided Reading and Study Worksheet: *Mosses, Liverworts, and Hornworts*
- Transparency A33

◉ **Student Edition on Audio CD**

Monitor Progress ———— ☐L2

Writing Have students write one or two sentences to describe the function of rhizoids.

Answers
Figure 11 The rhizoids

✓ **Reading Checkpoint** When dead plants collect at the bottom of a bog and become compressed into layers over time

Liverworts and Hornworts

Teach Key Concepts L2
Liverworts and Hornworts

Focus Direct attention to Figure 12.

Teach Have students identify the plant parts. Ask: **What part of the liverwort is the gametophyte?** *(The liver-shaped leaflike structures and the treelike structures that grow up from them)* **What gives the hornwort its name?** *(Its sporophytes; they look like horns.)*

Go Online
SciLINKS NSTA

For: Links on nonvascular plants
Visit: www.SciLinks.org
Web Code: scn-0143

Download a worksheet that will guide students' review of Internet resources on nonvascular plants.

Monitor Progress L2

Answer

✓ Reading Checkpoint The hornwort sporophyte looks like horns.

Assess

Reviewing Key Concepts

1. a. Nonvascular plants are low growing and live in moist environments where they can absorb water and nutrients directly from their environment. **b.** Nonvascular plants have no way to transport nutrients throughout a large plant body, so they remain small and low to the ground and live in moist surroundings that can quickly provide them what they need. **c.** They are all nonvascular plants. Moss grows in soil and on rocks and trees. Liverworts live in very moist areas near streams. Hornworts live in moist soil.

Reteach L1
Use Figure 11 to describe the life cycle of a moss.

Performance Assessment L2
Skills Check Have students make Venn diagrams to compare and contrast the three types of nonvascular plants.

All in One Teaching Resources

- Section Summary: *Mosses, Liverworts, and Hornworts*
- Review and Reinforce: *Mosses, Liverworts, and Hornworts*
- Enrich: *Mosses, Liverworts, and Hornworts*

FIGURE 12
Liverworts and Hornworts
Liverworts (left) have sporophytes that are too small to see. The leaf-like and treelike structures are part of the plants' gametophytes. Hornworts (right) have gametophytes that lie flat on the ground. The hornlike sporophytes are about one centimeter long.

Go Online
SciLINKS NSTA

For: Links on nonvascular plants
Visit: www.SciLinks.org
Web Code: scn-0143

Liverworts and Hornworts

Figure 12 shows examples of two other groups of nonvascular plants—liverworts and hornworts. There are more than 8,000 species of liverworts. This group of plants is named for the shape of the plant's body, which looks somewhat like a human liver. *Wort* is an old English word for "plant." Liverworts are often found growing as a thick crust on moist rocks or soil along the sides of a stream.

There are fewer than 100 species of hornworts. If you look closely at a hornwort, you can see slender, curved structures that look like horns growing out of the gametophytes. These hornlike structures, which give these plants their names, are the sporophytes. Unlike mosses or liverworts, hornworts are seldom found on rocks or tree trunks. Instead, hornworts usually live in moist soil, often mixed in with grass plants.

✓ Reading Checkpoint **What does a hornwort sporophyte look like?**

Section 3 Assessment

Target Reading Skill Identifying Main Ideas Use your graphic organizer about nonvascular plants to help you answer the questions below.

Reviewing Key Concepts

1. a. Describing Describe two characteristics that nonvascular plants share.
   b. Relating Cause and Effect Explain how the two characteristics of nonvascular plants are related.
   c. Comparing and Contrasting In what ways are mosses, liverworts, and hornworts similar? In what ways do they differ?

Lab zone At-Home **Activity**

Moss Hunt With a family member, go on a moss hunt in your neighborhood. Look for mosses in sidewalk cracks, on trees, or on other objects. For each location in which you find mosses, observe and record the sunlight and moisture conditions. Explain why mosses grow in the environments they do.

Lab zone At-Home **Activity**

Moss Hunt L1 Show students an actual moss plant so that they will have a better idea of what they are looking for during their moss search. Tell students to remember to take a notebook with them so that they can record the sun and moisture conditions. Encourage students to sketch the mosses they find.

Masses of Mosses

Problem
How is a moss plant adapted to carry out its life activities?

Skills Focus
observing, measuring

Materials
- clump of moss
- hand lens
- metric ruler
- toothpicks
- plastic dropper
- water

Procedure

1. Your teacher will give you a clump of moss. Examine the clump from all sides. Draw a diagram of what you see. Measure the size of the overall clump and the main parts of the clump. Record your observations.

2. Using toothpicks, gently separate five individual moss plants from the clump. Be sure to pull them totally apart so that you can observe each plant separately. If the moss plants start to dry out as you are working, moisten them with a few drops of water.

3. Measure the length of the leaflike, stemlike, and rootlike structures on each plant. If brown stalks and capsules are present, measure them. Find the average length of each structure.

4. Make a drawing of a single moss plant. Label the parts, give their sizes, and record the color of each part. When you are finished observing the moss, return it to your teacher. Wash your hands thoroughly.

5. Obtain class averages for the sizes of the structures you measured in Step 3. Also, if the moss that you observed had brown stalks and capsules, share your observations about those structures.

Analyze and Conclude

1. **Observing** Describe the overall appearance of the moss clump, including its color, size, and texture.

2. **Measuring** What was the typical size of the leaflike portion of the moss plants, the typical height of the stemlike portion, and the typical length of the rootlike portion?

3. **Inferring** In which part(s) of the moss does photosynthesis occur? How do you know?

4. **Communicating** Write a paragraph explaining what you learned about mosses from this investigation. Include explanations of why mosses cannot grow tall and why they live in moist environments.

More to Explore

Select a moss plant with stalks and capsules. Use toothpicks to release some of the spores, which can be as small as dust particles. Examine the spores under a microscope. Create a labeled drawing of what you see.

Analyze and Conclude
1. Sample answer: The moss clump is green and small but contains many individual plants, and has a leafy texture.
2. Leaflike: a few millimeters long by a fraction of a millimeter thick; stemlike: up to 15 cm high, usually much shorter; rootlike: very short.
3. In the green parts (leaflike and stemlike); only the green parts can carry out photosynthesis because only the green parts have chlorophyll.

4. Paragraphs should explain that mosses cannot transport water over long distances, so they cannot grow tall and they must live in moist environments.

Extend Inquiry

More to Explore Show students how to gently crush the moss capsules to release the spores. Students can then observe these structures with a microscope.

Masses of Mosses L2

Prepare for Inquiry

Key Concept
Students will observe a moss and describe its structures.

Skills Objectives
After this lab, students will be able to
- make detailed observations of a moss and communicate their observations
- measure the structures of a moss and calculate class averages

Class Time 45 minutes

Advance Planning
Provide a variety of species of mosses. If possible, obtain some moss clumps with sporophytes present.

Alternate Materials
If you have microscopes available, allow students to use them.

Safety
Students should wash their hands thoroughly after finishing the lab. If students use microscopes, review all relevant safety procedures. Review the safety guidelines in Appendix A.

All in One Teaching Resources
- Skills Lab: *Masses of Mosses*

Guide Inquiry

Troubleshooting the Experiment
Moss clumps from nature may contain more than one type. Have a field guide on hand for students to consult.

Expected Outcome
- Students should be able to identify all the parts of the moss plant.
- Measurements will vary, depending on the type of moss.

Objectives

After this lesson, students will be able to

A.4.4.1 Name some seedless vascular plants and list the characteristics they share.

A.4.4.2 Describe the structure of a fern plant and how it reproduces.

Target Reading Skill 🔄

Asking Questions Explain that changing a head into a question helps student anticipate the ideas, facts, and events they are about to read.

Answers

Possible questions and answers: **What are the characteristics of seedless vascular plants?** (*Seedless vascular plants have vascular tissue; they do not produce seeds; they reproduce by releasing spores.*) **How do ferns reproduce?** (*Ferns reproduce by spores that form on the underside of its fronds.*) **How do club moss differ from true mosses?** (*Club mosses have vascular tissue.*)

All in One Teaching Resources

• Transparency A34

Preteach

Build Background Knowledge L2

Identifying Fern Parts

Ask students to draw and label a picture of a plant. The picture should include leaves, stems, and roots. Then show students a potted fern and ask them to point out the leaves, stems, and roots of the fern.

Reading Preview

Key Concept

• What are the main characteristics of seedless vascular plants?

Key Term

• frond

🔄 Target Reading Skill

Asking Questions Before you read, preview the red headings. In a graphic organizer like the one below, ask a *what, how,* or *where* question for each heading. As you read, answer your questions.

Ferns, Club Mosses, and Horsetails

Question	Answer
What are the characteristics of seedless vascular plants?	Seedless vascular plants have . . .

Lab zone Discover **Activity**

How Quickly Can Water Move Upward?

1. Put on your goggles. Your teacher will give you a plastic petri dish as well as a narrow glass tube that is open at both ends.
2. Fill the petri dish half full of water. Add a drop of food coloring to the water.
3. Stand the tube on end in the water and hold it upright. Observe what happens. Record your observations.

Think It Over

Inferring Why might it be an advantage for the transporting cells of plants to be arranged in a tubelike way?

The time is 340 million years ago—long before the dinosaurs lived. The place is somewhere in the forests that covered most of Earth's land. If you could have walked through one of these ancient forests, it would have looked very strange to you. You might have recognized the mosses and liverworts that carpeted the moist soil. But overhead you would have seen very tall, odd-looking trees.

Among the trees were huge, tree-sized ferns. Other trees resembled giant sticks with leaves up to one meter long. The huge leaves stuck out from the branches. When the leaves dropped off, they left diamond-shaped scars that looked like the scales that cover a fish.

126 ♦ A

Lab zone Discover **Activity**

Skills Focus Inferring L1

Materials dropper, food coloring, goggles, narrow glass tube, plastic petri dish, water

Time 10 minutes

Tips Caution students to handle the glass tube gently. If they roughly push the glass

tube onto the bottom of the petri dish, the tube may shatter.

Expected Outcome The colored water should move quickly up the glass tube.

Think It Over Students should infer that a tubelike arrangement of cells will help water move quickly up the plant.

Characteristics of Seedless Vascular Plants

The odd-looking plants in the ancient forests were the ancestors of three groups of smaller plants alive today. **Ferns, club mosses, and horsetails share two characteristics. They have true vascular tissue and they do not produce seeds. Instead of seeds, these plants reproduce by releasing spores.**

Vascular Tissue What adaptations allowed the ancient trees to grow so tall? Unlike mosses, the trees were vascular plants. Vascular plants can grow tall because their vascular tissue provides an effective way of transporting materials throughout the plant.

The vascular tissue also strengthens the plants' bodies. The cells making up the vascular tissue have strong cell walls. Imagine a handful of drinking straws bundled together with rubber bands. The bundle of straws is stronger and more stable than a single straw would be. Arranged in a similar way, the strong tubelike structures in vascular plants give the plants strength and stability.

Spores for Reproduction Ferns, club mosses, and horsetails need to grow in moist surroundings just as mosses do. This is because the plants release spores into their surroundings, where they grow into gametophytes. When the gametophytes produce egg cells and sperm cells, there must be enough water available for the sperm to swim toward the eggs.

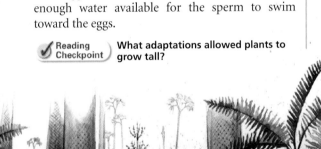

✓ **Reading Checkpoint** What adaptations allowed plants to grow tall?

FIGURE 13
An Ancient Forest
Giant ferns, club mosses, and horsetails dominated ancient forests on Earth.

A ◆ 127

Characteristics of Seedless Vascular Plants

Teach Key Concepts   L2
Vascular Tissue

Focus Have students study the pictures of the plants on these two pages. Ask: **How do these plants differ from mosses?** *(They are taller than mosses.)*

Teach Discuss with students how these plants differ from most larger plants today: They reproduce by spores, not seeds. Ask: **How are these plants similar to most larger plants today?** *(They have vascular tissue.)* **What structures give these seedless plants strength and stability?** *(Vascular tissue)* **Why is moisture important for reproduction in seedless vascular plants?** *(Sperm must swim through water to the eggs.)*

Apply Ask: **Why do you think seedless vascular plants are not as common today as in the past?** *(The environment is drier in most places than in the past.)* **learning modality: visual**

Independent Practice   L2

All in One Teaching Resources

• Guided Reading and Study Worksheet: *Characteristics of Seedless Vascular Plants*

◉ **Student Edition on Audio CD**

Monitor Progress _____   L2

Skills Check Have students list two functions of vascular tissue. *(Transports food and transports water through the plant's body, provides support)*

Answer

✓ **Reading Checkpoint** Vascular tissue

Differentiated Instruction

Special Needs Students   L1
Vascular Tissue Students who are visually impaired or need extra help may benefit by exploring a celery stalk's vascular tissue. Ask: **What do you feel on the outside of the celery stalk?** *(Narrow ridges)* Explain that these ridges are bundles of vascular tissue. Have students hold the base of a celery stalk in one hand and apply pressure to the top of the stalks with the other. Ask: **Why couldn't you crush or push together the celery stalk?** *(The vascular tissue is strong enough to resist the force of a hand pressing on it.)* **learning modality: kinesthetic**

Ferns

Teach Key Concepts L2

Fern Structure and Reproduction

Focus Remind students that vascular plants have true stems, roots, and leaves.

Teach Have students study the parts of the fern shown in Figure 14. Point out the underground stem. Ask: **How does this stem differ from most stems you are familiar with?** *(It is underground.)* **Which part of the fern is its leaf?** *(The frond)* Tell students that the upper surface of the frond is covered by a waxlike coating called the cuticle. Ask: **What advantage is the cuticle to the plant?** *(It helps prevent water loss from the plant.)* Point out the spores on the under surface of the fronds. Ask: **At what stage is the fern plant shown in the picture?** *(The sporophyte)* **learning modality: visual**

All in One **Teaching Resources**

• Transparency A35

Ferns

There are more than 12,000 species of ferns alive today. They range in size from tiny plants about the size of this letter "M" to tree ferns that grow up to 5 meters tall.

The Structure of Ferns Like other vascular plants, ferns have true stems, roots, and leaves. The stems of most ferns are underground. Leaves grow upward from the top side of the stems, while roots grow downward from the bottom of the stems. Roots are structures that anchor the fern to the ground and absorb water and nutrients from the soil. These substances enter the root's vascular tissue and travel through the tissue into the stems and leaves.

Figure 14 shows a fern's structure. Notice that the fern's leaves, or **fronds,** are divided into many smaller parts that look like small leaves. The upper surface of each frond is coated with a cuticle that helps the plant retain water. In many ferns, the developing leaves are coiled at first. Because they resemble the top of a violin, these young leaves are often called fiddleheads. As they mature, the fiddleheads uncurl.

Reproduction in Ferns The familiar fern, with its visible fronds, is the sporophyte stage of the plant. On the underside of mature fronds, spores develop in tiny spore cases. Wind and water can carry the spores great distances. If a spore lands in moist, shaded soil, it develops into a gametophyte. Fern gametophytes are tiny plants that grow low to the ground.

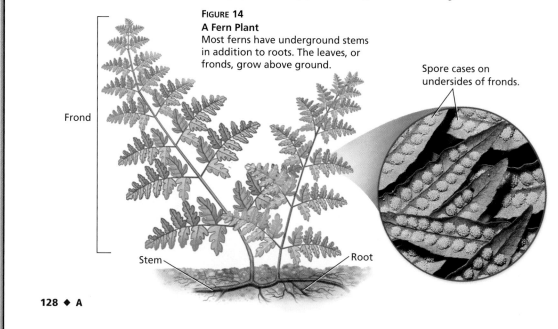

FIGURE 14
A Fern Plant
Most ferns have underground stems in addition to roots. The leaves, or fronds, grow above ground.

Spore cases on undersides of fronds.

Frond

Stem

Root

128 ◆ A

Lab zone Try This Activity

Skills Focus Inferring L2

Materials fern plant, hand lens, plastic dropper, water

Time 20 minutes

Tips Students should observe the fronds, the stem, and the roots. They should notice that the upper surface of a frond is smooth and shiny compared to the lower surface.

Spore cases may be visible on the underside of the blade. Water dropped onto the upper surface of the frond should run off.

Expected Outcome Students should note that the roots anchor the plant on land and absorb water. The cuticle on the upper surface reduces water loss.

Extend Suggest that students closely examine a spore case, and then release the spores from the case with a dissecting knife and examine them with a hand lens. **learning modality: visual**

Club Mosses and Horsetails

Like ferns, club mosses and horsetails have true stems, roots, and leaves. They also have a similar life cycle. However, there are relatively few species of club mosses and horsetails alive today.

Do not be confused by the name *club mosses*. Unlike true mosses, club mosses have vascular tissue. You may be familiar with the club moss in Figure 15. The plant, which looks a little like the small branch of a pine tree, is sometimes called ground pine or princess pine. Club mosses usually grow in moist woodlands and near streams.

There are about 30 species of horsetails on Earth today. As you can see in Figure 15, the stems of horsetails are jointed. Long, coarse, needlelike branches grow in a circle around each joint. Small leaves grow flat against the stem just above each joint. The whorled pattern of growth somewhat resembles the appearance of a horse's tail. The stems contain silica, a gritty substance also found in sand. During colonial times, Americans used the plants to scrub their pots and pans. Another common name for horsetails is scouring rushes.

 Reading Checkpoint Where do club mosses usually grow?

FIGURE 15
Club Mosses and Horsetails
Club mosses (left) look like tiny pine trees. Horsetails (right) have branches and leaves that grow in a circle around each joint. *Inferring Which grows taller—true mosses or club mosses?*

Section 4 Assessment

Target Reading Skill Asking Questions Use the answers to the questions you wrote about the headings to help you answer the questions below.

Reviewing Key Concepts

1. a. **Listing** What two characteristics do ferns, club mosses, and horsetails share?
   b. **Comparing and Contrasting** In what ways do ferns, club mosses, and horsetails differ from mosses? In what way are they similar to mosses?
   c. **Inferring** Although ferns have vascular tissue, they still must live in moist, shady environments. Explain why.

Writing in Science

Product Label Create a product label to be attached to pots of fern plants for sale at a garden shop. Describe the structure of ferns and growing instructions. Include other helpful information or diagrams.

Teach Key Concepts L1
Club Mosses and Horsetails

Focus Tell students that club mosses and true mosses are not the same.

Teach Ask: **How are club mosses different from true mosses?** (*Club mosses have vascular tissue, true mosses do not.*)

Apply Ask students to describe the appearance of the vascular tissue in horsetails. (*Sample: Long, jointed stems*)
learning modality: verbal

Monitor Progress _____ L2

Answers
Figure 15 Club mosses

 Reading Checkpoint In moist woodlands and near streams

Assess

Reviewing Key Concepts

1. **a.** Vascular tissue and the use of spores to reproduce **b.** They differ from mosses because they have true vascular tissue; mosses do not. They are similar in that they grow in moist places. **c.** So that the released spores can develop into gametophytes and that sperm can swim to the eggs.

Reteach L1

Have students draw and label diagrams showing the life cycle of ferns.

Performance Assessment L2
Skills Check Have students create Venn diagrams that compare ferns, club mosses, and horsetails.

All in One Teaching Resources

- Section Summary: *Ferns, Club Mosses, and Horsetails*
- Review and Reinforce: *Mosses, Ferns, Club Mosses, and Horsetails*
- Enrich: *Ferns, Club Mosses, and Horsetails*

Lab zone Chapter Project

Keep Students on Track Students should show the design of their interactive exhibit so some younger children and ask them if they can think of ways to make the exhibit easier to use or easier to understand. They should also ask if it should answer some overlooked question. Students should then revise their exhibit to accommodate the comments.

Writing in Science

Writing Mode Description
Scoring Rubric
4 Label includes detailed, accurate information about growth requirements; clearly presented
3 Includes all criteria; presentation somewhat unclear
2 Includes basic growth information; lacks details
1 Includes inaccurate information or is incomplete

nteractive Textbook

- Complete student edition
- Section and Chapter Self-Assessments
- Assessment reports for teachers

Help Students Read

Building Vocabulary

Word Part Analysis Before students read the chapter, list on the board the following word parts and meanings: *photo-*, "light"; *-phyte*, "plant"; *non-*, "not", *chloro-*, "green." Have students identify these word parts in the vocabulary terms. Discuss each term's meanings with students.

Words in Context Select key terms from the chapter. Have students write a sentence for each term that places the term in a correct context. Provide them with one example before they begin: *Cuticle: the cuticle of the plant helps prevent water loss.*

Connecting Concepts

Concept Maps Help students develop one way to show how information in this chapter is related. Have students brainstorm to identify the key concepts, key terms, details, and examples. Then write each one on a sticky note and attach it at random to chart paper or the board.

Tell students that this concept map can be organized in hierarchical order beginning at the top with the key concepts. Ask students these questions to guide them to categorize the information on the stickies. **What are characteristics of plants? How can plants be classified?**

Prompt students by using connecting words or phrases such as "is made up of," and "consists of" to indicate the basis for the organization of the map. The phrases should form a sentence between or among a set of concepts.

Answers

Accept logical presentations by students.

All in One Teaching Resources

- Key Terms Review: *Introduction to Plants*
- Connecting Concepts: *Introduction to Plants*

1 The Plant Kingdom

Key Concepts

- Nearly all plants are autotrophs, organisms that produce their own food. All plants are eukaryotes that contain many cells. In addition, all plant cells are surrounded by cell walls.

- For plants to survive on land, they must have ways to obtain water and other nutrients from their surroundings, retain water, transport materials in their bodies, support their bodies, and reproduce.

- Scientists informally group plants into two major groups—nonvascular plants and vascular plants.

- Plants have complex life cycles that include two different stages, the sporophyte stage and the gametophyte stage.

Key Terms

photosynthesis	zygote
tissue	nonvascular plant
chloroplast	vascular plant
vacuole	chlorophyll
cuticle	sporophyte
vascular tissue	gametophyte
fertilization	

2 Photosynthesis and Light

Key Concepts

- When light strikes the green leaves of a plant, most of the green part of the spectrum is reflected. Most of the other colors of light are absorbed.

- The many chemical reactions of photosynthesis can be summarized by this equation:

$$(CO_2) + (H_2O) \xrightarrow{\text{light energy}} (C_6H_{12}O_6) + (O_2)$$

Carbon dioxide and water combine in the presence of light to produce sugar and oxygen.

Key Terms

transmission	absorption
reflection	accessory pigment

3 Mosses, Liverworts, and Hornworts

Key Concept

- The three major groups of nonvascular plants are mosses, liverworts, and hornworts. These low-growing plants live in moist environments where they can absorb water and other nutrients directly from their environment.

Key Terms
rhizoid
bog
peat

4 Ferns, Club Mosses, and Horsetails

Key Concept

- Ferns, club mosses, and horsetails share two characteristics. They have true vascular tissue and they do not produce seeds. Instead of seeds, these plants reproduce by releasing spores.

Key Term
frond

Go Online
PHSchool.com
For: Self-Assessment
Visit: PHSchool.com
Web Code: cea-1040

Organizing Information

Comparing and Contrasting Copy the graphic organizer about mosses and ferns onto a separate sheet of paper. Then complete it and add a title. (For more on Comparing and Contrasting, see the Skills Handbook.)

Characteristic	Moss	Fern
Size	a. ____?	Can be tall
Environment	Moist	b. ____?
Body parts	Rootlike, stemlike, and leaflike structures	c. ____?
Familiar generation	d. ____?	Sporophyte
Is true vascular tissue present?	No	e. ____?

Reviewing Key Terms

Choose the letter of the best answer.

1. Mosses and trees are both
   a. vascular plants.
   b. nonvascular plants.
   c. seed plants.
   d. plants.

2. The structures in plant cells in which food is made are called
   a. cuticles.
   b. chloroplasts.
   c. vacuoles.
   d. vascular tissues.

3. When visible light strikes a green leaf, most of the green light is
   a. reflected.
   b. absorbed.
   c. transmitted.
   d. stored.

4. The familiar green, fuzzy moss is the
   a. frond.
   b. rhizoid.
   c. gametophyte.
   d. sporophyte.

5. The leaves of ferns are called
   a. rhizoids.   b. sporophytes.
   c. fronds.   d. cuticles.

If the statement is true, write *true*. If it is false, change the underlined word or words to make the statement true.

6. <u>Vascular tissue</u> is a system of tubelike structures through which water and food move.

7. The waxy, waterproof layer that covers the leaves of most plants is called the <u>cell wall</u>.

8. Leaves are green due to <u>accessory pigments</u>.

9. Sugars and oxygen are the products of <u>fertilization</u>.

10. Mosses are <u>vascular</u> plants.

Writing in Science

Firsthand Account You are a biologist who has studied plant life in various environments. Select one environment and describe in detail the plant life you found there. What features allowed the plants to survive?

Introduction to Plants
Video Preview
Video Field Trip
▶ Video Assessment

Go Online
PHSchool.com
For: Self-Assessment
Visit: PHSchool.com
Web Code: cea-1040

Students can take an online practice test that is automatically scored.

All in One Teaching Resources
- Transparency A36
- Chapter Test
- Performance Assessment Teacher Notes
- Performance Assessment Student Worksheet
- Performance Assessment Scoring Rubric

ExamView® Computer Test Bank CD-ROM

Organizing Information
a. Small and low
b. Moist
c. True roots, stems, and leaves
d. Gametophyte
e. Yes.
Possible title: Characteristics of Mosses and Ferns

Reviewing Key Terms
1. d 2. b 3. a 4. c 5. c
6. true
7. false; cuticle
8. false; chlorophyll
9. false; photosynthesis
10. false; nonvascular

Writing in Science

Writing Mode Description
Scoring Rubric
4 Includes accurate information with many details; writing is clear and organized
3 Includes all criteria but few details
2 Includes most criteria
1 Includes inaccurate or incomplete information

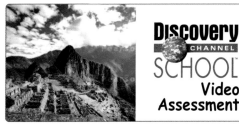

Video Assessment

Introduction to Plants

Show the Video Assessment to review chapter content and as a prompt for the writing assignment. Discussion questions: **Name and describe three different specialized adaptations of plants for living in extreme habitats.** (*Phototropism in places with short growing seasons—stems twist to keep plants pointed toward the sun; hairy stems in cold climates—help plants retain heat; hairy leaves in areas with low moisture—help collect water; long root systems in windy areas—keep plants firmly anchored*) **Explain how the Amazon water lily avoids self-pollination.** (*It blooms for only two days—the first day its white color and strong scent attract pollinators; the second day it changes to a color and scent that no longer attracts pollinators*)

Checking Concepts

11. Sample answer: a way to retain water; a way to obtain water and nutrients from soil; support for its body

12. A sporophyte produces a gametophyte. The gametophyte plant produces egg cells and sperm cells. Fertilization occurs when a sperm cell fuses with an egg cell to form a zygote. The zygote develops into a new sporophyte.

13. The bus appears yellow because its paint contains pigments that reflect the yellow part of visible light.

14. Chlorophyll absorbs most of the red and blue colors of light so the energy in these colors can be used to power photosynthesis.

15. Rhizoids anchor the plant and absorb water and nutrients. They are found in mosses.

16. Vascular tissue enables the fern to efficiently transport water and food to all its cells and support the plant so it can grow large.

17. Mosses are nonvascular plants; club mosses are vascular. Both need to grow in moist environments because they reproduce with spores.

Thinking Critically

18. As the taller plants grow, they block the light from the smaller ones. If light does not reach the smaller plants, they die.

19. The sporophyte generation produces the spores. The spores develop into the gametophyte stage, which produces two kinds of gametes—sperm cells and egg cells.

20. a. The apple reflects most of the red part of the spectrum. **b.** The mirror reflects all colors of light.

21. Students should indicate that their friend probably is mistaken. Mosses are nonvascular plants and cannot grow more than a few centimeters tall.

22. The north sides are cooler and get less sunlight. They are more moist.

Checking Concepts

11. Name one adaptation that distinguishes plants from algae.

12. Briefly describe the life cycle of a typical plant.

13. Explain why a yellow school bus appears yellow in color.

14. What role does chlorophyll play in the photosynthesis process?

15. What are two functions of rhizoids? In what plants are they found?

16. In what two ways is vascular tissue important to a fern plant?

17. In what ways do mosses and club mosses differ from each other? In what ways are they similar?

Thinking Critically

18. Relating Cause and Effect After a patch of land becomes bare, small plants often appear. Soon, slightly taller plants start to grow, while the small ones die. The new plants may be replaced by even taller plants. How might light play a role in these changes?

19. Comparing and Contrasting How does the sporophyte generation of a plant differ from the gametophyte generation?

20. Predicting Explain what would happen to light if it were to strike each object shown.

21. Applying Concepts A friend tells you that he has seen moss plants that are about 2 meters tall. Is your friend correct? Explain.

22. Inferring People have observed that mosses tend to grow on the north side of a tree rather than the south side. Why might this be so?

Applying Skills

Use the data table to answer Questions 23–27.

A scientist exposed a green plant to different colors of light. She then measured how much of each light the plant absorbed.

Absorption of Light by a Plant

Color of Light	Percentage of Light Absorbed
Red	55
Orange	10
Yellow	2
Green	1
Blue	85
Violet	40

23. Graphing Create a bar graph using the information in the data table. (For information on creating bar graphs, see the Skills Handbook.)

24. Interpreting Data What color of light did the plant absorb the most?

25. Drawing Conclusions List the three colors of light that are most important for photosynthesis in this plant.

26. Predicting If the plant were exposed only to yellow light, how might the plant be affected? Explain.

27. Inferring If a plant with reddish leaves were used in a similar experiment, how might the results differ? Explain.

Lab zone Chapter **Project**

Performance Assessment Present your exhibit to your classmates. Describe your original exhibit and how you changed it based on the feedback you received. Explain what you learned by doing this project. What factors are most important in creating a successful educational exhibit for children?

Lab zone Chapter **Project** L3

Project Wrap-Up Students' exhibits should be well organized and should contain detailed pictures and/or drawings of the process used to make their product. As students view one another's exhibits, have them take brief notes. After all exhibits are viewed, discuss any questions or comments students might have.

Standardized Test Prep

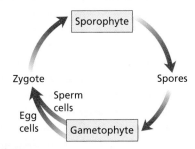
Choose the letter of the best answer.

1. Based on the diagram above, which of these statements about a plant's life cycle is true?
   A Plants spend part of their lives producing spores.
   B Plants spend part of their lives producing sperm and egg cells.
   C A zygote develops into the spore-producing stage of the plant.
   D all of the above

2. You examine plant cells under a microscope and notice many green round bodies within the cells.

The green structures are most likely involved in
   F directing the cell's functions.
   G photosynthesis.
   H storing food and water.
   J making proteins.

3. Both mosses and ferns
   A have true vascular tissue.
   B reproduce with spores.
   C have roots, stems, and leaves.
   D can only grow low to the ground.

4. Which of the following statements best explains why mosses and liverworts cannot grow tall?
   F They have no rootlike structures.
   G Taller plants in their surroundings release chemicals that slow down their growth.
   H They cannot take in enough oxygen from their surroundings.
   J They do not have true vascular tissue.

5. A houseplant that has not been watered for several days is droopy and wilted. What can you infer has happened to the plant's cells?
   A Water has filled the plant's nucleus.
   B Water has filled the plant's contractile vacuoles.
   C Water has filled the plant's chloroplasts.
   D Water has left the plant's vacuoles.

Constructed Response

6. Describe three adaptations that plants have for living on land. Explain why each adaptation is important for a plant to be able to survive on land.

Applying Skills

23. Graphs should show the percentage of light absorbed on the vertical axis, in increments of five or ten percentage points. The color of light should be placed along the horizontal axis. The height of each color's bar should correspond to the number in the table.

24. Blue

25. Red, blue, violet

26. Students should predict that little photosynthesis would occur. Without photosynthesis, the plant would die.

27. A plant with reddish leaves would reflect more red light and absorb more green light. The percentage of the red light would be a lower value, and the percentage of green light would be a higher value.

Standardized Test Prep

1. D **2.** G **3.** B **4.** J **5.** D

6. Sample answer: Land plants have roots that absorb water and minerals. A waxy cuticle helps prevent the loss of water from the plant. Vascular tissue transports materials throughout the plant.

Chapter at a Glance

PRENTICE HALL
Teacher EXPRESS™
Plan • Teach • Assess

 Chapter Project  *Cycle of a Lifetime*

Technology

Local Standards

All in One Teaching Resources
- Chapter Project Teacher Notes, pp. 272–273
- Chapter Project Student Overview, pp. 274–275
- Chapter Project Student Worksheets, pp. 276–277
- Chapter Project Scoring Rubric, p. 278

 Discovery SCHOOL Video Preview

Section 1 **The Characteristics of Seed Plants**

2–3 periods
1 1/2–2 blocks

A.5.1.1 Identify the characteristics that seed plants share.
A.5.1.2 Explain how seeds become new plants.
A.5.1.3 Describe the functions of roots, stems, and leaves.

 Discovery SCHOOL Video Field Trip

Section 2 **Gymnosperms**

2–3 periods
1 1/2–2 blocks

A.5.2.1 Identify the characteristics of gymnosperms.
A.5.2.2 Describe how gymnosperms reproduce.
A.5.2.3 List important products from gymnosperms.

 Go Online SCiLINKS NSTA

Section 3 **Angiosperms**

2–3 periods
1 1/2–2 blocks

A.5.3.1 Describe the characteristics shared by angiosperms.
A.5.3.2 State the function of an angiosperm's flowers.
A.5.3.3 Explain how angiosperms reproduce.
A.5.3.4 Tell how monocots differ from dicots.

 **Go Online** *active art*

Section 4 **Plant Responses and Growth**

2–3 periods
1 1/2–2 blocks

A.5.4.1 Identify three stimuli that produce plant responses.
A.5.4.2 Describe how plants respond to seasonal changes.
A.5.4.3 State how long different angiosperms live.

 **Go Online** SCiLINKS NSTA

Section 5 **Feeding the World**

1 periods
1/2 block

A.5.5.1 Identify technologies that may help farmers produce more crops.

 **Go Online** SCiLINKS NSTA

Review and Assessment

All in One Teaching Resources
- Key Terms Review, p. 321
- Transparency A51
- Performance Assessment Teacher Notes, p. 328
- Performance Assessment Scoring Rubric p. 329
- Performance Assessment Student Worksheet, p. 330
- Chapter Test, pp. 331–334

 Discovery SCHOOL Video Assessment

 Go Online PHSchool.com

Test Preparation

Test Preparation Blackline Masters

Chapter Activities Planner

Lab zone

Student Edition	Inquiry	Time	Materials	Skills	Resources
Chapter Project, p. 135	Open-Ended	Ongoing (3 to 4 weeks)	**All in One** Teaching Resources See p. 272	Posing questions, observing	**Lab zone Easy Planner** **All in One** Teaching Resources Support pp. 272–273
Section 1					
Discover Activity, p. 136	Guided	10 minutes	Foods from flowerless seed plants, such as carrots, parsnips, broccoli, cabbage, lettuce, celery, parsley, potato, onion	Classifying	**Lab zone Easy Planner**
Try This Activity, p. 138	Guided	10 minutes	Hand lens; dried kidney, lima, or black beans; dried yellow or green peas; shelled peanuts	Observing	**Lab zone Easy Planner**
Skills Activity, p. 142	Directed	35 minutes (20 wait time); 2 hours to test pre-diction	Calculator, celery stalk, clock or stopwatch, dropper, food coloring, lab apron, plastic container, spoon, timer, water	Calculating	**Lab zone Easy Planner**
Section 2					
Discover Activity, p. 146	Guided	10 minutes	Hand lens; metric ruler; 2 or 3 leaves from angiosperms, such as oak or maple tree, day lily, and rose; 2 or 3 leaves from gymnosperms, such as pine, yew, and spruce	Classifying	**Lab zone Easy Planner**
Try This Activity, p. 149	Guided	10 minutes	Mature female pine cone, hand lens, sheet of white paper	Inferring	**Lab zone Easy Planner**
Section 3					
Discover Activity, p. 151	Guided	15 minutes	Hand lens, metric ruler, three different fruits	Forming operational definitions	**Lab zone Easy Planner**
Skills Lab, pp. 158–159	Directed	40 minutes	Paper towels, plastic dropper, hand lens, microscope, slide, large flower, coverslip, scalpel, tape, water, metric ruler, lens paper	Observing, inferring, measuring	**Lab zone Easy Planner** **Lab Activity Video** **All in One** Teaching Resources Skills Lab: *A Close Look at Flowers*, pp. 302–304
Section 4					
Discover Activity, p. 160	Directed	10 minutes	Touch-sensitive plant, common houseplant	Inferring	**Lab zone Easy Planner**
Section 5					
Discover Activity, p. 165	Guided	20 minutes	Bags; tags; cooked rice, dry cereal, or raisins	Predicting	**Lab zone Easy Planner**
Technology Lab, pp. 168–169	Open-Ended	40 minutes first day; 10 minutes per day for 14 days, then repeat	Potted plant, 2 different types of plants, nutrient solution, empty 2-liter soda bottles, paper towels	Designing a solution, redesigning	**Lab zone Easy Planner** **Lab Activity Video** **All in One** Teaching Resources Technology Lab: *Design and Build a Hydroponic Garden*, pp. 319–321

Section 1 The Characteristics of Seed Plants

⏱ *2–3 periods, 1–1 1/2 blocks*

Objectives

A.5.1.1 Identify the characteristics that seed plants share.

A.5.1.2 Explain how seeds become new plants.

A.5.1.3 Describe the functions of roots, stems, and leaves.

Local Standards

Key Terms

• phloem • xylem • seed • embryo • cotyledon • germination • root cap
• cambium • stomata • transpiration

Preteach

Build Background Knowledge

Ask students to generate a list of plants they see often and identify which have seeds and which do not.

Lab zone Discover Activity *Which Plant Part Is It?*

Targeted Print and Technology Resources

All in One Teaching Resources

L2 Reading Strategy Transparency A37: Outlining

⊙ **Presentation-Pro CD-ROM**

Instruct

What Is a Seed Plant? Discuss that all seed plants have vascular tissue and produce seeds.

How Seeds Become New Plants Ask questions and use an illustration to discuss the structures of seeds and how they germinate.

Roots Identify the functions, types, and structures of roots.

Stems Use illustrations to describe the functions of stems.

Leaves Use a cross-section of a leaf to examine its functions.

Targeted Print and Technology Resources

All in One Teaching Resources

L2 Guided Reading, pp. 281–285

L2 Transparencies A38, A39, A40, A41, A42

PHSchool.com Web Code: ced-1051

⊙ **Student Edition on Audio CD**

Assess

Section Assessment Questions

↻ Have students use their outlines to help them answer the questions.

Reteach

Use the section figures to summarize the functions of roots, stems, and leaves.

Targeted Print and Technology Resources

All in One Teaching Resources

• Section Summary, p. 280

L1 Review and Reinforce, p. 286

L3 Enrich, p. 287

Section 2 Gymnosperms

⏱ *3 periods, 1 1/2–2 blocks*

ABILITY LEVELS
L1 Basic to Average
L2 For All Students
L3 Average to Advanced

Objectives
A.5.2.1 Identify the characteristics of gymnosperms.
A.5.2.2 Describe how gymnosperms reproduce.
A.5.2.3 List important products from gymnosperms.

Local Standards

Key Terms
• gymnosperm • cone • pollen • ovule • pollination

Preteach

Build Background Knowledge
Prompt students to name trees that stay green all year and describe their features.

Lab zone Discover Activity *Are All Leaves Alike?*

Targeted Print and Technology Resources

All in One Teaching Resources
L2 Reading Strategy Transparency A43: Previewing Visuals

💿 **Presentation-Pro CD-ROM**

Instruct

What Are Gymnosperms? Analyze the characteristics of gymnosperms.

Reproduction in Gymnosperms Use a cycle diagram to identify the steps in reproduction of gymnosperms.

Gymnosperms in Everyday Life Identify useful products that come from conifers.

Targeted Print and Technology Resources

All in One Teaching Resources
L2 Guided Reading, pp. 290–292
L2 Transparency A44

www.SciLinks.org Web Code: scn-0152

💿 **Student Edition on Audio CD**

Assess

Section Assessment Questions
🔄 Have students use their preview questions and answers to help them answer the questions.

Reteach
Have students fill in blanked out labels of the diagram showing reproduction of gymnosperms, then discuss as a class.

Targeted Print and Technology Resources

All in One Teaching Resources
• Section Summary, p. 289
L1 Review and Reinforce, p. 293
L3 Enrich, p. 294

Section Lesson Plans

Section 3 Angiosperms

 *2–3 periods, 1 1/2–2 blocks*

Objectives

A.5.3.1 Describe the characteristics shared by angiosperms.
A.5.3.2 State the function of an angiosperm's flowers.
A.5.3.3 Explain how angiosperms reproduce.
A.5.3.4 Tell how monocots differ from dicots.

Local Standards

Key Terms

• angiosperm • flower • sepal • petal • stamen • pistil • ovary • fruit
• monocot • dicot

Preteach

Build Background Knowledge

Invite students to describe flowers with which they are familiar.

 Discover Activity *What Is a Fruit?*

Targeted Print and Technology Resources

All in One Teaching Resources
L2 Reading Strategy: *Building Vocabulary*

⊙ Presentation-Pro CD-ROM

Instruct

The Structure of Flowers Use a diagram to examine the reproductive parts of a flower.

Reproduction in Angiosperms Ask questions to help students understand the steps in reproduction of angiosperms.

Types of Angiosperms Compare and contrast the structures of monocots and dicots.

Angiosperms in Everyday Life Identify commercial uses of angiosperms.

Skills Lab *A Close Look at Flowers*

Targeted Print and Technology Resources

All in One Teaching Resources
L2 Guided Reading, pp. 297–299
L2 Transparencies A45, A46, A47

PHSchool.com Web Code: cep-1053
L2 Skills Lab: *A Close Look at Flowers,* pp. 302–304

▄ Lab Activity Video/DVD
Skills Lab: *A Close Look at Flowers*

⊙ Student Edition on Audio CD

Assess

Section Assessment Questions

Have students use their definitions to answer the questions.

Reteach

Review the life cycle of angiosperms.

Targeted Print and Technology Resources

All in One Teaching Resources
• Section Summary, p. 296
L1 Review and Reinforce, p. 300
L3 Enrich, p. 301

Section 4 Plant Responses and Growth

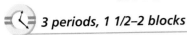 *3 periods, 1 1/2–2 blocks*

ABILITY LEVELS
L1 Basic to Average
L2 For All Students
L3 Average to Advanced

Objectives
A.5.4.1 Identify three stimuli that produce plant responses.
A.5.4.2 Describe how plants respond to seasonal changes.
A.5.4.3 State how long different angiosperms live.

Local Standards

Key Terms
• tropism • hormone • auxin • photoperiodism • short-day plant • long-day plant • day-neutral plant • dormancy • annual • biennial • perennial

Preteach

Build Background Knowledge
Have students describe the usual direction of plant stem and root growth.

Lab zone Discover Activity *Can a Plant Respond to Touch?*

Targeted Print and Technology Resources

All in One Teaching Resources
L2 Reading Strategy Transparency A48: Relating Cause and Effect

⊙ Presentation-Pro CD-ROM

Instruct

Tropisms Identify plant responses to the stimuli of touch, light, and gravity.

Seasonal Changes Analyze the different ways plants respond to changing seasons.

Life Spans of Angiosperms Contrast the life spans of annuals, biennials, and perennials.

Targeted Print and Technology Resources

All in One Teaching Resources
L2 Guided Reading, pp. 307–309
L2 Transparency A49

www.SciLinks.org Web Code: scn-0154

⊙ Student Edition on Audio CD

Assess

Section Assessment Questions
Have students use their cause and effect graphic organizer to answer the questions.

Reteach
Sketch examples of tropisms, photoperiodism, and dormancy, and have students describe them.

Targeted Print and Technology Resources

All in One Teaching Resources
• Section Summary, p. 306
L1 Review and Reinforce, p. 310
L3 Enrich, p. 311

Section 5 Feeding the World

 *2 periods, 1 block*

ABILITY LEVELS
L1 Basic to Average
L2 For All Students
L3 Average to Advanced

Objectives

A.5.5.1 Identify technologies that may help farmers produce more crops.

Local Standards

Key Terms

• precision farming • hydroponics • genetic engineering

Preteach

Build Background Knowledge

Elicit ideas of a typical farm 100 years ago, today, and 100 years from today.

 Discover Activity *Will There Be Enough to Eat?*

Targeted Print and Technology Resources

All in One Teaching Resources

L2 Reading Strategy Transparency A50: Identifying Main Ideas

Presentation-Pro CD-ROM

Instruct

Precision Farming Discuss precision farming and its benefits.

Hydroponics Describe hydroponics and identify an example of its use.

Engineering Better Plants State what genetic engineering is, and apply it to an example.

 Technology Lab *Design and Build a Hydroponic Garden*

Targeted Print and Technology Resources

All in One Teaching Resources

L2 Guided Reading, pp. 314–316

www.SciLinks.org Web Code: scn-0155

L3 Technology Lab: *Design and Build a Hydroponic Garden,* pp. 319–320

Lab Activity Video/DVD
Technology Lab: *Design and Build a Hydroponic Garden*

Assess

Section Assessment Questions

Have students use their graphic organizer of main ideas and details to answer the questions.

Reteach

Summarize the benefits of the technologies that increase crop yields.

Targeted Print and Technology Resources

All in One Teaching Resources

• Section Summary, p. 313
L1 Review and Reinforce, p. 317
L3 Enrich, p. 318

Chapter 5 Content Refresher

Section 1 The Characteristics of Seed Plants

Vascular Tissue The vascular systems of seed plants includes xylem and phloem tissues. In angiosperms, xylem has two components—tracheids and vessel elements. Both types of vessels are hollow and nonliving, but the vessel elements are larger and do not have transverse end walls. As a result they form a continuous, hollow tube for water and mineral transport.

A tracheid is a long, thick wall with ends that taper. Water moves from tracheid to tracheid through pores in the tracheid wall.

Phloem is made up of sieve-tube cells, which have cytoplasm but no nuclei. Their transverse walls contain channels through which sugars can pass. Lying next to each sieve tube cell is a companion cell that controls and maintains the life functions of both cells.

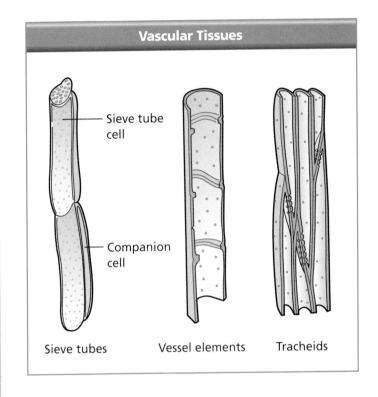

Vascular Tissues

Sieve tube cell

Companion cell

Sieve tubes · Vessel elements · Tracheids

Address Misconceptions

Many students think that trees "grow up" much the same way that grasses grow. However, trees grow by adding layers to the outside of the stem, so that the outer rings are newer than the inner rings. For a strategy for overcoming this misconception, see **Address Misconceptions** in the section The Characteristics of Seed Plants.

Section 2 Gymnosperms

History of Classifying Seed Plants In the 1820s, A Scottish botanist named Robert Brown became the first scientist to distinguish gymnosperms from plants whose seeds are contained inside fruits.

As a naturalist on the *Investigator* in 1801, Brown collected almost 4,000 different plants in Australia. He used the specimens to develop and refine his systems for classifying plants.

Brown's careful observations allowed him to see things that no one had ever seen before. He is credited with recognizing and naming the nucleus as a part of all plant cells. His most famous contribution, however, is the discovery and extensive study of a phenomenon known as Brownian motion—random movement of small particles in a fluid. Brown discovered the motion by observing pollen grains suspended in water.

Products From Gymnosperms Some of the most important products obtained from gymnosperms are resins, used for everything from art supplies to the production of medicine. Natural resin is a thick, yellowish liquid that is exuded from trees. Pine and fir trees are the source of most natural resin. Resin forms when the bark of the tree is injured, such as when it is affected by severe winds, fire, or lightning.

Turpentine is one form of resin. Oil of turpentine is used in the production of oil pastels, and artists use it to clean their paintbrushes. It is used extensively in the manufacture of chemical products such as insecticides, camphor, and synthetic resins, and in the production of plastic.

Section 3 Angiosperms

Scents of Flowers Many of the adaptations that attract pollinators to flowers—such as fragrance and color—also attract humans. For example, the flowers of many plants, such as jasmine, rose, and lavender, are used to create strong and attractive scents.

The art of making perfume requires knowledge of both chemistry and botany. For the best perfume, the flowers must be gathered at exactly the right time in the plant's life cycle. Isolating floral compounds often requires a large number of flowers. It takes approximately 113 kg of rose petals to make one ounce of attar of rose.

In addition to flowers, other parts of angiosperms are often valued for their scents. The seeds of the musk mallow tree of India are used for perfume.

Unusual Angiosperms Some of the most unusual angiosperms are insect-eating plants. These plants generally live in nitrogen-poor soils and receive vital nutrients from prey.

The pitcher plant uses a narrow, juglike structure to lure and trap insects. The pitcher has a strong scent and attractive color. The top of the pitcher has downward pointing bristles, which make escape difficult for any insect that is trapped. Further down the pitcher, the inside walls are very smooth, and the plant produces a sticky nectar. Insects slip down the side of the pitcher and fall into a bath of water and digestive juices.

Pitcher Plant

Section 4 Plant Responses and Growth

Rapid Responses Unlike animals, plants cannot move from one location to another. However, they do respond to some stimuli. All plants respond to light and gravity: plant shoots move upward toward light and against gravity, while roots move downward away from light and with gravity.

The response center for gravity appears to be in the root cap and may be governed by starch molecules. Response to light is governed by a plant hormone called auxin. Other plant hormones include gibberillins, cytokinins, and substances associated with the formation of flowers, tubers, bulbs, and buds.

Some plant responses do not involve growth. If the leaves of *Mimosa pudica,* appropriately called the "sensitive plant," are touched, its leaflets fold together completely within only two or three seconds. The secret to this movement is changes in osmotic pressure. Recall that osmotic pressure is caused by the diffusion of water into cells. The leaflets are held apart due to osmotic pressure at the base of the leaflets, where they join. When a leaf is touched, cells near the center of the leaflets pump out ions and lose water due to osmosis. Pressure from cells on the underside of the leaf, which do not lose water, force the leaflets together.

The carnivorous Venus' flytrap also demonstrates rapid responses. Each plant grows several kidney-shaped leaves with sensitive inner bristles. When a fly triggers sensory cells on the inside of the flytrap's leaf, electrical signals are sent from cell to cell. A combination of changes in osmotic pressure and cell wall expansion causes the leaf to snap shut, trapping the insect inside. Enzymes flood the inside of the trap and slowly digest the prey. Special glands absorb the nutrients. When the insect is fully digested, the trap opens again.

Venus' Flytrap

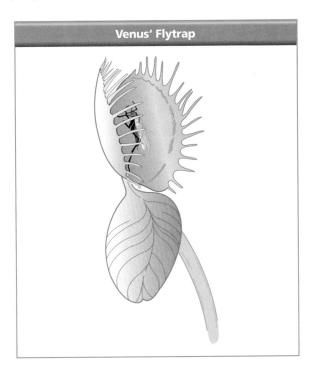

Section 5 Feeding the World

Controversy Over Genetic Engineering Genetic engineering, manipulating genetic code by artificial means, is significantly different from traditional selective breeding or hybridization, which relies on changes using members of the same species. Genetic engineering can go beyond the species boundary because DNA represents the universal language of life. For example, inserting a bacterial gene with useful traits into a plant's genome confers those qualities to the plant. Through genetic engineering, it is possible to create crops that can tolerate drought, produce medicines, or grow without pesticide.

However, many questions surround genetic engineering: "Are there long-term effects?" "If there are long-term effects, can we be certain they are not harmful?" and "What might happen if an undesirable genetically modified organism (GMO) makes its way into the general environment?" The answer to these questions is not yet known, but many people have concerns about genetic engineering and GMOs.

Help Students Read

Sequencing
Ordering Events

Strategy Help students understand and visualize the steps in a process, or the order in which events occur. Sequences frequently involve cause-effect relationships. Readers can construct graphic organizers to help themselves visualize and comprehend a sequence. For most sequences, flowcharts are the graphic of choice. However, cycle diagrams are more appropriate for cycles. Before students begin, locate a description in the chapter of a several-step process or a chain of causes and effects.

Example
1. Have students read the passage, thinking about what takes place first, second, third, and so on. Point out that the text will not always use order words such as *first, next, then,* and *finally.*
2. Review the passage, listing the steps or events in order.
3. If the passage describes a chain of steps or events, draw a flowchart on the board, having students tell the sequence of events, steps, or causes and effects, and writing each part of the process in a separate box.
4. If the passage describes a cycle, use a cycle diagram to show the sequence.
5. Have students locate additional examples of sequential relationships in the text or visuals of the chapter. Students can depict the steps or events using graphic organizers.

Chapter 5
Seed Plants

Chapter Preview

❶ The Characteristics of Seed Plants
Discover *Which Plant Part Is It?*
Try This *The In-Seed Story*
Skills Activity *Calculating*

❷ Gymnosperms
Discover *Are All Leaves Alike?*
Try This *The Scoop on Cones*
At-Home Activity *Everyday Gymnosperms*

❸ Angiosperms
Discover *What Is a Fruit?*
Active Art *The Structure of a Flower*
Math Skills *Multiples*
Skills Lab *A Close Look at Flowers*

❹ Plant Responses and Growth
Discover *Can a Plant Respond to Touch?*
Analyzing Data *Germination and Temperature*
At-Home Activity *Sun Seekers*

❺ Feeding the World
Discover *Will There Be Enough to Eat?*
Technology Lab *Design and Build a Hydroponic Garden*

The *Passiflora* plant produces delicate, highly scented flowers. ▶

134 ◆ A

Lab zone ▲ Chapter **Project**   L3

Objectives
During this project, students will grow plants from seeds and make detailed observations of the plant's life cycle from germination through growth, flowering, and pollination. After this Chapter Project, students will be able to

- pose questions about how seed plants grow and reproduce
- observe and measure different parts of a seed plant's life cycle
- create data tables
- apply chapter concepts to their observations
- communicate their findings about seed plants to classmates

Skills Focus
Posing questions, observing, measuring, creating data tables, applying concepts, communicating

Project Time Line 3 to 4 weeks

All in One Teaching Resources
- Chapter Project Teacher Notes
- Chapter Project Worksheet 1
- Chapter Project Worksheet 2
- Chapter Project Worksheet 3
- Chapter Project Scoring Rubric

134 ● A

Developing a Plan
Have students plant their seeds, discuss the life cycle of plants, and set up their data tables during the first week. Around week three, the plants should have flowers that are ready for pollination. Students can collect fresh seeds by the fourth week. At this time, advise them to prepare their displays and work on class presentations.

Possible Materials
- Provide gardening supplies such as potting trays, potting soil, fast-growing seeds that flower in about 28 days (such as tomatoes and peas), and cotton swabs for transferring pollen.
- Plant three or four seeds for the class to observe as well as to serve for replacement plants should any student plants fail.

Video Preview

Seed Plants

Show the Video Preview to introduce the Chapter Project and overview the chapter content. Discussion question: **Why do seeds have a better chance of survival if they are dispersed over a wide area?** *(Because they will have a better chance of landing in an environment where conditions are favorable for germination)*

Lab zone™ Chapter Project

Cycle of a Lifetime

How long is a seed plant's life? Redwood trees can live for thousands of years. Tomato plants die after only one season. Can organisms that seem so different have anything in common? In this chapter, you'll find out. Some answers will come from this chapter's project. In this project, you'll grow plants from seeds and then care for the plants until they produce seeds.

Your Goal To care for and observe a plant throughout its life cycle

To complete this project, you must

- grow a plant from a seed
- observe and describe key parts of your plant's life cycle, such as seed germination and pollination
- harvest and plant the seeds that your growing plant produces
- follow the safety guidelines in Appendix A

Plan It! Observe the seeds that your teacher gives you. In a small group, discuss what conditions the seeds might need to grow. What should you look for after you plant the seeds? What changes do you expect your plant to undergo during its life cycle? When you are ready, plant your seeds.

Chapter 5 A ◆ 135

Launching the Project

Ask: **How do we get more plants?** *(Accept student responses that indicate the need for "seeds.")* Then ask: **How do we get more seeds?** *(Accept all responses at this time.)*

Allow time for students to read the description of the project in their text.

Encourage discussion on the life cycle of seed plants and the materials that students will use. Make certain students understand that the most important activity in this project is caring for the plant so that it will grow well and provide useful information for their observations.

Performance Assessment

The Chapter Project Scoring Rubric will help you evaluate how well students complete the Chapter Project. You may want to share the scoring rubric with your students so they know what will be expected of them. Students will be assessed on

- How well and consistently they care for their plants
- Completeness of their observation entries, including measurements of stem, leaves, and flowers
- How well they apply chapter concepts to their observations
- Thoroughness and organization of their presentations **Portfolio**

The Characteristics of Seed Plants

Objectives

After this lesson, students will be able to

A.5.1.1 Identify the characteristics that seed plants share.

A.5.1.2 Explain how seeds become new plants.

A.5.1.3 Describe the functions of roots, stems, and leaves.

Target Reading Skill 🔄

Outlining Explain that using an outline format helps students organize information by main topic, subtopic, and details.

Answer

The Characteristics of Seed Plants
  I. What Is a Seed Plant?
      A. Vascular Tissue
      B. Seeds
  II. How Seeds Become New Plants
      A. Seed Structure
      B. Seed Dispersal
      C. Germination
  III. Roots
      A. Types of Roots
      B. The Structure of a Root
  IV. Stems
      A. The Structure of a Stem
      B. Annual Rings
  V. Leaves
      A. The Structure of a Leaf
      B. The Leaf and Photosynthesis
      C. Controlling Water Loss

All in One Teaching Resources

• Transparency A37

Preteach

Build Background Knowledge L2

Plants With and Without Seeds

Have students generate a list of plants they see everyday. Have them write the name of each plant under one of the following headings: *Has Seeds* or *Does Not Have Seeds*. Tell students that not only are most of the plants they are familiar with seed plants but that seed plants make up the greater number of all plants.

The Characteristics of Seed Plants

Reading Preview

Key Concepts
• What three characteristics do seed plants share?
• How do seeds become new plants?
• What are the main functions of roots, stems, and leaves?

Key Terms
• phloem • xylem • pollen
• seed • embryo • cotyledon
• germination • root cap
• cambium • stomata
• transpiration

🔄 Target Reading Skill

Outlining As you read, make an outline about seed plants that you can use for review. Use the red headings for the main ideas and the blue headings for the supporting ideas.

The Characteristics of Seed Plants
I. What is a seed plant?
A. Vascular tissue
B.
II. How seeds become new plants
A.
B.

Lab zone — Discover **Activity**

Which Plant Part Is It?

1. With a partner, carefully observe the items of food your teacher gives you.
2. Make a list of the food items.
3. For each food item, write the name of the plant part—root, stem, or leaf—from which you think it is obtained.

Think It Over

Classifying Classify the items into groups depending on the plant part from which the food is obtained. Compare your groupings with those of your classmates.

Have you ever planted seeds in a garden? If so, then you may remember how it seemed to take forever before those first green shoots emerged. Shortly afterwards, you saw one set of leaves, and then others. Then a flower may have appeared. Did you wonder where all those plant parts came from? How did they develop from one small seed? Read on to find out.

What Is a Seed Plant?

The plant growing in your garden was a seed plant. So are most of the other plants around you. In fact, seed plants outnumber seedless plants by more than ten to one. You eat many seed plants—rice, peas, and squash, for example. You wear clothes made from seed plants, such as cotton and flax. You may live in a home built from seed plants—oak, pine, or maple trees. In addition, seed plants produce much of the oxygen you breathe.

Seed plants share two important characteristics. They have vascular tissue, and they use pollen and seeds to reproduce. In addition, all seed plants have body plans that include roots, stems, and leaves. Like seedless plants, seed plants have complex life cycles that include the sporophyte and the gametophyte stages. In seed plants, the plants that you see are the sporophytes. The gametophytes are microscopic.

Lab zone — Discover **Activity**

Skills Focus Classifying L1

Materials edible parts of seed plants such as carrots, parsnips, broccoli, cabbage, lettuce, celery, parsley, potato, onion (do not use fruits, the mature ovary of flowers)

Time 10 minutes

Tips Mention that underground plant parts are not necessarily roots. For example, potatoes and onions are

underground stems. Celery is not a true stem, but a leaf stalk.

Expected Outcome Carrots and parsnips are roots, lettuce and cabbage are leaves, and broccoli is a stem.

Think It Over The foods should be classified as roots, stems, or leaves.

Vascular Tissue Most seed plants live on land. Recall from Chapter 4 that land plants face many challenges, including standing upright and supplying all their cells with food and water. Like ferns, seed plants meet these two challenges with vascular tissue. The thick walls of the cells in the vascular tissue help support the plants. In addition, food, water, and nutrients are transported throughout the plants in vascular tissue.

There are two types of vascular tissue. **Phloem** (FLOH um) is the vascular tissue through which food moves. When food is made in the leaves, it enters the phloem and travels to other parts of the plant. Water and minerals, on the other hand, travel in the vascular tissue called **xylem** (ZY lum). The roots absorb water and minerals from the soil. These materials enter the root's xylem and move upward into the stems and leaves.

Pollen and Seeds Unlike seedless plants, seed plants can live in a wide variety of environments. Recall that seedless plants need water in their surroundings for fertilization to occur. Seed plants do not need water for sperm to swim to the eggs. Instead, seed plants produce **pollen,** tiny structures that contain the cells that will later become sperm cells. Pollen delivers sperm cells directly near the eggs. After sperm cells fertilize the eggs, seeds develop. A **seed** is a structure that contains a young plant inside a protective covering. Seeds protect the young plant from drying out.

 Reading Checkpoint What material travels in phloem? What materials travel in xylem?

FIGURE 1
Harvesting Wild Rice
Like all seed plants, wild rice plants have vascular tissue and use seeds to reproduce. The seeds develop in shallow bodies of water, and the plants grow up above the water's surface. These men are harvesting the mature rice grains.

Differentiated Instruction

English Learners/Beginning L1
Vocabulary: Science Glossary Pair students with English proficient students. Have them work together to create a glossary that includes the phonetic English pronunciation and the definition for each key term. Students can draw and label their own diagrams of the structures. **learning modality: verbal**

English Learners/Intermediate L1
Vocabulary: Science Glossary Have students do the *Beginning* activity, then write a sentence that uses each of these words. Call on students to read their sentences aloud to give them an opportunity to practice pronunciation. **learning modality: verbal**

What Is a Seed Plant?

Teach Key Concepts L2
Characteristics of Seed Plants

Focus Remind students that ferns have vascular tissue and reproduce using spores.

Teach Ask: **What two characteristics are common to all seed plants?** (*Vascular tissue and seeds to reproduce*) **Which is different from ferns?** (*Ferns reproduce using spores.*) **What is the body structure of seed plants?** (*Plant bodies include roots, stems, and leaves.*)

Apply Remind students that seed plants evolved after mosses and ferns. Ask: **How did the evolution of seeds allow plants to live in places where mosses and ferns could not?** (*Seeds provide protection for the young plant inside. With seeds, plants can reproduce in drier environments.*) **learning modality: verbal**

Independent Practice L2

All in One Teaching Resources

- Guided Reading and Study Worksheet: *The Characteristics of Seed Plants*

Student Edition on Audio CD

Monitor Progress L2

Drawing Have students make flowcharts showing the movement of food, water, and nutrients through a vascular plant. (*Phloem—food moves from leaves to stems, roots, and other parts; xylem—water and minerals travel from roots into stems and leaves.*) Students can save their flowcharts in their portfolios.

Answer

Reading Checkpoint Food travels in phloem. Water and minerals travel in xylem.

How Seeds Become New Plants

Teach Key Concepts `L2`

What's Inside a Seed?

Focus Remind students that unlike seedless plants, seeds do not need water to be capable of surviving.

Teach Explain that one of the main parts of a seed is the seed coat, which keeps the seed from drying out. Ask: **What else is inside a seed?** (*A partially developed plant, or embryo*) **Why does the seed contain stored food?** (*The embryo uses the stored food until it can make its own food.*) **What is germination?** (*The early growth stage of the embryo*) Refer students to Figure 4 and ask them to describe the process of germination. (*The embryo uses its food, the roots grow downward, and the stem and leaves begin to grow upward.*)

Apply Ask: **Why is it an advantage for seeds to be able to remain inactive and not germinate immediately after the embryo forms?** (*This allows for them to be dispersed and to germinate under ideal growing conditions.*) **learning modality: verbal**

Use Visuals: Figure 2 `L2`

Seed Structure

Focus Have students locate the main parts in each seed.

Teach Ask: **What structures are common to all the seeds?** (*Seed coat, embryo, stored food, cotyledon*) **What plant characteristics can you see in the embryos?** (*The beginnings of roots, stems, and leaves*)

Apply Tell students to note the areas of stored food. Explain that when seeds absorb water, the food-storing tissues swell, which cracks open the seed coat. **learning modality: visual**

All in One Teaching Resources

• Transparency A38

FIGURE 2
Seed Structure

The structures of three different seeds are shown here.
Inferring *How is the stored food used?*

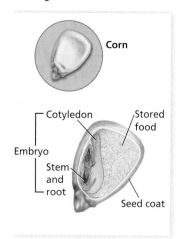
Corn — Cotyledon, Stored food, Embryo, Stem and root, Seed coat

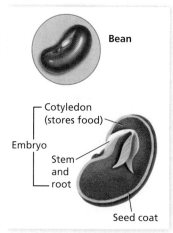
Bean — Cotyledon (stores food), Embryo, Stem and root, Seed coat

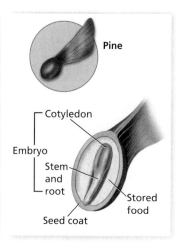
Pine — Cotyledon, Embryo, Stem and root, Stored food, Seed coat

---

 Lab zone Try This Activity

The In-Seed Story

1. Your teacher will give you a hand lens and two different seeds that have been soaked in water.
2. Carefully observe the outside of each seed. Draw what you see.
3. Gently remove the coverings of the seeds. Then carefully separate the parts of each seed. Use a hand lens to examine the inside of each seed. Draw what you see.

Observing Based on your observations, label the parts of each seed. Then describe the function of each part next to its label.

How Seeds Become New Plants

All seeds share important similarities. **Inside a seed is a partially developed plant. If a seed lands in an area where conditions are favorable, the plant sprouts out of the seed and begins to grow.**

Seed Structure A seed has three main parts—an embryo, stored food, and a seed coat. The young plant that develops from the zygote, or fertilized egg, is called the **embryo.** The embryo already has the beginnings of roots, stems, and leaves. In the seeds of most plants, the embryo stops growing when it is quite small. When the embryo begins to grow again, it uses the food stored in the seed until it can make its own food by photosynthesis. In all seeds, the embryo has one or more seed leaves, or **cotyledons** (kaht uh LEED unz). In some seeds, food is stored in the cotyledons. In others, food is stored outside the embryo. Figure 2 compares the structure of corn, bean, and pine seeds.

The outer covering of a seed is called the seed coat. Some familiar seed coats are the "skins" on lima beans and peanuts. The seed coat acts like plastic wrap, protecting the embryo and its food from drying out. This allows a seed to remain inactive for a long time. In many plants, the seeds are surrounded by a structure called a fruit, which you will learn more about in Section 3.

Lab zone Try This Activity

Skills Focus Observing `L2`

Materials hand lens; dried kidney, lima, or black beans; dried yellow or green peas; shelled peanuts

⚠ **CAUTION:** *Some students have severe reactions to eating peanuts or inhaling peanut dust. Do not use peanuts if any student is allergic to them.*

Time 10 minutes

Tips Before the activity, soak the beans for 2 hours and the peas for 24 hours. Remove peanuts from their shells 3 or 4 days before the activity, and store them in a moist place so the cotyledons will open.

Expected Outcome Students will observe that each of the seeds is composed of two

sections that can easily be separated. They will see the tiny leaves and root (and possibly the miniature stem) of the embryo plant. Sketches should include the seed coat, the cotyledons, and the embryo.

Extend Invite students to repeat the activity with other kinds of seeds. **learning modality: kinesthetic**

Seed Dispersal After seeds have formed, they are usually scattered, sometimes far from where they were produced. The scattering of seeds is called seed dispersal. Seeds are dispersed in many ways. One method involves other organisms. For example, some animals eat fruits, such as cherries or grapes. The seeds inside the fruits pass through the animal's digestive system and are deposited in new areas. Other seeds are enclosed in barblike structures that hook onto an animal's fur or a person's clothes. The structures then fall off the fur or clothes in a new area.

A second means of dispersal is water. Water can disperse seeds that fall into oceans and rivers. A third dispersal method involves wind. Wind disperses lightweight seeds that often have structures to catch the wind, such as those of dandelions and maple trees. Finally, some plants eject their seeds in a way that might remind you of popping popcorn. The force scatters the seeds in many directions.

FIGURE 3
Seed Dispersal
The seeds of these plants are enclosed in fruits with adaptations that help them disperse.

Dispersal by wind:
Dandelion fruits
with "parachutes" ▶

◀ Dispersal
by animals:
Barblike fruits

Dispersal by water:
Floating coconut
palm fruit ▶

Chapter 5 A ◆ 139

Lab zone Build **Inquiry**   L2

Modeling Seed Dispersal

Time 25 minutes

Materials tissue paper, modeling clay, plastic foam balls, plastic spoons, table tennis balls, hook-and-loop fastener strips, and other arts and crafts materials

Focus Use Figure 3 to review the different ways that plants disperse seeds.

Teach Explain to students that the structure (fruit) that encloses the seeds helps the seeds disperse. Have students work together to build model seeds that can be dispersed by wind, water, or by sticking to clothes or animal fur. Encourage students to predict how far their seeds will travel and then to test their predictions. Students can present their models to the class, identifying how their model seeds are similar to real seeds and how their models could be improved.

Apply Ask: **What properties or characteristics are most important for each method of dispersal?** *(Possible answers: Animal fur—seed must stick to fur with barbs or similar structures; water—seed must float; wind—seed has structures to catch the wind; mechanical—small, dense, compact)*
learning modality: kinesthetic

Differentiated Instruction

Less Proficient Readers   **L1**
Checking for Understanding After students have read the section, have them work in groups of four to write 10 questions about the characteristics of seed plants. Suggest they compose a variety of short-answer, fill in the blank, and matching questions. Remind them to create answer keys as well. Then have groups exchange questions and complete them. Students can check their answers using the answer keys. You may wish to make copies of the questions and answer keys for all students to use as study aids.
learning modality: verbal

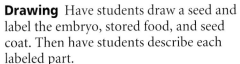

Monitor Progress   L2

Drawing Have students draw a seed and label the embryo, stored food, and seed coat. Then have students describe each labeled part.

Answer
Figure 2 Seeds store food so the embryo has food until it can make its own.

Seed Plants

Show the Video Field Trip to help students understand seed dispersal and development. Discussion question: **What are some ways in which seeds can be dispersed?** *(By wind, water, animal, or be ejected)*

Roots

Teach Key Concepts L2

Functions of Roots

Focus Point out to students that unlike nonvascular plants, seed plants are vascular plants and they have true roots.

Teach Ask: **What do roots do for a plant?** *(Anchor the plant in soil and absorb water and nutrients)* **What types of roots are there?** *(Some plants have a taproot, a long thick main root reaching down into the soil. Other plants have thin fibrous roots that form a tangled mass and take soil with them when they are pulled.)* **What is the purpose of a root cap?** *(It protects the root from injury.)*

Apply Ask: **Which root type is likely to be more useful in preventing soil erosion?** *(The fibrous root system holds soil between the root fibers so it works better than a tap root in preventing erosion.)* **learning modality: verbal**

All in One Teaching Resources

• Transparency A39

DISCOVERY
CHANNEL
SCHOOL

Seed Plants

Video Preview
▶ Video Field Trip
Video Assessment

Germination After a seed is dispersed, it may remain inactive for a while before it germinates. **Germination** (jur muh NAY shun) occurs when the embryo begins to grow again and pushes out of the seed. Germination begins when the seed absorbs water from the environment. Then the embryo uses its stored food to begin to grow. As shown in Figure 4, the embryo's roots first grow downward; then its stem and leaves grow upward. Once you can see a plant's leaves, the plant is called a seedling.

A seed that is dispersed far from its parent plant has a better chance of survival. When a seed does not have to compete with its parent for light, water, and nutrients, it has a better chance of becoming a seedling.

✓ **Reading Checkpoint** **What must happen in order for germination to begin?**

Roots

Have you ever tried to pull a dandelion out of the soil? It's not easy, is it? That is because most roots are good anchors. Roots have three main functions. **Roots anchor a plant in the ground, absorb water and minerals from the soil, and sometimes store food.** The more root area a plant has, the more water and minerals it can absorb.

Types of Roots The two main types of root systems are shown in Figure 5. A fibrous root system consists of many similarly sized roots that form a dense, tangled mass. Plants with fibrous roots take much soil with them when you pull them out of the ground. Lawn grass, corn, and onions have fibrous root systems. In contrast, a taproot system has one long, thick main root. Many smaller roots branch off the main root. A plant with a taproot system is hard to pull out of the ground. Carrots, dandelions, and cacti have taproots.

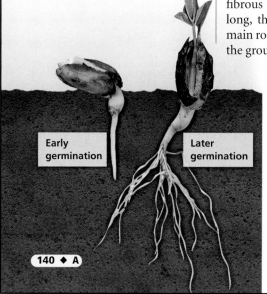

Early germination

Later germination

FIGURE 4
Germination
The embryo in this peanut seed uses its stored food to germinate. First, the embryo's roots grow downward. Then, its stem and leaves begin to grow upward.

140 ◆ A

The Structure of a Root In Figure 5, you can see the structure of a typical root. Notice that the tip of the root is rounded and is covered by a structure called the root cap. The **root cap** protects the root from injury from rocks as the root grows through the soil. Behind the root cap are the cells that divide to form new root cells.

Root hairs grow out of the root's surface. These tiny hairs can enter the spaces between soil particles, where they absorb water and minerals. By increasing the surface area of the root that touches the soil, root hairs help the plant absorb large amounts of substances. The root hairs also help to anchor the plant in the soil.

Locate the vascular tissue in the center of the root. The water and nutrients that are absorbed from the soil quickly move into the xylem. From there, these substances are transported upward to the plant's stems and leaves.

Phloem transports food manufactured in the leaves to the root. The root tissues may then use the food for growth or store it for future use by the plant.

> **Reading Checkpoint** What is a root cap?

FIGURE 5
Root Structure

Some plants have fibrous roots while others have taproots. A root's structure is adapted for absorbing water and minerals from the soil. **Relating Cause and Effect** *How do root hairs help absorb water and minerals?*

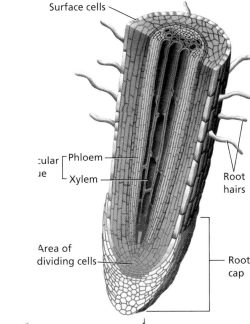

Surface cells

Vascular tissue — Phloem
— Xylem

Root hairs

Area of dividing cells

Root cap

Fibrous root system: Onion

Taproot system: Dandelion

A ◆ 141

Differentiated Instruction

Special Needs   [L1]
Relating Key Terms to Visuals Students who have difficulty processing information may benefit from relating key terms and structures of plants to visuals. Pair students with more able students. Have them write the key terms in this section on one side of an index card and draw a picture of the term on the other side. Encourage students to make up cards for key concepts as well. Then have partners form small groups of four students and guess the key terms of concepts by looking only at the illustrations. **learning modality: visual**

Teacher Demo   [L1]

Observing Roots

Materials small potted plant with a fibrous root system, such as a geranium; newspapers

Time 10 minutes

Focus Review the two types of roots.

Teach Loosen the geranium from the container and hold it over newspapers to collect dirt. Gently tap the soil around the roots to make the root system visible. Have students sketch the root system for both plants, labeling the structures.

Apply Ask students to explain how the structure of roots is related to their function. *(They are long so they can stretch out into the spaces between soil particles to anchor the plant and absorb water and minerals.)*
learning modality: visual

Use Visuals: Figure 5   [L2]
Root Structure

Focus Encourage students to study the diagram of a root in Figure 5.

Teach Ask: **What tissue is made up of the phloem and xylem?** *(Vascular tissue)* **Where is the vascular tissue located?** *(In the center)*

Apply Ask: **Which part of the root would you expect to grow longer as the root grows?** *(The area of dividing cells; the root cap contains dead cells and cannot grow.)*
learning modality: visual

Monitor Progress   [L2]

Writing Have students write a description of roots that includes their purposes, types, and structure.

Answers
Figure 5 They increase the amount of water and minerals aborbed by the plant.

> **Reading Checkpoint** A seed must absorb water from the environment.

> **Reading Checkpoint** A structure that covers and protects the tip of the root

A ● 141

Stems

Help Students Read

Active Comprehension Have students read the first paragraph of *Stems*. Then ask: **What would you like to know about stems?** *(Possible answers: Are the stems of trees and flowers similar? How are substances transported through stems?)* Write student responses on the board and have students read the remainder of the selection. After students are finished reading, ask them to respond to each question.

Teach Key Concepts [L2]

The Functions of Stems

Focus Remind students that nonvascular plants grow very close to the ground so that they can obtain the water they need. Indicate that stems are unique to vascular plants.

Teach Ask students to name the functions of stems. *(Stems carry water and nutrients from roots to leaves and food from leaves to roots. Stems support plants and hold leaves so that they are exposed to sunlight. Some stems also store food.)* Point out the structures in Figures 6 and 7. Ask: **How can you distinguish between the two types of stems? What are their names?** *(Woody stems contain wood and are hard and rigid; herbaceous stems are often soft and flexible and do not contain wood.)*

Apply Ask: **What will happen to a tree if a wound encircling the tree cuts through to the inner bark?** *(Because the inner bark is the phloem, the tree will be unable to transport food from leaves to other parts of the tree. It will die.)* **learning modality: verbal**

All in One Teaching Resources
• Transparencies A40, A41

Lab zone Skills Activity

Calculating

In this activity, you will calculate the speed at which water moves up a celery stalk.

1. Pour about 1 cm of water into a tall plastic container. Stir in several drops of red food coloring.
2. Place the freshly cut end of a celery stalk in the water. Lean the stalk against the container's side.
3. After 20 minutes, remove the celery. Use a metric ruler to measure the height of the water in the stalk.
4. Use the measurement and the following formula to calculate how fast the water moved up the stalk.

$$\text{Speed} = \frac{\text{Height}}{\text{Time}}$$

Based on your calculation, predict how far the water would move in 2 hours. Then test your prediction.

Stems

The stem of a plant has two main functions. **The stem carries substances between the plant's roots and leaves. The stem also provides support for the plant and holds up the leaves so they are exposed to the sun.** In addition, some stems, such as those of asparagus, store food.

The Structure of a Stem Stems can be either herbaceous (hur BAY shus) or woody. Herbaceous stems contain no wood and are often soft. Coneflowers and pepper plants have herbaceous stems. In contrast, woody stems are hard and rigid. Maple trees and roses have woody stems.

Both herbaceous and woody stems consist of phloem and xylem tissue as well as many other supporting cells. Figure 6 shows the inner structure of one type of herbaceous stem.

As you can see in Figure 7, a woody stem contains several layers of tissue. The outermost layer is bark. Bark includes an outer protective layer and an inner layer of living phloem, which transports food through the stem. Next is a layer of cells called the **cambium** (KAM bee um), which divide to produce new phloem and xylem. It is xylem that makes up most of what you call "wood." Sapwood is active xylem that transports water and minerals through the stem. The older, darker, heartwood is inactive but provides support.

Reading Checkpoint What function does the bark of a woody stem perform?

FIGURE 6
A Herbaceous Stem
Herbaceous stems, like those on these coneflowers, are often soft. The inset shows the inner structure of one type of herbaceous stem.

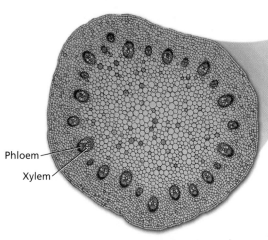

Phloem —
Xylem —

Lab zone Skills Activity

Skills Focus calculating [L2]

Materials calculator, celery stalk, clock or stopwatch, dropper, food coloring, lab apron, plastic container (tall and narrow), spoon, water

Time 35 minutes (20 wait time); 2 hours wait time to test prediction

Tips Make sure students wear lab aprons. Choose stalks 15–30 cm long. Before the activity, cut the end of each stalk, and peel a thin layer off the back of each.

Expected Outcome The water moves about 1.5 mm/min (30 mm ÷ 20 min). After 2 hours, it should rise 180 mm (120 min × 1.5 mm/min).

Extend Have students repeat the activity with another plant, such as a green onion or a leek. **learning modality: logical/mathematical**

Annual Rings Have you ever looked at a tree stump and seen a pattern of circles that looks something like a target? These circles are called annual rings because they represent a tree's yearly growth. Annual rings are made of xylem. Xylem cells that form in the spring are large and have thin walls because they grow rapidly. They produce a wide, light brown ring. Xylem cells that form in the summer grow slowly and, therefore, are small and have thick walls. They produce a thin, dark ring. One pair of light and dark rings represents one year's growth. You can estimate a tree's age by counting its annual rings.

The width of a tree's annual rings can provide important clues about past weather conditions, such as rainfall. In rainy years, more xylem is produced, so the tree's annual rings are wide. In dry years, rings are narrow. By examining annual rings from some trees in the southwestern United States, scientists were able to infer that severe droughts occurred in the years 840, 1067, 1379, and 1632.

FIGURE 7
A Woody Stem
Trees like these maples have woody stems. A typical woody stem is made up of many layers. The layers of xylem form annual rings that can reveal the age of the tree and the growing conditions it has experienced.
Interpreting Diagrams *Where is the cambium located?*

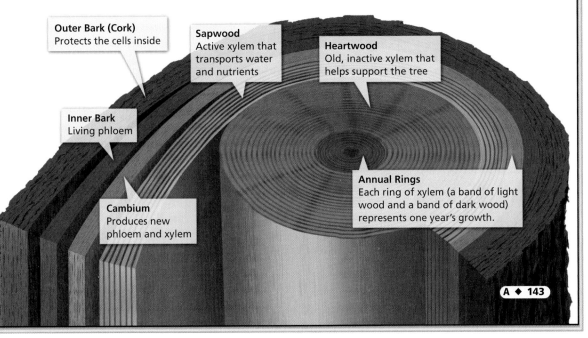

Outer Bark (Cork)
Protects the cells inside

Sapwood
Active xylem that transports water and nutrients

Heartwood
Old, inactive xylem that helps support the tree

Inner Bark
Living phloem

Cambium
Produces new phloem and xylem

Annual Rings
Each ring of xylem (a band of light wood and a band of dark wood) represents one year's growth.

A ◆ 143

Leaves

Teach Key Concepts　L2
The Functions of Leaves

Focus Remind students that plants are autotrophs—they make their own food.

Teach Ask: **How do leaves provide food for a plant?** *(They capture energy from sunlight and use it to carry out photosynthesis.)* Have students examine Figure 8 as you ask questions such as **Where are the stomata mostly found?** *(On a leaf's underside)* **What do they do?** *(They open to let in carbon dioxide, and allow water vapor and oxygen to leave. They close to conserve water.)* **What happens to the sugars made in the leaf during photosynthesis?** *(They enter the phloem and travel to other parts of the plant.)*

Apply Ask: **If the temperature is not very hot, when would stomata generally be open and closed?** *(Open during the daytime when sunlight is available and photosynthesis is active; closed at night when open stomata would only lead to water loss)* **learning modality: verbal**

All in One Teaching Resources
• Transparency A42

Use Visuals: Figure 8　L2
The Structure of a Leaf

Focus Ask student volunteers to read each caption in the figure.

Teach Ask: **Where is the leaf cuticle and what does it do?** *(It covers the leaf's surface and prevents water loss.)* **Where are the chloroplasts?** *(In the upper and lower leaf cells)* **What structure contains the xylem and phloem?** *(Vein)*

Apply Ask: **What is the benefit of upper leaf cells that are densely packed, rather than loosely packed?** *(Densely packed cells can collect more energy for photosynthesis.)* **learning modality: visual**

FIGURE 8
The Structure of a Leaf
A leaf is a well-adapted food factory. Each structure helps the leaf produce food.

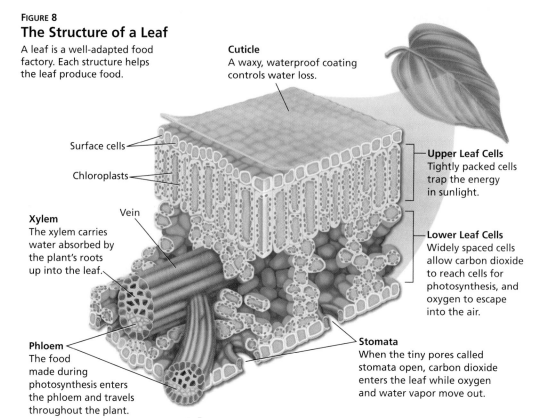

Cuticle
A waxy, waterproof coating controls water loss.

Surface cells

Chloroplasts

Upper Leaf Cells
Tightly packed cells trap the energy in sunlight.

Xylem
The xylem carries water absorbed by the plant's roots up into the leaf.

Vein

Lower Leaf Cells
Widely spaced cells allow carbon dioxide to reach cells for photosynthesis, and oxygen to escape into the air.

Phloem
The food made during photosynthesis enters the phloem and travels throughout the plant.

Stomata
When the tiny pores called stomata open, carbon dioxide enters the leaf while oxygen and water vapor move out.

Leaves

Leaves vary greatly in size and shape. Pine trees, for example, have needle-shaped leaves. Birch trees have small rounded leaves with jagged edges. Regardless of their shape, leaves play an important role in a plant. **Leaves capture the sun's energy and carry out the food-making process of photosynthesis.**

The Structure of a Leaf If you were to cut through a leaf and look at the edge under a microscope, you would see the structures in Figure 8. The leaf's top and bottom surface layers protect the cells inside. Between the layers of cells are veins that contain xylem and phloem.

The surface layers of the leaf have small openings, or pores, called **stomata** (STOH muh tuh) (singular *stoma*). The Greek word *stoma* means "mouth"—and stomata do look like tiny mouths. The stomata open and close to control when gases enter and leave the leaf. When the stomata are open, carbon dioxide enters the leaf, and oxygen and water vapor exit.

The Leaf and Photosynthesis The structure of a leaf is ideal for carrying out photosynthesis. The cells that contain the most chloroplasts are located near the leaf's upper surface, where they get the most light. The chlorophyll in the chloroplasts traps the sun's energy.

Carbon dioxide enters the leaf through open stomata. Water, which is absorbed by the plant's roots, travels up the stem to the leaf through the xylem. During photosynthesis, sugar and oxygen are produced from the carbon dioxide and water. Oxygen passes out of the leaf through the open stomata. The sugar enters the phloem and then travels throughout the plant.

Controlling Water Loss Because such a large area of a leaf is exposed to the air, water can quickly evaporate, or be lost, from a leaf into the air. The process by which water evaporates from a plant's leaves is called **transpiration.** A plant can lose a lot of water through transpiration. A corn plant, for example, can lose almost 4 liters of water on a hot summer day. Without a way to slow down the process of transpiration, a plant would shrivel up and die.

Fortunately, plants have ways to slow down transpiration. One way that plants retain water is by closing the stomata. The stomata often close when leaves start to dry out.

✓ Reading Checkpoint How does water get into a leaf?

FIGURE 9
Stomata
Stomata open (top) and close (bottom) to control when gases enter and exit the leaf.
Relating Cause and Effect *What gases enter and exit when the stomata open?*

Section 1 Assessment

 Target Reading Skill Outlining Use the information in your outline about seed plants to help you answer the questions below.

Reviewing Key Concepts

1. a. Reviewing What two characteristics do all seed plants share?
   b. Relating Cause and Effect What characteristics enable seed plants to live in a wide variety of environments? Explain.
2. a. Listing Name the three main parts of a seed.
   b. Sequencing List the steps in the sequence in which they must occur for a seed to grow into a new plant.
   c. Applying Concepts If a cherry seed were to take root right below its parent tree, what three challenges might the cherry seedling face?

3. a. Identifying What are the main functions of a plant's roots, stems, and leaves?
   b. Comparing and Contrasting Compare the path on which water moves through a plant to the path on which sugar moves through a plant.
   c. Applying Concepts How are the structures of a tree's roots and leaves well-suited for their roles in supplying the tree with water and sugar?

Writing in Science

Product Label Write a "packaging label" for a seed. Include a name and description for each part of the seed. Be sure to describe the role of each part in producing a new plant.

Chapter 5 A ◆ 145

Monitor Progress **L2**
Answers
Figure 9 Carbon dioxide enters the leaf, and water vapor and oxygen exit.

✓ Reading Checkpoint It is absorbed by the roots and travels up the stem to the leaf through the xylem.

Assess

Reviewing Key Concepts

1. a. They have vascular tissue and they use pollen and seeds to reproduce. **b.** They have structures to bring water and nutrients to all parts of the plant, and they do not need water for fertilization to occur.
2. a. Embryo, stored food, seed coat **b.** Dispersal, absorb water, germination, embryo begins to grow, plant leaves emerge **c.** It would compete with the parent tree for light, water, and minerals.
3. a. Roots—anchor plant, absorb water and nutrients from soil, some store food; stems—carry substances between roots and leaves, some store food; leaves—capture sun's energy and carry out photosynthesis **b.** Water moves from roots to leaves through the xylem; sugar moves from leaves to stems, roots, and other parts, through phloem. **c.** Tree roots have root hairs that help absorb water from the soil. Roots have xylem to carry water to leaves. Sugar made by the chloroplasts in the leaves moves to phloem and then travels to all parts of the plant.

Reteach **L1**
Use the section figures to summarize the functions of roots, stems, and leaves.

Performance Assessment **L2**
Oral Presentation Have groups of students make posters showing the functions of leaves, stems, or roots, then present their posters to the class.

All in One Teaching Resources
• Section Summary: *The Characteristics of Seed Plants*
• Review and Reinforce: *The Characteristics of Seed Plants*
• Enrich: *The Characteristics of Seed Plants*

Lab zone Chapter Project

Keep Students on Track By now seeds should have germinated and students begun making their observations. If some seeds have not germinated, allow students to start over or to observe seeds that have germinated. Make certain students are preparing detailed diagrams, drawings, or photographs of their observations.

Writing in Science

Writing Mode Description
Scoring Rubric
4 Includes the name, function, and description for each part of a seed; uses vivid descriptions that resemble a real label and engage the reader
3 Includes all criteria, but descriptions are uninteresting
2 Includes brief but accurate descriptions
1 Includes incomplete or inaccurate descriptions

Objectives

After this lesson, students will be able to
A.5.2.1 Identify the characteristics of gymnosperms.
A.5.2.2 Describe how gymnosperms reproduce.
A.5.2.3 List important products from gymnosperms.

Target Reading Skill

Previewing Visuals Explain that looking at visuals before they read helps students activate prior knowledge and predict what they are about to read.

Answers

Possible questions and answers include:
How does gymnosperm pollination occur? *(Pollen is transferred from a male reproductive structure to a female reproductive structure; wind often carries pollen from male to female cones.)* **How does gymnosperm fertilization occur?** *(Pollen collects in a sticky substance produced by ovules. Female scales close to seal in pollen and fertilization occurs.)*

All in One Teaching Resources

• Transparency A43

Preteach

Build Background Knowledge   L1

Green Trees in Winter

Ask students to name trees that stay green all winter and describe their features. *(Possible answers: Fir, pine; tall with needles for leaves, cones, needle-like leaves, sticky sap)*

Reading Preview

Key Concepts

• What are the characteristics of gymnosperms?
• How do gymnosperms reproduce?
• What important products come from gymnosperms?

Key Terms

• gymnosperm • cone • ovule
• pollination

Target Reading Skill

Previewing Visuals Before you read, preview Figure 11. Then write two questions that you have about the diagram in a graphic organizer like the one below. As you read, answer your questions.

The Life Cycle of a Gymnosperm

Q.	How does gymnosperm pollination occur?
A.	
Q.	

Go Online
SciLINKS NSTA

For: Links on gymnosperms
Visit: www.SciLinks.org
Web Code: scn-0152

Lab zone Discover Activity

Are All Leaves Alike?

1. Your teacher will give you a hand lens, a ruler, and the leaves from some seed plants.
2. Using the hand lens, examine each leaf. Sketch each leaf in your notebook.
3. Measure the length and width of each leaf. Record your measurements in your notebook.

Think It Over
Classifying Divide the leaves into two groups on the basis of your observations. Explain why you grouped the leaves as you did.

Have you ever seen a tree that is wider than a car? Do trees this huge really exist? The answer is yes. Some giant sequoia trees, which grow almost exclusively in central California, are more than 10 meters wide. You can understand why giant sequoias are commonly referred to as "giants of the forest." It takes a long time for a tree to grow so big. Scientists think that the largest giant sequoias may be about 2,000 years old. One reason they live so long is because their bark is fire resistant.

What Are Gymnosperms?

The giant sequoia trees belong to the group of seed plants known as gymnosperms. A **gymnosperm** (JIM nuh spurm) is a seed plant that produces naked seeds. The seeds of gymnosperms are referred to as "naked" because they are not enclosed by a protective fruit.

Every gymnosperm produces naked seeds. In addition, many gymnosperms have needle-like or scalelike leaves, and deep-growing root systems. Gymnosperms are the oldest type of seed plant. According to fossil evidence, gymnosperms first appeared on Earth about 360 million years ago. Fossils also indicate that there were many more species of gymnosperms on Earth in the past than there are today. Four groups of gymnosperms exist today.

Lab zone Discover Activity

Skills Focus Classifying   L1

Materials hand lens; metric ruler; 2 or 3 leaves from angiosperms, such as oak tree, maple tree, day lily, and rose; 2 or 3 leaves from gymnosperms, such as pine, yew, and spruce

Time 10 minutes

Tips Encourage students to include a detailed description of the leaf's features.

Direct students to wash their hands after handling the leaves.

Expected Outcome Students will observe differences in size, length, width, and thickness.

Think It Over Groups should be needlelike shapes and broad shaped leaves. Students' reasons may include the difference in thickness and broadness of the leaves.

FIGURE 10
Types of Gymnosperms

Gymnosperms are the oldest seed plants. Cycads, conifers, ginkgoes, and gnetophytes are the only groups that exist today.

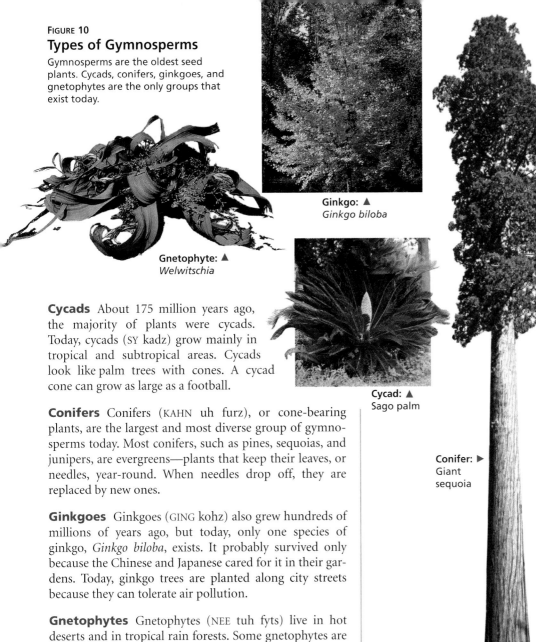

Gnetophyte: ▲
Welwitschia

Ginkgo: ▲
Ginkgo biloba

Cycad: ▲
Sago palm

Conifer: ▶
Giant sequoia

Cycads About 175 million years ago, the majority of plants were cycads. Today, cycads (SY kadz) grow mainly in tropical and subtropical areas. Cycads look like palm trees with cones. A cycad cone can grow as large as a football.

Conifers Conifers (KAHN uh furz), or cone-bearing plants, are the largest and most diverse group of gymnosperms today. Most conifers, such as pines, sequoias, and junipers, are evergreens—plants that keep their leaves, or needles, year-round. When needles drop off, they are replaced by new ones.

Ginkgoes Ginkgoes (GING kohz) also grew hundreds of millions of years ago, but today, only one species of ginkgo, *Ginkgo biloba*, exists. It probably survived only because the Chinese and Japanese cared for it in their gardens. Today, ginkgo trees are planted along city streets because they can tolerate air pollution.

Gnetophytes Gnetophytes (NEE tuh fyts) live in hot deserts and in tropical rain forests. Some gnetophytes are trees, some are shrubs, and others are vines. The *Welwitschia* shown in Figure 10 grows in the deserts of West Africa and can live for more than 1,000 years.

✓ **Reading Checkpoint** What are the four types of gymnosperms?

A ◆ 147

Instruct

Go Online
SciLINKS™ NSTA

For: Links on gymnosperms
Visit: www.SciLinks.org
Web Code: scn-0152

Download a worksheet to guide students' review of gymnosperms.

What Are Gymnosperms?

Teach Key Concepts L2
Characteristics of Gymnosperms

Focus Explain that *gymnosperm* comes from the Greek root *gymno*, meaning "naked" and *sperma*, meaning "seed."

Teach Ask: **What characteristic of a gymnosperm gives the plant its name?** (*Gymnosperms have naked seeds.*) **What other characteristics are common to most gymnosperms?** (*Needlelike leaves and deep-growing root systems*)

Apply Ask students to infer why the conifers are the largest group of gymnosperms. (*Possible answer: They have adaptations that allow them to live in a wide variety of places. For example, many conifers can live in dry conditions because their long, thin needles limit water loss.*)
learning modality: verbal

All in One Teaching Resources

• Guided Reading and Study Worksheet: *Gymnosperms*

○ **Student Edition on Audio CD**

Differentiated Instruction

Special Needs L1
Visual Science Glossary Have students draw a characteristic of a typical gymnosperm, as well as a characteristic of each group of gymnosperms, based on the text description. Drawings should include needlelike or scalelike leaves, deep-growing root systems, and seeds that are not enclosed in a fruit. Encourage students to add a mnemonic device or memory jogger to their drawings that will help them remember the characteristic shown. (*Examples: A sewing needle for needlelike leaves, a marble for unprotected seeds, a ladder for deep-growing root systems*)
learning modality: visual

Monitor Progress L2

Oral Presentation Have students state the characteristics common to gymnosperms.

Answers

✓ **Reading Checkpoint** Cycads, conifers, ginkoes, and gnetophytes

Interpreting Data on Gymnosperms

Materials references on gymnosperms, including Web sites; state map, map pins

Time 20 minutes

Focus Challenge students to create a map showing the distribution of gymnosperms in your state.

Teach Allow students to research gymnosperms, then place pins on the map (one color for each type of gymnosperm) as they locate an area where each type grows.

Apply Ask students to explain which type of gymnosperm is most common in your state and why. *(Answers should include climate conditions in your state.)* **learning modality: visual**

Reproduction in Gymnosperms

Teach Key Concepts
L2

Pollination and Fertilization

Focus Refer students to Figure 11.

Teach Ask: **What process occurs in the male cone?** *(Male cones produce pollen.)* **What processes occur in the female cone before fertilization?** *(First, an egg cell forms inside an ovule on a scale of a female cone. Next, pollination takes place on the scales. After pollen falls from a male cone onto a female cone, a sperm cell and an egg cell join in an ovule on the female cone.)* **What process follows fertilization but occurs before seeds mature and disperse?** *(The fertilized egg develops into an embryo.)* **Once the embryo develops, what else must happen for a seed to be ready to disperse?** *(The seed must mature—the seed coat and its stored food develops.)*

Apply Ask: **Is pollen more or less likely to be dispersed by wind during rainy weather?** *(Less, because the rain moistens the pollen; the pollen falls to the ground instead of being in the air.)* **learning modality: logical/ mathematical**

All in One Teaching Resources
• Transparency A44

Lab zone Try This Activity

The Scoop on Cones
In this activity, you will observe the structure of a female cone.

1. Use a hand lens to look closely at the female cone. Gently shake the cone over a piece of white paper. Observe what happens.
2. Break off one scale from the cone. Examine its base. If the scale contains a seed, remove the seed.
3. With a hand lens, examine the seed from Step 2 or examine a seed that fell on the paper in Step 1.
4. Wash your hands.

Inferring How does the structure of the cone protect the seeds?

148 ◆ A

Lab zone Try This Activity

Skills Focus Inferring
L2

Materials mature female pine cone, hand lens, sheet of white paper

Time 10 minutes 10 minutes

Tips CAUTION: *Check for student allergies before this lab.* Make certain that cones have some seeds inside the scales. Remind students to wash their hands afterwards.

Expected Outcome The scales probably protect developing seeds from wind, rain, and very cold temperatures.

Extend Have students compare, then sketch, male and female pine cones. Sketches should indicate differences in size, shape, and structure of the scales. **learning modality: visual**

Reproduction in Gymnosperms

Most gymnosperms have reproductive structures called **cones.** Cones are covered with scales. Most gymnosperms produce two types of cones: male cones and female cones. Usually, a single plant produces both male and female cones. In some types of gymnosperms, however, individual trees produce either male cones or female cones. A few types of gymnosperms produce no cones at all.

In Figure 11, you can see the male and female cones of a Ponderosa pine. Male cones produce tiny grains of pollen—the male gametophyte. Pollen contains the cells that will later become sperm cells. Each scale on a male cone produces thousands of pollen grains.

The female gametophyte develops in structures called ovules. An **ovule** (OH vyool) is a structure that contains an egg cell. Female cones contain at least one ovule at the base of each scale. After fertilization occurs, the ovule develops into a seed.

You can follow the process of gymnosperm reproduction in Figure 11. **First, pollen falls from a male cone onto a female cone. In time, a sperm cell and an egg cell join together in an ovule on the female cone.** After fertilization occurs, the seed develops on the scale of the female cone.

Pollination The transfer of pollen from a male reproductive structure to a female reproductive structure is called **pollination.** In gymnosperms, wind often carries the pollen from the male cones to the female cones. The pollen collects in a sticky substance produced by each ovule.

Fertilization Once pollination has occurred, the ovule closes and seals in the pollen. The scales also close, and a sperm cell fertilizes an egg cell inside each ovule. The fertilized egg then develops into the embryo part of the seed.

Seed Development Female cones remain on the tree while the seeds mature. As the seeds develop, the female cone increases in size. It can take up to two years for the seeds of some gymnosperms to mature. Male cones, however, usually fall off the tree after they have shed their pollen.

Seed Dispersal When the seeds are mature, the scales open. The wind shakes the seeds out of the cone and carries them away. Only a few seeds will land in suitable places and grow into new plants.

 Reading Checkpoint What is pollen and where is it produced?

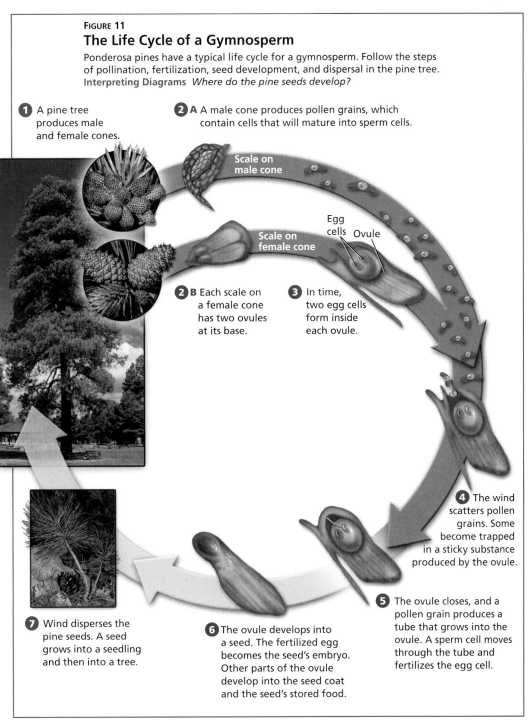

FIGURE 11

The Life Cycle of a Gymnosperm

Ponderosa pines have a typical life cycle for a gymnosperm. Follow the steps of pollination, fertilization, seed development, and dispersal in the pine tree.
Interpreting Diagrams *Where do the pine seeds develop?*

1 A pine tree produces male and female cones.

2 A A male cone produces pollen grains, which contain cells that will mature into sperm cells.

Scale on male cone

Scale on female cone

Egg cells Ovule

2 B Each scale on a female cone has two ovules at its base.

3 In time, two egg cells form inside each ovule.

4 The wind scatters pollen grains. Some become trapped in a sticky substance produced by the ovule.

5 The ovule closes, and a pollen grain produces a tube that grows into the ovule. A sperm cell moves through the tube and fertilizes the egg cell.

6 The ovule develops into a seed. The fertilized egg becomes the seed's embryo. Other parts of the ovule develop into the seed coat and the seed's stored food.

7 Wind disperses the pine seeds. A seed grows into a seedling and then into a tree.

Chapter 5 A ◆ 149

Help Students Read

Reciprocal Teaching Have students read *Reproduction in Gymnosperms* with a partner. One partner reads a paragraph out loud. Then, the other partner summarizes the paragraph's contents and explains the main concepts. The partners continue to switch roles with each new paragraph.

Use Visuals: Figure 11   L2

Life Cycle of a Gymnosperm

Focus Encourage students to study the photographs of the male and female cones in Figure 11.

Teach Ask: **How is pollen transferred from the male to the female cone?** *(Wind)* **Why are male cones at the tips of branches rather than closer to the trunk?** *(Branch tips allow more efficient pollen distribution.)* **What happens to male cones after they shed their pollen?** *(They fall from the tree.)* **What happens to female cones after fertilization?** *(They stay on the tree as the seed matures.)*

Apply Ask: **How does the shape of the seed affect its motion in the wind?** *(The shape of the seed allows the wind to carry the seed some distance away from the parent tree.)* **learning modality: logical/mathematical**

Monitor Progress   L2

Writing Have students use the following words in paragraphs to describe gymnosperm reproduction: *ovule, pollen, male, female, fertilization, seed,* and *scales.*

Answers
Figure 11 On the female cones

Reading Checkpoint Pollen contains cells that mature into sperm cells. It is produced in male cones.

Gymnosperms in Everyday Life

Teach Key Concepts
Useful Gymnosperms

Focus Tell students that the U.S. is the world's leading producer and consumer of forest products.

Teach Ask: **What useful products come from conifers?** *(Paper, lumber, rayon fiber, cellophane, and turpentine)*

Apply Ask: **How are managed forests renewable resources?** *(New trees are planted to replace trees that are cut down.)* **learning modality: verbal**

Monitor Progress
Answer

Reading Checkpoint Turpentine and rosin

Assess

Reviewing Key Concepts

1. a. They produce unprotected seeds; many have needlelike or scalelike leaves and deep root systems. **b.** Gymnosperm seeds are not enclosed by a protective fruit. **c.** Not likely; the seeds aren't enclosed in fruits that animals are attracted to.
2. a. The reproductive structure of a gymnosperm **b.** Male cones produce pollen. Female cones have ovules in which eggs are produced. **c.** Pollen falls from a male cone onto a female cone. Fertilization occurs when a sperm cell and an egg cell join inside the ovule. The fertilized egg becomes the seed's embryo.
3. a. Paper and lumber **b.** Possible answer: No; demand could increase or bad weather could decrease the yield.

Reteach [L1]

Provide students with a copy of Figure 11 with the labels blanked out. Ask students to fill in the labels, then discuss the life cycle of gymnosperms as a class.

All in One Teaching Resources

- Section Summary: *Gymnosperms*
- Review and Reinforce: *Gymnosperms*
- Enrich: *Gymnosperms*

FIGURE 12
Uses of Gymnosperms
Conifers provided the lumber for this new house.

Gymnosperms in Everyday Life

Gymnosperms, especially conifers, provide many useful products. **Paper and other products, such as the lumber used to build homes, come from conifers.** The rayon fibers in clothes as well as the cellophane wrappers on some food products also come from conifers. Other products, such as turpentine and the rosin used by baseball pitchers, gymnasts, and musicians, are made from the sap produced by some conifers.

Because conifers are so useful to humans, they are grown in large, managed forests in many regions of the United States. When adult trees in managed forests are cut down, young trees are planted to replace them. Since different parts of the forest are usually cut at different times, there are always adult trees that can be harvested. These management efforts help ensure a steady supply of these important trees.

Reading Checkpoint What are two products made from the sap of conifers?

Section 2 Assessment

Target Reading Skill Previewing Visuals Refer to your questions and answers about Figure 11 to answer Question 2.

Reviewing Key Concepts
1. a. **Listing** What characteristics do all gymnosperms share? What other characteristics do many gymnosperms have?
   b. **Comparing and Contrasting** In what way do gymnosperm seeds differ from corn or bean seeds, which are not gymnosperms?
   c. **Predicting** Do you think that the seeds of gymnosperms would likely be dispersed by animals? Why or why not?
2. a. **Reviewing** What is a cone?
   b. **Comparing and Contrasting** What are the two different types of cones? What role does each cone play in gymnosperm reproduction?
   c. **Sequencing** Briefly describe the steps in the reproduction of a gymnosperm.

3. a. **Identifying** Name two important products that come from conifers.
   b. **Making Judgments** Do you think that managed forests guarantee that there will be a steady supply of conifers? Why or why not?

Lab zone At-Home Activity

Everyday Gymnosperms Describe the characteristics of gymnosperms to a family member. Then, with that family member, make a list of things in your home that are made from gymnosperms. Also list the gymnosperms that grow where you live.

Lab zone At Home Activity

Everyday Gymnosperms [L1] As a class, review the characteristics of gymnosperms and compile a list of gymnosperms that grow in your area of the country. After students look in their homes for gymnosperm products such as furniture, cellophane, and turpentine, have them bring their lists to class for comparisons. Encourage students to highlight any unusual products or uses.

Reading Preview

Key Concepts
• What characteristics do angiosperms share?
• What is the function of an angiosperm's flowers?
• How do angiosperms reproduce?
• How do monocots differ from dicots?

Key Terms
• angiosperm • flower • sepal
• petal • stamen • pistil
• ovary • fruit • monocot
• dicot

Target Reading Skill
Building Vocabulary Using a word in a sentence helps you think about how best to explain the word. After you read the section, reread the paragraphs that contain definitions of Key Terms. Use all the information you have learned to write a meaningful sentence using each Key Term.

Lab zone Discover **Activity**

What Is a Fruit?

1. Your teacher will give you three different fruits that have been cut in half.
2. Use a hand lens to carefully observe the outside of each fruit. For each fruit, record its color, shape, size, and other external features. Record your observations in your notebook.
3. Carefully observe the structures inside the fruit. Record your observations.

Think It Over
Forming Operational Definitions Based on your observations, how would you define the term *fruit*?

You probably associate the word *flower* with a sweet-smelling plant growing in a garden. You certainly wouldn't think of something that smells like rotting meat. But that's exactly what the corpse flower, or rafflesia, smells like. These flowers, which grow on vines in Asia, are huge—nearly 1 meter across! You won't be seeing rafflesia in your local florist shop any time soon.

Rafflesia belongs to the group of seed plants known as **angiosperms** (AN jee uh spurmz). **All angiosperms, or flowering plants, share two important characteristics. First, they produce flowers. Second, in contrast to gymnosperms, which produce uncovered seeds, angiosperms produce seeds that are enclosed in fruits.**

Angiosperms live almost everywhere on Earth. They grow in frozen areas in the Arctic, tropical jungles, and barren deserts. A few angiosperms, such as mangrove trees, can live at the ocean's edge.

◀ Rafflesia

Chapter 5 A ◆ 151

Objectives
After this lesson, students will be able to
A.5.3.1 Describe the characteristics shared by angiosperms.
A.5.3.2 State the function of an angiosperm's flowers.
A.5.3.3 Explain how angiosperms reproduce
A.5.3.4 Tell how monocots differ from dicots.

Target Reading Skill ↻

Building Vocabulary Explain that using a vocabulary strategy such as using the words in a sentence helps students define key-concept words.

Answers
Have students write what they know about each key term before reading the definitions in the section. Explain that connecting what they already know about key terms helps them to remember the terms. As they read each passage that contains key terms, remind them to write the definitions in their own words.

All in One Teaching Resources
• Guided Reading Study Worksheet: *Angiosperms, Use Target Reading Skills*

Preteach

Build Background Knowledge   L2

Flower Descriptions
Ask students to describe how the flowering plants or trees they are familiar with change throughout the year. Encourage students to use specific examples, such as a tree in the schoolyard or a flowering house plant. Post several pictures of a single flowering plant taken at different times of the year. Have students describe the changes that take place in chronological order. Prompt students to include times of increased insect or animal activity in their descriptions, if applicable.

Lab zone Discover **Activity**

Skills Focus Forming operational definitions   L1

Materials hand lens; metric ruler; three different fruits, such as apples, cherries, peaches, plums, tomatoes, or peppers

Time 15 minutes

Tips CAUTION: *Tell students not to taste or eat the fruit. Check for food allergies before*

beginning this activity. Students may not think that some vegetables, such as tomatoes and peppers, are considered by botanists to be fruits. Challenge students to determine why.

Think It Over Possible definition: Fruits contain seeds and have a fleshy edible part. They vary in color, shape, and the number of seeds they contain.

The Structure of Flowers

Teach Key Concepts   L2

Flowers Are Reproductive Organs

Focus Remind students that in gymnosperms, the cone is the reproductive structure.

Teach Explain that in angiosperms, a flower is the reproductive structure. Ask: **What is the function of flowers?** *(To reproduce)* **What kinds of structures do you expect to find in a flower?** *(Male and female reproductive structures of the plant)* Refer students to Figure 13. Ask them to examine each part as student volunteers read the captions and the sentences in the passage containing key terms. Ask: **What structures make up the male parts of a flower?** *(Stamens with their filaments and anthers)* **The female parts?** *(Pistils, which have stigmas, styles, and an ovary)* **What purpose do the color and shape of the petals serve?** *(To help ensure pollination)*

Apply Ask: **How is it an advantage for a plant to have many flowers together in a single structure?** *(More flowers might attract more pollinators, which increases the chance of pollination.)* **learning modality: visual**

Extend The Active Art will show students how the structures of flowers are specialized for reproduction.

All in One **Teaching Resources**

• Transparency A45

Independent Practice   L2

All in One **Teaching Resources**

• Guided Reading and Study Worksheet: *Angiosperms*

🔘 **Student Edition on Audio CD**

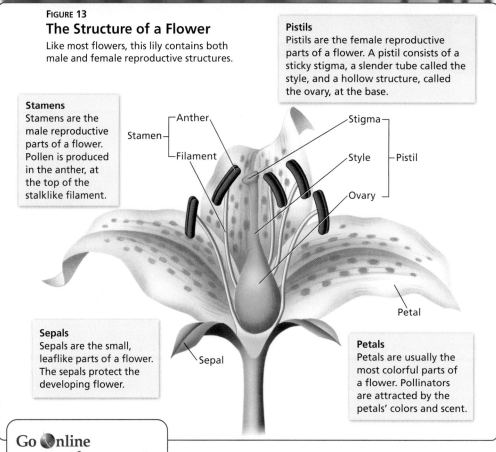

FIGURE 13
The Structure of a Flower
Like most flowers, this lily contains both male and female reproductive structures.

Pistils
Pistils are the female reproductive parts of a flower. A pistil consists of a sticky stigma, a slender tube called the style, and a hollow structure, called the ovary, at the base.

Stamens
Stamens are the male reproductive parts of a flower. Pollen is produced in the anther, at the top of the stalklike filament.

Stamen — Anther
— Filament

Stigma
Style — Pistil
Ovary

Petal

Sepals
Sepals are the small, leaflike parts of a flower. The sepals protect the developing flower.

Sepal

Petals
Petals are usually the most colorful parts of a flower. Pollinators are attracted by the petals' colors and scent.

The Structure of Flowers

Flowers come in all sorts of shapes, sizes, and colors. But, despite their differences, all flowers have the same function—reproduction. A **flower** is the reproductive structure of an angiosperm. Figure 13 shows the parts of a typical flower. As you read about the parts, keep in mind that some flowers lack one or more of the parts. For example, some flowers have only male reproductive parts, and some flowers lack petals.

Sepals and Petals When a flower is still a bud, it is enclosed by leaflike structures called **sepals** (SEE pulz). Sepals protect the developing flower and are often green in color. When the sepals fold back, they reveal the flower's colorful, leaflike **petals.** The petals are generally the most colorful parts of a flower. The shapes, sizes, and number of petals vary greatly from flower to flower.

Stamens Within the petals are the flower's male and female reproductive parts. The **stamens** (STAY munz) are the male reproductive parts. Locate the stamens inside the flower in Figure 13. The thin stalk of the stamen is called the filament. Pollen is produced in the anther, at the top of the filament.

Pistils The female parts, or **pistils** (PIS tulz), are found in the center of most flowers. Some flowers have two or more pistils; others have only one. The sticky tip of the pistil is called the stigma. A slender tube, called a style, connects the stigma to a hollow structure at the base of the flower. This hollow structure is the **ovary,** which protects the seeds as they develop. An ovary contains one or more ovules.

Pollinators The colors and shapes of most petals and the scents produced by most flowers attract insects and other animals. These organisms ensure that pollination occurs. Pollinators include birds, bats, and insects such as bees and flies. The rafflesia flower you read about at the beginning of the section is pollinated by flies. The flies are attracted by the strong smell of rotting meat.

 Reading Checkpoint What are the male and female reproductive parts of a flower?

FIGURE 14
Pollinators
Pollinators, such as insects, birds, and bats, are attracted to a flower's color, shape, or scent. *Inferring How might the white color of the cactus flower aid in attracting bats?*

◄ A honeybee is covered in the pollen of an orange flower.

▲ A hummingbird pollinates a bright red flower.

A bat pollinates an organ ► pipe cactus flower at night.

Chapter 5 A ◆ 153

Reproduction in Angiosperms

Teach Key Concepts

Processes in Angiosperm Reproduction

Focus Ask: **What reproductive structures are unique to angiosperms?** (*Flowers and fruits*)

Teach Ask: **After a plant has produced a mature flower, what is the first step in reproduction?** (*Pollen falls on the stigma.*) **What is this process called?** (*Pollination*) **What happens next?** (*A sperm cell in the pollen joins with an egg cell inside the ovary.*) **What is the process called? What is the result of the process?** (*Fertilization, a zygote*) **What happens to the ovary as the seed develops?** (*The ovary changes into a fruit.*)

Apply Have students suppose they have discovered a new plant that has tiny green flowers against a background of green leaves. Ask: **How do you think this plant is pollinated?** (*Probably the wind because it does not have colorful flowers to attract animal pollinators*) **learning modality: visual**

All in One Teaching Resources
• Transparency A46

 Build Inquiry L2

Comparing and Contrasting Fruit

Materials whole fruit and fruit slices, such as grapes, coconut, apples, bananas, tomatoes, and so on

Time 10 minutes

Focus Review the definition of a fruit.

Teach CAUTION: *Check for allergies before allowing students to handle fruit. Make certain students do not eat or taste the fruit.* Encourage students to feel the shape, weight, and texture of several fruits. Ask students to describe how the physical characteristics of each fruit and its seeds might be related to the way in which its seeds are dispersed.

Apply Ask: **What is the purpose of fruits being sweet and fleshy?** (*Animals are more likely to eat the fruit, which helps the plants disperse its seeds.*) **learning modality: kinesthetic**

Reproduction in Angiosperms

You can follow the process of angiosperm reproduction in Figure 16. **First, pollen falls on a flower's stigma. In time, the sperm cell and egg cell join together in the flower's ovule. The zygote develops into the embryo part of the seed.**

Pollination A flower is pollinated when a grain of pollen falls on the stigma. Like gymnosperms, some angiosperms are pollinated by the wind. But most angiosperms rely on birds, bats, or insects for pollination. Nectar, a sugar-rich food, is located deep inside a flower. When an animal enters a flower to obtain the nectar, it brushes against the anthers and becomes coated with pollen. Some of the pollen can drop onto the flower's stigma as the animal leaves the flower. The pollen can also be brushed onto the sticky stigma of the next flower the animal visits.

Fertilization If the pollen falls on the stigma of a similar plant, fertilization can occur. A sperm cell joins with an egg cell inside an ovule within the ovary at the base of the flower. The zygote then begins to develop into the seed's embryo. Other parts of the ovule develop into the rest of the seed.

Fruit Development and Seed Dispersal As the seed develops after fertilization, the ovary changes into a **fruit**—a ripened ovary and other structures that enclose one or more seeds. Apples and cherries are fruits. So are many foods you usually call vegetables, such as tomatoes and squash. Fruits are the means by which angiosperm seeds are dispersed. Animals that eat fruits help to disperse their seeds.

 **Reading Checkpoint** What flower part develops into a fruit?

FIGURE 15
Fruits
The seeds of angiosperms are enclosed in fruits, which protect and help disperse the seeds.

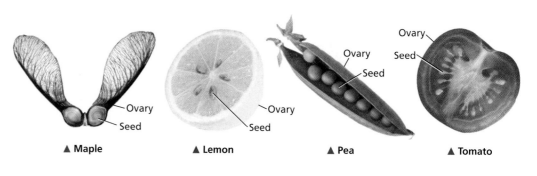

▲ Maple   ▲ Lemon   ▲ Pea   ▲ Tomato

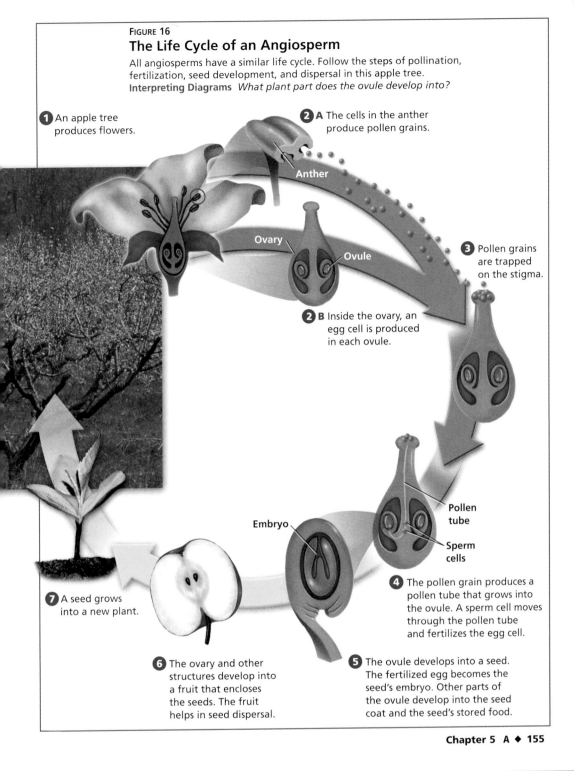

FIGURE 16
The Life Cycle of an Angiosperm
All angiosperms have a similar life cycle. Follow the steps of pollination, fertilization, seed development, and dispersal in this apple tree.
Interpreting Diagrams *What plant part does the ovule develop into?*

1 An apple tree produces flowers.

2 A The cells in the anther produce pollen grains.

Anther

Ovary

Ovule

3 Pollen grains are trapped on the stigma.

2 B Inside the ovary, an egg cell is produced in each ovule.

Embryo

Pollen tube

Sperm cells

4 The pollen grain produces a pollen tube that grows into the ovule. A sperm cell moves through the pollen tube and fertilizes the egg cell.

7 A seed grows into a new plant.

6 The ovary and other structures develop into a fruit that encloses the seeds. The fruit helps in seed dispersal.

5 The ovule develops into a seed. The fertilized egg becomes the seed's embryo. Other parts of the ovule develop into the seed coat and the seed's stored food.

Chapter 5 A ◆ 155

Focus Encourage students to follow the reproductive process of flowering plants shown in Figure 16.

Teach Make sure students can identify the ovary and anther in Step 1. Ask: **Why are there Steps 2A and 2B?** (*One step is the male—cells in the anther produce pollen; the other step is the female—cells in each ovule produce egg cells.*) As students review the steps in the visual, have them record what each of these structures produces and its role in the life cycle: anther (*Pollen grains*), ovule (*Egg cell, seed*), pollen grain (*Pollen tube*), ovule's wall (*Seed coat*), and ovary (*Fruit*). Ask: **What is the purpose of the stigma?** (*To trap pollen*) **What happens to the ovule parts that are not the embryo?** (*They develop into a seed coat and stored food.*) **What is the purpose of fruit?** (*Enclose seeds and aid in seed dispersal.*)

Apply Call students' attention to Step 6. Ask students to infer how animals that eat fruit help to ensure the germination of seeds. (*When animals eat fruits, the seeds pass through the animals' digestive system. When the animals travel, they disperse seeds away from the parent plant. Seeds may then have a better chance of germinating because they won't have to compete with the parent plant for resources.*) **learning modality: visual**

Differentiated Instruction

English Learners/Beginning **L1**
Comprehension: Link to Visual Help students construct a table listing each reproductive structure, what it produces, and what role the structure plays in the plant's life cycle. Use the headings *Plant Part*, *Produces*, and *Role*. Entries in the *Plant Part* column should include *anther*, *ovule*, *ovary*, *sperm cells*, and so on.
learning modality: visual

English Learners/Intermediate **L2**
Comprehension: Modified Cloze Have student pairs write sentences with blanks for key terms and concepts, then switch with another pair to fill in the blanks. Example: **The *anther* produces *pollen grains* that fertilize the *egg*. learning modality: verbal**

Monitor Progress **L2**

Oral Presentation Have students describe the roles of an orange blossom and an orange in the reproduction of an orange tree.

Answers
Figure 15 A seed

✔ Reading Checkpoint — The ovary and other structures

Types of Angiosperms

Teach Key Concepts L2
Monocots and Dicots

Focus Remind students that a cotyledon is a seed leaf that sometimes stores food for the plant embryo.

Teach Ask: **How can you classify angiosperms by the number of cotyledons?** *(A monocot has one seed leaf; a dicot has two seed leaves.)* **How are the petals of each type different?** *(A monocot has petals in groups of three or multiples of three; a dicot has petals in groups of four or five or multiples of four or five.)*

Apply Ask: **What can you infer about a cross-section of a fossilized stem that has holes scattered randomly throughout?** *(It was vascular because it had a stem with vascular tissue. It probably was seed bearing and a monocot because the vascular tissue was scattered throughout the stem.)* **learning modality: verbal**

All in One Teaching Resources
• Transparency A47

Math Skills Whole number operations

Focus Reinforce that monocots may have more than 3 petals.

Teach Ask: **How can you use the number of petals to determine if a flower is a monocot or a dicot?** *(Divide the number of petals by 3. It is a monocot if you get a whole number.)*

Answer 12 and 16

Angiosperms in Everyday Life

Teach Key Concepts L2
Uses of Angiosperms

Focus Tell students that angiosperms have greater commercial use than gymnosperms, except in forest products.

Teach Ask: **Besides for food, how do people use angiosperms?** *(Clothing, rubber, furniture, medications)*

Apply Ask students to name specific food crops that are angiosperms. *(Rice, wheat, corn, all types of fruits and vegetables)*

learning modality: verbal

FIGURE 17
Monocots and Dicots
Monocots and dicots differ in the number of cotyledons, the pattern of veins and vascular tissue, and the number of petals.
Interpreting Tables
How do monocot and dicot leaves differ?

Comparing Monocots and Dicots

Plant Part	Monocots		Dicots	
Seed	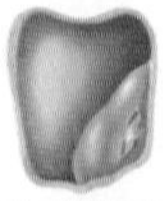	One cotyledon	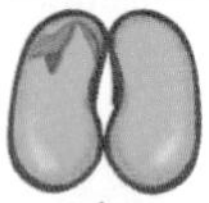	Two cotyledons
Leaf		Parallel veins		Branching veins
Stem	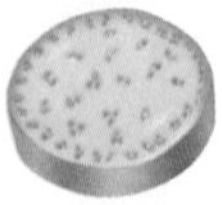	Bundles of vascular tissue scattered throughout stem		Bundles of vascular tissue arranged in a ring
Flower		Flower parts in threes		Flower parts in fours or fives

Math Skills

Multiples

Is a flower with 6 petals a monocot? To answer this question, you need to determine if 6 is a multiple of 3. A number is a multiple of 3 if there is a nonzero whole number that, when multiplied by 3, gives you that number.

In this case, 6 is a multiple of 3 because you can multiply 2 (a nonzero whole number) by 3 to get 6.

$$2 \times 3 = 6$$

Therefore, a flower with 6 petals is a monocot. Other multiples of 3 include 9 and 12.

Practice Problem Which of these numbers are multiples of 4?

6, 10, 12, 16

Types of Angiosperms

Angiosperms are divided into two major groups: monocots and dicots. "Cot" is short for *cotyledon*. Recall from Section 1 that the cotyledon, or seed leaf, provides food for the embryo. *Mono* means "one" and *di* means "two." **Monocots** are angiosperms that have only one seed leaf. **Dicots,** on the other hand, produce seeds with two seed leaves. In Figure 17, you can compare the characteristics of monocots and dicots.

Monocots Grasses, including corn, wheat, and rice, and plants such as lilies and tulips are monocots. The flowers of a monocot usually have either three petals or a multiple of three petals. Monocots usually have long, slender leaves with veins that run parallel to one another like train rails. The bundles of vascular tissue in monocot stems are usually scattered randomly throughout the stem.

Dicots Dicots include plants such as roses and violets, as well as dandelions. Both oak and maple trees are dicots, as are food plants such as beans and apples. The flowers of dicots often have either four or five petals or multiples of these numbers. The leaves are usually wide, with veins that branch many times. Dicot stems usually have bundles of vascular tissue arranged in a ring.

 Reading Checkpoint How do the petals of monocots and dicots differ in number?

Angiosperms in Everyday Life

Angiosperms are an important source of food, clothing, and medicine for other organisms. Plant-eating animals, such as cows, elephants, and beetles, eat flowering plants such as grasses as well as the leaves of trees. People eat vegetables, fruits, and cereals, all of which are angiosperms.

People also produce clothing and other products from angiosperms. For example, the seeds of cotton plants, like the ones you see in Figure 18, are covered with cotton fibers. The stems of flax plants provide linen fibers. The sap of rubber trees is used to make rubber for tires and other products. Furniture is often made from the wood of maple, cherry, and oak trees. Some important medications come from angiosperms, too. For example, the heart medication digitalis comes from the leaves of the foxglove plant.

FIGURE 18
Cotton Bolls
Angiosperms, such as cotton plants, provide many important products. Cotton seeds, which develop in fruits called bolls, are covered with fibers that are manufactured into cotton fabric.

Reading Checkpoint — *What are two angiosperms from which people produce clothing?*

Section 3 Assessment

 Target Reading Skill Building Vocabulary Use your sentences to help you answer the questions below.

Reviewing Key Concepts

1. **a. Reviewing** What two characteristics do all angiosperms share?
   b. Comparing and Contrasting Do gymnosperms share either of the two characteristics with angiosperms? Explain.

2. **a. Identifying** What is the function of an angiosperm's flowers?
   b. Describing Describe the role of a flower's sepals, petals, stamens, and pistil.

3. **a. Reviewing** On what part of a flower must pollen land for pollination to occur?
   b. Sequencing Briefly describe the steps in the reproduction of an angiosperm, from pollination to seed dispersal.
   c. Making Judgments Do you agree or disagree with the following statement? Animals are essential in order for reproduction in angiosperms to occur. Explain your answer.

4. **a. Listing** Name the two major groups of angiosperms.
   b. Comparing and Contrasting How do the seeds, leaves, stems, and flowers of these two groups differ?
   c. Classifying A plant's leaves have parallel veins, and each of its flowers has six petals. To which group does it belong? Explain.

Math Practice

5. **Multiples** Which of the following numbers are multiples of 3? Which of the numbers are multiples of 4?

   5, 6, 8, 10, 12, 15

6. **Multiples** Suppose you found a flower with 12 petals. Would you know from the number of petals whether the flower is a monocot or a dicot? Explain.

Monitor Progress _____ L2

Answers
Figure 17 The leaves of monocots have parallel veins. The leaves of dicots have branching veins.

Reading Checkpoint — Monocots have petals in multiples of three; dicots have petals in multiples of four or five.

Reading Checkpoint — Cotton plant and flax plant.

Assess

Reviewing Key Concepts

1. **a.** They produce flowers and seeds encased in fruits. **b.** No; gymnosperms do not produce flowers and their seeds are naked.

2. **a.** Reproduction **b.** Sepals—protect the developing flower; petals—attract pollinators; stamens—male reproductive part; pistil—female reproductive part

3. **a.** Stigma **b.** Pollen falls on a stigma. The sperm cell and egg cell join in the ovule and a zygote develops into the embryo part of the seed. The seed matures, a fruit develops around it, and the seed is dispersed, often with the help of animals. **c.** Possible answer: Agree; animals help pollinate flowers and disperse seeds, and thus help plants reproduce and develop into new plants.

4. **a.** Monocots and dicots **b.** Monocots: one cotyledon, leaves with parallel veins, stems show scattered bundles of vascular tissue, flower parts are three or multiples of three; dicots: two cotyledons, leaves with branching veins, stem contains a circle of vascular tissue, flower parts are four or five or multiples of four or five **c.** Monocot; its leaves have parallel veins, and six is a multiple of three.

5. Math Practice 6, 12, 15; 8, 12

6. Math Practice No; 12 is a multiple of 3 and 4.

Reteach L1
Review the life cycle of angiosperms.

All in One Teaching Resources
• Section Summary: *Angiosperms*
• Review and Reinforce: *Angiosperms*
• Enrich: *Angiosperms*

Lab zone Chapter Project

Keep Students on Track Observe the growth of plants. If some of them are dying, discuss their care with students. When the plants flower, help students pollinate them. The two best methods are to use the bee parts that come in a seed-growing kit, or tap the flower gently, collecting the pollen that falls on a sheet of paper. The pollen can then be placed in the stigma of the plant. A third method is to use a cotton swab, but this may not be as successful. Discuss with students how these methods compare to the way plants are pollinated in nature.

A Close Look at Flowers

Prepare for Inquiry

Key Concept
Flowers contain several distinct parts whose structures can be studied for a more complete understanding of their functions.

Skills Objectives
After this lab, students will be able to
- Observe the structures of flowers
- Infer the method of pollination and classify the plant as a monocot or a dicot
- Measure petal size, and the heights of pistil and stamen

 Class Time 40 minutes

All in One Teaching Resources
- Lab Worksheet: *A Close Look at Flowers*

Advance Planning
Provide a variety of flowers so that students can observe more than one type. Use large- or medium-sized flowers that have all the essential structures, such as tulips, lilies, gladiolas, daffodils, petunias, and others.

Safety
 Before starting the lab, find out which students may be allergic to pollen. Provide a substitute activity for these students, or make other arrangements. Make sure all students wash their hands immediately after this activity. Teach scalpel safety. Substitute scissors for scalpels whenever possible. Advise students to take care not to drop the glass microscope slides. Review the safety guidelines in Appendix A.

A Close Look at Flowers

Problem
What is the function of a flower, and what roles do its different parts play?

Skills Focus
observing, inferring, measuring

Materials
- paper towels
- plastic dropper
- hand lens
- microscope
- slide
- large flower
- coverslip
- scalpel
- tape
- water
- metric ruler
- lens paper

Procedure

PART 1 The Outer Parts of the Flower

1. Tape four paper towel sheets on your work area. Obtain a flower from your teacher. While handling the flower gently, observe its shape and color. Use the ruler to measure it. Notice whether the petals have any spots or other markings. Does the flower have a scent? Record your observations with sketches and descriptions.

2. Observe the sepals. How many are there? How do they relate to the rest of the flower? (*Hint:* The sepals are often green, but not always.) Record your observations.

3. Use a scalpel to carefully cut off the sepals without damaging the structures beneath them. **CAUTION:** *Scalpels are sharp. Cut in a direction away from yourself and others.*

4. Observe the petals. How many are there? Are all the petals the same, or are they different? Record your observations.

PART 2 The Male Part of the Flower

5. Carefully pull off the petals to examine the male part of the flower. Try not to damage the structures beneath the petals.

6. Observe the stamens. How many are there? How are they shaped? How tall are they? Record your observations.

7. Use a scalpel to carefully cut the stamens away from the rest of the flower without damaging the structures beneath them. Lay the stamens on the paper towel.

8. Obtain a clean slide and coverslip. Hold a stamen over the slide, and gently tap some pollen grains from the anther onto the slide. Add a drop of water to the pollen. Then place the coverslip over the water and pollen.

9. Observe the pollen under both the low-power objective and the high-power objective of a microscope. Draw and label a pollen grain.

Guide Inquiry

Invitation
Ask: **What is the function of the flower?** (*Reproduction*) Ask students to think about how each structure of the flower relates to the two stages of reproduction in angiosperms—pollination and fertilization.

Introduce the Procedure
- Introduce or review the use of a microscope and how to make a wet mount.
- To obtain pollen samples, students can simply tap the stamen of the flower if sufficiently developed. If the flower has just opened, demonstrate how to crush the stamen against the slide.

PART 3 The Female Part of the Flower

10. Use a scalpel to cut the pistil away from the rest of the flower. Measure the height of the pistil. Examine its shape. Observe the top of the pistil. Determine if that surface will stick to and lift a tiny piece of lens paper. Record your observations.

11. Lay the pistil on the paper towel. Holding it firmly at its base, use a scalpel to cut the pistil in half at its widest point, as shown in the diagram below. **CAUTION:** *Cut away from your fingers.* How many compartments do you see? How many ovules do you see? Record your observations.

Analyze and Conclude

1. **Observing** Based on your observations, describe how the sepals, petals, stamens, and pistils of a flower are arranged.

2. **Inferring** How are the sepals, petals, stamens, and pistil involved in the function of this flower?

3. **Measuring** Based on your measurements of the heights of the pistil and stamens, how do you think the flower you examined is pollinated? Use additional observations to support your answer.

4. **Classifying** Did you find any patterns in the number of sepals, petals, stamens, or other structures in your flower? If so, describe that pattern. Is your flower a monocot or a dicot?

5. **Communicating** Write a paragraph explaining all you can learn about a plant by examining one of its flowers. Use your observations in this lab to support your conclusions.

More to Explore

Some kinds of flowers do not have all the parts found in the flower in this lab. Obtain a different flower. Find out which parts that flower has, and which parts are missing. *Obtain your teacher's permission before carrying out your investigation.*

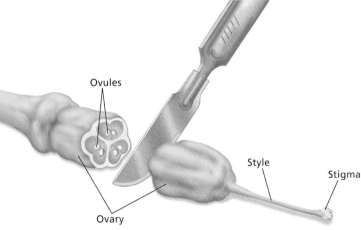

Ovules

Ovary

Style

Stigma

- If pollen begins to fall off as students handle the flowers, they can collect it on a sheet of paper and put it aside for Steps 8–9.
- Make sure students do not grip the test tubes too tightly. Remind students to tell you immediately if any glass is broken.

Expected Outcome

- The top of the pistil (the stigma) may be rough, smooth, sticky, branched, or feathery.
- The number of chambers in the ovary is equal to or is a multiple of the number of petals and stamens.

Analyze and Conclude

1. In circles, in this order: sepals on the outside, then petals, then stamens, the pistil at the center.

2. The sepals protect the flower as it develops and support the base of the flower. The petals may attract the attention of animals by color or scent. Stamens produce pollen, which releases sperm cells. Pistils hold the egg cells.

3. Answers will vary. Possible answers: Colorful petals suggest the flower is pollinated by organisms attracted to colors. A pistil that is taller than the stamens may suggest that the flower does not self-pollinate. A flower structure in which the anthers and stigma are located deep within the flower suggests pollination by small pollinators such as insects or hummingbirds.

4. Flower parts of monocots are usually in threes or multiples of threes. Flower parts of dicots are usually in fives or fours, or multiples of those numbers.

5. Answers will depend on students' observations. Paragraphs should indicate that examination of the flower parts can determine how the structures are arranged in a flower, how the flower parts function relative to one another, the most likely way the flower is pollinated, and whether the flower is a monocot or a dicot.

Extend Inquiry

More to Explore Make certain students' second flower is different from the first flower they examined. Upon comparing flowers, students will discover that flowers vary greatly in structure. For example, some plants have separate male and female flowers, whereas some have male and female parts in different relative positions.

Objectives

After this lesson, students will be able to

A.5.4.1 Identify three stimuli that produce plant responses.

A.5.4.2 Describe how plants respond to seasonal changes.

A.5.4.3 State how long different angiosperms live.

Target Reading Skill ⊙

Relating Cause and Effect Explain that cause is the reason for what happens. The effect is what happens because of the cause. Relating cause and effect helps students relate the reason for what happens to what happens as a result.

Answers

Effects: Tropisms; Germination; Forming flowers, stems, leaves; Shedding leaves; Development and ripening of fruit

All in One Teaching Resources

• Transparency A48

Preteach

Build Background Knowledge   **L2**

Descriptions of Plant Growth

Ask students to describe the usual direction of root and stem growth for plants on Earth. *(Roots grow downward; stems grow upward.)* Tell students that researchers are studying how plants grow in low gravity conditions. This knowledge could help them develop food crops for future space expeditions. Challenge students to speculate how low gravity conditions might affect plant growth. *(Possible answer: Plants might not grow in the same orientation as they do on Earth.)*

160 ● A

---

4 Plant Responses and Growth

Reading Preview

Key Concepts
• What are three stimuli that produce plant responses?
• How do plants respond to seasonal changes?
• How long do different angiosperms live?

Key Terms
• tropism • hormone
• auxin • photoperiodism
• short-day plant
• long-day plant
• critical night length
• day-neutral plant • dormancy
• annual • biennial • perennial

⊙ Target Reading Skill
Relating Cause and Effect
A cause makes something happen. An effect is what happens. As you read through the paragraphs under the heading Hormones and Tropisms, identify four effects of plant hormones. Write the information in a graphic organizer like the one below.

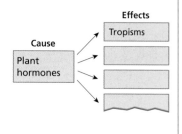

```
                        Effects
                    ┌──────────┐
                    │ Tropisms │
           Cause    └──────────┘
         ┌────────┐ ┌──────────┐
         │ Plant  │→│          │
         │hormones│ └──────────┘
         └────────┘ ┌──────────┐
                    │          │
                    └──────────┘
                    ┌──────────┐
                    │          │
                    └──────────┘
```

160 ◆ A

Can a Plant Respond to Touch?

1. 🖐 Your teacher will give you two plants. Observe the first plant. Gently touch a leaf with the tip of a pencil. Observe what happens over the next three minutes. Record your observations.

2. Repeat Step 1 with the second plant. Record your observations.

3. Wash your hands with soap and water.

Think It Over
Inferring What advantage might a plant have if its leaves responded to touch?

The bladderwort is a freshwater plant with small yellow flowers. Attached to its floating stems are open structures called bladders. When a water flea touches a sensitive hair on a bladder, the bladder flicks open. Faster than you can blink, the water flea is sucked inside, and the bladder snaps shut. The plant then digests the trapped flea.

A bladderwort responds quickly—faster than many animals respond to a similar stimulus. You may be surprised to learn that some plants have lightning-quick responses. In fact, you might have thought that plants do not respond to stimuli at all. But plants do respond to some stimuli, although they usually do so more slowly than the bladderwort.

Tropisms

Animals usually respond to stimuli by moving. Unlike animals, plants commonly respond by growing either toward or away from a stimulus. A plant's growth response toward or away from a stimulus is called a **tropism** (TROH piz um). If a plant grows toward the stimulus, it is said to show a positive tropism. If a plant grows away from a stimulus, it shows a negative tropism. **Touch, light, and gravity are three important stimuli to which plants show growth responses, or tropisms.**

Skills Focus Inferring   **L1**

Materials touch-sensitive plant such as a Venus' flytrap or mimosa; common houseplant such as a geranium or impatiens

Time 10 minutes

Tips If you have difficulty obtaining sensitive plants, contact a biological supply house or specialty gardening shop.

Remind students to wash their hands after touching the plants.

Expected Outcome The leaf of the sensitive plant closes when it is touched. The leaf of the houseplant does not respond.

Think It Over Students might infer that having sensitive leaves helps protect a plant from predators and environmental conditions.

Touch Some plants, such as bladderworts, show a response to touch called thigmotropism. The prefix *thigmo-* comes from a Greek word that means "touch." The stems of many vines, such as grapes and morning glories, show a positive thigmotropism. As the vines grow, they coil around any object that they touch.

Light Have you ever noticed plants on a windowsill with their leaves and stems facing the sun? All plants exhibit a response to light called phototropism. The leaves, stems, and flowers of plants grow toward light, showing a positive phototropism. By growing towards the light, a plant receives more energy for photosynthesis.

Gravity Plants also respond to gravity. This response is called gravitropism. Roots show positive gravitropism—they grow downward. Stems, on the other hand, show negative gravitropism—they grow upward.

Hormones and Tropisms Plants are able to respond to touch, light, and gravity because they produce hormones. A **hormone** produced by a plant is a chemical that affects how the plant grows and develops.

One important plant hormone is named **auxin** (AWK sin). Auxin speeds up the rate at which a plant's cells grow. Auxin controls a plant's response to light. When light shines on one side of a plant's stem, auxin builds up in the shaded side of the stem. The cells on the shaded side begin to grow faster. Eventually, the cells on the stem's shaded side are longer than those on its sunny side. So the stem bends toward the light.

In addition to tropisms, plant hormones also control many other plant activities. Some of these activities are germination, the formation of flowers, stems, and leaves, the shedding of leaves, and the development and ripening of fruit.

 Reading Checkpoint What is one role that the plant hormone auxin plays?

FIGURE 19
Tropisms
Touch, light, and gravity are three stimuli to which plants show growth responses, or tropisms.

▲ **Touch** A vine coiling around a wire shows positive thigmotropism.

▲ **Light** A plant's stems and flowers growing toward light show positive phototropism.

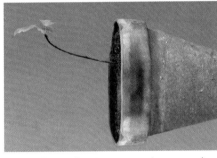

▲ **Gravity** A plant's stem growing upward, against the pull of gravity, shows negative gravitropism.

Chapter 5 A ◆ 161

Seasonal Changes

Teach Key Concepts   L2

The Factor of Darkness in Blooming

Focus Ask: **Why don't some plants bloom in winter in locations that have seasonal changes?** *(Temperatures are too low and days are too short.)*

Teach Ask: **What environmental factor triggers plants to flower?** *(The amount of darkness a plant receives)* **What is photoperiodism?** *(A plant's response to hours of light and darkness)* **When does a short-day plant flower?** *(When nights are longer than its critical night length)* **A long-day plant?** *(When nights are shorter than its critical night length)* **If a long-day plant has a critical night length of 10 hours, when will it flower?** *(When nights are shorter than 10 hours)* **What are plants that bloom no matter what the periods of darkness called?** *(Day-neutral plants)*

Apply Ask students to infer the advantage of different plants flowering at different times of the year. *(Possible answers: The plant's pollinators may pollinate only during certain times of the year. Plants have adapted to the climate—for example, a particular plant may not be able to flower during the summer.)* **learning modality: logical/ mathematical**

All in One Teaching Resources

• Transparency A49

Help Students Read

Sequencing Refer to the Content Refresher for guidelines on sequencing. After students have read the passage *Winter Dormancy,* have them sketch the steps showing the changes a tree undergoes when winter approaches. Have them label each step and write in their own words what happens.

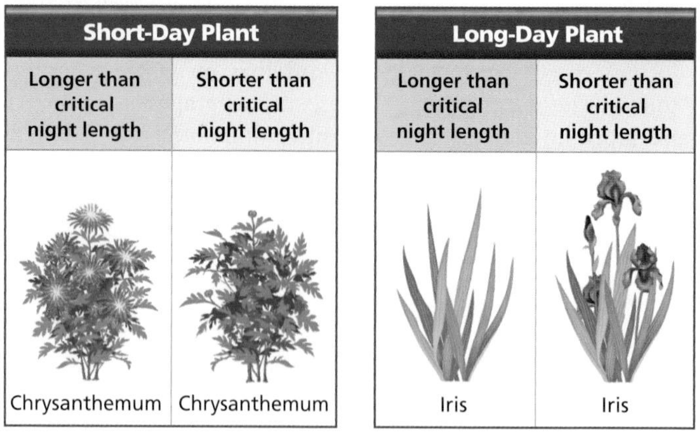

FIGURE 20
Short-day and Long-day Plants
A short-day plant flowers when nights are longer than the critical night length. A long-day plant flowers when nights are shorter than the critical night length.
Applying Concepts *Which plant—chrysanthemum or iris— would most likely flower in the early summer?*

Short-Day Plant		Long-Day Plant	
Longer than critical night length	Shorter than critical night length	Longer than critical night length	Shorter than critical night length
Chrysanthemum	Chrysanthemum	Iris	Iris

Seasonal Changes

You may have heard the saying "April showers bring May flowers," but have you ever wondered whether it's true? Do all flowers bloom in May? Is it really rain that makes flowers bloom?

People have long observed that plants respond to the changing seasons. Some plants bloom in early spring, while others don't bloom until summer. The leaves on some trees change color in autumn and then fall off by winter.

Photoperiodism What environmental factor triggers a plant to flower? **The amount of darkness a plant receives determines the time of flowering in many plants.** A plant's response to seasonal changes in length of night and day is called **photoperiodism.**

Plants differ in how they respond to the length of nights. **Short-day plants** flower when nights are *longer* than a critical length. **Long-day plants** flower when nights are *shorter* than a critical length. This critical length, called the **critical night length,** is the number of hours of darkness that determines whether or not a plant will flower. For example, if a short-day plant has a critical night length of 11 hours, it will flower only when nights are longer than 11 hours.

Short-day plants bloom in the fall or winter, when nights are growing longer. Chrysanthemums and poinsettias are short-day plants. In contrast, long-day plants flower in the spring or summer, when nights are getting shorter. Long-day plants include irises and lettuce.

Other plants, such as dandelions, rice, and tomatoes, are **day-neutral plants.** Their flowering cycle is not sensitive to periods of light and dark.

FIGURE 21
Winter Dormancy
As winter approaches, the leaves on this sugar maple turn color and then fall to the ground.

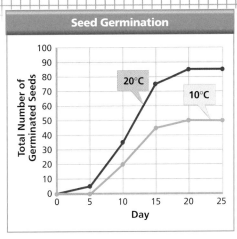

Winter Dormancy As winter draws near, many plants prepare to go into a state of dormancy. **Dormancy is a period when an organism's growth or activity stops. Dormancy helps plants survive freezing temperatures and the lack of liquid water.**

With many trees, the first change is that the leaves begin to turn color. Cooler weather and shorter days cause the leaves to stop making chlorophyll. As chlorophyll breaks down, yellow and orange pigments become visible. In addition, the plant begins to produce new red pigments. The brilliant colors of autumn leaves result.

Over the next few weeks, all of the remaining sugar and water are transported out of the tree's leaves. The leaves then fall to the ground, and the tree is ready for winter.

✓ **Reading Checkpoint**) What is dormancy?

Math ⟩ Analyzing Data

Germination and Temperature

One hundred radish seeds were planted in each of two identical trays of soil. One tray was kept at 10°C, and one tray was kept at 20°C. The trays received equal amounts of water and sunlight. The graph shows how many seeds germinated over time at each temperature.

1. **Reading Graphs** What variable is plotted on the horizontal axis? What variable is plotted on the vertical axis?

2. **Interpreting Data** How did the number of seeds that germinated change between day 20 and day 25 at 10°C? At 20°C?

3. **Drawing Conclusions** According to the graph, at which temperature did more seeds eventually germinate? What can you conclude about the relationship between temperature and germination?

Seed Germination

[Line graph: Total Number of Germinated Seeds (vertical axis, 0–100) vs. Day (horizontal axis, 0–25). Two curves labeled 20°C and 10°C.]

4. **Predicting** Predict what the graph would look like for a tray of 100 radish seeds kept at 5°C. Give a reason for your prediction.

Chapter 5   A ◆ 163

Math ⟩ Analyzing Data

Math Skill Interpreting graphs

Focus Explain that line graphs compare variables over time.

Teach Tell students to find "20 days" on the horizontal axis, then follow that line upward until it meets the line for "10°C." Read across to the vertical axis value—50 seeds.

Answers
1. Days; total number of germinated seeds
2. The numbers did not change.
3. 20°C; the number of germinating seeds increases as the temperature increases.
4. The slope would be less steep because fewer seeds would germinate.

Differentiated Instruction

Gifted and Talented   **L3**
Investigating Flower Induction Invite students to research how greenhouse managers bring flowers to bloom for specific seasons, such as poinsettas, and how they induce seasonal plants, such as chrysanthemums, to bloom all year.
learning modality: verbal

Less Proficient Readers   **L1**
Outlining Provide students with copies of an outline with the headings and subheadings of this section and blank lines under each heading. Have students fill in details under each heading as they read. Direct student pairs to generate questions from their outlines and quiz one another.
learning modality: verbal

Monitor Progress _____ **L2**

Skills Check Have students make a compare/contrast table of the types of photoperiodism in plants. Students can place their tables in their portfolios.

Portfolio

Answers
Figure 20 Iris

✓ **Reading Checkpoint**) A period when an organism's growth or activity stops

Life Spans of Angiosperms

Teach Key Concepts L2
Annuals, Biennials, and Perennials

Focus Review the meanings of the terms *annual*, *biennial*, and *perennial*.

Teach Ask: **What are the life spans of angiosperms?** *(Annuals—one growing season, biennial—two years; perennials—many years)*

Apply Ask: **Why are trees sold as seedlings rather than seeds?** *(Trees are perennials and too slow-growing to start as seeds.)* **learning modality: verbal**

Monitor Progress _____ L2
Answer

✓ **Reading Checkpoint** Two years

Assess

Reviewing Key Concepts

1. a. Thigmotropism—a plant's response to touch; phototropism—a plant's response to light; gravitropism—a plant's response to gravity **b.** It makes the cells on the shaded side grow longer than other cells. **c.** Possible answer: The plants display positive thigmotropism to cling to something for support.
2. a. A plant's response to seasonal changes in length of night and day; a period when an organism's growth or activity stops
b. Short-day plants bloom when nights are longer than a critical length. Long-day plants bloom when nights are shorter than a critical length. **c.** Leaves stop making chlorophyll. Chlorophyll breaks down. Pigments masked by chlorophyll become visible. New red pigments are produced. Remaining sugar and water leave the leaves. Leaves fall to the ground.
3. a. Annuals complete a life cycle within one growing year, biennials within two years, and perennials more than two years.
b. Perennial; it lives for many years.

Reteach L1
Sketch examples of tropisms, photoperiodism, and dormancy, and have students describe them.

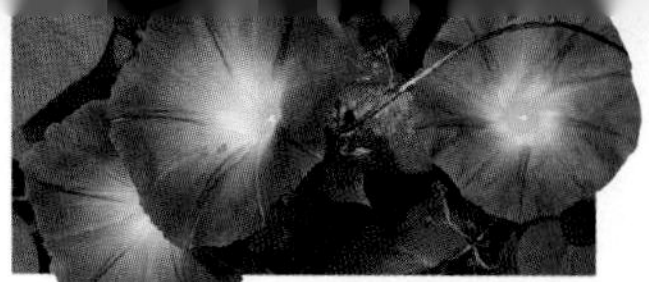

164 ● A

▲ **Annual:** Morning glory

► **Biennial:** Foxglove

FIGURE 22
Life Spans of Angiosperms
Annuals live for one year. Biennials live for two years, and perennials live for many years.

▲ **Perennial:** Peony

Life Spans of Angiosperms

Angiosperms are classified as annuals, biennials, or perennials based on the length of their life cycles. Flowering plants that complete a life cycle within one growing season are called **annuals.** Most annuals have herbaceous stems. Annuals include marigolds, petunias, wheat, and cucumbers.

Angiosperms that complete their life cycle in two years are called **biennials** (by EN ee ulz). In the first year, biennials germinate and grow roots, very short stems, and leaves. During their second year, biennials lengthen their stems, grow new leaves, and then produce flowers and seeds. Once the flowers produce seeds, the plant dies. Parsley, celery, and foxglove are biennials.

Flowering plants that live for more than two years are called **perennials.** Most perennials flower every year. Some perennials, such as peonies, have herbaceous stems. The leaves and stems of these plants die each winter, and new ones are produced each spring. Most perennials, however, have woody stems that live through the winter. Maple trees are examples of woody perennials.

 Reading Checkpoint How long does a biennial live?

Section 4 Assessment

🎯 **Target Reading Skill Relating Cause and Effect** Refer to your graphic organizer about plant hormones to help you answer Question 1 below.

Reviewing Key Concepts
1. a. Describing Describe three tropisms that take place in plants.
b. Explaining How does auxin control a plant's response to light?
c. Developing Hypotheses The stems of your morning glory plants have wrapped around your garden fence. Explain why this has occurred.
2. a. Defining What is photoperiodism? What is winter dormancy?
b. Comparing and Contrasting How do short-day plants and long-day plants differ?
c. Sequencing List in order the changes that a tree undergoes as winter approaches.

3. a. Defining How do annuals, biennials, and perennials differ?
b. Applying Concepts Is the grass that grows on most lawns an annual, a biennial, or a perennial? Explain.

Lab zone At-Home **Activity**

Sun Seekers With a family member, soak some corn seeds or lima bean seeds in water overnight. Then push them gently into some soil in a paper cup until they are just covered. Keep the soil moist. When you see the stems break through the soil, place the cup in a sunny window. After a few days, explain to your family member why the plants grew in the direction they did.

164 ◆ A

All in One Teaching Resources
- Section Summary: *Plant Responses and Growth*
- Review and Reinforce: *Plant Responses and Growth*
- Enrich: *Plant Responses and Growth*

Lab zone At Home **Activity**

Sun Seekers L2 Review the explanation with students: the plants respond with positive phototropism because they grow toward light. Ask students to identify what part of the seedling demonstrated positive gravitropism. *(Roots)*

Reading Preview

Key Concept
• What technologies may help farmers produce more crops?

Key Terms
• precision farming • hydroponics
• genetic engineering

Target Reading Skill
Identifying Main Ideas As you read the section, write the main idea in a graphic organizer like the one below. Then write three supporting details that give examples of the main idea.

Main Idea

| Technologies that may help produce more food include . . . |

| Detail | Detail | Detail |

Lab zone Discover Activity

Will There Be Enough to Eat?

1. Choose a numbered tag from the bag that your teacher provides. If you pick a tag with the number *1* on it, you're from a wealthy country. If you pick a tag with the number *2*, you're from a middle-income country. If you pick a tag with the number *3*, you're from a poor country.

2. Find classmates that have the same number on their tag. Sit down as a group.

3. Your teacher will serve your group a meal. The amount of food you receive will depend on the number on your tag.

4. As you eat, observe the people in your group and in the other groups. After you eat, record your observations. Also, record how you felt and what you were thinking during the meal.

Think It Over

Predicting Based on this activity, predict what effect an increase in the world's population would have on the world's food supply.

More than 6 billion people live on Earth today. By the year 2050, the population could grow as large as 10 billion. Think about how much food will be needed to feed the growing population. How will farmers be able to grow enough food?

Farmers and scientists are hard at work trying to find answers to this question. Farmers are using new technologies that make farming more efficient. People are developing methods for growing crops in areas with poor soil. In addition, scientists are developing plants that are more resistant to insects, diseases, and drought.

◄ A food market in Turkey

A ◆ 165

Lab zone Discover Activity

Skills Focus Predicting **L1**

Materials bags; tags; cooked rice, dry cereal, or raisins

Time 20 minutes

Tips For a class of 30, make 3 #1 tags, 5 #2 tags, and 22 #3 tags. Divide the food into three equal portions, and then divide each portion by the number of students in each group. Group 1 should have the largest portions, Group 3 the smallest.

CAUTION: *Check for food allergies among students.*

Expected Outcome Students may feel guilt, pity, envy, anger, resentment, or gratefulness.

Think It Over Food is already scarce in some countries. As world population increases, even less food will be available.

Objectives
After this lesson, students will be able to
A.5.5.1 Identify technologies that may help farmers produce more crops.

Target Reading Skill
Identifying Main Ideas Explain that identifying main ideas and details helps students sort the facts from the information into groups. Each group can have a main topic, subtopics, and details.

Answers
Possible details: Precision farming—uses satellite images and computers to determine the amount of water and fertilizer needed; Hydroponics—plants are grown in solutions of nutrients instead of in soil; Genetic engineering—genetic material is altered to produce plants with useful qualities

All in One Teaching Resources
• Transparency A50

Preteach

Build Background Knowledge **L2**
Comparing Farming Methods
Ask students to describe their idea of a typical farm from 100 years ago. (*Most will say it was small, one family worked on it, and it grew only enough food for the family.*) Then, have students describe a contemporary farm. (*Farms exist in all sizes, from the small family farm to very large agribusiness that grow food for many people.*) Ask students to speculate on what a farm will be like in 100 years. (*Accept all reasonable responses.*)

Precision Farming

Teach Key Concepts   L2
Benefits of Precision Farming

Focus Tell students that in the U.S., irrigation represents the largest demand for freshwater withdrawal.

Teach Ask: **What variables can be manipulated in precision farming?** *(Amount of water and fertilizer)* **What are the benefits?** *(More food per plant, more plants per field, increased harvests)* **How can precision farming help the environment?** *(It can minimize the amount of water and fertilizer used. Decreased fertilizer use leads to less runoff into streams, lakes, and rivers.)*

Apply Ask students to infer additional way data from satellites can be used on farms. *(Data can be collected and analyzed over time, allowing farmers to evaluate the effects of new methods or products.)* **learning modality: verbal**

Hydroponics

Teach Key Concepts   L2
Farming Without Soil

Focus Tell students that *hydro* is the Latin word for water.

Teach Ask: **What is hydroponics?** *(A farming method relying on solutions of nutrients rather than soil)* **What is the benefit?** *(It allows crops to grow in areas with poor soil.)*

Apply Ask students to identify a location that would benefit from hydroponics. *(Possible answer: salty soil near the ocean)* **learning modality: logical/ mathematical**

Independent Practice   L2

 **Teaching Resources**

- Guided Reading and Study Worksheet: *Feeding the World*

🔘 **Student Edition on Audio CD**

FIGURE 23
Precision Farming
The map on this tractor's computer screen shows the makeup of the soil in a farm's fields. The map was obtained by satellite imaging.
Relating Cause and Effect *How can precision farming benefit the environment?*

166 ◆ A

Precision Farming

On the farms of the future, satellite images and computers will be just as important as tractors and harvesters. Such technologies will allow farmers to practice **precision farming,** a farming method in which farmers fine-tune the amount of water and fertilizer they use to the requirements of a specific field.

First, satellite images of a farmer's fields are taken. Then, a computer analyzes the images to determine the makeup of the soil in the different fields. The computer uses the data to prepare a watering and fertilizing plan for each field.

Precision farming can benefit farmers by saving time and money. It also increases crop yields by helping farmers maintain ideal conditions in all fields. Precision farming would also benefit the environment because farmers use only as much fertilizer as the soil needs. When less fertilizer is used, fewer nutrients wash off the land into lakes and rivers. As you read in Chapter 3, reducing the use of fertilizers is one way to prevent algal blooms from damaging bodies of water.

Hydroponics

In some areas, people cannot grow crops because the soil is so poor. For example, on some islands in the Pacific Ocean, the soil contains large amounts of salt from the surrounding ocean. Food crops will not grow in salty soil.

On these islands, people may soon use hydroponics to grow food crops. **Hydroponics** (hy druh PAHN iks) is a farming method in which plants are grown in solutions of nutrients instead of in soil. Usually, the plants are grown in containers in which their roots are anchored in gravel or sand. The nutrient solution is pumped through the gravel or sand. **Hydroponics allows people to grow crops in areas with poor soil to help feed a growing population.** Unfortunately, hydroponics is a costly method of growing food crops.

 Reading Checkpoint   What is hydroponics?

Differentiated Instruction

English Learners/Beginning   L1
Comprehension: Prior Knowledge
Write the first sentence under *Engineering Better Plants* on the board. Write a list of food crops commonly grown in your region of the U.S. Ask students to name or draw a picture of the main food crops grown in their native country. **learning modality: visual**

English Learners/Intermediate   L2
Comprehension: Prior Knowledge
Pair students with students proficient in English. Have them make two columns and list foods and the plants they are from, for example, Bread/Wheat and Corn/Tortilla. Make sure the list includes foods from the students' native countries. **learning modality: verbal**

Engineering Better Plants

Wheat, corn, rice, and potatoes are the major sources of food today. To feed more people, the yields of these crops must be increased. This is not an easy task. One challenge facing farmers is that these crops grow only in certain climates. Another challenge is that the size and structure of these plants limit how much food they can produce.

One technique scientists are using to address these challenges is called genetic engineering. In **genetic engineering,** scientists alter an organism's genetic material to produce an organism with qualities that people find useful.

Scientists are using genetic engineering to produce plants that can grow in a wider range of climates. They are also engineering plants to be more resistant to damage from insects. For example, scientists have inserted genetic material from a bacterium into corn and tomato plants. This bacterium is harmless to humans. But its genetic material enables the plants to produce substances that kill insects. Caterpillars or other insects that bite into the leaves of these plants are killed. Today, farmers grow many kinds of genetically engineered plants.

 Reading Checkpoint What is one way that genetic engineering can help farmers produce more food?

 Go Online
SC_LINKS_ NSTA

For: Links on plants as food
Visit: www.SciLinks.org
Web Code: scn-0155

Section 5 Assessment

 **Target Reading Skill** Identifying Main Ideas Use your graphic organizer to help you answer the questions below.

Reviewing Key Concepts

1. **a. Listing** Name three technologies that farmers can use to increase crop yields.
   b. Explaining Describe one farming challenge that each technology addresses.
   c. Making Judgments Which technology do you think holds the most promise for the future? Support your answer with reasons.

Writing in Science

Interview Suppose you could interview a farmer who uses precision farming. Write a one-page interview in which you ask the farmer to explain the technology and its benefits.

Writing in Science

Writing Mode Interview

Scoring Rubric

4 Includes description and benefits of precision farming in an interview style; goes beyond requirements, for example, describes traditional farming methods

3 Includes all criteria but does not go beyond requirements

2 Includes only brief description

1 Includes incomplete or inaccurate descriptions

Lab zone Chapter Project

Keep Students on Track Help students collect seeds. Find the average number of seeds produced per plant for each group of students. If time permits, have students plant these seeds to begin the life cycle again. Emphasize that this second cycle should be similar to the one they just observed. Check student's data tables for completeness and make sure their diagrams are labeled properly.

Engineering Better Plants

 **Go Online**
SC_LINKS_ NSTA

For: Links on plants as food
Visit: www.SciLinks.org
Web Code: scn-0155

Download a worksheet that will guide students' review of Internet resources on plants as food.

Teach Key Concepts L2

Better Plants Through Genetics

Focus Tell students that in 2000, 25 percent of the corn grown in the U.S. was genetically modified.

Teach Ask: **What is genetic engineering?** *(The process of altering an organism's genetic material)*

Apply Ask: **What is the benefit of plants that produce a natural insecticide?** *(They do not have to be sprayed with synthetic pesticides.)* **learning modality: verbal**

Monitor Progress L2

Answers

Figure 23 Less fertilizer is used.

Reading Checkpoint A farming method of growing plants in nutrient-rich water and without soil

Reading Checkpoint Making organisms that are resistant to harmful insects

Assess

Reviewing Key Concepts

1. **a.** Precision farming, hydroponics, genetic engineering **b.** Increases crop yields; grows crops in areas with poor soil; makes plants resistant to insects **c.** Answers will vary. Possible answer: Hydroponics because plants can be grown in various locations without soil

Reteach L1

Summarize the benefits of the technologies that increase crop yields.

All in One Teaching Resources

- Section Summary: *Feeding the World*
- Review and Reinforce: *Feeding the World*
- Enrich: *Feeding the World*

Design and Build a Hydroponic Garden

Prepare for Inquiry

Key Concept
To design and build a hydroponic garden, students evaluate building materials and control variables for maximum plant growth.

Skills Objectives
After this lab, students will be able to
- Design an effective hydroponic garden
- Measure and record data concerning plant growth and health
- Evaluate an initial design and determine changes or adaptations

Class Time 40 minutes design and set up, 10 minutes a day for 14 days for observation; 40 minutes for design adjustments, 10 minutes a day for a second 14 day interval of observation

All in One Teaching Resources
- Lab Worksheet: *Design and Build a Hydroponic Garden*

Advance Planning
Provide a variety of plants or flowers such as lettuce, spinach, tomatoes, peppers, nasturtiums, and morning glories. Prepare a nutrient solution using nitrogen, phosphorous, and potassium. Or, use a commercially available nutrient solution. Provide students with materials useful for anchoring plants—perlite, sand, small gravel, or rock wool are useful alternatives. If photoperiod is not designated as an independent variable, leave lights on 24 hours a day for rapid growth in the system.

Design and Build a Hydroponic Garden

Problem
Can you design and build a system for growing plants without soil?

Skills Focus
designing a solution, redesigning

Materials
- potted plant
- 2 different types of seedlings
- nutrient solution
- empty 2-liter soda bottles
- paper towels
- optional materials provided by your teacher

Procedure 🔧

PART 1 Research and Investigate
1. Copy the data table onto a sheet of paper.
2. Carefully examine the potted plant your teacher gives you. Think about all the factors that are required in order for the plant to grow. List these factors in the first column of the data table.
3. Use your knowledge of plants and additional research to fill in the second column of the data table.
4. For each factor listed in the table, decide whether or not it is "essential" for plant growth. Write this information in the third column of the data table.

PART 2 Design and Build
5. To test whether soil is essential for plant growth, design a "garden" system for growing plants without soil. Your garden must
   - include at least two different types of seedlings
   - use only the amount of nutrient solution provided by your teacher
   - be built using materials that are small and lightweight, yet durable
6. Sketch your garden design on a sheet of paper and make a list of the materials you will use. Then obtain your teacher's approval and build your garden.

PART 3 Evaluate and Redesign
7. Test your garden design by growing your plants for 2 weeks. Each day, measure and record the height of your plants and the number of leaves. Also note the overall appearance of your plants.
8. Evaluate your design by comparing your garden and plants with those of your classmates. Based on your comparison, decide how you might improve your garden's design. Then make any needed changes and monitor plant growth for one more week.

Data Table		
Factor Required for Plant Growth	What This Factor Provides for the Plant	Essential or Nonessential?

Safety
🔧⚠️ Make sure all students wash their hands immediately after handling plants and any time they handle the nutrient solution. Review the safety guidelines in Appendix A.

Guide Inquiry

Introduce the Procedure
- Have sketches of several simple hydroponic systems—milk carton and rock wool, soda bottle, floating foam raft, basic wick, and rudimentary ebb and flow—available as references.
- Make sure students understand that the anchoring materials are not soil substitutes.

Analyze and Conclude

1. **Identifying a Need** In Part 1, did you list soil as a factor required for plant growth? If so, did you think it was an essential or nonessential factor? Explain your thinking.

2. **Designing a Solution** How did the information you gathered in Part 1 help you in designing your garden in Part 2? How did your garden design provide for each of the essential growth factors you listed?

3. **Redesigning** What changes did you make to your garden design and why? Did the changes lead to improved plant growth?

4. **Working With Design Constraints** How did the design constraints in Step 5 limit your design? How did you overcome those limitations?

5. **Evaluating the Impact on Society** Hydroponic gardens are planned for future space flights and as a way to grow plants in cold climates. Explain why hydroponic gardens are a good choice for each of these situations. Then, identify two more situations in which hydroponic gardens would be a good choice and explain why.

Communicate

Create a brochure highlighting the benefits of hydroponic gardening. Be sure to provide details about how a plant's needs are met and about the problems that hydroponic gardens could solve.

Extend Inquiry

Communicate Encourage students to create a brochure that is interesting to read and holds the reader's attention. Supporting details should be included, including results of the student's experiences with designing a hydroponic garden.

Troubleshooting the Experiment

- Remind students that their designs should include a way to recycle nutrient solution not absorbed as it passes through the plant roots.
- Make sure all gardens have approximately the same amount of light in a day. Use artificial plant lights and natural light if available.

Expected Outcome

- A successfully designed garden should show growth by the end of 2 weeks. Healthy gardens with 24 hours of light a day can produce a crop of spinach or soft-leaved lettuce in about 4 weeks.
- Students recognize that given an adequate supply of nutrients, plants can grow—and thrive—without soil.

Analyze and Conclude

1. Students most likely listed soil because it provided nutrients. Students may have concluded that if plants received nutrients in an alternate manner, soil could become nonessential.

2. Answers should indicate that students recognized that the factors listed in Part 1 determined some aspects of the garden setup and how their design addressed each essential factor, including light, nutrients, and water.

3. Answers will vary. Any changes made should be tied to initial garden performance.

4. Answers will vary. For example, students might explain how they made the nutrient solution last for the two week duration of the activity.

5. Answers will depend on students' observations. Answers should include that a lightweight, durable hydroponic garden could supply food on long space voyages and that because hydroponics is independent of soil, crops can be grown indoors in cold climates. Hydroponics offers a solution for areas with only salt water sources or land with poor soil.

Interactive Textbook

- Complete student edition
- Section and chapter self-assessments
- Assessment reports for teachers

Help Students Read

Building Vocabulary

Word-Part Analysis Have students use a dictionary to find the meanings of the prefixes of *annual, biennial*, and *perennial* and relate them to their definitions. *(Annual comes from the Latin word* annus, *meaning "year." Annuals live for only one season. Biennial has the prefix* bi- *meaning "two." Biennials live for two years. Perennial has the prefix* per- *meaning "throughout." Perennials live for many years.)*

Vocabulary Knowledge Rating Chart

Have students construct a chart with four columns: Term, Can Define or Use It, Have Heard or Seen It, Don't Know. Students can copy the vocabulary terms for this chapter under column 1, then place a checkmark under one of the other columns for each term. If students did not check the Can Define or Use It column, have them re-read passages with those terms.

Connecting Concepts

Concept Maps Help students develop one way to show how the information in this chapter is related. Seed plants have vascular tissue and use seeds to reproduce, and are divided into monocots and dicots. Have students brainstorm to identify the key concepts, key terms, details, and examples, then write each one on a sticky note and attach it at random on chart paper or on the board.

Tell students that this concept map will be organized in hierarchical order and to begin at the top with the key concepts. Ask students these questions to guide them to categorize the information on the stickies: **What are the characteristics of seed plants? How are angiosperms classified into monocots and dicots?**

① The Characteristics of Seed Plants

Key Concepts

- Seed plants have vascular tissue and use pollen and seeds to reproduce.
- Inside a seed is a partially developed plant. If a seed lands in an area where conditions are favorable, it can begin to develop into a plant.
- Roots anchor a plant in the ground and absorb water and minerals. Stems carry substances between roots and leaves, provide support, and hold up the leaves. Leaves capture the sun's energy for photosynthesis.

Key Terms

phloem	germination
xylem	root cap
pollen	cambium
seed	stomata
embryo	transpiration
cotyledon	

② Gymnosperms

Key Concepts

- Every gymnosperm produces naked seeds. In addition, many gymnosperms have needle-like or scalelike leaves, and deep-growing roots.
- During reproduction, pollen falls from a male cone onto a female cone. In time, sperm and egg cells join in an ovule on the female cone.
- Paper and other products, such as the lumber used to build homes, come from conifers.

Key Terms

gymnosperm	ovule
cone	pollination

170 ◆ A

③ Angiosperms

Key Concepts

- All angiosperms produce flowers and fruits.
- All flowers function in reproduction.
- During reproduction, pollen falls on a flower's stigma. In time, sperm and egg cells join in the flower's ovule. The zygote develops into the embryo part of the seed.
- Angiosperms are divided into two major groups: monocots and dicots.

Key Terms

angiosperm	pistil
flower	ovary
sepal	fruit
petal	monocot
stamen	dicot

④ Plant Responses and Growth

Key Concepts

- Touch, light, and gravity are stimuli to which plants have growth responses, or tropisms.
- The amount of darkness that a plant receives determines the time of flowering in many plants.
- Dormancy helps plants survive winter.
- Angiosperms are classified as annuals, biennials, or perennials.

Key Terms

tropism	critical night length
hormone	day-neutral plant
auxin	dormancy
photoperiodism	annual
short-day plant	biennial
long-day plant	perennial

⑤ Feeding the World

Key Concept

- Precision farming, hydroponics, and genetic engineering can help farmers produce more crops to feed the world's population.

Key Terms

precision farming	genetic engineering
hydroponics	

Prompt students by using connecting words or phrases, such as "may be" and "have," to indicate the basis for the organization of the map. The phrases should form a sentence between or among a set of concepts.

Answer
Accept logical presentations by students.

All in One Teaching Resources

- Key Terms Review: *Seed Plants*
- Connecting Concepts: *Seed plants*

Review and Assessment

Go Online
PHSchool.com
For: Self-Assessment
Visit: PHSchool.com
Web Code: cea-1050

Organizing Information

Concept Mapping Copy the concept map about seed plants onto a sheet of paper. Then complete it and add a title. (For more on Concept Mapping, see the Skills Handbook.)

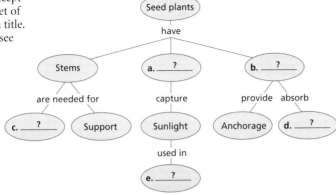

Reviewing Key Terms

Choose the letter of the best answer.

1. The process by which a seed sprouts is called
   a. pollination.
   b. fertilization.
   c. dispersal.
   d. germination.

2. In woody stems, new xylem cells are produced by the
   a. bark.
   b. cambium.
   c. phloem.
   d. pith.

3. Which of the following is the male part of a flower?
   a. pistil
   b. ovule
   c. stamen
   d. petal

4. What kind of tropism do roots display when they grow downward into the soil?
   a. positive gravitropism
   b. negative gravitropism
   c. phototropism
   d. thigmotropism

5. The process of growing crops in a nutrient solution is called
   a. genetic engineering.
   b. hydroponics.
   c. precision farming.
   d. satellite imaging.

If the statement is true, write *true*. If it is false, change the underlined word or words to make the statement true.

6. <u>Stems</u> anchor plants in the soil.

7. The needles of a pine tree are actually its <u>leaves</u>.

8. <u>Gymnosperm</u> seeds are dispersed in fruits.

9. Flowering plants that live for more than two years are called <u>annuals</u>.

10. <u>Precision farming</u> uses technology to fine-tune water and fertilizer requirements.

Writing in Science

Firsthand Account Write a story from the viewpoint of a seedling. Describe how you were dispersed as a seed and how you grew into a seedling.

Discovery CHANNEL SCHOOL

Seed Plants
Video Preview
Video Field Trip
▶ Video Assessment

Go Online
PHSchool.com
For: Self-Assessment
Visit: PHSchool.com
Web Code: cfa-1050

Students can take a practice test online that is automatically scored.

All in One Teaching Resources
- Transparency A51
- Chapter Test
- Performance Assessment Teacher Notes
- Performance Assessment Student Worksheet
- Performance Assessment Scoring Rubric

ExamView® Computer Test Bank CD-ROM

Review and Assessment

Organizing Information
a. Leaves
b. Roots
c. Transport
d. Water and minerals
e. Photosynthesis

Reviewing Key Terms
1. d 2. b 3. c 4. a 5. b
6. false; Roots
7. true
8. false; Angiosperm
9. false; perennials
10. true

Writing in Science

Writing Mode Description
Scoring Rubric
4 Includes complete description of dispersal, the conditions under which it germinates, and the parts of a seed; goes beyond requirements, for example, includes the functions of its stems, leaves, and roots
3 Includes all criteria but does not go beyond requirements
2 Includes only brief description
1 Includes incomplete and inaccurate description

Discovery CHANNEL SCHOOL
Video Assessment

Seed Plants

Show the Video Assessment to review chapter content and as a prompt for the writing assignment. Discussion questions: **What are the three basic parts of a seed?** (*Embryo, stored food, seed coat*) **What conditions are necessary for seeds to germinate?** (*Favorable temperature, water, and oxygen conditions*)

Checking Concepts

11. Seeds can be dispersed by wind, water, or animals. Some plants shoot out their seeds.

12. Stomata open and allow carbon dioxide to enter the leaf and also allow the oxygen and water vapor produced during photosynthesis to escape into the air. Stomata close and retain water in leaf cells during warm temperatures.

13. Female cones are covered by scales that contain at least one ovule each.

14. Pollination is the process by which pollen, containing male reproductive cells, is transferred to the female reproductive structures. Fertilization is the joining of a sperm cell and an egg cell.

15. Fruits attract and are eaten by animals that help to disperse the seeds, increasing the areas that the angiosperms inhabit.

16. The plant hormone auxin is involved in phototropism. Auxin speeds up the rate at which plant cells grow. It builds up on the shadier side of a plant, causing those cells to grow faster than the cells on the sunny side of the plant. With longer cells on one side than the other, the stem bends toward the light.

17. Food can be grown in more places on Earth, including places that have poor soil.

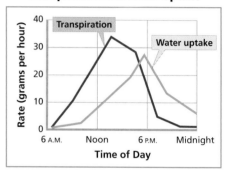

Review and Assessment

Checking Concepts

11. Describe four different ways that seeds can be dispersed.

12. Explain the role that stomata play in leaves.

13. Describe the structure of a female cone.

14. What is the difference between pollination and fertilization?

15. What role does a fruit play in an angiosperm's life cycle?

16. What role do plant hormones play in phototropism?

17. How can the use of hydroponics help increase the amount of food that can be grown on Earth?

Thinking Critically

18. Inferring Sometimes undersea volcanoes erupt, and new islands form far away from other land masses. Years later, seed plants may be found growing on those islands. How can the presence of those plants be explained?

19. Relating Cause and Effect When a strip of bark is removed all the way around the trunk of a tree, the tree dies. Explain why.

20. Predicting Pesticides are designed to kill harmful insects. Sometimes, however, pesticides kill helpful insects as well. What effect could this have on angiosperms?

21. Comparing and Contrasting Which of the plants below is a monocot? Which is a dicot? Explain your conclusions.

22. Applying Concepts Explain why people who grow houseplants on windowsills should turn the plants every week or so.

Math Practice

23. Multiples Use what you know about multiples to determine which flower is a monocot and which is a dicot: a flower with nine petals; a flower with ten petals. Explain.

Applying Skills

Use the data in the graph below to answer Questions 24–26.

A scientist measured transpiration in an ash tree over an 18-hour period. She also measured how much water the tree's roots took up in the same period.

Transpiration and Water Uptake

[Graph: Rate (grams per hour) on y-axis from 0 to 40; Time of Day on x-axis from 6 A.M. to Midnight. Two curves labeled "Transpiration" and "Water uptake."]

24. Interpreting Data At what time is the rate of transpiration highest? At what time is the rate of water uptake highest?

25. Inferring Why do you think the transpiration rate increases and decreases as it does during the 18-hour period?

26. Drawing Conclusions Based on the graph, what is one conclusion you can reach about the pattern of water loss and gain in the ash tree?

Lab zone Chapter **Project**

Performance Assessment Design a poster that shows the results of your investigation. You may wish to use a cycle diagram to show the main events in the plant's life. What new information did you learn about seed plants by doing this project?

Lab zone Chapter **Project**

Project Wrap-Up Encourage students to use the cycle diagram to describe their observations during the life span of the plant in this project. Remind students to include what will happen after the new seeds are germinated. Find a space for students to display their exhibits.

Reflect and Record Discuss the project with students. Make sure they understand the cyclic nature of plant life. Students may suggest using their plants to investigate tropisms or hydroponics. If time permits, allow students to try their new experiments after you approve their plans.

Standardized Test Prep

Choose the letter of the best answer.

1. The diagram below shows the parts of a flower. In which flower part does pollen formation take place?

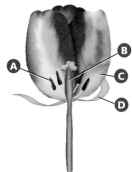

A part A
C part C
B part B
D part D

2. Which of the following is the correct path that water takes once it enters a plant?
   F leaves, stems, roots
   G roots, leaves, stems
   H stems, roots, leaves
   J roots, stems, leaves

3. A scientist examining the annual rings of a tree observes a section with wide rings. What inference can be made from this observation?
   A There was a drought during the years the wide rings were produced.
   B Rainfall was plentiful during the years the wide rings were produced.
   C Forest fires produced the wide rings.
   D There were severe springtime frosts during the years the wide rings were produced.

4. Which would a student expect to find when examining a dicot?
   F one cotyledon
   G flower parts in multiples of threes
   H stems with bundles of vascular tissue arranged in a ring
   J leaves with parallel veins

5. Which of the following statements is a valid comparison of gymnosperms and angiosperms?
   A Both gymnosperms and angiosperms produce flowers.
   B Gymnosperms produce flowers, while angiosperms produce cones.
   C Most gymnosperms have broad leaves, while angiosperms do not.
   D Angiosperm seeds are enclosed within fruits, while gymnosperm seeds are not.

Constructed Response

6. Explain how positive phototropism can help a plant survive. Use the following terms in your answer: food, leaves, photosynthesis, energy, and sunlight.

Thinking Critically

18. Pollen and seeds are carried by the wind or by birds flying to an island.

19. The inner part of bark is phloem. If the bark is stripped around the entire base of a tree, all the phloem is removed in that space. Food made in the leaves can no longer reach the lower parts of the tree. These cells die, followed by the entire tree.

20. If helpful insects are killed by a pesticide, the plants that depend on these insects for pollination may not be pollinated.

21. Plant B is a monocot because it has parallel veins, and it has three petals—the petals of monocots are present in groups of three. Plant A is a dicot because it has branching veins and ten petals—the petals of dicots are present in groups of four or five.

22. If plants near the window are not turned often, they will not grow evenly, and all their leaves will grow toward the window.

Math Practice

23. A flower with nine petals is a monocot because 9 can be divided by 3 to produce a whole number ($9 \div 3 = 3$). A flower with 10 petals is a dicot because 10 can be divided by 5 to produce a whole number ($10 \div 5 = 2$).

Applying Skills

24. Transpiration is at its highest at about 1:00 P.M. Water uptake is at its highest at about 6:00 P.M.

25. The transpiration rate increases throughout the morning until early afternoon, then starts to decrease because most evaporation occurs during the hot middle part of the day. Not much water evaporates in the cool evening.

26. The maximum amount of transpiration occurs about 5 hours before the peak in water uptake.

Standardized Test Prep

1. A **2.** J **3.** B **4.** H **5.** D

6. Leaves carry out photosynthesis by trapping energy from sunlight to make food. Positive phototropism helps a plant survive by causing the leaves to grow toward sunlight, therefore capturing as much energy as possible.

Corn—The Amazing Grain

This interdisciplinary feature presents the central theme of corn by connecting four different disciplines: social studies, science, mathematics, and language arts. The four explorations are designed to capture students' interest and help them see how the content they are studying in science relates to other school subjects and real-world events. Share with others for a team-teaching experience.

All in One Teaching Resources

- Interdisciplinary Exploration: *Social Studies*
- Interdisciplinary Exploration: *Science*
- Interdisciplinary Exploration: *Mathematics*
- Interdisciplinary Exploration: *Language Arts*

Build Background Knowledge
Corn Is a Seed Plant

Help students recall what they know about seed plants. Ask: **What are some examples of seed plants?** *(Corn, tomatoes, peppers, oak trees, maple trees)*

Introduce the Exploration

Have students brainstorm a list of foods made from corn. *(Corn on the cob, cornbread, popcorn, cereal, tortillas, corn chips, flour)* Ask: **What other products are derived from corn?** *(Cornstarch is used as a smoothing and thickening agent in many products. Corn syrup is used as a sweetener. Corn oil is used in cooking and to make salad dressings. The sugar from corn is used to make alcohol, which is combined with gasoline to produce an alternative fuel—ethanol.)* Ask students whether they know where corn originated. Write students' ideas on the board, and tell them that they will learn about the origin of corn in the Interdisciplinary Exploration.

Corn—The Amazing Grain

What common grain is—

- dried, then popped and eaten at the movies?
- ground into meal?
- eaten in flakes for breakfast?

People have been eating corn in hundreds of different ways for thousands of years—since corn was first grown for food by ancient cultures in Mexico.

Because corn is useful, people have valued it throughout history. It tastes good, is nourishing, and stores well. Over time, knowledge of corn has spread among people and cultures. Christopher Columbus introduced corn to Europe. Columbus called it *mahiz*, meaning "a kind of grain."

Today in many countries of the world, corn is a basic part of people's diet, whether in the form of kernels, meal, oil, syrup, or flour. The United States grows billions of bushels a year. But people eat only a tiny portion of this yield as corn. About 80 percent of the United States corn crop is fed to livestock to supply eggs, milk, and meat. Hundreds of other products—from chewing gum to fireworks—are also made from parts of the plant.

Machu Picchu
The ruins of Machu Picchu, an Incan city, are in the Andes Mountains of Peru.

Village Market
A Peruvian farmer sells different types of corn.

174 ◆ A

Maize Through the Ages

Some people say, "Wherever corn went, civilization followed." Corn—or maize—was probably cultivated from a wild grass in Mexico around 8000 B.C. Early farmers planted seeds and harvested crops in planned spaces. They passed on their knowledge of corn to their children and to other farmers. Having plenty of corn is believed to be one reason the ancient agricultural empires of the Mayas and Incas developed and flourished.

In Central America, the Mayan civilization was at its height between A.D. 300 and A.D. 800. In Mayan cities, the people built pyramid-shaped temples where they worshipped gods of the sun, rain, and corn. Maize was grown in fields around the cities. The timing of the stages for growing corn affected all Mayan activities. The life cycle of maize and its plant parts—leaves, silk, tassels, and kernels—became the basis for words in the Mayan language.

In South America, the Incan empire thrived between the 1400s and 1535. A powerful ruler of the Incas came to power in Peru in 1438. In less than a century, the Incas expanded their territory from a small area around Cuzco, Peru, to a vast empire. The Inca empire stretched through the Andes Mountains, from Chile to Ecuador. It was the last of Peru's thriving ancient civilizations. The Incan empire was destroyed by Spaniards who arrived in the 1530s in search of gold. In Cuzco, they found an eye-dazzling garden where corn stalks, leaves, husks, and cobs were crafted in silver and gold. To the Incas, corn was more precious than the metal the Spaniards sought.

Though the empires of the Mayas and Incas collapsed, corn-growing spread to other regions. Eventually, the plant was brought north to the Mississippi and Ohio river valleys and east to the Caribbean islands.

Early Civilizations of Central and South America

Atlantic Ocean

Yucatán Peninsula

Tikal

Central America

Caribbean Sea

Amazon River

South America

Cuzco

Andes Mountains

Pacific Ocean

KEY

Mayan Empire
A.D. 300 – A.D. 900

Incan Empire
A.D. 1400s – A.D. 1535

| 0 | 1000 km |
| 0 | 600 mi |

Civilizations of the Americas
The Mayan civilization in Central America and the Incan civilization in South America flourished before Europeans arrived.

Social Studies Activity

Use a map of Central and South America today.

- Trace the approximate boundaries of the Mayan and Incan empires.
- Name the countries that are now located in these areas.
- Identify the geographical features within the empires.
- Find out about the climate. Why were these lands well suited to growing corn?

A ◆ 175

Explore Social Studies Concepts

Teacher Demo Some students may never have seen corn plants or even an ear of corn still in the husk. Display photographs of the different varieties of corn plants. Bring to class a whole corn plant or some unhusked corn on the cob.

Discuss Have students think about what the statement "Wherever corn went, civilization followed" means. Ask: **Why would it be important for a civilization to know that a grain such as corn will grow successfully in a new location?** (*Grains, such as corn, were the staple of the diet for many ancient civilizations. Before moving to a new location, it would be an advantage to know that a grain would grow successfully. This means that a population of people could be supported by food resources in the new location.*)

Research Have students find out more about the Incas and the Mayas. What were their cultures like? How were they similar? How were they different?

Connect Culture Explain that *maize* and *corn* are different names for the same plant. In the United States, we call the plant *corn*. In many other countries, the plant is called *maize*. Throughout history, different cultures used various names for this plant. Have students research the etiology of *corn*.

Social Studies Activity

Focus Group students into fours. Students will likely need to use different sources to find the countries and geographic features.

Teach Use this activity to help students recognize the link between geography and farming. Corn cannot be grown in all climates because it needs particular weather conditions.

Expected Outcome Students should find that the Mayan empire included all or parts of Ecuador, Peru, Chile, Bolivia, and Argentina and that the Incan empire included all or parts of Mexico, Guatemala, and Belize. Geographical features of the Mayan empire include the Pacific coast, the Andes mountains, and Lake Titicaca. Features of the Incan empire include highlands along the Pacific coast and lowlands along the Caribbean coast. The climate of these areas includes wet and warm summers, which are necessary conditions for growing corn.

Background

History Europeans probably first tasted corn in 1492, when Roderigo de Jerez and Luiz Torres were given corn by the Arawaks who lived in what is now Cuba. Jerez and Torres were members of Christopher Columbus's crew. On their return to Europe, Columbus described the "mahiz" as a kind of grain, "well tasted."

After landing in November of 1620, the Pilgrims who survived the first hard winter in America learned to plant life-saving kernels from a Native American named Squanto. By the 1700s, many people in colonial America were growing corn, including George Washington and Thomas Jefferson. Increasingly, corn became a staple food for the expanding United States population.

Explore Science Concepts

Organize Information After students read "A Kernel Goes a Long Way," help them create a sequence graphic organizer that shows the steps in processing field corn. Ask questions such as: **What happens to field corn after it is picked?** *(It is trucked to refineries.)* **What process takes place at the refinery?** *(The corn is cleaned and soaked.)*

Discuss Point out the process that is used to separate the embryo from the kernel. Tell students that the process in which the material is spun horizontally is called centrifuging. When a sample is centrifuged, its components separate out according to their densities, with the heavier component migrating farthest from center.

Use Visuals Display an ear of corn with the husk and dried silk fibers still attached. Point out the husk, fibers, and kernels on the ear. You might have students do a simple dissection of the corn kernels. They can use the diagram on this page to identify the seed coat, the stored food, and the embryo.

Science Activity

Focus Have students work in pairs. For students not testing popcorn, suggest that they compare the nutritional information between different brands of the same product. For example, they might test the assumption that the most expensive product has the most nutritional value.

Teach Check students' written procedures for safety and practicality before allowing them to perform any experiments. Be sure students understand that even if the results do not support their initial assumption, their experiment was still a success.

Scoring Rubric

4 Includes clearly identified criteria, a stated prediction, a well thought-out experiment, detailed observations, and logical conclusions.
3 Includes all criteria but observations are not detailed.
2 Includes all criteria but conclusion is not supported by experiment results.
1 Some criteria are missing.

A Kernel Goes a Long Way

Did you know that corn and corn products are used as fuel? Or, did you know that corn is found in some brands of baby food, crayons, soap, and tires? It's even found in ketchup, hot dogs, and toothpaste.

Today, only a small portion of the corn that is planted is sweet corn. Sweet corn is sold fresh or used to produce canned or frozen corn. But millions of bushels of field corn, which is less sweet, are trucked to refineries. There, the kernels are turned into oil, starch, sugar, or fuel.

When ears of field corn arrive at a refinery, the corn is cleaned and soaked. Next, corn kernels are milled—crushed and ground. The milled substance is spun in giant tanks to separate out the embryos. Oil is extracted from the embryo of the kernel. The seed coat may be removed by sifting and can be dried to produce corn bran.

The remaining substance—the stored food—is ground into corn meal. One part of the ground meal is rich in proteins and is used for animal feed. The other part of the corn meal is the starch.

From cornstarch, corn sugars and syrups are processed. You eat these in breads, breakfast cereals, colas, ice cream, and salad dressings, to name only a few products. Cornstarch is also processed into glues and powders for the paper and textile industries, and into ethanol, a fuel.

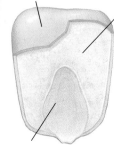

Corn Ear
Corn plants grow from kernels on corn ears like this one.

Seed Coat
The seed coat protects the kernel. Bran is made from the seed coat.

Stored Food
The stored food is the inner starchy part that feeds the embryo. Many things are made from the starchy part of the corn kernel, including
• cornstarch
• corn sugar
• corn syrups
• ice cream
• animal feed
• glue
• fuel

Embryo
The embryo is the part of the seed that will develop into a new corn plant. Corn oil is made from the embryo.

Science Activity

When you're at the supermarket, how do you decide which brand of a particular product to buy? What criteria do you use? Working with a partner, choose a corn product, such as tortillas, corn flakes, or popcorn, to investigate.

• Collect several brands of the product to test.

• Decide what you will test for. For example, you might want to test which brand of popcorn produces more popped kernels.

• Before you begin, predict what your results will be.

• Design your own experiment. Write out the step-by-step procedure you will follow. Make sure that you keep all variables the same as you test each product.

• Make observations and collect data.

• Interpret the data and draw your conclusion. How did your results compare with your prediction?

176 ◆ A

Background

Facts and Figures Most ears of corn have between 750 and 1,000 kernels arranged in 16 rows. Farmers have been breeding new varieties of corn since ancient times. A new variety might be developed to thrive in a harsh climate or in poor soils. Most new varieties are intended to yield more kernels per ear and more ears per acre, meaning more corn produced in a growing season.

Not all corn grows to the same height. Some dwarf varieties are only 60 cm high when they mature. Other types may reach heights of 6 meters or more. The average height is about 2.5 meters. According to the *Guinness Book of Records,* the tallest corn plant in the United States was grown in Iowa in 1946. It was 9.3 meters in height.

Mind-Boggling Corn Data

Every continent in the world except Antarctica produces some corn each year. The largest corn-producing country is the United States, growing 42 percent of the world's corn. The graph shows the leading corn-producing countries. China is next largest, growing 19 percent. The other countries in the world grow smaller amounts.

In the United States, corn is grown in nearly every state, producing about 9 billion bushels of corn a year. A bushel of corn contains about 72,800 kernels. Most of that corn is grown in a group of midwestern states known as the "Corn Belt." Iowa, Illinois, Nebraska, and Minnesota are the four major corn-growing states. Indiana, Missouri, Kansas, Ohio, South Dakota, Wisconsin, Michigan, and Kentucky are the other Corn Belt states.

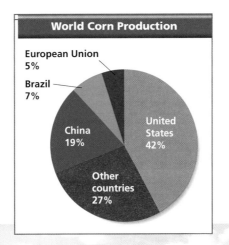

World Corn Production

- European Union 5%
- Brazil 7%
- China 19%
- United States 42%
- Other countries 27%

Math Activity

Make a circle graph to show corn production in the United States. To create your graph, follow the steps in the Skills Handbook.

- Use the data in the table below to set up proportions to find the number of degrees in each slice. Then figure percents for Major Corn Belt States, Other Corn Belt States, and States Outside the Corn Belt. Round to the nearest tenth.
- Use a compass to draw a circle.
- Determine the size of each of the three slices.
- Measure out and mark off each slice in the circle.

What percent should you get when you add up these numbers?

United States Corn Production	
	Billions of Bushels
Major Corn Belt States (Iowa, Illinois, Nebraska, Minnesota)	5.45
Other Corn Belt States (Indiana, Missouri, Kansas, Ohio, South Dakota, Wisconsin, Michigan, and Kentucky)	2.49
States Outside the Corn Belt	1.06
Total for the United States	9.00

A ◆ 177

Mathematics

Explore Mathematics Concepts

Discuss Direct attention to the circle graph. Tell students that a circle graph is a good way to show parts (percentages) of a whole. Ask: **What does the graph show?** (*The percentage of world corn production by various areas of the world*)

Research Encourage students to find out what weather conditions are needed to grow corn. Have them find out why the corn belt is ideal for growing corn.

Math Activity

Focus Point out the table. Tell students that the circle graph that they make should have three slices, not four. Ask: **What is the fourth line in the table?** (*The total*)

Teach Help students determine the size of one of the slices of their circle graph. Explain that, for each slice of the graph, they will need to set up a proportion where x equals the number of degrees in a slice. As an example, write the following on the board:

$$\frac{\text{production of major corn belt states}}{\text{total corn production}} = \frac{x}{\text{degrees in a circle}}$$

Then help students solve for x by substituting in the known values and rearranging the equation.

$$\frac{5{,}450{,}000{,}000}{9{,}000{,}000{,}000} = \frac{x}{360}$$

$$9{,}000{,}000{,}000x = 5{,}450{,}000{,}000 \times 360$$

$$x = 5{,}450{,}000{,}000 \times \frac{360}{9{,}000{,}000{,}000}$$

$$x = 218 \text{ degrees}$$

Therefore, the slice for the Major Corn Belt States should contain 218 degrees. The number of degrees for the other slices are as follows: Other Corn Belt States, 99.6 degrees; States Outside the Corn Belt, 42.4 degrees.

Expected Outcome Major Corn Belt States, 60.55%; Other Corn Belt States, 27.66%; States Outside the Corn Belt, 11.77%. Total is 100% when rounded. Make sure the size of each segment is the right size for the percentage.

Explore Language Arts Concepts

Discuss A folk tale may often teach a lesson as part of the story. Ask: **What moral lesson do you think this folk tale is trying to teach?** *(Possible answer: If a gift is not appreciated, it may be taken away.)* **What events in the story lead you to this conclusion?** *(The hunter's brother did not like the bread and threw it on the ground. This was taken as a sign of not appreciating the gift of the Great Spirit. As punishment, the corn is ruined and the people are hungry.)* **What does the word *dishonored* mean in the second paragraph?** *(Treated in a degrading way)* **What does the word *game* mean in the fourth paragraph?** *(Wild animals that people hunt for sport or food)* Point out that in the story, only the brother appears to be unappreciative of the corn gift, yet the entire group is punished for his behavior. Ask: **Do you think it is fair to punish a group of people for the behavior of one person? What is the purpose of this?** *(Students should debate whether they think this is fair or not. The purpose may be to use peer pressure to motivate people to exhibit proper behavior and follow rules. If the entire group is punished for one person's behavior, that person will likely not be well liked by others.)*

Use Visuals Direct students' attention to the corn husk mask. Some students may not know that the husk is the outer leaves of the corn cob. Point out that there are several crafts that use corn husks, such as the making of corn husk dolls.

From the Garden in the Sky

The word for corn in some Native American languages means "that which gives us life." No one knows how humans discovered corn. But many cultures have myths and stories to explain how the plant came to be. To the Pawnee on the Nebraska plains, corn was Evening Star, the mother of all things. The Navajo in the southwestern United States tell a story of a turkey hen that flew in a straight line. As it traveled, it shook an ear of corn from its feathers. The following folk tale comes from the Iroquois in Canada.

The Corn Goddess

The Great Spirit gave seeds of corn to a mysterious maiden who became the wife of a great hunter. The wife taught the hunter's people how to plant and harvest the corn, and how to grind it and bake it into bread. The people were pleased.

But the great hunter's brother disliked the bread and threw it to the ground. The wife was alarmed that he had dishonored the gift of the Great Spirit. That night she told her husband that she must leave his people.

Shortly before dawn, the people heard the sound of falling rain. But it was not rain. It was the sound of thousands of kernels dropping from the ears of corn. Soon all the stalks were empty.

The men hunted but found little game. Before long the children cried because they were so hungry. The great hunter was sad. He decided to leave and find his wife. She had told him, "If ever you want to find me, walk east. When you reach a lake, rest and listen for the cry of a child. Then you should plant an arrow in the ground, point it in the direction of the sound, and sleep. When you wake, the arrow will show you the way."

The great hunter went east to the big lake and lit a fire. Late that night he heard crying. He planted his arrow and lay down to sleep. At dawn, he walked as the arrow pointed. He walked all day, then stopped to rest at night. He lit another fire. Again he heard crying, placed his arrow, and slept. On the third night, his wife appeared.

He said his people were starving and he asked for her help. When winter passed, the great hunter returned to his people with corn from his wife. That year, the harvest was abundant. He rejoiced, but he missed his wife and left to find her again. He traveled to the lake and listened for crying, but he did not hear it. He traveled another day, and another, thinking he knew the direction to go. He searched day after day, listening for the cry. Perhaps he is still looking for her.

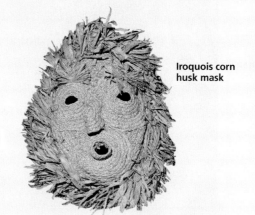

Iroquois corn husk mask

————Adapted from *The Corn Goddess and Other Tales from Indian Canada*, National Museum, Canada

178 ◆ A

Background

Facts and Figures Although corn is native to the Americas, the origin of corn is still unknown. Corn was used as a staple grain in the diets of civilizations that inhabited the Americas long before the Europeans arrived. Evidence from archaeological studies dated corn pollen found buried beneath Mexico City to be 80,000 years old. A corn cob found in a bat cave in New Mexico was dated at 5,600 years old. Wild corn existed in southern Mexico as many as 4,600 years ago. Scientific evidence also shows that cultivated corn has been growing in the southwestern United States for about 3,000 years.

A folk tale is a story that is passed down from person to person. It may explain something in nature, as this story does, or teach a lesson. Find words and phrases that show that this tale was created a long time ago.

Write your own story about how corn came to be found in nature. Use a modern-day setting and characters in your story.

Tie It Together

Plan a Corn Ball

Organize a corn carnival for your school. To advertise the carnival, create a huge popcorn ball with popped corn and glue made from a cornstarch and water mixture. (The largest popcorn ball on record weighed over a ton.)

Here are some suggestions for activities.

- Display a variety of products made from corn.
- Bring in food made from corn.
- Set up a booth to explain how popcorn pops.
- Have a contest for visitors to guess the number of popcorn kernels.
- Set up a booth for telling corny jokes.
- Collect corn facts, pictures, and photographs that show corn in art or in history.
- Collect information on agriculture in the Mayan or Incan cultures.

Corn on the Cob
It's a favorite American food.

A ◆ 179

Language Arts Activity

Focus Remind students that their folk tales should somehow explain where corn came from.

Teach Encourage students to be creative. For example, in their folk tale, corn could be a gift from a god, could be brought by an animal, or any number of other explanations. Remind students that if their tale includes dialog, students should use quotations marks and begin a new paragraph every time the person speaking changes.

Expected Outcome The words and phrases that students choose from the story may vary. Reference to the Great Spirit indicates a long time ago, as does the fact that the husband walks when he searches for his wife. Students' stories should provide a creative explanation about the origin of corn. The story should be well constructed, show good use of adjectives, and be grammatically correct.

Tie It Together

Plan a Corn Ball

Time 1 week (2 days for research, 2 days for preparing booths, 1 day for the carnival)

Tips Have students work in groups of three or four. Assign groups a booth or have them draw slips of paper to determine their booth. If necessary, help groups divide up the tasks and make a plan for compiling materials and preparing for the carnival.
- Most information that students must research should be available from encyclopedias or gardening books.
- Students may want to use the Internet to search for information.

Extend If the carnival is a success, students may wish to keep their materials and ideas to hold the carnival again as a fund-raiser for the school.

Think Like a Scientist

The Skills Handbook is designed as a reference for students to use whenever they need to review inquiry, reading, or math skills. You can use the activities in this part of the Skills Handbook to teach or reinforce inquiry skills.

Observing

Focus Remind students that an observation is what they can see, hear, smell, taste, or feel.

Teach Invite students to make observations of the classroom. List these observations on the board. Challenge students to identify the senses they used to make each observation. Then, ask: **Which senses will you use to make observations from the photograph on this page?** (*Sight is the only sense that can be used to make observations from the photograph.*)

Activity

Some observations that students might make include that the boy is skateboarding, wearing a white helmet, and flying in the air. Make sure that students' observations are confined to only things that they can actually see in the photograph.

Inferring

Focus Choose one or two of the classroom observations listed on the board, and challenge students to interpret them. Guide students by asking why something appears as it does.

Teach Encourage students to describe their thought processes in making their inferences. Point out where they used their knowledge and experience to interpret the observations. Then invite students to suggest other possible interpretations for the observations. Ask: **How can you find out whether an inference is correct?** (*By further investigation*)

Activity

One possible inference is that the boy just skated off a ramp at a skate park. Invite students to share their experiences that helped them make the inference.

Predicting

Focus Discuss the weather forecast for the next day. Point out that this prediction is an inference about what will happen in the

---

Think Like a Scientist

Scientists have a particular way of looking at the world, or scientific habits of mind. Whenever you ask a question and explore possible answers, you use many of the same skills that scientists do. Some of these skills are described on this page.

Observing

When you use one or more of your five senses to gather information about the world, you are **observing.** Hearing a dog bark, counting twelve green seeds, and smelling smoke are all observations. To increase the power of their senses, scientists sometimes use microscopes, telescopes, or other instruments that help them make more detailed observations.

An observation must be an accurate report of what your senses detect. It is important to keep careful records of your observations in science class by writing or drawing in a notebook. The information collected through observations is called evidence, or data.

Inferring

When you interpret an observation, you are **inferring,** or making an inference. For example, if you hear your dog barking, you may infer that someone is at your front door. To make this inference, you combine the evidence—the barking dog—and your experience or knowledge—you know that your dog barks when strangers approach—to reach a logical conclusion.

Notice that an inference is not a fact; it is only one of many possible interpretations for an observation. For example, your dog may be barking because it wants to go for a walk. An inference may turn out to be incorrect even if it is based on accurate observations and logical reasoning. The only way to find out if an inference is correct is to investigate further.

Predicting

When you listen to the weather forecast, you hear many predictions about the next day's weather—what the temperature will be, whether it will rain, and how windy it will be. Weather forecasters use observations and knowledge of weather patterns to predict the weather. The skill of **predicting** involves making an inference about a future event based on current evidence or past experience.

Because a prediction is an inference, it may prove to be false. In science class, you can test some of your predictions by doing experiments. For example, suppose you predict that larger paper airplanes can fly farther than smaller airplanes. How could you test your prediction?

Activity

Use the photograph to answer the questions below.

Observing Look closely at the photograph. List at least three observations.

Inferring Use your observations to make an inference about what has happened. What experience or knowledge did you use to make the inference?

Predicting Predict what will happen next. On what evidence or experience do you base your prediction?

---

future based on observations and experience.

Teach Help students differentiate between a prediction and an inference. You might organize the similarities and differences in a Venn diagram on the board. Both are interpretations of observations using experience and knowledge, and both can be incorrect. Inferences describe current or past events. Predictions describe future events.

Activity

Students might predict that the boy will land and skate to the other side. Others might predict that the boy will fall. Students should also describe the evidence or experience on which they based their predictions.

Classifying

Could you imagine searching for a book in the library if the books were shelved in no particular order? Your trip to the library would be an all-day event! Luckily, librarians group together books on similar topics or by the same author. Grouping together items that are alike in some way is called **classifying**. You can classify items in many ways: by size, by shape, by use, and by other important characteristics.

Like librarians, scientists use the skill of classifying to organize information and objects. When things are sorted into groups, the relationships among them become easier to understand.

Activity

Classify the objects in the photograph into two groups based on any characteristic you choose. Then use another characteristic to classify the objects into three groups.

Making Models

Have you ever drawn a picture to help someone understand what you were saying? Such a drawing is one type of model. A model is a picture, diagram, computer image, or other representation of a complex object or process. **Making models** helps people understand things that they cannot observe directly.

Scientists often use models to represent things that are either very large or very small, such as the planets in the solar system, or the parts of a cell. Such models are physical models—drawings or three-dimensional structures that look like the real thing. Other models are mental models—mathematical equations or words that describe how something works.

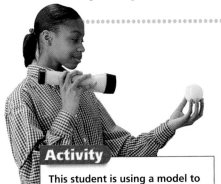

Activity

This student is using a model to demonstrate what causes day and night on Earth. What do the flashlight and the tennis ball in the model represent?

Communicating

Whenever you talk on the phone, write a report, or listen to your teacher at school, you are communicating. **Communicating** is the process of sharing ideas and information with other people. Communicating effectively requires many skills, including writing, reading, speaking, listening, and making models.

Scientists communicate to share results, information, and opinions. Scientists often communicate about their work in journals, over the telephone, in letters, and on the Internet.

They also attend scientific meetings where they share their ideas with one another in person.

Activity

On a sheet of paper, write out clear, detailed directions for tying your shoe. Then exchange directions with a partner. Follow your partner's directions exactly. How successful were you at tying your shoe? How could your partner have communicated more clearly?

Skills Handbook ◆ 181

Classifying

Focus Encourage students to think of common things that are classified.

Teach Ask: **What things at home are classified?** *(Clothing might be classified in order to place it in the appropriate dresser drawer; glasses, plates, and silverware are grouped in different parts of the kitchen; screws, nuts, bolts, washers, and nails might be separated into small containers.)* **What are some things that scientists classify?** *(Scientists classify many things they study, including organisms, geological features and processes, and kinds of machines.)*

Activity

Some characteristics students might use include color, pattern of color, use of balls, and size. Students' criteria for classification should clearly divide the balls into two, and then three, distinct groups.

Making Models

Focus Ask: **What are some models you have used to study science?** *(Students might have used human anatomical models, solar system models, maps, or stream tables.)* **How have these models helped you?** *(Models can help you learn about things that are difficult to study because they are very large, very small, or highly complex.)*

Teach Be sure students understand that a model does not have to be three-dimensional. For example, a map is a model, as is a mathematical equation. Have students look at the photograph of the student modeling the causes of day and night on Earth. Ask: **What quality of each item makes this a good model?** *(The flashlight gives off light, and the ball is round and can be rotated by the student.)*

Activity

The flashlight represents the sun and the ball represents Earth.

Communicating

Focus Have students identify the methods of communication they have used today.

Teach Ask: **How is the way you communicate with a friend similar to and different from the way scientists communicate about their work to other scientists?** *(Both may communicate using various methods, but scientists must be very detailed and precise, whereas communication between friends may be less detailed and precise.)* Encourage students to communicate like a scientist as they carry out the activity.

Activity

Students' answers will vary but should identify a step-by-step process for tying a shoe. Help students identify communication errors such as leaving out a step, putting steps in the wrong order, or disregarding the person's handedness.

A ● 181

Making Measurements

Students can refer to this part of the Skills Handbook whenever they need to review how to make measurements with SI units. You can use the activities here to teach or reinforce SI units.

Measuring in SI

Focus Review SI units with students. Begin by providing metric rulers, graduated cylinders, balances, and Celsius thermometers. Use these tools to reinforce that the meter is the unit of length, the liter is the unit of volume, the gram is the unit of mass, and the degree Celsius is the unit of temperature.

Teach Ask: **If you want to measure the length and the width of the classroom, which SI unit would you use?** *(Meter)* **Which unit would you use to measure the amount of mass in your textbook?** *(Gram)* **Which would you use to measure how much water a drinking glass holds?** *(Liter)* **When would you use the Celsius scale?** *(To measure the temperature of something)* Then use the measuring equipment to review SI prefixes. For example, ask: **What are the smallest units on the metric ruler?** *(Millimeters)* **How many millimeters are there in one centimeter?** *(10 millimeters)* **How many in 10 centimeters?** *(100 millimeters)* **How many centimeters are there in one meter?** *(100 centimeters)* **What does 1,000 meters equal?** *(One kilometer)*

Activity

Length The length of the shell is 7.8 centimeters, or 78 millimeters. If students need more practice measuring length, have them use meter sticks and metric rulers to measure various objects in the classroom.

Activity

Liquid Volume The volume of water in the graduated cylinder is 62 milliliters. If students need more practice, have them use a graduated cylinder to measure different volumes of water.

Making Measurements

By measuring, scientists can express their observations more precisely and communicate more information about what they observe.

Measuring in SI

The standard system of measurement used by scientists around the world is known as the International System of Units, which is abbreviated as SI (**Système International d'Unités,** in French). SI units are easy to use because they are based on multiples of 10. Each unit is ten times larger than the next smallest unit and one tenth the size of the next largest unit. The table lists the prefixes used to name the most common SI units.

Common SI Prefixes		
Prefix	Symbol	Meaning
kilo-	k	1,000
hecto-	h	100
deka-	da	10
deci-	d	0.1 (one tenth)
centi-	c	0.01 (one hundredth)
milli-	m	0.001 (one thousandth)

Length To measure length, or the distance between two points, the unit of measure is the **meter (m).** The distance from the floor to a doorknob is approximately one meter. Long distances, such as the distance between two cities, are measured in kilometers (km). Small lengths are measured in centimeters (cm) or millimeters (mm). Scientists use metric rulers and meter sticks to measure length.

Common Conversions	
1 km	= 1,000 m
1 m	= 100 cm
1 m	= 1,000 mm
1 cm	= 10 mm

Activity

The larger lines on the metric ruler in the picture show centimeter divisions, while the smaller, unnumbered lines show millimeter divisions. How many centimeters long is the shell? How many millimeters long is it?

Liquid Volume To measure the volume of a liquid, or the amount of space it takes up, you will use a unit of measure known as the **liter (L).** One liter is the approximate volume of a medium-size carton of milk. Smaller volumes are measured in milliliters (mL). Scientists use graduated cylinders to measure liquid volume.

Activity

The graduated cylinder in the picture is marked in milliliter divisions. Notice that the water in the cylinder has a curved surface. This curved surface is called the *meniscus.* To measure the volume, you must read the level at the lowest point of the meniscus. What is the volume of water in this graduated cylinder?

Common Conversion
1 L = 1,000 mL

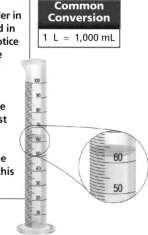

Mass To measure mass, or the amount of matter in an object, you will use a unit of measure known as the **gram (g).** One gram is approximately the mass of a paper clip. Larger masses are measured in kilograms (kg). Scientists use a balance to find the mass of an object.

Common Conversion

1 kg = 1,000 g

Activity

The mass of the potato in the picture is measured in kilograms. What is the mass of the potato? Suppose a recipe for potato salad called for one kilogram of potatoes. About how many potatoes would you need?

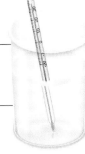

0.25 KG

Temperature To measure the temperature of a substance, you will use the **Celsius scale.** Temperature is measured in degrees Celsius (°C) using a Celsius thermometer. Water freezes at 0°C and boils at 100°C.

Time The unit scientists use to measure time is the **second (s).**

Activity

What is the temperature of the liquid in degrees Celsius?

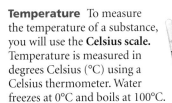

Converting SI Units

To use the SI system, you must know how to convert between units. Converting from one unit to another involves the skill of **calculating,** or using mathematical operations. Converting between SI units is similar to converting between dollars and dimes because both systems are based on multiples of ten.

Suppose you want to convert a length of 80 centimeters to meters. Follow these steps to convert between units.

1. Begin by writing down the measurement you want to convert—in this example, 80 centimeters.

2. Write a conversion factor that represents the relationship between the two units you are converting. In this example, the relationship is 1 meter = 100 centimeters. Write this conversion factor as a fraction, making sure to place the units you are converting from (centimeters, in this example) in the denominator.

3. Multiply the measurement you want to convert by the fraction. When you do this, the units in the first measurement will cancel out with the units in the denominator. Your answer will be in the units you are converting to (meters, in this example).

Example

80 centimeters = ▮ meters

$$80 \text{ centimeters} \times \frac{1 \text{ meter}}{100 \text{ centimeters}} = \frac{80 \text{ meters}}{100}$$

$$= 0.8 \text{ meters}$$

Activity

Convert between the following units.
1. 600 millimeters = ▮ meters
2. 0.35 liters = ▮ milliliters
3. 1,050 grams = ▮ kilograms

Skills Handbook ◆ 183

Activity

Mass The mass of the potato is 0.25 kilograms. You would need 4 potatoes to make one kilogram. If students need more practice, give them various objects, such as coins, paper clips, and books, to measure mass.

Activity

Temperature The temperature of the liquid is 35°C. Students who need more practice can measure the temperatures of various water samples.

Converting SI Units

Focus Review the steps for converting SI units, and work through the example with students.

Teach Ask: **How many millimeters are in 80 centimeters?** (*With the relationship 10 millimeters = 1 centimeter, students should follow the steps to calculate that 80 centimeters is equal to 800 millimeters.*) Have students do the conversion problems in the activity.

Activity

1. *600 millimeters = 0.6 meters*
2. *0.35 liters = 350 milliliters*
3. *1,050 grams = 1.05 kilograms*
If students need more practice converting SI units, have them make up conversion problems to trade with partners.

Conducting a Scientific Investigation

Students can refer to this part of the Skills Handbook whenever they need to review the steps of a scientific investigation. You can use the activities here to teach or reinforce these steps.

Posing Questions

Focus Ask: **What do you do when you want to learn about something?** (*Answers might include asking questions about it or looking for information in books or on the Internet.*) Explain that scientists go through the same process to learn about something.

Teach Tell students that the questions scientists ask may have no answers or many different answers. To answer their questions, scientists often conduct experiments. Ask: **Why is a scientific question important to a scientific investigation?** (*It helps the scientist decide if an experiment is necessary; the answer might already be known. It also helps focus the idea so that the scientist can form a hypothesis.*) **What is the scientific question in the activity on the next page?** (*Is a ball's bounce affected by the height from which it is dropped?*)

Developing a Hypothesis

Focus Emphasize that a hypothesis is one possible explanation for a set of observations. It is *not* a guess. It is often based on an inference.

Teach Ask: **On what information do scientists base their hypotheses?** (*Their observations and previous knowledge or experience*) Point out that a hypothesis does not always turn out to be correct. Ask: **When a hypothesis turns out to be incorrect, do you think the scientist wasted his or her time? Explain.** (*No. The scientist learned from the investigation and will develop another hypothesis that could prove to be correct.*)

Designing an Experiment

Focus Have a volunteer read the Experimental Procedure in the box. Invite students to identify the manipulated variable (*amount of salt*), the variables kept constant (*amount and temperature of water, location of containers*), the control (*Container 3*), and the responding variable (*time required for the water to freeze*).

Conducting a Scientific Investigation

In some ways, scientists are like detectives, piecing together clues to learn about a process or event. One way that scientists gather clues is by carrying out experiments. An experiment tests an idea in a careful, orderly manner. Although experiments do not all follow the same steps in the same order, many follow a pattern similar to the one described here.

Posing Questions

Experiments begin by asking a scientific question. A scientific question is one that can be answered by gathering evidence. For example, the question "Which freezes faster—fresh water or salt water?" is a scientific question because you can carry out an investigation and gather information to answer the question.

Developing a Hypothesis

The next step is to form a hypothesis. A **hypothesis** is a possible explanation for a set of observations or answer to a scientific question. In science, a hypothesis must be something that can be tested. A hypothesis can be worded as an *If . . . then . . .* statement. For example, a hypothesis might be *"If I add salt to fresh water, then the water will take longer to freeze."* A hypothesis worded this way serves as a rough outline of the experiment you should perform.

184 ◆ A

Teach Ask: **How might the experiment be affected if Container 1 had only 100 milliliters of water?** (*It wouldn't be an accurate comparison with the containers that have more water.*) Also make sure that students understand the importance of the control. Then, ask: **What operational definition is used in this experiment?** (*"Frozen" means the time at which a wooden stick can no longer move in a container.*)

Designing an Experiment

Next you need to plan a way to test your hypothesis. Your plan should be written out as a step-by-step procedure and should describe the observations or measurements you will make.

Two important steps involved in designing an experiment are controlling variables and forming operational definitions.

Controlling Variables In a well-designed experiment, you need to keep all variables the same except for one. A **variable** is any factor that can change in an experiment. The factor that you change is called the **manipulated variable**. In this experiment, the manipulated variable is the amount of salt added to the water. Other factors, such as the amount of water or the starting temperature, are kept constant.

The factor that changes as a result of the manipulated variable is called the **responding variable.** The responding variable is what you measure or observe to obtain your results. In this experiment, the responding variable is how long the water takes to freeze.

An experiment in which all factors except one are kept constant is called a **controlled experiment.** Most controlled experiments include a test called the control. In this experiment, Container 3 is the control. Because no salt is added to Container 3, you can compare the results from the other containers to it. Any difference in results must be due to the addition of salt alone.

Forming Operational Definitions Another important aspect of a well-designed experiment is having clear operational definitions. An **operational definition** is a statement that describes how a particular variable is to be measured or how a term is to be defined. For example, in this experiment, how will you determine if the water has frozen? You might decide to insert a stick in each container at the start of the experiment. Your operational definition of "frozen" would be the time at which the stick can no longer move.

Experimental Procedure
1. Fill 3 containers with 300 milliliters of cold tap water.
2. Add 10 grams of salt to Container 1; stir. Add 20 grams of salt to Container 2; stir. Add no salt to Container 3.
3. Place the 3 containers in a freezer.
4. Check the containers every 15 minutes. Record your observations.

Interpreting Data

The observations and measurements you make in an experiment are called **data.** At the end of an experiment, you need to analyze the data to look for any patterns or trends. Patterns often become clear if you organize your data in a data table or graph. Then think through what the data reveal. Do they support your hypothesis? Do they point out a flaw in your experiment? Do you need to collect more data?

Drawing Conclusions

A **conclusion** is a statement that sums up what you have learned from an experiment. When you draw a conclusion, you need to decide whether the data you collected support your hypothesis or not. You may need to repeat an experiment several times before you can draw any conclusions from it. Conclusions often lead you to pose new questions and plan new experiments to answer them.

Activity

Is a ball's bounce affected by the height from which it is dropped? Using the steps just described, plan a controlled experiment to investigate this problem.

Skills Handbook ♦ 185

Interpreting Data

Focus Ask: **What kind of data would you collect from the experiment with freezing salt water?** *(Time and state of the water)*

Teach Ask: **What if you forgot to record some data during an investigation?** *(You wouldn't be able to draw valid conclusions because some data are missing.)* Then, ask: **Why are data tables and graphs a good way to organize data?** *(They make it easier to record data accurately, as well as compare and analyze data.)* **What kind of data table and graph might you use for this experiment?** *(A table would have columns for each container with a row for each time interval in which the state of water is recorded. A bar graph would show the time elapsed until water froze for each container.)*

Drawing Conclusions

Focus Help students understand that a conclusion is not necessarily the end of a scientific investigation. A conclusion about one experiment may lead right into another experiment.

Teach Point out that in scientific investigations, a conclusion is a summary and explanation of the results of an experiment. For the Experimental Procedure described on this page, tell students to suppose that they obtained the following results: Container 1 froze in 45 minutes, Container 2 in 80 minutes, and Container 3 in 25 minutes. Ask: **What conclusions can you draw from this experiment?** *(Students might conclude that water takes longer to freeze as more salt is added to it. The hypothesis is supported, and the question of which freezes faster is answered—fresh water.)*

Activity

You might wish to have students work in pairs to plan the controlled experiment. Students should develop a hypothesis, such as, "If I increase the height from which a ball is dropped, then the height of its bounce will increase." They can test the hypothesis by dropping a ball from varying heights (the manipulated variable). All trials should be done with the same kind of ball and on the same surface (constants). For each trial, they should measure the height of the bounce (responding variable). After students have designed the experiment, provide rubber balls, and invite them to carry out the experiment so they can collect and interpret data and draw conclusions.

Technology Design Skills

Students can refer to this part of the Skills Handbook whenever they need to review the process of designing new technologies. You can use the activities here to teach or reinforce the steps in this process.

Identify a Need

Focus Solicit from students any situations in which they have thought that a tool, machine, or other object would be really helpful to them or others. Explain that this is the first step in the design of new products.

Teach Point out that identifying specific needs is very important to the design process. Ask: **If it was specified that the toy boat be wind-powered, how might that affect the design?** (*The boat would likely be designed with sails.*)

Research the Problem

Focus Explain that research focuses the problem so that the design is more specific.

Teach Ask: **What might happen if you didn't research the problem before designing the solution?** (*Answers include developing a design that has already been found to fail, using materials that aren't the best, or designing a solution that already exists.*) **What would you research before designing your toy boat?** (*Students might research designs and materials.*)

Design a Solution

Focus Emphasize the importance of a design team. Ask: **Why are brainstorming sessions important in product design?** (*A group will propose more new ideas than one person.*)

Teach Divide the class into teams to design the toy boat. Instruct them to brainstorm design ideas. Then, ask: **Why do you think engineers evaluate constraints after brainstorming?** (*Evaluating constraints while brainstorming often stops the flow of new ideas.*) **What design constraints do you have for your toy boat?** (*Materials must be readily available and teacher-approved. The boat must be 15 centimeters or less in length and must travel 2 meters in a straight line carrying a load of 20 pennies.*)

Technology Design Skills

Engineers are people who use scientific and technological knowledge to solve practical problems. To design new products, engineers usually follow the process described here, even though they may not follow these steps in the exact order. As you read the steps, think about how you might apply them in technology labs.

Identify a Need

Before engineers begin designing a new product, they must first identify the need they are trying to meet. For example, suppose you are a member of a design team in a company that makes toys. Your team has identified a need: a toy boat that is inexpensive and easy to assemble.

Research the Problem

Engineers often begin by gathering information that will help them with their new design. This research may include finding articles in books, magazines, or on the Internet. It may also include talking to other engineers who have solved similar problems. Engineers often perform experiments related to the product they want to design.

For your toy boat, you could look at toys that are similar to the one you want to design. You might do research on the Internet. You could also test some materials to see whether they will work well in a toy boat.

Drawing for a boat design ▼

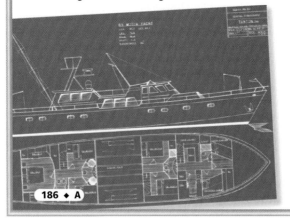

186 ● A

Design a Solution

Research gives engineers information that helps them design a product. When engineers design new products, they usually work in teams.

Generating Ideas Often design teams hold brainstorming meetings in which any team member can contribute ideas. **Brainstorming** is a creative process in which one team member's suggestions often spark ideas in other group members. Brainstorming can lead to new approaches to solving a design problem.

Evaluating Constraints During brainstorming, a design team will often come up with several possible designs. The team must then evaluate each one.

As part of their evaluation, engineers consider constraints. **Constraints** are factors that limit or restrict a product design. Physical characteristics, such as the properties of materials used to make your toy boat, are constraints. Money and time are also constraints. If the materials in a product cost a lot, or if the product takes a long time to make, the design may be impractical.

Making Trade-offs Design teams usually need to make trade-offs. In a **trade-off,** engineers give up one benefit of a proposed design in order to obtain another. In designing your toy boat, you will have to make trade-offs. For example, suppose one material is sturdy but not fully waterproof. Another material is more waterproof, but breakable. You may decide to give up the benefit of sturdiness in order to obtain the benefit of waterproofing.

Build and Evaluate a Prototype

Once the team has chosen a design plan, the engineers build a prototype of the product. A **prototype** is a working model used to test a design. Engineers evaluate the prototype to see whether it works well, is easy to operate, is safe to use, and holds up to repeated use.

Think of your toy boat. What would the prototype be like? Of what materials would it be made? How would you test it?

Troubleshoot and Redesign

Few prototypes work perfectly, which is why they need to be tested. Once a design team has tested a prototype, the members analyze the results and identify any problems. The team then tries to **troubleshoot,** or fix the design problems. For example, if your toy boat leaks or wobbles, the boat should be redesigned to eliminate those problems.

Communicate the Solution

A team needs to communicate the final design to the people who will manufacture and use the product. To do this, teams may use sketches, detailed drawings, computer simulations, and word descriptions.

You can use the technology design process to design and build a toy boat.

Research and Investigate

1. Visit the library or go online to research toy boats.
2. Investigate how a toy boat can be powered, including wind, rubber bands, or baking soda and vinegar.
3. Brainstorm materials, shapes, and steering for your boat.

Design and Build

4. Based on your research, design a toy boat that
   • is made of readily available materials
   • is no larger than 15 cm long and 10 cm wide

   • includes a power system, a rudder, and an area for cargo
   • travels 2 meters in a straight line carrying a load of 20 pennies

5. Sketch your design and write a step-by-step plan for building your boat. After your teacher approves your plan, build your boat.

Evaluate and Redesign

6. Test your boat, evaluate the results, and troubleshoot any problems.
7. Based on your evaluation, redesign your toy boat so it performs better.

Skills Handbook ◆ 187

Build and Evaluate a Prototype

Focus Explain that building a prototype enables engineers to test design ideas.

Teach Relate building and testing a prototype to conducting an experiment. Explain that engineers set up controlled experiments to test the prototype. Ask: **Why do you think engineers set up controlled experiments?** *(From the data, they can determine which component of the design is working and which is failing.)* **How would you test your prototype of the toy boat?** *(Answers will vary depending on the toy boat's propulsion system.)*

Troubleshoot and Redesign

Focus Make sure students know what it means to troubleshoot. If necessary, give an example. One example is a stapler that isn't working. In that case, you would check to see if it is out of staples or if the staples are jammed. Then you would fix the problem and try stapling again. If it still didn't work, you might check the position of staples and try again.

Teach Explain that engineers often are not surprised if the prototype doesn't work. Ask: **Why isn't it a failure if the prototype doesn't work?** *(Engineers learn from the problems and make changes to address the problems. This process makes the design better.)* Emphasize that prototypes are completely tested before the product is made in the factory.

Communicate the Solution

Focus Inquire whether students have ever read the instruction manual that comes with a new toy or electronic device.

Teach Emphasize the importance of good communication in the design process. Ask: **What might happen if engineers did not communicate their design ideas clearly?** *(The product might not be manufactured correctly or used properly.)*

Activity

The design possibilities are endless. Students might use small plastic containers, wood, foil, or plastic drinking cups for the boat. Materials may also include toothpicks, straws, or small wooden dowels. Brainstorm with students the different ways in which a toy boat can be propelled. The boats may be any shape, but must be no longer than 15 centimeters.

As student groups follow the steps in the design process, have them record their sources, brainstorming ideas, and prototype design in a logbook. Also give them time to troubleshoot and redesign their boats. When students turn in their boats, they should include assembly directions with a diagram, as well as instructions for use.

Creating Data Tables and Graphs

Students can refer to this part of the Skills Handbook whenever they need to review the skills required to create data tables and graphs. You can use the activities provided here to teach or reinforce these skills.

Data Tables

Focus Emphasize the importance of organizing data. Ask: **What might happen if you didn't use a data table for an experiment?** (*Possible answers include that data might not be collected or they might be forgotten.*)

Teach Have students create a data table to show how much time they spend on different activities during one week. Suggest that students first list the main activities they do every week. Then they should determine the amount of time they spend on each activity each day. Remind students to give the data table a title. A sample data table is shown below.

Bar Graphs

Focus Have students compare and contrast the data table and the bar graph on this page. Ask: **Why would you make a bar graph if the data are already organized in a table?** (*The bar graph organizes the data in a visual way that makes them easier to interpret.*)

Teach Students can use the data from the data table they created to make a bar graph that shows the amount of time they spend on different activities during a week. The vertical axis should be divided into units of time, such as hours. Remind students to label both axes and give their graph a title. A sample bar graph is shown below.

Creating Data Tables and Graphs

How can you make sense of the data in a science experiment? The first step is to organize the data to help you understand them. Data tables and graphs are helpful tools for organizing data.

Data Tables

You have gathered your materials and set up your experiment. But before you start, you need to plan a way to record what happens during the experiment. By creating a data table, you can record your observations and measurements in an orderly way.

Suppose, for example, that a scientist conducted an experiment to find out how many Calories people of different body masses burn while doing various activities. The data table shows the results.

Notice in this data table that the manipulated variable (body mass) is the heading of one column. The responding variable (for

Calories Burned in 30 Minutes			
Body Mass	Experiment 1: Bicycling	Experiment 2: Playing Basketball	Experiment 3: Watching Television
30 kg	60 Calories	120 Calories	21 Calories
40 kg	77 Calories	164 Calories	27 Calories
50 kg	95 Calories	206 Calories	33 Calories
60 kg	114 Calories	248 Calories	38 Calories

Experiment 1, the number of Calories burned while bicycling) is the heading of the next column. Additional columns were added for related experiments.

Bar Graphs

To compare how many Calories a person burns doing various activities, you could create a bar graph. A bar graph is used to display data in a number of separate, or distinct, categories. In this example, bicycling, playing basketball, and watching television are the three categories.

To create a bar graph, follow these steps.

1. On graph paper, draw a horizontal, or *x*-, axis and a vertical, or *y*-, axis.
2. Write the names of the categories to be graphed along the horizontal axis. Include an overall label for the axis as well.
3. Label the vertical axis with the name of the responding variable. Include units of measurement. Then create a scale along the axis by marking off equally spaced numbers that cover the range of the data collected.

4. For each category, draw a solid bar using the scale on the vertical axis to determine the height. Make all the bars the same width.
5. Add a title that describes the graph.

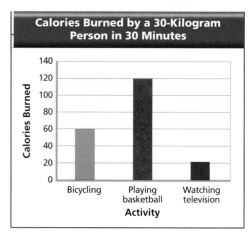

Calories Burned by a 30-Kilogram Person in 30 Minutes

Time Spent on Different Activities in a Week				
	Going to Classes	Eating Meals	Playing Soccer	Watching Television
Monday	6	2	2	0.5
Tuesday	6	1.5	1.5	1.5
Wednesday	6	2	1	2
Thursday	6	2	2	1.5
Friday	6	2	2	0.5
Saturday	0	2.5	2.5	1
Sunday	0	3	1	2

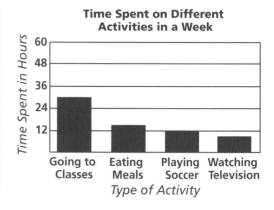

Time Spent on Different Activities in a Week

Line Graphs

To see whether a relationship exists between body mass and the number of Calories burned while bicycling, you could create a line graph. A line graph is used to display data that show how one variable (the responding variable) changes in response to another variable (the manipulated variable). You can use a line graph when your manipulated variable is **continuous,** that is, when there are other points between the ones that you tested. In this example, body mass is a continuous variable because there are other body masses between 30 and 40 kilograms (for example, 31 kilograms). Time is another example of a continuous variable.

Line graphs are powerful tools because they allow you to estimate values for conditions that you did not test in the experiment. For example, you can use the line graph to estimate that a 35-kilogram person would burn 68 Calories while bicycling.

To create a line graph, follow these steps.

1. On graph paper, draw a horizontal, or *x*-, axis and a vertical, or *y*-, axis.
2. Label the horizontal axis with the name of the manipulated variable. Label the vertical axis with the name of the responding variable. Include units of measurement.
3. Create a scale on each axis by marking off equally spaced numbers that cover the range of the data collected.
4. Plot a point on the graph for each piece of data. In the line graph above, the dotted lines show how to plot the first data point (30 kilograms and 60 Calories). Follow an imaginary vertical line extending up from the horizontal axis at the 30-kilogram mark. Then follow an imaginary horizontal line extending across from the vertical axis at the 60-Calorie mark. Plot the point where the two lines intersect.

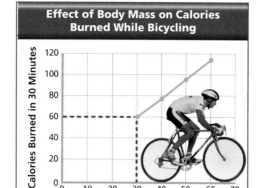

Effect of Body Mass on Calories Burned While Bicycling

5. Connect the plotted points with a solid line. (In some cases, it may be more appropriate to draw a line that shows the general trend of the plotted points. In those cases, some of the points may fall above or below the line. Also, not all graphs are linear. It may be more appropriate to draw a curve to connect the points.)
6. Add a title that identifies the variables or relationship in the graph.

Activity

Create line graphs to display the data from Experiment 2 and Experiment 3 in the data table.

Activity

You read in the newspaper that a total of 4 centimeters of rain fell in your area in June, 2.5 centimeters fell in July, and 1.5 centimeters fell in August. What type of graph would you use to display these data? Use graph paper to create the graph.

Skills Handbook ◆ 189

Line Graphs

Focus Ask: **Would a bar graph show the relationship between body mass and the number of Calories burned in 30 minutes?** *(No. Bar graphs can only show data in distinct categories.)* Explain that line graphs are used to show how one variable changes in response to another variable.

Teach Walk students through the steps involved in creating a line graph using the example illustrated on the page. For example, ask: **What is the label on the horizontal axis? On the vertical axis?** *(Body Mass (kg); Calories Burned in 30 Minutes)* **What scale is used on each axis?** *(10 kg on the x-axis and 20 Calories on the y-axis)* **What does the second data point represent?** *(77 Calories burned for a body mass of 40 kg)* **What trend or pattern does the graph show?** *(The number of Calories burned in 30 minutes of cycling increases with body mass.)*

Activity

Students should make a different graph for each experiment. Each graph should have a different *x*-axis scale that is appropriate for the data. See sample graphs below.

Activity

Students should conclude that a bar graph would be best for displaying the data.

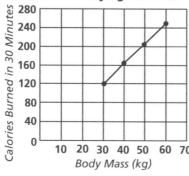

Effect of Body Mass on Calories Burned While Playing Basketball

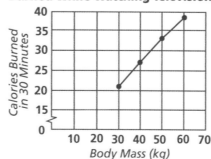

Effect of Body Mass on Calories Burned While Watching Television

A ● 189

Circle Graphs

Focus Emphasize that a circle graph must include 100 percent of the categories for the topic being graphed. For example, ask: **Could the data in the bar graph titled "Calories Burned by a 30-kilogram Person in Various Activities" (on the previous page) be shown in a circle graph? Why or why not?** (*No. It does not include all the possible ways a 30-kilogram person can burn Calories.*)

Teach Walk students through the steps for making a circle graph. If necessary, help them with the compass and the protractor. Use the protractor to illustrate that a circle has 360 degrees. Make sure students understand the mathematical calculations involved in making a circle graph.

Activity

You might have students work in pairs to complete the activity. Students' circle graphs should look like the graph below.

Ways Students Get to School

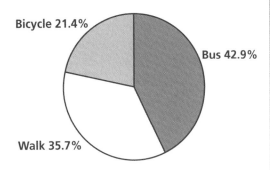

Bicycle 21.4%

Bus 42.9%

Walk 35.7%

Circle Graphs

Like bar graphs, circle graphs can be used to display data in a number of separate categories. Unlike bar graphs, however, circle graphs can only be used when you have data for *all* the categories that make up a given topic. A circle graph is sometimes called a pie chart. The pie represents the entire topic, while the slices represent the individual categories. The size of a slice indicates what percentage of the whole a particular category makes up.

The data table below shows the results of a survey in which 24 teenagers were asked to identify their favorite sport. The data were then used to create the circle graph at the right.

Favorite Sports

Sport	Students
Soccer	8
Basketball	6
Bicycling	6
Swimming	4

To create a circle graph, follow these steps.

1. Use a compass to draw a circle. Mark the center with a point. Then draw a line from the center point to the top of the circle.

2. Determine the size of each "slice" by setting up a proportion where *x* equals the number of degrees in a slice. (*Note:* A circle contains 360 degrees.) For example, to find the number of degrees in the "soccer" slice, set up the following proportion:

$$\frac{\text{Students who prefer soccer}}{\text{Total number of students}} = \frac{x}{\text{Total number of degrees in a circle}}$$

$$\frac{8}{24} = \frac{x}{360}$$

Cross-multiply and solve for x.

$$24x = 8 \times 360$$
$$x = 120$$

The "soccer" slice should contain 120 degrees.

Sports That Teens Prefer

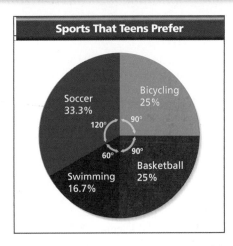

Soccer 33.3%

Bicycling 25%

Swimming 16.7%

Basketball 25%

3. Use a protractor to measure the angle of the first slice, using the line you drew to the top of the circle as the 0° line. Draw a line from the center of the circle to the edge for the angle you measured.

4. Continue around the circle by measuring the size of each slice with the protractor. Start measuring from the edge of the previous slice so the wedges do not overlap. When you are done, the entire circle should be filled in.

5. Determine the percentage of the whole circle that each slice represents. To do this, divide the number of degrees in a slice by the total number of degrees in a circle (360), and multiply by 100%. For the "soccer" slice, you can find the percentage as follows:

$$\frac{120}{360} \times 100\% = 33.3\%$$

6. Use a different color for each slice. Label each slice with the category and with the percentage of the whole it represents.

7. Add a title to the circle graph.

Activity

In a class of 28 students, 12 students take the bus to school, 10 students walk, and 6 students ride their bicycles. Create a circle graph to display these data.

Math Review

Scientists use math to organize, analyze, and present data.
This appendix will help you review some basic math skills.

Mean, Median, and Mode

The **mean** is the average, or the sum of the data divided by the number of data items. The middle number in a set of ordered data is called the **median**. The **mode** is the number that appears most often in a set of data.

> **Example**
>
> A scientist counted the number of distinct songs sung by seven different male birds and collected the data shown below.
>
> | Male Bird Songs | | | | | | | |
> |---|---|---|---|---|---|---|---|
> | Bird | A | B | C | D | E | F | G |
> | Number of Songs | 36 | 29 | 40 | 35 | 28 | 36 | 27 |
>
> To determine the mean number of songs, add the total number of songs and divide by the number of data items—in this case, the number of male birds.
>
> $$\text{Mean} = \frac{231}{7} = 33 \text{ songs}$$
>
> To find the median number of songs, arrange the data in numerical order and find the number in the middle of the series.
>
> **27 28 29 35 36 36 40**
>
> The number in the middle is 35, so the median number of songs is 35.
>
> The mode is the value that appears most frequently. In the data, 36 appears twice, while each other item appears only once. Therefore, 36 songs is the mode.

> **Practice**
>
> Find out how many minutes it takes each student in your class to get to school. Then find the mean, median, and mode for the data.

Probability

Probability is the chance that an event will occur. Probability can be expressed as a ratio, a fraction, or a percentage. For example, when you flip a coin, the probability that the coin will land heads up is 1 in 2, or $\frac{1}{2}$, or 50 percent.

The probability that an event will happen can be expressed in the following formula.

$$P(\text{event}) = \frac{\text{Number of times the event can occur}}{\text{Total number of possible events}}$$

> **Example**
>
> A paper bag contains 25 blue marbles, 5 green marbles, 5 orange marbles, and 15 yellow marbles. If you close your eyes and pick a marble from the bag, what is the probability that it will be yellow?
>
> $$P(\text{yellow marbles}) = \frac{15 \text{ yellow marbles}}{50 \text{ marbles total}}$$
>
> $$P = \frac{15}{50}, \text{ or } \frac{3}{10}, \text{ or } 30\%$$

> **Practice**
>
> Each side of a cube has a letter on it. Two sides have A, three sides have B, and one side has C. If you roll the cube, what is the probability that A will land on top?

Math Review

Students can refer to this part of the Skills Handbook whenever they need to review some basic math skills. You can use the activities provided here to teach or reinforce these skills.

Mean, Median, and Mode

Focus Remind students that data from an experiment might consist of hundreds or thousands of numbers. Unless analyzed, the numbers likely will not be helpful.

Teach Work through the process of determining mean, median, and mode using the example in the book. Make sure students realize that these three numbers do not always equal each other. Point out that taken together, these three numbers give more information about the data than just one of the numbers alone.

> **Practice**
>
> Answers will vary based on class data. The mean should equal the total number of minutes divided by the number of students. The median should equal the number in the middle after arranging the data in numerical order. The mode should equal the number of minutes that is given most frequently.

Probability

Focus Show students a coin and ask: **What is the chance that I will get tails when I flip the coin?** (*Some students might know that there is a 1 in 2, or 50 percent, chance of getting tails.*)

Teach Set up a bag of marbles like the one in the example. Allow students to practice determining the probabilities of picking marbles of different colors. Then, encourage them to actually pick marbles and compare their actual results with those results predicted by probability.

> **Practice**
>
> $P(A) = 2$ sides with $\frac{A}{6}$ sides total
> $P = \frac{2}{6}$, or $\frac{1}{3}$, or 33%

Area

Focus Ask: **Who knows what area is?** *(Area is equal to the number of square units needed to cover a certain shape or object.)* On the board, write the formulas for the area of a rectangle and a circle.

Teach Give students various objects of different shapes. Have them measure each object and determine its area based on the measurements. Point out that the units of the answer are squared because they are multiplied together. If students are interested, you might also explain that π is equal to the ratio of the circumference of a circle to its diameter. For circles of all sizes, π is approximately equal to the number 3.14, or $\frac{22}{7}$.

Practice

The area of the circle is equal to
$21 \text{ m} \times 21 \text{ m} \times \frac{22}{7}$, or 1,386 m^2.

Circumference

Focus Draw a circle on the board. Then trace the outline with your finger and explain that this is the circumference of the circle, or the distance around it.

Teach Show students that the radius is equal to the distance from the center of the circle to any point on it. Point out that the diameter of a circle is equal to two times the radius. Give students paper circles of various sizes, and have them calculate the circumference of each.

Practice

The circumference is equal to $2 \times 28 \text{ m} \times \frac{22}{7}$, or 176 m.

Volume

Focus Fill a beaker with 100 milliliters of water. Ask: **What is the volume of water?** *(100 milliliters)* Explain that volume is the amount of space that something takes up. Then point out that one milliliter is equal to one cubic centimeter (cm^3).

Teach Write on the board the formulas for calculating the volumes of a rectangle and a cylinder. Point out that volume is equal to the area of an object multiplied by its height. Then measure the beaker to show students the relationship between liquid volume (100 milliliters) and the number of cubic units it contains (100 cubic centimeters).

Area

The **area** of a surface is the number of square units that cover it. The front cover of your textbook has an area of about 600 cm^2.

Area of a Rectangle and a Square To find the area of a rectangle, multiply its length times its width. The formula for the area of a rectangle is

$$A = \ell \times w, \text{ or } A = \ell w$$

Since all four sides of a square have the same length, the area of a square is the length of one side multiplied by itself, or squared.

$$A = s \times s, \text{ or } A = s^2$$

Example

A scientist is studying the plants in a field that measures 75 m $\times$ 45 m. What is the area of the field?

$$A = \ell \times w$$
$$A = 75 \text{ m} \times 45 \text{ m}$$
$$A = 3,375 \text{ m}^2$$

Area of a Circle The formula for the area of a circle is

$$A = \pi \times r \times r, \text{ or } A = \pi r^2$$

The length of the radius is represented by r, and the value of π is approximately $\frac{22}{7}$.

Example

Find the area of a circle with a radius of 14 cm.

$$A = \pi r^2$$
$$A = 14 \times 14 \times \frac{22}{7}$$
$$A = 616 \text{ cm}^2$$

Practice

Find the area of a circle that has a radius of 21 m.

Circumference

The distance around a circle is called the circumference. The formula for finding the circumference of a circle is

$$C = 2 \times \pi \times r, \text{ or } C = 2\pi r$$

Example

The radius of a circle is 35 cm. What is its circumference?

$$C = 2\pi r$$
$$C = 2 \times 35 \times \frac{22}{7}$$
$$C = 220 \text{ cm}$$

Practice

What is the circumference of a circle with a radius of 28 m?

Volume

The volume of an object is the number of cubic units it contains. The volume of a wastebasket, for example, might be about 26,000 cm^3.

Volume of a Rectangular Object To find the volume of a rectangular object, multiply the object's length times its width times its height.

$$V = \ell \times w \times h, \text{ or } V = \ell w h$$

Example

Find the volume of a box with length 24 cm, width 12 cm, and height 9 cm.

$$V = \ell w h$$
$$V = 24 \text{ cm} \times 12 \text{ cm} \times 9 \text{ cm}$$
$$V = 2,592 \text{ cm}^3$$

Practice

What is the volume of a rectangular object with length 17 cm, width 11 cm, and height 6 cm?

Practice

The volume of the rectangular object is equal to 17 cm $\times$ 11 cm $\times$ 6 cm, or 1,122 cm^3.

Fractions

A **fraction** is a way to express a part of a whole. In the fraction $\frac{4}{7}$, 4 is the numerator and 7 is the denominator.

Adding and Subtracting Fractions To add or subtract two or more fractions that have a common denominator, first add or subtract the numerators. Then write the sum or difference over the common denominator.

To find the sum or difference of fractions with different denominators, first find the least common multiple of the denominators. This is known as the least common denominator. Then convert each fraction to equivalent fractions with the least common denominator. Add or subtract the numerators. Then write the sum or difference over the common denominator.

Example

$$\frac{5}{6} - \frac{3}{4} = \frac{10}{12} - \frac{9}{12} = \frac{10-9}{12} = \frac{1}{12}$$

Multiplying Fractions To multiply two fractions, first multiply the two numerators, then multiply the two denominators.

Example

$$\frac{5}{6} \times \frac{2}{3} = \frac{5 \times 2}{6 \times 3} = \frac{10}{18} = \frac{5}{9}$$

Dividing Fractions Dividing by a fraction is the same as multiplying by its reciprocal. Reciprocals are numbers whose numerators and denominators have been switched. To divide one fraction by another, first invert the fraction you are dividing by—in other words, turn it upside down. Then multiply the two fractions.

Example

$$\frac{2}{5} \div \frac{7}{8} = \frac{2}{5} \times \frac{8}{7} = \frac{2 \times 8}{5 \times 7} = \frac{16}{35}$$

Practice

Solve the following: $\frac{3}{7} \div \frac{4}{5}$.

Decimals

Fractions whose denominators are 10, 100, or some other power of 10 are often expressed as decimals. For example, the fraction $\frac{9}{10}$ can be expressed as the decimal 0.9, and the fraction $\frac{7}{100}$ can be written as 0.07.

Adding and Subtracting With Decimals To add or subtract decimals, line up the decimal points before you carry out the operation.

Example

```
  27.4          278.635
+  6.19        − 191.4
-------        --------
  33.59          87.235
```

Multiplying With Decimals When you multiply two numbers with decimals, the number of decimal places in the product is equal to the total number of decimal places in each number being multiplied.

Example

```
   46.2    (one decimal place)
 ×  2.37   (two decimal places)
 -------
 109.494   (three decimal places)
```

Dividing With Decimals To divide a decimal by a whole number, put the decimal point in the quotient above the decimal point in the dividend.

Example

$$15.5 \div 5$$
```
    3.1
 5)15.5
```

To divide a decimal by a decimal, you need to rewrite the divisor as a whole number. Do this by multiplying both the divisor and dividend by the same multiple of 10.

Example

$$1.68 \div 4.2 = 16.8 \div 42$$
```
     0.4
 42)16.8
```

Practice

Multiply 6.21 by 8.5.

Fractions

Focus Draw a circle on the board, and divide it into eight equal sections. Shade in one of the sections, and explain that one out of eight, or one eighth, of the sections is shaded. Also use the circle to show that four eighths is the same as one half.

Teach Write the fraction $\frac{3}{4}$ on the board. Ask: **What is the numerator?** *(Three)* **What is the denominator?** *(Four)* Emphasize that when adding and subtracting fractions, the denominators of the two fractions must be the same. If necessary, review how to find the least common denominator. Remind students that when multiplying and dividing, the denominators do not have to be the same.

Practice

$$\frac{3}{7} \div \frac{4}{5} = \frac{3}{7} \times \frac{5}{4} = \frac{15}{28}$$

Decimals

Focus Write the number *129.835* on the board. Ask: **What number is in the ones position?** *(9)* **The tenths position?** *(8)* **The hundredths position?** *(3)* Make sure students know that 0.8 is equal to $\frac{8}{10}$ and 0.03 is equal to $\frac{3}{100}$.

Teach Use the examples in the book to review addition, subtraction, multiplication, and division with decimals. Make up a worksheet of similar problems to give students additional practice. Also show students how a fraction is converted to a decimal by dividing the numerator by the denominator. For example, $\frac{1}{2}$ is equal to 0.5.

Practice

$$6.21 \times 8.5 = 52.785$$

Ratio and Proportion

Focus Differentiate a ratio from a fraction. Remind students that a fraction tells how many parts of the whole. In contrast, a ratio compares two different numbers. For example, $\frac{12}{22}$, or $\frac{6}{11}$, of a class are girls. But the ratio of boys to girls in the class is 10 to 12, or $\frac{5}{6}$.

Teach Use the example in the book to explain how to use a proportion to find an unknown quantity. Provide students with additional practice problems, if needed.

Practice

$6 \times 49 = 7x$
$294 = 7x$
$294 \div 7 = x$
$x = 42$

Percentage

Focus On the board, write $50\% = \frac{50}{100}$. Explain that a percentage is a ratio that compares a number to 100.

Teach Point out that when calculating percentages, you are usually using numbers other than 100. In this case, you set up a proportion. Go over the example in the book. Emphasize that the number representing the total goes on the bottom of the ratio, as does the 100%.

Practice

Students should set up the proportion

$\frac{42 \text{ marbles}}{300 \text{ marbles}} = \frac{x\%}{100\%}$

$42 \times 100 = 300x$

$4200 = 300x$

$4200 \div 300 = 14\%$

Ratio and Proportion

A **ratio** compares two numbers by division. For example, suppose a scientist counts 800 wolves and 1,200 moose on an island. The ratio of wolves to moose can be written as a fraction, $\frac{800}{1,200}$, which can be reduced to $\frac{2}{3}$. The same ratio can also be expressed as 2 to 3 or 2 : 3.

A **proportion** is a mathematical sentence saying that two ratios are equivalent. For example, a proportion could state that $\frac{800 \text{ wolves}}{1,200 \text{ moose}} = \frac{2 \text{ wolves}}{3 \text{ moose}}$. You can sometimes set up a proportion to determine or estimate an unknown quantity. For example, suppose a scientist counts 25 beetles in an area of 10 square meters. The scientist wants to estimate the number of beetles in 100 square meters.

Example

1. Express the relationship between beetles and area as a ratio: $\frac{25}{10}$, simplified to $\frac{5}{2}$.
2. Set up a proportion, with x representing the number of beetles. The proportion can be stated as $\frac{5}{2} = \frac{x}{100}$.
3. Begin by cross-multiplying. In other words, multiply each fraction's numerator by the other fraction's denominator.

   $5 \times 100 = 2 \times x$, or $500 = 2x$

4. To find the value of x, divide both sides by 2. The result is 250, or 250 beetles in 100 square meters.

Practice

Find the value of x in the following proportion: $\frac{6}{7} = \frac{x}{49}$.

Percentage

A **percentage** is a ratio that compares a number to 100. For example, there are 37 granite rocks in a collection that consists of 100 rocks. The ratio $\frac{37}{100}$ can be written as 37%. Granite rocks make up 37% of the rock collection.

You can calculate percentages of numbers other than 100 by setting up a proportion.

Example

Rain falls on 9 days out of 30 in June. What percentage of the days in June were rainy?

$\frac{9 \text{ days}}{30 \text{ days}} = \frac{d\%}{100\%}$

To find the value of d, begin by cross-multiplying, as for any proportion:

$9 \times 100 = 30 \times d$ $d = \frac{900}{30}$ $d = 30$

Practice

There are 300 marbles in a jar, and 42 of those marbles are blue. What percentage of the marbles are blue?

Significant Figures

The **precision** of a measurement depends on the instrument you use to take the measurement. For example, if the smallest unit on the ruler is millimeters, then the most precise measurement you can make will be in millimeters.

The sum or difference of measurements can only be as precise as the least precise measurement being added or subtracted. Round your answer so that it has the same number of digits after the decimal as the least precise measurement. Round up if the last digit is 5 or more, and round down if the last digit is 4 or less.

Example

Subtract a temperature of 5.2°C from the temperature 75.46°C.

75.46 − 5.2 = 70.26

5.2 has the fewest digits after the decimal, so it is the least precise measurement. Since the last digit of the answer is 6, round up to 3. The most precise difference between the measurements is 70.3°C.

Practice

Add 26.4 m to 8.37 m. Round your answer according to the precision of the measurements.

Significant figures are the number of nonzero digits in a measurement. Zeroes between nonzero digits are also significant. For example, the measurements 12,500 L, 0.125 cm, and 2.05 kg all have three significant figures. When you multiply and divide measurements, the one with the fewest significant figures determines the number of significant figures in your answer.

Example

Multiply 110 g by 5.75 g.

110 × 5.75 = 632.5

Because 110 has only two significant figures, round the answer to 630 g.

Scientific Notation

A **factor** is a number that divides into another number with no remainder. In the example, the number 3 is used as a factor four times.

An **exponent** tells how many times a number is used as a factor. For example, $3 \times 3 \times 3 \times 3$ can be written as 3^4. The exponent 4 indicates that the number 3 is used as a factor four times. Another way of expressing this is to say that 81 is equal to 3 to the fourth power.

Example

$$3^4 = 3 \times 3 \times 3 \times 3 = 81$$

Scientific notation uses exponents and powers of ten to write very large or very small numbers in shorter form. When you write a number in scientific notation, you write the number as two factors. The first factor is any number between 1 and 10. The second factor is a power of 10, such as 10^3 or 10^6.

Example

The average distance between the planet Mercury and the sun is 58,000,000 km. To write the first factor in scientific notation, insert a decimal point in the original number so that you have a number between 1 and 10. In the case of 58,000,000, the number is 5.8.

To determine the power of 10, count the number of places that the decimal point moved. In this case, it moved 7 places.

58,000,000 km = 5.8 × 10^7 km

Practice

Express 6,590,000 in scientific notation.

Significant Figures

Focus Measure the length of a paper clip using two different rulers. Use one ruler that is less precise than the other. Compare the two measurements. Ask: **Which measurement is more precise?** *(The ruler with the smallest units will give the more precise measurement.)*

Teach Give students the opportunity to take measurements of an object using tools with different precision. Encourage students to add and subtract their measurements, making sure that they round the answers to reflect the precision of the instruments. Go over the example for significant digits. Check for understanding by asking: **How many significant digits are in the number 324,000?** *(Three)* **In the number 5, 901?** *(Four)* **In the number 0.706?** *(Three)* If students need additional practice, create a worksheet with problems in multiplying and dividing numbers with various significant digits.

Practice

26.4 m + 8.37 m = 34.77 m
This answer should be rounded to 34.8 m because the least precise measurement has only one digit after the decimal. This number is rounded up to 8 because the last digit is more than 5.

Scientific Notation

Focus Write a very large number on the board, such as 100 million, using all the zeros. Then, write the number using scientific notation. Ask: **Why do you think scientists prefer to write very large numbers using scientific notation?** *(Possible answers include that it is easier to do calculations, convert units, and make comparisons with other numbers.)*

Teach Go over the examples, and ask: **In the second example, which numbers are the factors?** *(5.8 and 10^7)* **Which number is the exponent?** *(7)* Explain that very small numbers have a negative exponent because the decimal point is moved to the right to produce the first factor. For example, 0.00000628 is equal to 6.28×10^{-6}.

Practice

$6,590,000 = 6.59 \times 10^6$

A ● 195

Reading Comprehension Skills

Students can refer to this part of the Skills Handbook whenever they need to review a reading skill. You can use the activities provided here to teach or reinforce these skills.

Learning From Science Textbooks

Reading in a content area presents challenges different from those encountered when reading fiction. Science texts often have more new vocabulary and more unfamiliar concepts that place greater emphasis on inferential reasoning. Students who can apply reading skills and information-organizing strategies will be more successful in reading and understanding a science textbook.

Activity

Turn with students to the first page of any section. Walk through the Reading Preview with students, showing them the Key Concepts that provide a guiding set of questions that students can answer from the text. Next, point out the Key Terms list, which highlights the science vocabulary. Last, have students find the Target Reading Skill with graphic organizer. Make the connection for students to the help in this Skills Handbook.

All in One Teaching Resources

• Target Reading Skills Handbook

Building Vocabulary

Focus Explain to students that knowing the definitions of key concept words can help them understand what they read.

Teach List on the board strategies to learn the definitions of new terms. Also solicit from students strategies that work for them—drawing a picture for the term, acting it out, or using it in conversation. Challenge students to choose a new strategy to learn the Key Terms in your next section.

Using Prior Knowledge

Focus Explain to students that using prior knowledge helps connect what they already know to what they are about to read.

Teach Point out that prior knowledge might not be accurate because memories have faded or perspectives have changed. Encourage students to ask questions to

---

Reading Comprehension Skills

Your textbook is an important source of science information. As you read your science textbook, you will find that the book has been written to assist you in understanding the science concepts.

Learning From Science Textbooks

As you study science in school, you will learn science concepts in a variety of ways. Sometimes you will do interesting activities and experiments to explore science ideas. To fully understand what you observe in experiments and activities, you will need to read your science textbook. To help you read, some of the important ideas are highlighted so that you can easily recognize what they are. In addition, a target reading skill in each section will help you understand what you read.

By using the target reading skills, you will improve your reading comprehension—that is, you will improve your ability to understand what you read. As you learn science, you will build knowledge that will help you understand even more of what you read. This knowledge will help you learn about all the topics presented in this textbook.

And—guess what?—these reading skills can be useful whenever you are reading. Reading to learn is important for your entire life. You have an opportunity to begin that process now.

The target reading skills that will improve your reading comprehension are described below.

Building Vocabulary

To understand the science concepts taught in this textbook, you need to remember the meanings of the Key Terms. One strategy consists of writing the definitions of these terms in your own words. You can also practice using the terms in sentences and make lists of words or phrases you associate with each term.

Using Prior Knowledge

Your prior knowledge is what you already know before you begin to read about a topic. Building on what you already know gives you a head start on learning new information. Before you begin a new assignment, think about what you know. You might page through your reading assignment, looking at the headings and the visuals to spark your memory. You can list what you know in the graphic organizer provided in the section opener. Then, as you read, consider questions like the ones below to connect what you learn to what you already know.

• How does what you learn relate to what you know?
• How did something you already know help you learn something new?
• Did your original ideas agree with what you have just learned? If not, how would you revise your original ideas?

Asking Questions

Asking yourself questions is an excellent way to focus on and remember new information in your textbook. You can learn how to ask good questions.

One way is to turn the text headings into questions. Then your questions can guide you to identify and remember the important information as you read. Look at these examples:

Heading: Using Seismographic Data
Question: How are seismographic data used?
Heading: Kinds of Faults
Question: What are the kinds of faults?

---

resolve discrepancies between their prior knowledge and what they have learned.

Asking Questions

Focus Demonstrate to students how to change a text heading into a question to help them anticipate the concepts, facts, and events they will read about.

Teach Encourage students to use this reading skill for the next section they read. Instruct them to turn the text headings into questions. Also challenge students to write at least four *what, how, why, who, when,* or *where* questions. Then, have students evaluate the skill. Ask: **Did asking questions about the text help you focus on the reading and remember what you read?** (*Answers will vary, but encourage honesty.*) If this reading skill didn't help, challenge them to assess why not.

You do not have to limit your questions to the text headings. Ask questions about anything that you need to clarify or that will help you understand the content. *What* and *how* are probably the most common question words, but you may also ask *why, who, when,* or *where* questions. Here is an example:

Properties of Waves

Question	Answer
What is amplitude?	Amplitude is . . .

Previewing Visuals

Visuals are photographs, graphs, tables, diagrams, and illustrations. Visuals, such as this diagram of a normal fault, contain important information. Look at visuals and their captions before you read. This will help you prepare for what you will be reading about.

Often you will be asked what you want to learn about a visual. For example, after you look at the normal fault diagram, you might ask: What is the movement along a normal fault? Questions about visuals give you a purpose for reading—to answer your questions. Previewing visuals also helps you see what you already know.

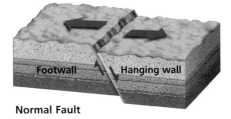

Footwall   Hanging wall

Normal Fault

Outlining

An outline shows the relationship between main ideas and supporting ideas. An outline has a formal structure. You write the main ideas, called topics, next to Roman numerals. The supporting ideas, sometimes called subtopics, are written under the main ideas and labeled A, B, C, and so on. An outline looks like this:

Technology and Society

I. Technology through history

II. The impact of technology on society

   A.

   B.

When you have completed an outline like this, you can see at a glance the structure of the section. You can use this outline as a study tool.

Identifying Main Ideas

When you are reading, it is important to try to understand the ideas and concepts that are in a passage. As you read science material, you will recognize that each paragraph has a lot of information and detail. Good readers try to identify the most important—or biggest—idea in every paragraph or section. That's the main idea. The other information in the paragraph supports or further explains the main idea.

Sometimes main ideas are stated directly. In this book, some main ideas are identified for you as key concepts. These are printed in boldface type. However, you must identify other main ideas yourself. In order to do this, you must identify all the ideas within a paragraph or section. Then ask yourself which idea is big enough to include all the other ideas.

Previewing Visuals

Focus Explain to students that looking at the visuals before reading will help them activate prior knowledge and predict what they are about to read.

Teach Assign a section for students to preview the visuals. First, instruct them to write a sentence describing what the section will be about. Then, encourage them to write one or two questions for each visual to give purpose to their reading. Also have them list any prior knowledge about the subject.

Outlining

Focus Explain that using an outline format helps organize information by main topic, subtopic, and details.

Teach Choose a section in the book, and demonstrate how to make an outline for it. Make sure students understand the structure of the outline by asking: **Is this a topic or a subtopic? Where does this information go in the outline? Would I write this heading next to a Roman numeral or a capital letter?** (*Answers depend on the section being outlined.*) Also show them how to indent and add details to the outline using numerals and lowercase letters.

Identifying Main Ideas

Focus Explain that identifying main ideas and details helps sort the facts from the information into groups. Each group can have a main topic, subtopics, and details.

Teach Tell students that paragraphs are often written so that the main idea is in the first or second sentence, or in the last sentence. Assign students a page in the book. Instruct them to write the main idea for each paragraph on that page. If students have difficulty finding the main idea, suggest that they list all of the ideas given in the paragraph, and then choose the idea that is big enough to include all the others.

Comparing and Contrasting

Focus Explain that comparing and contrasting information shows how concepts, facts, and events are similar or different. The results of the comparison can have importance.

Teach Point out that Venn diagrams work best when comparing two things. To compare more than two things, students should use a compare/contrast table. Have students make a Venn diagram or compare/contrast table using two or more different sports or other activities, such as playing musical instruments. Emphasize that students should select characteristics that highlight the similarities and differences in the activities.

Sequencing

Focus Tell students that organizing information from beginning to end will help them understand a step-by-step process.

Teach Encourage students to create a flowchart to show the things they did this morning to get ready for school. Remind students that a flowchart should show the correct order in which events occur. *(A typical flowchart might include: got up → took a shower → got dressed → ate breakfast → brushed teeth → gathered books and homework → put on jacket.)* Then explain that a cycle diagram shows a sequence of events that is continuous. Challenge students to create a cycle diagram that shows how the weather changes with the seasons where they live. *(Most cycle diagrams will include four steps, one for each season.)*

Comparing and Contrasting

When you compare and contrast, you examine the similarities and differences between things. You can compare and contrast in a Venn diagram or in a table. Your completed diagram or table shows you how the items are alike and how they are different.

Venn Diagram A Venn diagram consists of two overlapping circles. In the space where the circles overlap, you write the characteristics that the two items have in common. In one of the circles outside the area of overlap, you write the differing features or characteristics of one of the items. In the other circle outside the area of overlap, you write the differing characteristics of the other item.

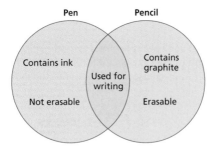

Table In a compare/contrast table, you list the items to be compared across the top of the table. Then list the characteristics or features to be compared in the left column. Complete the table by filling in information about each characteristic or feature.

Blood Vessel	Function	Structure of Wall
Artery	Carries blood away from heart	
Capillary		
Vein		

Sequencing

A sequence is the order in which a series of events occurs. Recognizing and remembering the sequence of events is important to understanding many processes in science. Sometimes the text uses words like *first, next, during,* and *after* to signal a sequence. A flowchart or a cycle diagram can help you visualize a sequence.

Flowchart To make a flowchart, write a brief description of each step or event in a box. Place the boxes in order, with the first event at the top of the page. Then draw an arrow to connect each step or event to the next.

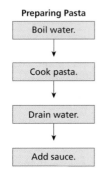

Cycle Diagram A cycle diagram shows a sequence that is continuous, or cyclical. A continuous sequence does not have an end because when the final event is over, the first event begins again. To create a cycle diagram, write the starting event in a box placed at the top of a page in the center. Then, moving in a clockwise direction around an imaginary circle, write each event in a box in its proper sequence. Draw arrows that connect each event to the one that occurs next, forming a continuous circle.

Identifying Supporting Evidence

A hypothesis is a possible explanation for observations made by scientists or an answer to a scientific question. A hypothesis is tested over and over again. The tests may produce evidence that supports the hypothesis. When enough supporting evidence is collected, a hypothesis may become a theory.

Identifying the supporting evidence for a hypothesis or theory can help you understand the hypothesis or theory. Evidence consists of facts—information whose accuracy can be confirmed by testing or observation.

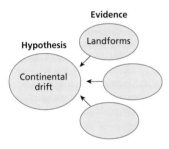

Relating Cause and Effect

Identifying causes and effects helps you understand relationships among events. A cause makes something happen. An effect is what happens. When you recognize that one event causes another, you are relating cause and effect. Words like *cause, because, effect, affect,* and *result* often signal a cause or an effect.

Sometimes an effect can have more than one cause, or a cause can produce several effects. For example, car exhaust and smoke from industrial plants are two causes of air pollution. Some effects of air pollution include breathing difficulties for some people, death of plants along some highways, and damage to some building surfaces.

Science involves many cause-and-effect relationships. Seeing and understanding these relationships helps you understand science processes.

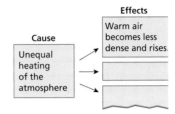

Concept Mapping

Concept maps are useful tools for organizing information on any topic. A concept map begins with a main idea or core concept and shows how the idea can be subdivided into related subconcepts or smaller ideas. In this way, relationships between concepts become clearer and easier to understand.

You construct a concept map by placing concepts (usually nouns) in ovals and connecting them with linking words. The biggest concept or idea is placed in an oval at the top of the map. Related concepts are arranged in ovals below the big idea. The linking words are often verbs and verb phrases and are written on the lines that connect the ovals.

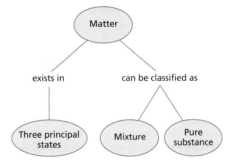

Identifying Supporting Evidence

Focus Explain to students that identifying the supporting evidence will help them to understand the relationship between the facts and the hypothesis.

Teach Remind students that a hypothesis is neither right nor wrong, but it is either supported or not supported by the evidence from testing or observation. If evidence is found that does not support a hypothesis, the hypothesis can be changed to accommodate the new evidence, or it can be dropped.

Relating Cause and Effect

Focus Explain to students that cause is the reason for what happens. The effect is what happens in response to the cause. Relating cause and effect helps students relate the reason for what happens to what happens as a result.

Teach Emphasize that not all events that occur together have a cause-and-effect relationship. For example, tell students that you went to the grocery store and your car stalled. Ask: **Is there a cause-and-effect relationship in this situation? Explain.** (*No. Going to the grocery store could not cause a car to stall. There must be another cause to make the car stall.*)

Concept Mapping

Focus Elicit from students how a map shows the relationship of one geographic area to another. Connect this idea to how a concept map shows the relationship between terms and concepts.

Teach Challenge students to make a concept map with at least three levels of concepts to organize information about types of transportation. All students should start with the phrase *Types of transportation* at the top of the concept map. After that point, their concepts may vary. (*For example, some students might place* private transportation *and* public transportation *at the next level, while other students might choose* human-powered *and* gas-powered.) Make sure students connect the concepts with linking words.

Interactive Textbook

- Complete student edition
- Video and audio
- Simulations and activities
- Section and chapter activities

Laboratory Safety

Laboratory safety is an essential element of a successful science class. Students need to understand exactly what is safe and unsafe behavior and what the rationale is behind each safety rule.

All in One Teaching Resources

- Laboratory Safety Teacher Notes
- Laboratory Safety Rules
- Laboratory Safety Symbols
- Laboratory Safety Contract

General Precautions

- Post safety rules in the classroom, and review them regularly with students before beginning every science activity.
- Familiarize yourself with the safety procedures for each activity before introducing it to your students.
- For open-ended activities like Chapter Projects, have students submit their procedures or design plans in writing and check them for safety considerations.
- Always act as an exemplary role model by displaying safe behavior.
- Know how to use safety equipment, such as fire extinguishers and fire blankets, and always have it accessible.
- Have students practice leaving the classroom quickly and orderly to prepare them for emergencies.
- Explain to students how to use the intercom or other available means of communication to get help during an emergency.
- Never leave students unattended while they are engaged in science activities.
- Provide enough space for students to safely carry out science activities.
- Instruct students to report all accidents and injuries to you immediately.

Safety Symbols

These symbols warn of possible dangers in the laboratory and remind you to work carefully.

 Safety Goggles Wear safety goggles to protect your eyes in any activity involving chemicals, flames or heating, or glassware.

 Lab Apron Wear a laboratory apron to protect your skin and clothing from damage.

 Breakage Handle breakable materials, such as glassware, with care. Do not touch broken glassware.

 Heat-Resistant Gloves Use an oven mitt or other hand protection when handling hot materials such as hot plates or hot glassware.

 Plastic Gloves Wear disposable plastic gloves when working with harmful chemicals and organisms. Keep your hands away from your face, and dispose of the gloves according to your teacher's instructions.

 Heating Use a clamp or tongs to pick up hot glassware. Do not touch hot objects with your bare hands.

 Flames Before you work with flames, tie back loose hair and clothing. Follow instructions from your teacher about lighting and extinguishing flames.

 No Flames When using flammable materials, make sure there are no flames, sparks, or other exposed heat sources present.

 Corrosive Chemical Avoid getting acid or other corrosive chemicals on your skin or clothing or in your eyes. Do not inhale the vapors. Wash your hands after the activity.

 Poison Do not let any poisonous chemical come into contact with your skin, and do not inhale its vapors. Wash your hands when you are finished with the activity.

 Fumes Work in a ventilated area when harmful vapors may be involved. Avoid inhaling vapors directly. Only test an odor when directed to do so by your teacher, and use a wafting motion to direct the vapor toward your nose.

 Sharp Object Scissors, scalpels, knives, needles, pins, and tacks can cut your skin. Always direct a sharp edge or point away from yourself and others.

 Animal Safety Treat live or preserved animals or animal parts with care to avoid harming the animals or yourself. Wash your hands when you are finished with the activity.

 Plant Safety Handle plants only as directed by your teacher. If you are allergic to certain plants, tell your teacher; do not do an activity involving those plants. Avoid touching harmful plants such as poison ivy. Wash your hands when you are finished with the activity.

 Electric Shock To avoid electric shock, never use electrical equipment around water, or when the equipment is wet or your hands are wet. Be sure cords are untangled and cannot trip anyone. Unplug equipment not in use.

 Physical Safety When an experiment involves physical activity, avoid injuring yourself or others. Alert your teacher if there is any reason you should not participate.

 Disposal Dispose of chemicals and other laboratory materials safely. Follow the instructions from your teacher.

 Hand Washing Wash your hands thoroughly when finished with the activity. Use antibacterial soap and warm water. Rinse well.

⚠️ **General Safety Awareness** When this symbol appears, follow the instructions provided. When you are asked to develop your own procedure in a lab, have your teacher approve your plan before you go further.

End-of-Experiment Rules

- Always have students use warm water and soap for washing their hands.

Heating and Fire Safety

- No flammable substances should be in use around hot plates, light bulbs, or open flames.
- Test tubes should be heated only in water baths.

- Students should be permitted to strike matches to light candles or burners *only* with strict supervision. When possible, you should light the flames, especially when working with younger students.
- Be sure to have proper ventilation when fumes are produced during a procedure.
- All electrical equipment used in the lab should have GFI (Ground Fault Interrupter) switches.

Science Safety Rules

General Precautions

Follow all instructions. Never perform activities without the approval and supervision of your teacher. Do not engage in horseplay. Never eat or drink in the laboratory. Keep work areas clean and uncluttered.

Dress Code

Wear safety goggles whenever you work with chemicals, glassware, heat sources such as burners, or any substance that might get into your eyes. If you wear contact lenses, notify your teacher.

Wear a lab apron or coat whenever you work with corrosive chemicals or substances that can stain. Wear disposable plastic gloves when working with organisms and harmful chemicals. Tie back long hair. Remove or tie back any article of clothing or jewelry that can hang down and touch chemicals, flames, or equipment. Roll up long sleeves. Never wear open shoes or sandals.

First Aid

Report all accidents, injuries, or fires to your teacher, no matter how minor. Be aware of the location of the first-aid kit, emergency equipment such as the fire extinguisher and fire blanket, and the nearest telephone. Know whom to contact in an emergency.

Heating and Fire Safety

Keep all combustible materials away from flames. When heating a substance in a test tube, make sure that the mouth of the tube is not pointed at you or anyone else. Never heat a liquid in a closed container. Use an oven mitt to pick up a container that has been heated.

Using Chemicals Safely

Never put your face near the mouth of a container that holds chemicals. Never touch, taste, or smell a chemical unless your teacher tells you to.

Use only those chemicals needed in the activity. Keep all containers closed when chemicals are not being used. Pour all chemicals over the sink or a container, not over your work surface. Dispose of excess chemicals as instructed by your teacher.

Be extra careful when working with acids or bases. When mixing an acid and water, always pour the water into the container first and then add the acid to the water. Never pour water into an acid. Wash chemical spills and splashes immediately with plenty of water.

Using Glassware Safely

If glassware is broken or chipped, notify your teacher immediately. Never handle broken or chipped glass with your bare hands.

Never force glass tubing or thermometers into a rubber stopper or rubber tubing. Have your teacher insert the glass tubing or thermometer if required for an activity.

Using Sharp Instruments

Handle sharp instruments with extreme care. Never cut material toward you; cut away from you.

Animal and Plant Safety

Never perform experiments that cause pain, discomfort, or harm to animals. Only handle animals if absolutely necessary. If you know that you are allergic to certain plants, molds, or animals, tell your teacher before doing an activity in which these are used. Wash your hands thoroughly after any activity involving animals, animal parts, plants, plant parts, or soil.

During field work, wear long pants, long sleeves, socks, and closed shoes. Avoid poisonous plants and fungi as well as plants with thorns.

End-of-Experiment Rules

Unplug all electrical equipment. Clean up your work area. Dispose of waste materials as instructed by your teacher. Wash your hands after every experiment.

Handling Organisms Safely

- In an activity where students are directed to taste something, be sure to store the material in clean, *nonscience* containers. Distribute the material to students in *new* plastic or paper dispensables, which should be discarded after the tasting. Tasting or eating should never be done in a lab classroom.

- When growing bacterial cultures, use only disposable petri dishes. After streaking, the dishes should be sealed and not opened again by students. After the lab, students should return the unopened dishes to you.

- Two methods are recommended for the safe disposal of bacterial cultures. *First method:* Autoclave the petri dishes and discard them without opening. *Second method:* If no autoclave is available, carefully open the dishes (never have a student do this), pour full-strength bleach into the dishes, and let them stand for a day. Then pour the bleach from the petri dishes down a drain, and flush the drain with lots of water. Tape the petri dishes back together, and place them in a sealed plastic bag. Wrap the plastic bag with a brown paper bag or newspaper, and tape securely. Throw the sealed package in the trash. Thoroughly disinfect the work area with bleach.

- To grow mold, use a new, sealable plastic bag that is two to three times larger than the material to be placed inside. Seal the bag and tape it shut. After the bag is sealed, students should not open it. To dispose of the bag and mold culture, make a small cut near an edge of the bag, and cook the bag in a microwave oven on a high setting for at least one minute. Discard the bag according to local ordinance, usually in the trash.

- Students should wear disposable nitrile, latex, or food-handling gloves when handling live animals or nonliving specimens.

Using Glassware Safely

- Use plastic containers, graduated cylinders, and beakers whenever possible. If using glass, students should wear safety goggles.
- Use only nonmercury thermometers with anti-roll protectors.

Using Chemicals Safely

- When students use both chemicals and microscopes in one activity, microscopes should be in a separate part of the room from the chemicals so that when students remove their goggles to use the microscopes, their eyes are not at risk.

The microscope is an essential tool in the study of life science. It allows you to see things that are too small to be seen with the unaided eye.

You will probably use a compound microscope like the one you see here. The compound microscope has more than one lens that magnifies the object you view.

Typically, a compound microscope has one lens in the eyepiece, the part you look through. The eyepiece lens usually magnifies 10 ×. Any object you view through this lens would appear 10 times larger than it is.

The compound microscope may contain one or two other lenses called objective lenses. If there are two objective lenses, they are called the low-power and high-power objective lenses. The low-power objective lens usually magnifies 10 ×. The high-power objective lens usually magnifies 40 ×.

To calculate the total magnification with which you are viewing an object, multiply the magnification of the eyepiece lens by the magnification of the objective lens you are using. For example, the eyepiece's magnification of 10 × multiplied by the low-power objective's magnification of 10 × equals a total magnification of 100 ×.

Use the photo of the compound microscope to become familiar with the parts of the microscope and their functions.

The Parts of a Compound Microscope

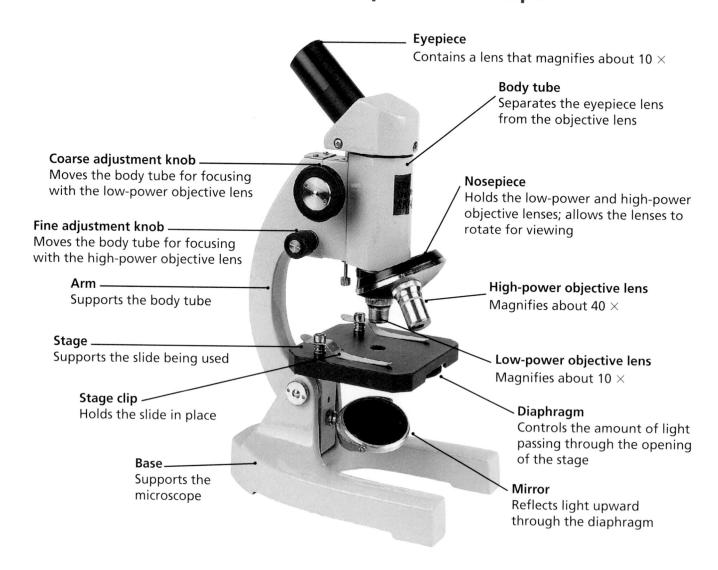

Eyepiece
Contains a lens that magnifies about 10 ×

Body tube
Separates the eyepiece lens from the objective lens

Coarse adjustment knob
Moves the body tube for focusing with the low-power objective lens

Nosepiece
Holds the low-power and high-power objective lenses; allows the lenses to rotate for viewing

Fine adjustment knob
Moves the body tube for focusing with the high-power objective lens

Arm
Supports the body tube

High-power objective lens
Magnifies about 40 ×

Stage
Supports the slide being used

Low-power objective lens
Magnifies about 10 ×

Stage clip
Holds the slide in place

Diaphragm
Controls the amount of light passing through the opening of the stage

Base
Supports the microscope

Mirror
Reflects light upward through the diaphragm

Using the Microscope

Use the following procedures when you are working with a microscope.

1. To carry the microscope, grasp the microscope's arm with one hand. Place your other hand under the base.
2. Place the microscope on a table with the arm toward you.
3. Turn the coarse adjustment knob to raise the body tube.
4. Revolve the nosepiece until the low-power objective lens clicks into place.
5. Adjust the diaphragm. While looking through the eyepiece, also adjust the mirror until you see a bright white circle of light. **CAUTION:** *Never use direct sunlight as a light source.*
6. Place a slide on the stage. Center the specimen over the opening on the stage. Use the stage clips to hold the slide in place. **CAUTION:** *Glass slides are fragile.*
7. Look at the stage from the side. Carefully turn the coarse adjustment knob to lower the body tube until the low-power objective almost touches the slide.
8. Looking through the eyepiece, very slowly turn the coarse adjustment knob until the specimen comes into focus.
9. To switch to the high-power objective lens, look at the microscope from the side. Carefully revolve the nosepiece until the high-power objective lens clicks into place. Make sure the lens does not hit the slide.
10. Looking through the eyepiece, turn the fine adjustment knob until the specimen comes into focus.

Making a Wet-Mount Slide

Use the following procedures to make a wet-mount slide of a specimen.

1. Obtain a clean microscope slide and a coverslip. **CAUTION:** *Glass slides and coverslips are fragile.*
2. Place the specimen on the slide. The specimen must be thin enough for light to pass through it.
3. Using a plastic dropper, place a drop of water on the specimen.
4. Gently place one edge of the coverslip against the slide so that it touches the edge of the water drop at a 45° angle. Slowly lower the coverslip over the specimen. If air bubbles are trapped beneath the coverslip, tap the coverslip gently with the eraser end of a pencil.
5. Remove any excess water at the edge of the coverslip with a paper towel.

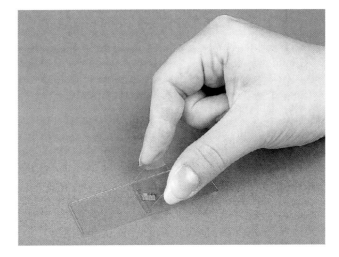

English and Spanish Glossary

A

absorption The process by which an object takes in, or absorbs, light. (p. 115)
absorción Proceso por el cual un objeto absorbe la luz.

accessory pigment A pigment other than chlorophyll found in plant cells. (p. 116)
pigmento accesorio Pigmento diferente de la clorofila que se halla en las células vegetales.

algae Plantlike protists. (p. 79)
algas Protistas con características vegetales.

algal bloom The rapid growth of a population of algae. (p. 84)
floración de algas Rápido crecimiento de una población de algas.

angiosperm A flowering plant that produces seeds enclosed in a protective structure. (p. 151)
angiosperma Planta con flores que produce semillas encerradas en una estructura protectora.

annual A flowering plant that completes its life cycle in one growing season. (p. 164)
anual Planta con flores que completa su ciclo de vida en una sola temporada de crecimiento.

antibiotic A chemical that can kill bacteria without harming a person's cells. (p. 62)
antibiótico Sustancia química que puede matar bacterias sin dañar las células humanas.

antibiotic resistance The ability of bacteria to withstand the effects of an antibiotic. (p. 63)
resistencia a antibióticos Capacidad de la bacteria a resistir los efectos de los antibióticos.

asexual reproduction A reproductive process that involves only one parent and produces offspring that are identical to the parent. (p. 52)
reproducción asexual Proceso de reproducción que implica a sólo un progenitor y produce descendencia que es idéntica al progenitor.

autotroph An organism that makes its own food. (p. 12)
autótrofo Organismo que produce su propio alimento.

auxin A plant hormone that speeds up the rate of growth of plant cells. (p. 161)
auxina Una hormona vegetal que acelera el crecimiento de las células de la planta.

B

bacteria Single-celled organisms that lack a nucleus; prokaryotes. (p. 49)
bacteria Organismos unicelulares que no tienen núcleo; procariotas.

bacteriophage A virus that infects bacteria. (p. 41)
bacteriófago Virus que infecta bacterias.

biennial A flowering plant that completes its life cycle in two years. (p. 164)
bienal Planta con flores que completa su ciclo de vida en dos años.

binary fission A form of asexual reproduction in which one cell divides to form two identical cells.
fisión binaria Forma de reproducción asexual en la que una célula se divide para formar dos células idénticas. (p. 52)

binomial nomenclature The system for naming organisms in which each organism is given a unique, two-part scientific name indicating its genus and species. (p. 18)
nomenclatura binaria Sistema para nombrar organismos, en el cual a cada organismo se le da un nombre científico único de dos partes, que indica su género y especie.

bog A wetland where sphagnum moss grows on top of acidic water. (p. 123)
ciénaga Pantano en donde crecen los musgos esfagnáceos encima de agua ácida.

budding A form of asexual reproduction of yeast in which a new cell grows out of the body of a parent.
gemación Forma de reproducción asexual de las levaduras, en la que una nueva célula crece del cuerpo de su progenitor. (p. 90)

C

cambium A layer of cells in a plant that produces new phloem and xylem cells. (p. 142)
cámbium Una capa de células de una planta que produce nuevas células de floema y xilema.

cell The basic unit of structure and function in an organism. (p. 7)
célula Unidad básica de estructura y función en los seres vivos.

chlorophyll A green pigment found in the chloroplasts of plants, algae, and some bacteria. (p. 110)
clorofila Pigmento verde que se halla en los cloroplastos de las plantas, en algas y algunas bacterias.

chloroplast A plant cell structure in which photosynthesis occurs. (p. 105)
cloroplasto Estructura en las células vegetales en la que occurre fotosíntesis.

cilia The hairlike projections on the outside of cells that move in a wavelike manner. (p. 77)
cilios Proyecciones finas en el exterior de las células, que se mueven de manera ondulante.

classification The process of grouping things based on their similarities. (p. 17)
clasificación Proceso de agrupar cosas según sus semejanzas.

cone The reproductive structure of a gymnosperm.
cono Estructura reproductora de una gimnosperma. (p. 148)

conjugation The process in which a unicellular organism transfers some of its genetic material to another unicellular organism. (p. 52)
conjugación Proceso por el cual un organismo unicelular transfiere parte de su material genético a otro organismo unicelular.

contractile vacuole The cell structure that collects extra water from the cytoplasm and then expels it from the cell. (p. 76)
vacuola contráctil Estructura celular que recoge el agua sobrante del citoplasma y luego la expulsa de la célula.

controlled experiment An experiment in which all factors are identical except one. (p. 10)
experimento controlado Experimento en el que todos los factores son iguales excepto uno.

cotyledon A seed leaf; sometimes stores food. (p. 138)
cotiledón Hoja de una semilla; en la que a veces se almacena alimento.

critical night length The number of hours of darkness that determines whether or not a plant will flower. (p. 162)
duración crítica de noche El número de horas de oscuridad que determina si floreza una planta o no.

cuticle The waxy, waterproof layer that covers the leaves and stems of most plants. (p. 106)
cutícula Capa cerosa e impermeable que cubre las hojas y los tallos de la mayoría de las plantas.

cytoplasm The region of a cell located inside the cell membrane (in prokaryotes) or between the cell membrane and nucleus (in eukaryotes); contains a gel-like material and cell structures. (p. 49)
citoplasma Región de una célula ubicada dentro de la membrana celular (en procariotas), o entre la membrana celular y el núcleo (en eucariotas); contiene un material gelatinoso y estructuras celulares.

D

day-neutral plant A plant with a flowering cycle that is not sensitive to periods of light and dark. (p. 162)
planta de día neutro Planta cuyo ciclo de floración no es sensible a la duración de los períodos de luz y oscuridad.

decomposer An organism that breaks down chemicals from dead organisms and returns important materials to the soil and water. (p. 56)
descomponedor Organismo que separa sustancias químicas de los organismos muertos y devuelve materiales importantes al suelo y al agua.

development The process of change that occurs during an organism's life to produce a more complex organism. (p. 9)
desarrollo Proceso de cambio que ocurre durante la vida de un organismo, mediante el cual se desarrolla un organismo más complejo.

dicot An angiosperm that has two seed leaves. (p. 156)
dicotiledónea Angiosperma cuyas semillas tienen dos cotiledones.

dormancy A period when an organism's growth or activity stops. (p. 163)
latencia Periodo durante el cual se suspende el crecimiento o la actividad de un organismo.

E

embryo The young organism that develops from a zygote. (p. 138)
embrión Organismo joven que se desarrolla a partir de un cigoto.

endospore A small, rounded, thick-walled, resting cell that forms inside a bacterial cell. (p. 53)
endospora Célula pequeña y redonda de paredes gruesas que se encuentra en reposo, que se forma dentro de una célula bacterial.

eukaryote An organism whose cells contain nuclei.
eucariota Organismo cuyas células contienen núcleos. (p. 28)

eutrophication The buildup over time of nutrients in freshwater lakes and ponds that leads to an increase in the growth of algae. (p. 86)
eutroficación Acumulación gradual de nutrientes en lagos y estanques de agua dulce que produce un aumento en el crecimiento de algas.

evolution The process by which species gradually change over time. (p. 23)
evolución Proceso mediante el cual las especies cambian gradualmente con el tiempo.

fertilization The joining of a sperm cell and an egg cell. (p. 107)
fertilización Unión de un espermatozoide y de un óvulo.

flagellum A long, whiplike structure that helps a cell to move. (p. 49)
flagelo Estructura larga con forma de látigo, que ayuda a la célula para moverse.

flower The reproductive structure of an angiosperm. (p. 152)
flor Estructura reproductora de una angiosperma.

fossil A trace of an ancient organism that has been preserved in rock or other substance. (p. 32)
fósil Restos de un organismo antiguo que se ha preservado en la roca u otra sustancia.

frond The leaf of a fern plant. (p. 128)
fronda Hoja de un helecho.

fruit The ripened ovary and other structures of an angiosperm that enclose one or more seeds. (p. 155)
frut Ovario maduro y otras estructuras que encierran una o más semillas de una angiosperma.

fruiting body The reproductive structure of a fungus that contains many hyphae and produces spores.
órgano fructífero Estructura reproductora de un hongo, que contiene muchas hifas y produce esporas.(p. 90)

fungus A eukaryotic organism that has cell walls, uses spores to reproduce, and is a heterotroph that feeds by absorbing its food. (p. 88)
hongo Organismo eucariótico que posee paredes celulares, usa esporas para reproducirse y es un heterótrofo que se alimenta absorbiendo su comida.

gametophyte The stage in the life cycle of a plant in which the plant produces gametes, or sex cells.
gametofito Etapa en el ciclo vital de una planta en la cual la planta produce gametos, es decir, células sexuales. (p. 110)

genetic engineering The process of altering an organism's genetic material to produce an organism with qualities that people find useful. (p. 167)
ingeniería genética Proceso por el cual se altera el material genético de un organismo para producir otro organismo con cualidades que se consideran útiles.

genus A classification grouping that consists of a number of similar, closely related species. (p. 18)
género Clasificación por grupo formada por un número de especies similares y muy relacionadas.

germination The sprouting of the embryo out of a seed; occurs when the embryo resumes its growth. (p. 140)
germinación La brotadura del embrión de una semilla; se occura cuando el embrión resuma su crecimiento.

gymnosperm A plant that produces seeds that are not enclosed by a protective fruit.
gimnosperma Planta cuyas semillas no están encerradas en una fruta protectora. (p. 146)

heterotroph An organism that cannot make its own food. (p. 12)
heterótrofo Organismo que no puede producir su propio alimento.

homeostasis The maintenance of stable internal conditions. (p. 14)
homeostasis Mantenimiento de condiciones internas estables.

hormone A chemical that affects growth and development. (p. 161)
hormona Sustancia química que afecta el crecimiento y el desarrollo.

host An organism that provides a source of energy or a suitable environment for a virus or another organism to live. (p. 41)
huésped Organismo que provee una fuente de energía o un ambiente apropiado para que viva un virus u otro organismo.

hydroponics A farming method in which plants are grown in solutions of nutrients instead of soil. (p. 166)
hidroponía Método de cultivo de plantas en el que se usan soluciones de nutrientes en vez de suelos.

hyphae The branching, threadlike tubes that make up the bodies of multicellular fungi. (p. 89)
hifas Delgados tubos ramificados que constituyen el cuerpo de los hongos multicelulares.

I

infectious disease An illness that can pass from one organism to another. (p. 60)
enfermedad infecciosa Enfermedad que puede pasar de un organismo a otro.

L

lichen The combination of a fungus and either an alga or an autotrophic bacterium that live together in a mutualistic relationship. (p. 95)
liquen Combinación de un hongo y una alga o bien una bacteria autótrofa, que viven juntos en una relación de mutualismo.

long-day plant A plant that flowers when the nights are shorter than the plant's critical night length. (p. 162)
planta de día largo Una planta que florece cuando las noches son más cortas que la duración critical de noche de la planta.

M

monocot An angiosperm that has only one seed leaf.
monocotiledónea Angiosperma cuyas semillas tienen un solo cotiledón. (p. 156)

multicellular Consisting of many cells. (p. 7)
multicelular Que se compone de muchas células.

mutualism A type of symbiosis in which both partners benefit from living together. (p. 78)
mutualismo Tipo de simbiosis en la que ambos participantes se benefician de vivir juntos.

N

nonvascular plant A low-growing plant that lacks true vascular tissue. (p. 108)
planta no vascular Planta de crecimiento lento que carece de tejido vascular verdadero.

nucleus The dense area in a eukaryotic cell that contains nucleic acids, the chemical instructions that direct the cell's activities. (p. 27)
núcleo Área densa en una célula eucariota que contiene ácidos nucleicos, es decir, las instrucciones químicas que dirigen las actividades de la célula.

O

organism A living thing. (p. 7)
organismo Ser vivo.

ovary A flower structure that encloses and protects ovules and seeds as they develop. (p. 153)
ovario Estructura de la flor que encierra y protege a los óvulos y a las semillas durante su desarrollo.

ovule A plant structure in seed plants that produces the female gametophyte; contains an egg cell. (p. 148)
óvulo Estructura de las plantas de semilla que se produce el gametofito femenino; contiene una célula reproductora femenina.

P

parasite An organism that lives on or in a host and causes harm to the host. (p. 41)
parásito Organismo que vive sobre o dentro de un huésped y le causa daño.

pasteurization A process of heating food to a temperature that is high enough to kill most harmful bacteria without changing the taste of the food. (p. 55)
pasteurización Proceso de calentamiento del alimento a una temperatura suficientemente alta como para matar la mayoría de las bacterias dañinas sin cambiar el sabor de la comida.

peat Compressed layers of dead sphagnum mosses that accumulate in bogs. (p. 123)
turba Capas comprimidas de musgos esfagnáceos muertos que se acumulan en las marismas.

perennial A flowering plant that lives for more than two years. (p. 164)
perenne Planta con flores que vive más de dos años.

petal A colorful, leaflike structure of some flowers.
pétalo Estructura de color brillante que tienen algunas flores. (p. 152)

phloem The vascular tissue through which food moves in some plants. (p. 137)
floema Tejido vascular por el que circula el alimento en algunas plantas.

photoperiodism A plant's response to seasonal changes in length of night and day. (p. 162)
fotoperiodicidad Respuesta de una planta a los cambios de día y noche por las estaciones.

photosynthesis The process by which plants and some other organisms capture and use light energy to make food from carbon dioxide and water. (p. 104)
fotosíntesis Proceso por el que las plantas y otros organismos captan energía luminosa y la usan para producir alimento a partir del dióxido de carbono y del agua.

pigment A chemical that produces color. (p. 79)
pigmento Sustancia química que produce color.

pistil The female reproductive part of a flower. (p. 153)
pistilo Parte reproductora femenina de una flor.

pollen Tiny particles (male gametophytes) produced by seed plants that contain the cells that later become sperm cells. (p. 137)
polen Partículas diminutas (gametofitos masculinos) producidas por las plantas semillas que contienen las células que posteriormente se convierten en células reproductoras masculinas.

pollination The transfer of pollen from male reproductive structures to female reproductive structures in plants. (p. 149)
polinización Transferencia de polen de las estructuras reproductoras masculinas a las estructuras reproductoras femeninas de las plantas.

precision farming A farming method in which farmers use technology to fine-tune the amount of water and fertilizer they use to match the requirements of a specific field. (p. 166)
agricultura de precisión Método de cultivo en el que los agricultores usan la tecnología para determinar con precisión la cantidad de agua y fertilizante que emplearán, para suplir las necesidades de un terreno específico.

prokaryote An organism whose cells lack a nucleus and some other cell structures. (p. 27)
procariota Organismo cuyas células carecen de núcleo y otras estructuras celulares.

protist A eukaryotic organism that cannot be classified as an animal, plant, or fungus. (p. 75)
protista Organismo eucariótico que no se puede clasificar como animal, planta ni hongo.

protozoan An animal-like protist. (p. 75)
protozoario Protista con características animales.

pseudopod A "false foot" or temporary bulge of cytoplasm used for feeding and movement in some protozoans. (p. 76)
seudópodo "Pie falso" o abultamiento temporal del citoplasma, que algunos protozoarios usan para alimentarse o desplazarse.

red tide An algal bloom that occurs in salt water. (p. 85)
marea roja Floración de algas que se presenta en agua salada.

reflection The process by which light bounces off an object. (p. 115)
reflexión Proceso por el cual la luz rebota en un objeto.

respiration The process of breaking down food to release its energy. (p. 51)
respiración Proceso de descomposición de alimentos para liberar su energía.

response An action or change in behavior that occurs as a result of a stimulus. (p. 9)
respuesta Acción o cambio en el comportamiento que ocurre como resultado de un estímulo.

rhizoid A thin, rootlike structure that anchors a moss and absorbs water and nutrients for the plant. (p. 123)
rizoide Estructura fina parecida a una raíz que sujeta un musgo al suelo, y que absorbe el agua y los nutrientes para la planta.

ribosome A tiny structure located in the cytoplasm of a cell where proteins are produced. (p. 49)
ribosoma Estructura diminuta ubicada en el citoplasma de una célula donde se producen las proteínas.

root cap A structure that covers the tip of a root, protecting the root from injury. (p. 141)
cofia Estructura que cubre la punta de una raíz y la protege contra daños.

seed The plant structure that contains a young plant inside a protective covering. (p. 137)
semilla Estructura de una planta, que contiene una planta joven dentro de una cubierta protectora.

sepal A leaflike structure that encloses the bud of a flower. (p. 152)
sépalo Estructura, parecida a una hoja, que encierra el botón de una flor.

sexual reproduction A reproductive process that involves two parents that combine their genetic material to produce a new organism, which differs from both parents. (p. 52)
reproducción sexual Proceso de reproducción que implica a dos progenitores que combinan su material genético para producir un nuevo organismo diferente a los dos progenitores.

short-day plant A plant that flowers when the nights are longer than the plant's critical night length. (p. 162)
planta del día corto Una planta que florece cuando las noches son más largos que la duración critical de noche de la planta.

species A group of similar organisms that can mate with each other and produce offspring that can also mate and reproduce. (p. 18)
especie Grupo de organismos semejantes que pueden cruzarse entre ellos y producir descendencia fértil.

spontaneous generation The mistaken idea that living things arise from nonliving sources. (p. 10)
generación espontánea Idea equivocada de que los seres vivos surgen de fuentes inertes.

spore A tiny cell that is able to grow into a new organism. (p. 82)
espora Célula diminuta que, al crecer, puede convertirse en un nuevo organismo.

sporophyte The stage in the life cycle of a plant in which the plant produces spores. (p. 110)
esporofito Etapa en el ciclo vital de una planta en la que la planta produce esporas.

stamen The male reproductive part of a flower. (p. 153)
estambre Parte reproductora masculina de una flor.

stimulus A change in an organism's surroundings that causes the organism to react. (p. 8)
estímulo Cambio en el entorno de un organismo que le hace reaccionar.

stomata The small openings on the surfaces of most leaves through which gases can move.
estomas Pequeñas aberturas en las superficies de casi todas las hojas, a través de las cuales pasan los gases. (p. 144)

symbiosis A close relationship between two organisms in which at least one of the organisms benefits. (p. 78)
simbiosis Relación estrecha entre dos organismos, en la que al menos uno de los organismos se beneficia.

taxonomy The scientific study of how living things are classified. (p. 17)
taxonomía Estudio científico de cómo se clasifican los seres vivos.

tissue A group of similar cells that perform a specific function in an organism. (p. 105)
tejido Grupo de células semejantes que realizan una función específica en un organismo.

toxin A poison that can harm an organism. (p. 61)
toxina Veneno que puede dañar a un organismo.

transmission The process by which light passes through an object. (p. 115)
transmisión Proceso por el cual la luz pasa a través de un objeto.

transpiration The process by which water is lost through a plant's leaves. (p. 145)
transpiración Proceso por el cual las hojas de una planta pierden agua.

tropism The growth response of a plant toward or away from a stimulus. (p. 160)
tropismo Respuesta de una planta a un estímulo, que consiste en crecer hacia el estímulo o en la dirección opuesta.

unicellular Made of a single cell. (p. 7)
unicelular Compuesto por una sola célula.

vaccine A substance introduced into the body to stimulate the production of chemicals that destroy specific disease-causing viruses and organisms. (p. 65)
vacuna Sustancia introducida en el cuerpo para estimular la producción de sustancias químicas que destruyen a los virus y organismos específicos causantes de enfermedades.

vacuole A large sac-like storage area in a cell. (p. 105)
vacuola Gran área de almacenamiento parecida a un saco en una célula.

vascular plant A plant that has true vascular tissue. (p. 108)
planta vascular Planta que tiene tejido vascular verdadero.

vascular tissue The internal transporting tissue in some plants that is made up of tubelike structures.
tejido vascular Tejido de transporte interno en algunas plantas que está formado por estructuras parecidas a tubos. (p. 107)

virus A tiny, nonliving particle that invades and then reproduces inside a living cell. (p. 41)
virus Partícula diminuta no viva que invade una célula viva y luego se reproduce dentro de ella.

xylem The vascular tissue through which water and nutrients move in some plants. (p. 137)
xilema Tejido vascular por el que circulan agua y nutrientes en algunas plantas.

zygote A fertilized egg. (p. 107)
cigoto Huevo fertilizado.

Index

Page numbers for key terms are printed in **boldface** type.
Page numbers for illustrations, maps, and charts are printed in *italics*.

Index

Index

Page numbers for key terms are printed in **boldface** type.
Page numbers for illustrations, maps, and charts are printed in *italics*.

Index

Index

Acknowledgments

Acknowledgment for page 178: Excerpt from *The Corn Goddess and Other Tales from Indian Canada* by Diamond Jenness, Bulletin no. 141, Anthropological Series no. 39, National Museum of Canada, 1956. © Canadian Museum of Civilization.

Illustration

Patrice Rossi Calkin: 44–45, 76–77; **John Edwards and Associates:** 23 insets, 43, 80, 116b, 138; **David Fuller:** 175; **Kevin Jones Associates:** 142; **Richard McMahon:** 118; **Karen Minot:** 26, 100, 162, 172; **Morgan-Cain & Associates:** 10, 11, 36t, 92, 144; **Laurie O'Keefe:** 23; **Stephanie Pershing:** 31; **Walter Stuart:** 89t, 123, 128, 176; **Cynthia Turner:** 156; **J/B Woolsey Associates:** 21, 22, 81, 90, 141, 152, 159. **All charts and graphs by Matt Mayerchak.**

Photography

Photo Research Sue McDermott
Cover image top, Lester Lefkowitz/Corbis; **bottom,** Zefa Biotic/Photonica

Page vi l, Dr. Brad Fute/Peter Arnold, Inc.; **vi m,** Dr. Linda Stannard, UCT/Photo Researchers, Inc.; **vi r,** Tektoff-RM/CNRI/Photo Researchers, Inc.; **vii,** Richard Haynes; **viii,** Richard Haynes; **x b,** USDA/S.S./Photo Researchers; **x t,** Courtesy of Cindy Friedman; **2,** Reinhard Dirscher/Alamy Images; **3,** Courtesy of Cindy Friedman.

Pages 4–5, Roland Birke/Peter Arnold, Inc.; **5 inset,** Richard Haynes; **6b,** Beatty/Visuals Unlimited; **6t,** Russ Lappa; **7br,** Biodisc/Visuals Unlimited; **7l,** Michael & Patricia Fogden/Corbis; **7tr,** Michael Abbey/Photo Researchers, Inc.; **8,** Norvia Behling/Animals Animals; **9l,** Steve Callahan/Visuals Unlimited; **9m,** Dan Suzio/Photo Researchers, Inc.; **9r,** Porterfield-Chickering/Photo Researchers, Inc.; **10,** Breck Kent/Animals Animals; **11,** Superstock; **12 inset,** Tom Brakefield/DRK Photo; **12–13b,** Stephen J. Krasemann/DRK Photo; **13 inset l,** Kennan Ward/Corbis; **13 inset r,** W. Perry Conway/Corbis; **14,** Michael Newman/PhotoEdit; **15,** Russ Lappa; **16b,** Inga Spence/The Picture Cube, Inc.; **16t,** Russ Lappa; **17,** Biophoto Associates/Photo Researchers, Inc.; **18l,** Gerard Lacz/Animals Animals; **18m,** Gavriel Jecan/Art Wolfe, Inc.; **18r,** Ron Kimball Studios; **19,** Lynn Stone/Animals Animals; **21,** Thomas Kitchin/Tom Stack & Associates, Inc.; **24l,** Richard Day/Animals Animals; **24r,** Phil Dotson/Photo Researchers, Inc.; **25 all,** Russ Lappa; **27b,** Alan Schietzch/Bruce Coleman; **27 inset b,** BBoonyaratanakornkit & D.S. Clark, G. Vrdolijak/EM Lab, U. of C Berkeley/Visuals Unlimited; **27t,** Lennart Nilsson/Albert Bonniers Forlag AB; **27 inset t,** Eye of Science/Photo Researchers, Inc.; **28 inset l,** Carolina Biological/Visuals Unlimited; **28 inset r,** W. Wayne Lockwood, M.D./Corbis; **28–29t,** Daniel J. Krasemann/DRK Photo; **29 inset l,** Photodisc/Getty Images, Inc.; **29 inset r,** E.R. Degginger/Animals Animals; **30,** Russ Lappa; **32l,** Biological Photo Service; **32r,** Reg Morrison/Auscape; **33,** Peggy/Yoram Kahana/Peter Arnold, Inc.; **34l,** W. Wayne Lockwood, M.D./Corbis; **34r,** E.R. Degginger/Animals Animals.

Pages 38–39, Dennis Kunkel/Phototake; **39 inset,** Richard Haynes; **40bl,** Institut Pasteur/CNRI/Phototake; **40br,** Lee D. Simon/Photo Researchers, Inc.; **40t,** Getty Images, Inc.; **41l,** Dr. Brad Fute/Peter Arnold, Inc.; **41m,** Dr. Linda Stannard, UCT/Photo Researchers, Inc.; **41r,** Tektoff-RM/CNRI/Photo Researchers, Inc.; **44–45,** Peter Minister/Dorling Kindersley; **46,** Esbin-Anderson/Omni-Photo; **47b,** Dr. Linda Stannard, UCT/Photo Researchers, Inc.; **47t,** Custom Medical Stock; **48,** Richard Haynes; **49b,** Geoff Brightling/Dorling Kindersley; **49t,** USDA/Visuals Unlimited; **50b,** David M. Phillips/Visuals Unlimited; **50r,** Oliver Meckes/Photo Researchers, Inc.; **50t,** Scott Camazine/Photo Researchers, Inc.; **51b,** Dr. Jeremy Burgess/Photo Researchers, Inc.; **51 inset b,** Dennis Kunkel/Phototake; **51l,** Steve Dunwell/Index Stock Imagery; **51 inset l,** Dennis Kunkel/Phototake; **51t,** Alan L. Detrick/Photo Researchers, Inc.; **51 inset t,** Photo courtesy of Agriculture and Agri-Food Canada ; **52b,** Dr. Dennis Kunkel/Phototake; **52t,** Dr. K.S. Kim/Peter Arnold, Inc.; **53,** Alfred Pasieka/Peter Arnold, Inc.; **54l,** StockFood/Raben; **54r,** Richard Haynes; **55l,** Dorling Kindersley; **55m,** J. C. Carton/Bruce Coleman; **55r,** Neil Marsh/Dorling Kindersley; **56b,** Ben Osborne; **56 inset,** Michael Abbey/Photo Researchers, Inc.; **56t,** John Riley/Getty Images, Inc.; **57,** David Young-Wolff/PhotoEdit; **59,** Richard Haynes; **60,** Richard Haynes; **61b,** Getty Images, Inc.; **61bm,** David M. Dennis/Tom Stack & Associates, Inc.; **61t,** Grapes/Michaud/Photo Researchers, Inc.; **61tm,** Richard Haynes; **62l,** Clouds Hill Imaging, Ltd.; **62r,** Dennis Kunkel/Phototake; **63,** Dr. Gary Gaugler/Photo Researchers, Inc.; **64,** Institut Pasteur/CNRI/Phototake; **65,** David Young-Wolff/PhotoEdit; **66–67 boy,** Richard Haynes; **66 stomach ulcers,** Veronika Burmeister/Visuals Unlimited; **66 tuberculosis,** Dennis Kunkel/Phototake; **66 cavities,** Dr. David Phillips/Visuals Unlimited; **66 pneumonia,** BSIP/Photo Researchers, Inc.; **66 strep throat,** Dr. Gary Gaugler/Photo Researchers, Inc.; **66 ear infection,** David M. Phillips/Photo Researchers, Inc.; **66 conjunctivitis,** Dr. Gary Gaugler/Visuals Unlimited; **66 meningitis,** Dr. Dennis Kunkel/Visuals Unlimited; **67 impetigo,** Dr. Stanley Flegler/Visuals Unlimited; **67r,** C. Swartzell/Visuals Unlimited; **68b,** Geoff Brightling/Dorling Kindersley; **68t,** Lee D. Simon/Photo Researchers, Inc.; **70l,** Dennis Kunkel; **70r,** Science Photo Library.

Pages 72–73, Michael Fogden/DRK Photo; **73 inset,** Richard Haynes; **74b,** Jan Hinsch/Science Photo Library/Photo Researchers, Inc.; **74t,** Science VU/Visuals Unlimited; **75b,** Gregory G. Dimijian/Photo Researchers, Inc.; **75m,** A. Le Toquin/Photo Researchers, Inc.; **75t,** O.S.F./Animals Animals/Earth Scenes; **76,** Astrid & Hanns-Frieder Michler/Photo Researchers, Inc.; **77,** Eric Grave/Photo Researchers, Inc.; **78b,** Oliver Meckes/Photo Researchers, Inc.; **78 inset,** Jerome Paulin/Visuals Unlimited; **78t,** Layne Kennedy/Corbis; **79,** David M. Phillips/Visuals Unlimited; **80,** Sinclair Stammers Oxford Scientific Films/Animals Animals/Earth Scenes; **81,** Barry Runk/Stan/Grant Heilman Photography; **82 both,** David M. Dennis/Tom Stack & Associates, Inc.; **83b,** G.R. Roberts/Omni-Photo; **83t,** Dwight R. Kuhn; **84,** Doug Perrine/Hawaii Whale Research Foundation/Innerspace Visions; **85,** Sanford Berry/Visuals Unlimited; **85 inset,** Dr. David Phillips/Visuals Unlimited; **86,** Doug Sokell/Visuals Unlimited; **87,** Russ Lappa; **88b,** Michael Fogden/Animals Animals/Earth Scenes; **88t,** Russ Lappa; **89,** Fred Unverhau/Animals Animals/Earth Scenes; **90t,** Nobel Proctor/Science Source/Photo Researchers, Inc.; **90b,** David Scharf/Peter Arnold, Inc.; **91t,** Carolina Biological/Visuals Unlimited; **91bl,** Michael Fogden/Animals Animals/Earth Scenes; **91bl inset,** Scott Camazine; **91br,** Runk/Schoenberger/Grant Heilman Photography, Inc.; **91br inset,** E.R. Degginger/Photo Researchers, Inc.; **92l,** Viard/Jacana /Photo Researchers, Inc.; **92r,** Owen Franken/Corbis; **93bl,** Eye of Science/Photo Researchers, Inc.; **93br,** ISM/Phototake; **93t,** C. James Webb/Phototake; **94,** Photo courtesy of David Read; **95,** Rod Planck/Tom Stack & Associates, Inc.; **95 inset,** V. Ahmadjian/Visuals Unlimited; **96,** Richard Haynes; **97,** Richard Haynes; **98,** Michael Fogden/Animals Animals/Earth Scenes.

Pages 102–103, Norbert Rosing/National Geographic Image Collection; **103 inset,** Richard Haynes; **104,** Richard Haynes; **105l,** Michael J. Doolittle/The Image Works; **105 inset,** Runk/Schoenberger/Grant Heilman Photography, Inc.; **106,** Kjell B. Sandved/Photo Researchers, Inc.; **107,** Ludovic Maisant/Corbis; **108l,** Randy M. Ury/Corbis; **108r,** John Shaw/Bruce Coleman; **109bl,** Ron Thomas/Getty Images, Inc.; **109br,** Eastcott Momatiuk/Getty Images, Inc.; **109m,** Barry Runk/Stan/Grant Heilman Photography; **109tl,** R. Van Nostrand/Photo Researchers, Inc.; **109tr,** Brenda Tharp/Photo Researchers, Inc.; **110b,** Frans Lanting/Minden Pictures; **110tl,** Runk/Schoenberger/ Grant Heilman Photography, Inc.; **110tr,** Peter Chadwick/Dorling Kindersley; **112,** Royalty Free/Corbis; **113,** Lester Lefkowitz/Corbis; **114b,** Peter A. Simon/Corbis; **114t,** Richard Haynes; **115,** Christi Carter/Grant Heilman Photography; **116,** Runk/Schoenberger/Grant Heilman Photography; **117b,** Georg Gerster/Photo Researchers, Inc.; **117t,** Interfoto-Pressebild-Agentur; **118,** Biophoto Associates/ Photo Researchers, Inc.; **119,** Michael Keller/Corbis; **120,** Richard Haynes; **121,** Richard Haynes; **122t,** Russ Lappa; **122–123b,** J. Lotter Gurling/Tom Stack & Associates, Inc.; **123 inset,** Runk/Schoenberger/Grant Heilman Photography, Inc.; **124l,** Runk/Schoenberger/Grant Heilman Photography, Inc.; **124r,** William E. Ferguson; **125,** Richard Haynes; **126,** Richard Haynes; **128,** Milton Rand/Tom Stack & Associates, Inc.; **129l,** Runk/Schoenberger/Grant Heilman Photography, Inc.; **129r,** Gerald Moore; **130,** J. Lotter Gurling/Tom Stack & Associates, Inc.; **133,** Runk/Schoenberger/Grant Heilman Photography, Inc.

Pages 134–135, Barrett and MacKay; **135 inset,** Jon Chomitz; **136,** Russ Lappa; **137 both,** Phil Schermeister/Corbis; **138l,** Barry Runk/Grant Heilman Photography, Inc.; **138m,** Dave King/Dorling Kindersley; **138r,** Anna W. Schoettle, USDA Forest Service; **139bl,** D. Cavagnaro/Visuals Unlimited; **139br,** Frans Lanting/Minden Pictures; **139m,** Heather Angel/Natural Visions; **139mr,** Color-Pic/Animals Animals/Earth Scenes; **139ml,** John Pontier/Animals Animals/Earth Scenes; **139t,** J.A.L. Cooke/OSF/Earth Scenes; **140 background,** Color-Pic/Earth Scenes; **140 inset both,** Runk/Schoenberger/Grant Heilman Photography, Inc.; **141 background,** Color-Pic/Earth Scenes; **141l inset,** Max Stuart/Alamy; **141r inset,** Runk/Schoenberger/Grant Heilman Photography, Inc.; **142l,** Barry Runk/Stan/Grant Heilman; **142r,** Richard Shiell/Animals Animals/Earth Scenes; **143,** Darrell Gulin/Getty Images, Inc.; **145 both,** Dr.Jeremy Burgess/Photo Researchers, Inc.; **146,** Richard Haynes; **147b,** Ken Brate/Photo Researchers, Inc.; **147l,** Michael Fogden/Animals Animals/Earth Scenes; **147r,** Breck Kent/Animals Animals/Earth Scenes; **147t,** Jim Strawser/Grant Heilman Photography, Inc.; **149t,** Grant Heilman/Grant Heilman Photography, Inc.; **149t inset,** Breck P. Kent/Animals Animals/Earth Scenes; **149b inset,** Breck P. Kent; **149b,** Patti Murray/Animals Animals/Earth Scenes; **150,** Martin Rogers/Stock Boston; **151b,** Frans Lanting/Minden Pictures; **151t,** Russ Lappa; **153bl,** Ian Tait/Natural Visions; **153br,** Merlin D. Tuttle, Bat Conservation International; **153t,** Anthony Bannister/Animals Animals; **154l,** Perennou et Nuridsany/Photo Researchers, Inc.; **154ml,** Russ Lappa; **154mr,** Philip Dowell/Dorling Kindersley; **154r,** Jules Selmes and Debi Treloar/Dorling Kindersley; **155t,** Nancy Rotenberg/Animals Animals/Earth Scenes; **155b,** Dwight Kuhn; **157,** Alan Pitcairn/Grant Heilman Photography, Inc.; **158,** Richard Haynes; **160,** David Sieren /Visuals Unlimited; **161b,** E.R. Degginger; **161m,** Heather Angel/Natural Visions; **161t,** Barry Runk/Stan/Grant Heilman Photography; **163 both,** Scott Smith/Animals Animals/Earth Scenes; **164b,** Larry Lefever/Grant Heilman Photography, Inc.; **164m,** Mark E. Gibson/Corbis; **164t,** E. R. Degginger; **165,** Robert Frerck/Odyssey Productions, Inc.; **166b,** Arthur C. Smith III/Grant Heilman Photography, Inc.; **166–167t,** Patti McConville/Getty Images, Inc.; **168,** Richard Haynes; **169,** Richard Haynes; **170,** Ken Brate/Photo Researchers, Inc.; **174b,** Ed Simpson/Getty Images, Inc.; **174 inset,** Robert Frerck, Odyssey Productions, Chicago; **174–175t,** Monica Stevenson/Getty Images, Inc.; **176,** David Frazier Photo Library; **177,** Ed Bock/Corbis; **178b,** C.M. Dixon; **178t,** Tim Spransy; **179,** David Young Wolff/PhotoEdit; **180,** Tony Freeman/PhotoEdit; **181b,** Russ Lappa; **181m,** Richard Haynes; **181t,** Russ Lappa; **182,** Richard Haynes; **184,** Richard Haynes; **186,** Morton Beebe/Corbis; **187,** Richard Haynes; **189b,** Richard Haynes; **189t,** Dorling Kinderlsey; **191,** Image Stop/Phototake; **194,** Richard Haynes; **201,** Richard Haynes; **203 both,** Richard Haynes.